Myth and the American Experience

Myth and the American Experience

Volume One

Nicholas Cords
& Patrick Gerster

Lakewood State Junior College
White Bear Lake, Minnesota

GLENCOE PRESS
A division of Benziger Bruce & Glencoe, Inc.
New York • Beverly Hills

GLENCOE PRESS
A division of Benziger Bruce & Glencoe, Inc.
8701 Wilshire Boulevard
Beverly Hills, California 90211
Collier-Macmillan Canada, Ltd., Toronto, Canada

Library of Congress catalog card number: 72-91271

Printed in the United States of America

First Printing, 1973

To
Maggie & Carole

Contents

Preface

It would be scarcely novel to suggest that America's historical past has been, at least in some measure, subject to distortion and myth. Comparatively, it appears that American history is more myth-laden than that of any other western nation. Indeed, Henry Steele Commager, in an article included in this work, demonstrates that during the period 1789–1860, at least, Americans set out with a vengeance to create a "usable past"—myths included.

Accuracy, it is said, must be the constant companion of the historian. It has been out of this constant concern for accuracy that one of the major thrusts of American historiography (at least in the twentieth century) has been the reinterpretation of America's historical myths, many of which were the products of historians themselves. Yet it seems equally true that such historical observations, though uttered consistently, have been expressed with a somewhat fragmented voice.

C. Vann Woodward, in a review article written in 1962 (also included in this work), challenged historians to face up to "the relationship between myth and history." Reminding us that "myth has more than pejorative usages and that it can be used to denote more than what one deems false about another man's beliefs," Professor Woodward goes on to suggest not the destruction of myths, but their serious critique. This collection of readings, focusing on the dichotomy of myth and reality in American history, is a partial reply to that challenge.

We do not intend here to supply a definitive answer as to why such a predisposition has intrigued professional historians and students of the American past, nor to suggest that this work supplies the final word as to what is myth and what is reality in American history. Realizing that one man's myth may well be another man's reality, we wish merely to bring together various myths that have been isolated and identified by members of the American historical community. Certainly we have selected the individual articles, but it is the individual historians represented in the selections who have identified the myths. Each article stands on its own arguments and its own merits, yet in some measure each seems to suggest the validity of studying the past within the framework of myth and reality.

In a more pragmatic sense, this work emanates from a course developed and taught by one of the editors, Patrick Gerster, which focused on the theme of myth and reality in American history. The course's marked success with lower division college students demonstrated the viability of the approach and the pervasiveness of myth, as well as its relevance to the study of America's past.

Perhaps we should make a further observation concerning the relationship between myth and reality: The black-and-white distinction between the two is used in this work as a tool for historical analysis. Remember that there is a point at which myth and reality intersect; thus, at given points, they can become one and the same thing. Myth becomes reality precisely when man reacts as if the myth were true and bases his beliefs and conduct upon it. Thus, the difficulty seems to lie not so much with the myth itself, but rather with the fact that myth often serves as the basis for mores and cultural attitudes—for canons and laws. All men, then, to a degree live in accordance with the norms and principles that have been drawn from myth. If one accepts the idea or perception of myth as an important ingredient in man's past and present, then the recognition and understanding of myth seems absolutely essential to the study of history.

As historians have continued to reinterpret and revise, and to demonstrate that history is more than a catalogue of great wars, crusading generals, and the decisions of presidents, increasingly they have discovered that discrepancies often exist between history as actuality and history as perceived. As a result of this process, history's scholarly practitioners have left ample and enviable commentary on America's myth-encrusted past. Significant examples of their findings comprise this work.

White Bear Lake, Minnesota
January 1973

NICHOLAS CORDS
PATRICK GERSTER

Acknowledgments

It is customary to acknowledge myriad debts—both intellectual and personal—to those who have contributed to publication. Often, the catalogue is sweeping: historians (from Herodotus to Handlin), sources (from *The Peloponnesian War* to *The Pentagon Papers*), teachers (from K through Ph.D.), students, colleagues, publishers, editors, research assistants (what are they?), typists, et al. Also included are wives, parents ("without whom this work would not have been possible"), children, in-laws and other sundry relatives and friends. Further sources of inspiration may well be represented. Having somewhat facetiously recited the litany, yet struck by the amount of truth therein, we selectively acknowledge our obligations to the above. More specifically, a word of thanks is extended to Clarke Chambers, Professor of History and Department Chairman, University of Minnesota, who has been aware of the project from its beginning, and who has strategically provided both constructive criticism and enthusiastic support as the occasion warranted. Finally, special thanks to those authors and publishers who have granted reprint privileges, particularly those who were financially considerate and those whose permissions were accompanied by notes of encouragement, interest and good will.

INTRODUCTION: HISTORY AND MYTH

The Mythmakers of American History

Thomas A. Bailey

Thomas A. Bailey, long an established American diplomatic historian, and now Byrne Professor of American History, Emeritus, at Stanford University, has been one of the most consistent and articulate spokesman on the topic of myth in American history. In an expanded version of a presidential address given before the Organization of American Historians in 1968, Professor Bailey provides his own definition of "historical myth" and highlights what he feels are the major sources of America's historical myths—from poets and presidents to historians themselves. Mr. Bailey's selection does much to set both the tone and the perspective for the chapters that follow.

False historical beliefs are so essential to our culture that if they did not exist, like Voltaire's God, they would have to be invented. In this uncertain world we crave certainties, and if an iconoclast were suddenly to shatter all myths, our social structure would suffer a traumatic shock. We need only imagine how different our national history would be if countless millions of our citizens had not been brought up to believe in the manifestly destined superiority of the American people, in the supremacy of the white race, in the primacy of the Nordics within the white race, in the safety-valve "free" land in the West, in completely rugged individualism, and in the rags-to-riches dream of a millionaire's blank check in every workingman's lunch box.[1]

Historical myths and legends are needful in establishing national identity and stimulating patriotic pride.[2] If Switzerland has its William Tell and the arrowed apple, and if Scotland has its Robert Bruce and the persevering spider, the United States has its George Washington and the chopped cherry tree. The American colonials, having jettisoned George III, were under compulsion to fabricate home-grown tales of their own in a hurry; and this perhaps explains why so many of our heroic legends are associated with the "glorious" War of Independence.[3]

American children are indoctrinated with nonhistorical myths before they are hardly out of the bassinet. Santa Claus keeps small fry better behaved before Christmas, while the stork keeps them—or used to keep them—from asking embarrassing questions between Christmases. The youngster also hears

From "The Mythmakers of American History," by Thomas A. Bailey, in *Journal of American History*, Vol. LV (June 1968), pp. 5–21; reprinted by permission of the author and publisher.

hero tales about Washington kneeling in the snow at Valley Forge and Abraham Lincoln reading by the light of a flickering fireplace. Yet there is no credible evidence that either did either.

Many elementary teachers of history and literature are not well enough informed to separate the legend from the truth. They are only too happy to keep the children entertained. Others, I find, know the facts but continue to tell the time-tested stories, including the Parson Weems tale about the cherry tree. Many teachers have discovered that the pupil does not remember the stories anyhow, so the end result does not make much difference. If the children are taught the debunked account, they might become unsettled. They might even repeat it in garbled form in a superpatriotic home, thereby stirring up trouble with the school authorities and jeopardizing their jobs. The safest course for the instructor is to perpetuate the hallowed myths and not rock the boat.[4]

The poets studied in school have also done their part in creating historical mythology. John Keats had poetical license on his side when he had Cortés rather than Balboa discover the Pacific, but this was carrying his license a bit too far. The stirring tale of Paul Revere's ride was a legend in search of a poet, and it found Henry Wadsworth Longfellow, who put the resolute rider on the wrong side of the river and had him thunder into Concord, which he failed to reach.[5] The playwrights, as cousins of the poets, have likewise sinned. Robert E. Sherwood's *Abe Lincoln in Illinois* (1938), whether on the stage or on the screen, has probably done more than any other single medium to implant the maudlin legend of Lincoln's grief-stricken love affair with Ann Rutledge.

Historical novels are among our most effective teachers, but they are naturally more concerned with dramatic effect than undramatic truth. Nathaniel Hawthorne's harsh image of the blue-nosed Puritan, as portrayed in *The Scarlet Letter*, persists in the face of recent scholarship. The fading picture that many high school graduates retain of the Civil War and Reconstruction from their dessicated textbooks is probably overshadowed by Margaret Mitchell's *Gone With The Wind*, which presents the story with a southern exposure and a rebel yell. Literature, including historical novels and novelized history, is often the continuation of war by other means.

Star-spangled history textbooks still dish up much mythology, shaped as they are in part by patriotic pressure groups. In our dealings with foreign countries, especially Britain, we are not only about one hundred percent right but one hundred percent righteous. (It is only fair to add that British versions of the two Anglo-American wars generally reverse the process.[6]) Professional patriots, like the Sons of the American Revolution and Texans for America, are still demanding that we teach patriotism above all. They would exalt the "Spirit of '76," restore Nathan Hale and his undying dying regret, and combat socialism or any other "ism" that foreshadows social change. The United

Daughters of the Confederacy are by no means mute more than a hundred years after the guns fell silent at Appomattox. The hyphenates are still vocal, especially the Italian-Americans, who insist on having Columbus, rather than the Norsemen, discover America.[7] The Italians are generally successful, except in Minnesota, where the Scandinavians, clinging to their questionable Kensington Stone, have more votes.

A newly formed hyphenate group, but not a new element, consists of African-Americans. Seeking a quasi-national identity, much as white America did after 1776, they are now understandably clamoring for historical recognition. For many generations they were the "invisible men" of American history—the dusky hoers of weeds and pluckers of cotton. Now, with black balloting power and portentous rioting power, they are insisting on visibility, if not overvisibility, in the textbooks. In at least two of our great cities—New York and Detroit—the school authorities have issued separate booklets, a hundred or so pages in length, detailing the contributions of the Negro.[8]

This belated recognition, though praiseworthy in many respects, is fraught with danger. Most non-militant Negroes would probably like to think of themselves as dark-skinned Americans, and this self-imposed Jim Crowism can be self-defeating. Pressure-group history of any kind is deplorable, especially when significant white men are bumped out to make room for much less significant black men in the interests of social harmony.[9] If this kind of distortion gets completely out of hand, we can visualize what will happen when the Negroes become the dominant group in all our largest cities, as they already are in Washington, D.C. Coexistence may end, and we may even have hard-backed Negro histories of the United States, with the white man's achievements relegated to a subsidiary treatment.

The apotheosis of Crispus Attucks is illuminating. He was a runaway Negro slave, we are told, whose blood was the first to be shed in the American struggle for independence. We have long known that he was fatally shot in the so-called Boston Massacre of March 5, 1770. But we do not know for a certainty whether he was a Negro or an Indian or even a runaway. He and his fellows were guilty of hooliganism that night; several other people had earlier lost their lives in the struggle against British authority since 1763; and the armed outburst at Lexington and Concord was a full five years in the offing.[10]

This determination to stand American history on its head, so characteristic of minority groups, may stimulate pride among Negroes, but it can win little support from true scholarship. The luckless African-Americans while in slavery were essentially in jail; and we certainly would not write the story of a nation in terms of its prison population. Yet the pressure is on to overstress Negro initiative in organizing revolts, in escaping from bondage, and in securing emancipation. President Andrew Johnson, who was once downgraded by James Ford Rhodes and John W. Burgess because he messed up Reconstruction for the southern whites, is again being downgraded, this time because he messed it up for the unfortunate blacks.[11]

Once the pupil, white or black, has escaped the tyranny of the timid teacher and timeserving textbook, he is at the mercy of the journalists. He scans the columns of his daily newspaper, probably unaware that dramatic historical tales are the stock-in-trade of the newsman, and that a good reporter never exaggerates unless he improves the story.[12] Mr. Drew Pearson, for example, has continued to give currency to the fabrication that the official purchase price of Alaska contained a secret payment for the costs of bringing the two Russian fleets to American waters during the Civil War.[13] Mr. Walter Lippmann, in a hands-across-the-seas book published during the war year 1943, falsely but patriotically described the Monroe Doctrine as a quasi-alliance with Britain.[14]

Pictorial history, including cartoons and faked photographs, also presents numerous pitfalls.[15] The artist, like the poet, is entitled to draw on his imagination for details, as did John Trumbull, the painter of the American Revolution. But Benjamin West's famous painting of Penn's Treaty with the Indians depicts a colorful scene which cannot be documented. The celebration which accompanied the dramatic "wedding of the rails," near Ogden, Utah, in 1869, was fortunately photographed. Yet the pasteurized painting of the scene, as later authorized by former Governor Leland Stanford of California, neatly eliminated the liquor bottles, included prominent men who had not been there, and excluded the numerous ladies of negotiable virtue who definitely were there.[16]

The television tube, in more ways than one, has helped to get the picture out of focus. We now discover Daniel Boone operating near West Point to rescue that key fortress from the treachery of Benedict Arnold. Television has turned murderous "hoods," like Jesse James and Billy the Kid, into veritable Robin Hoods. It has also contributed an additional encrustation of legend to such dubious frontier characters as Wyatt Earp and "Wild Bill" Hickok.[17]

Much of our historical mythology is created by the motion picture industry, which often spends enormous sums to get the facts straight and then proceeds to make them crooked. The pioneer cinema classic, *The Birth of a Nation* (1915), set back Reconstruction history by a generation or so by glorifying the hooded hoodlums of the old Ku Klux Klan and stimulating the besheeted bigots of the new.

The politician must also take high rank among the most prolific of mythmakers. His primary objective is to get into office and stay there, and his so-called history is apt to be hand tooled for these ends. I invariably cringe when a politician voices the sonorous "History teaches," because I know that he is going to make it teach whatever he wants it to teach.[18] Thomas Jefferson set an unfortunate example in the Declaration of Independence when he accused George III of many sins that the ill-starred monarch never dreamed of committing.

The worst history teachers of all in some respects are the Presidents of the United States, one of whose many roles is "Teacher-in-Chief." Only three of them could claim fairly solid credentials as historians—Theodore Roosevelt, Woodrow Wilson, and John F. Kennedy—and of these only Wilson had graduate training.[19] With tens of millions of listeners now in the living-room classroom, the President is keenly aware that he is making history, rather than writing it. A "credibility gap"—the phrase employed by journalists whose own credibility is often suspect—has existed since the days of George Washington. . . . President Lyndon B. Johnson's real problem was not so much misusing history as making statements that were obviously false. Perhaps he did not know enough about it to misuse it skillfully. The historian is a little disturbed to find him referring to the late President Diem (not Ho Chi Minh) as the Winston Churchill of Vietnam, to the Dominican intervention as "just like the Alamo," and to the Vietnam War as a hunt which must end, in Davy Crockett fashion, "with that coonskin on the wall."[20] The historical Big Lie is just as much a lie when it comes from the banks of the Potomac as from the beer halls of Munich.

It is easy enough for historians to pillory the politicians and the press while overlooking their own faults. Samuel Butler, the English essayist, is quoted as saying that since God himself cannot change the past, he is obliged to tolerate the existence of historians. Other cynics have wondered why history is so dull when so much of it is obviously fiction. The ugly fact is that the professional keeper of the record does not have a good public "image": Clio, wrote Arthur Schopenhauer, "is as permeated with lies as a street-whore with syphilis."[21]

Too many so-called historians are really "hysterians"; their thinking is often more visceral than cerebral. When their duties as citizens clash with their responsibilities as scholars, Clio frequently takes a back seat. How many of us can march in Mississippi one week and teach Negro history with reasonable objectivity the next? How many of us can be shining eggheads for Adlai Stevenson in the evening and sober spokesmen for scholarship the next morning? How many of us who are professional Southerners or New Englanders can deal fairly with other sections?[22] How many of us can forget that we are white or black when writing about whites or blacks? How many of us can avoid the academic homosexuality of falling in love with our own hero? We recall with scholarly shame that for some twenty-five years the only reasonably respectable one-volume biography of Woodrow Wilson was written with sticky adulation by an eminent American historian.[23]

How many of us can forget that we are Americans, presumably loyal Americans? To be sure, we have ample, if not admirable precedent, in the patriotic effusions of George Bancroft, whose every page seemingly voted for Andrew Jackson or American democracy or both. We remember without pride how certain prominent historians sprang to the colors in 1917 and prostituted their art in an effort to hamstring the Hun and make the world safe for normalcy.[24] The conduct of scholars during World War II was more commendable. Both they and the American people were more sophisticated, and, with Hitler on the loose, the issues were clearer cut. But even today our history texts suffer from being too America-centered, as though we were the hub of the universe and all other nations were barbarians dwelling in outer darkness.[25]

How many of us, seeking an instant reputation at the expense of some towering figure, have embarked upon dubious revisionism for the sake of sensationalism or in response to faddism? No one will deny that fresh interpretations are desirable, or that history becomes more meaningful when rewritten by succeeding generations in the light of their own experience, as it invariably is. But much of our revisionism comes about as a result of a flair for novelty or a reaction against the monotony of repeating the eternal verities year after year. And let us not forget that revisionists, like evangelists, universally overstate their case in their effort to get a hearing.

Sometimes revisionism comes from a conspiratorial complex, for which mankind has a natural affinity, as recently demonstrated anew by the Kennedy assassination case. The eminent historian who warned us most emphatically against the Devil Theory of history, ironically enough, stumbled into his own well-described trap. Near the end of a memorable career, he published two books that portrayed Franklin D. Roosevelt as a veritable Mephistopheles, bent on having war at almost any price, including the destruction of our Pacific fleet.[26]

The scholar often falls into the error of failing to understand the mentality of the masses, who obviously are not all fellow historians. Ensconced in his book-lined study, a century or two after the event, he betrays a species of arrogance when he assumes that men living in a bygone era did not have the fuzziest idea of what was going on about them or what they wanted. This assumption has led to what may be called "the flight from the obvious." We should take heed of Ralph Waldo Emerson's warning in 1836, "In analysing history do not be too profound, for often the causes are quite superficial."[27]

Let us look at America's wars. The men of 1776 thought they were fighting for liberty; the revisionists of the twentieth century played up economic motivations. Now, in something of a back-to-Bancroft movement, we are again stressing liberty. The men of 1812 believed they were fighting for a free sea; the revisionists of the 1920s had them fighting for Canada. Now we have left Tippecanoe Creek and are back again on the bounding main. The men of 1861, including Lincoln, assumed that slavery was the principal villain in the coming of the war. In the 1920s Beard and others shifted emphasis to the North's alleged industrial imperialism—a thesis which the Southerners happily embraced as taking a load off their consciences. Now we think that slavery, directly or indirectly, had much to do with the guns of April. The men of 1917 concluded that the submarine plunged us into hostilities with imperial Germany. The revisionists of the 1930s blamed the financiers, the "munitioneers," the "propagandeers," and the "sloganeers."[28] Now, scores of volumes and millions of casualties later, we are back, at the risk of some oversimplification, with the submarine.

Much of our revisionism has come from premature and half-baked hypotheses, launched, in Carl Becker's immortal phrase, "without fear and without research." New hypotheses should certainly be encouraged, but if the evidence is lacking or scanty, they should be advanced with the utmost tentativeness. Charles A. Beard, in his pathbreaking study of the Constitution, modestly acknowledged in his preface that his research was "frankly fragmentary," and he implied that he was advancing views which would be more firmly established by later evidence. His modesty was fully justified by the revelations of subsequent hatchet-wielders.

Sometimes historians degenerate into polemicists, as did Harry Elmer Barnes, with an inevitable distortion of the record. Their diatribes can become so shrill that they cannot secure reputable publishers, whereupon they raise pained cries of "Court History" or "historical blackout."[29] David Starr Jordan once observed that no man can shout and at the same time tell the truth.

Some scholars run to the other extreme. They are so afraid of being labeled debunkers that they cling like barnacles to the tried and true bunk. Anatole France, in a classic passage in the preface of *Penguin Island,* points out that people do not like to be jolted but prefer the comfort of the old sillinesses (*les sottises*). The mythmaker simplifies and soothes; the critic complicates and agitates. The word "debunker," evidently coined by W. E. Woodward in 1923, has unfortunate overtones.[30] We certainly cannot get at the solid timber of truth unless we first clear away the underbrush of myth and legend. But the historian who spends his life hacking at underbrush in search of shockers is misapplying his talents. This Weemsianism-in-reverse runs the risk of "rebunking"—that is, substituting new bunk for old. And if the debunker manages to dig up dirt about our national heroes, say Lincoln, he is not likely to get a Book-of-the-Month Club adoption or even a *Reader's Digest* abridgment.[31] He who strikes at patriotic myths strikes at the foundations of our society; he is deemed guilty of sacrilege, at least by the anti-revolutionary Daughters of the American Revolution.

Too many historical writers are the votaries of cults, which, by definition, are dedicated to whitewashing warts and hanging halos. Many of us have developed a warping bias for or against Jefferson, Andrew Jackson, Lincoln, Wilson, or the Roosevelts. The overnight birth in this city of a Kennedy cult, complete with an eternal flame, should provide a poignant reminder of the pitfalls of apotheosis. We recall that Kennedy's Secretary of the Navy, Fred Korth, was accused of involvement in a conflict-of-interest scandal, which led to his hush-hush resignation. By a tasteful coincidence this episode is not even mentioned in either of the lengthy books by Sorensen and Schlesinger, two of the President's close associates and admirers.[32]

Presidents of the American Historical Association, no less than those of the United States, are exposed to cultism, as evidenced by the embarrassing adoration of impressionable disciples. Frederick Jackson Turner, Beard, and Herbert Eugene Bolton were among those historians so honored. Their devotees have not only defended the mistakes of the master but have sometimes carried his theories beyond all reasonable bounds.

Special dangers lurk in a vested interest in a given interpretation, whether by the master or his students. The temptation is almost overpowering to ignore negative evidence or to manipulate positive evidence, in the Procrustean-bed fashion of an Arnold Toynbee. A case in point came to my attention some twenty-five years ago. A well-known defender of southern slavery urged a colleague to be on the alert, in his related researches, for as many instances as he could find of northern husbands beating their wives.

A close cousin of cultism is monocausationism. Turner was by no means a monocausationist, but many of his followers tended to view the entire spectrum through the chinks of a log cabin. Karl Marx's lucubrations have led to an overemphasis on economic factors, as presently exemplified by some younger writers of the so-called New Left.[33] Beard's block-busting book on the Constitution was an attempt to deal with one set of causes—the economic. Narrowing the problem in this way is a perfectly legitimate historical exercise, given one's interest and available time. But such an approach invariably leads to distortion, no matter how emphatically the author sets forth his intentions in the preface, which all too often is skipped.[34]

Monocausation has also led the unwary to confuse causes with objectives. The major military goal of the Americans in the War of 1812 was Canada, because that was the only place where Britain was getatable. But the battle cry "On to Canada" has deceived short-sighted observers, then as now, into concluding that we went to war primarily because we lusted after the timbered lands of our semi-defenseless northern neighbor, rather than the right to sail the high seas unhindered.

Dexter Perkins has spoken eloquently of the scholarly joy of revising one's conclusions in the light of more information or reflection. Not all historians experience this praiseworthy thrill. Loyalty to one's errors is one of the lowest forms of loyalty, and repetition in the classroom for thirty-five years does not make truths of untruths or half-truths. Rigidity is a major vice in the historian, be he a teacher, writer, or editor. Some twenty years ago I was puzzled by an eminent Lincoln scholar who flatly refused to accept new evidence that reflected unfavorably on Wilson. I began to wonder what he did with new evidence that reflected unfavorably on Lincoln. I later found the answer—he suppressed it.

The historian, despite his training in historical method and his presumed objectivity, is often unjustifiably emotional or gullible.[35] The diary of William E. Dodd, published under dubious auspices, is still too highly respected as a primary source.[36] After some humbling experience, I have concluded that most, if not all, of the pretty little stories of history are in some degree false, if pursued to their smallest details. In the absence of expert shorthand or mechanical recording, I would question all or most of the stirring utterances that have come down to us from John Paul Jones to Ronald Reagan. The text of Patrick Henry's famous "liberty-or-death" speech, for example, was pieced together some forty years after the event with the help of old men who contributed their motheaten recollections.[37] I now have less confidence than I had forty-five years ago in the memories of elderly men.

"Presentitis" is another cardinal sin of the myth-making writer of history. Coupling historical events with current events can be most useful in stimulating classroom discussion and clarifying thought, but this practice may be carried to extremes, especially in strained analogies. The historian who attempts to interpret the past to the present in terms of present-day values often undertakes the almost impossible task of serving two masters—of trying to be both a chronicler and a chameleon. Surely we misuse the evidence when we read back into the Jackson era the beginnings of the New Deal, or when we apply to the so-called "Robber Barons" of the nineteenth century the same ethical standards that were finally sanctified in 1914 by the Federal Trade Commission Act. Recent scholarship tends to regard the "Robber Barons" as industrial statesmen, more baronial than piratical.[38]

Textbook writers, from McGuffey on up, have been among the most active preservers of hoary myths. If they do not know any better, they are in beyond their depth. But if they deliberately falsify the record to secure lucrative state adoptions, they are prostitutes. Publishers have perhaps been more guilty than authors, for they have different ethical standards. But we can only look with shame upon the numerous textbooks dealing with the Negro and the Civil War that have been published in two editions: one for the North and one for the South, as though there could be a northern truth and a southern truth, on a take-your-pick basis.[39]

Perhaps the most fruitful contributor to historical mythology is sheer ignorance. Wilson once wondered how the conscientious scholar could sleep nights. The historian should be more than cautious in using such treacherous words as "the only," "always," "the first," and "never before"; and especially the superlatives "oldest," "best," "richest," and "greatest." For many years I told my students that Eli Whitney invented the cotton gin in 1793, and then I discovered that a successful gin was employed on a considerable scale by the French in San Domingo as early as the 1740s.[40] For many years I assured my classes that the American Civil War was the bloodiest thus far in history, with a loss of some 600,000 lives. I changed my tune somewhat when I finally learned that the contemporaneous Taiping Rebellion in China (c. 1850–1864) lasted about fourteen years and cost some 20,000,000 lives.

The rising flood of books and articles is such a mighty torrent that there is an acute "Digestion Gap." The teacher of history simply cannot keep on top of all this material. Those of us who write books do not have time to read books—or at least not all the books and journals we should. In 1939 I published a lengthy article in the *American Historical Review* based on manuscript materials from the archives of three nations. It demonstrated that the British did *not* save George Dewey's fleet from the German fleet at Manila Bay in August 1898. Yet the myth lives merrily on in works by distinguished scholars, including a brilliant survey by a onetime president of the American Historical Association who has shown unusual interest in ship movements. Aside from the "Digestion Gap," this particular tale endures, like other myths that endure, largely because it serves or has served a useful purpose: hands-across-the-sea for the British and fists-across-the-Rhine for the Germans.[41] One is tempted to say that old myths never die; they just become embedded in the textbooks.

Every year dozens of articles of a myth-shattering nature appear in the two hundred or so American magazines, often in journals so obscure that the overburdened teacher never heard of them. I herewith propose, in all earnestness, that the Organization of American Historians and the American Historical Association jointly set up in an appropriate place a centralized Myth Registry, for both articles and books. Abstracts of discredited myths can be recorded, much as dissertation titles are registered, either by the author or by an appropriate abstracting agency.[42] Then, with the marvelous data-recovery processes now being perfected, the requisite information can be made speedily available on request. Such an agency should be a gold mine for teachers, researchers, and especially textbook writers, who have a heavy obligation to keep abreast of this verbal Niagara.

Most historical myths, I suppose, are not dangerous. The cherry tree yarn does no real harm, except perhaps to make young George an insufferable prig. It may even do some good in building youthful character by telling a lie to discourage lie telling. But a little history, to paraphrase Alexander Pope, can be a dangerous thing, and certain historical myths are infinitely mischievous, especially in the area of foreign relations.[43] As John F. Kennedy remarked in 1961 "Domestic policy can only defeat us, but foreign policy can kill us."[44]

The *Herrenvolk* myth, American style, has been with us since the early days of Massachusetts Bay. The conviction that we were God's chosen people, and that we had a divine mandate to spread our ennobling democratic institutions over the rest of the benighted globe, encouraged us to shoulder the White Man's Burden in the Philippines and elsewhere at the turn of the century. We Americans continue to believe that we are a mighty nation, not primarily because we were endowed with magnificent natural resources, but because there was something inherent in our genes that enabled us to become great. This superiority complex has strengthened the conviction that we can impose our democracy on illiterate peasants in faraway rice paddies, including those of Vietnam.

The myth of American omnipotence has led us into some strange and steamy jungles. We find in our America-centered textbooks that we won all our wars, although we certainly did not win the War of 1812 or the Korean War, second phase; neither did we lose them. The pride of unbroken victory —a false pride—pushed us ever deeper into the vortex of Vietnam at a time when face-saving negotiations held some promise of success. President Johnson, with his Alamo complex, has been charged with not wanting to be known as the first President of the United States who failed to win a war for which he was responsible.[45]

The myth that we won all our wars, in spite of being unready for them, has repeatedly caused us to skate to the brink of disaster. This was painfully true in 1916–1917 and later in the pre-Pearl Harbor years, when we clung to the minuteman policy of not preparing until we saw the whites of the enemy's eyes. The myth of unlimited American might has also seduced our policy makers into assuming that we can halt Communist aggression all over the world, including Vietnam.[46] Many hawkish Americans still feel that we could have saved China with American troops in the mid-1940s. The recent costly experience in relatively tiny Vietnam should silence some of the criticism in that quarter.

The myth of permanent victory, fortified by the illusion of invariable "unconditional surrender," has resulted in some expensive but ill-learned lessons. We Americans seem not to realize that impermanence is one of the most permanent features of history, and that victory does not keep. We whipped the Kaiser in 1918 and then brought the doughboys home before the fire was out. We repeated the same process in 1945, when the "I Wanna Go Home" movement reached mutinous proportions. Some wag has said that history repeats itself because no one was listening the first time.

The myth of American righteousness has resulted in some glaring inconsistencies. Our nationalistic textbooks tend to stress the view that there are two sides to every international dispute: our side and the wrong side. We excuse our sins, if excuse them we must, by pointing the accusing finger at other nations, as was notably true of our countercharges when the U–2 spy plane went down in 1960, along with America's holier-than-thou reputation. When the Cuban crunch came in 1962, relatively few Americans, including some near the throne, saw anything inconsistent about encircling the Soviet Union with missiles, while denying Moscow the right to emplace missiles in Cuba.[47]

The Munich myth has likewise borne a lush harvest of evil fruit. Before 1938 the word "appeasement" was in reasonably good odor; after Munich it became a dirty word. The Munich agreement was a compromise, although lopsided and morally vulnerable. Peacetime negotiation, as we know, is normally impossible without mutual compromise and concession. But after Munich countless two-fisted Americans inevitably branded all compromise as appeasement. One basic reason why we refused to sign the Geneva Accords of 1954 regarding Vietnam was that cries of base surrender were being raised in the United States. Bad though the Munich sellout was, the misapplication of its so-called lessons since then may already have caused even greater damage.[48]

Perhaps more harmful has been the myth of the Communist monolith, which has flourished not only in patriotic textbooks but among the planners on the Potomac. Fearful of this Kremlin-directed behemoth, we have fought two undeclared wars and disbursed over 100 billion dollars in foreign aid. But international communism was never a monolith, and most of the time not even communistic. Lenin, Trotsky, and Stalin were never in complete accord, and Trotsky paid for his dissent with exile and a smashed skull. But after China fell to the Reds in 1949, the monolith seemed all the more menacing. The next year, in May 1950, President Harry S. Truman committed the United States to support the French in Vietnam with dollars and military hardware, and since then we have sunk ever deeper into the bottomless bed of snakes.

The irony is that the absence of a monolith was noisily advertised when Red China openly split with Red Russia in the 1960s. The men of Moscow had every reason to believe that they had reared up a nuclear Frankenstein's monster. "Who lost China?" was a question that could be more appropriately asked in the Kremlin than in Congress. The Sino-Soviet split removed the basic reason for our being in Vietnam, yet by this time we were too heavily bemired in the monsoon mud to pull out and had to stress other reasons for remaining. The crack in the so-called monolith presented Washington with a heaven-sent opportunity, yet our Vietnam policies, based in part on false assumptions, tended to narrow, rather than widen, the split between the once-intimate ideological bedfellows.

This by no means exhausts the list of costly or dangerous myths in the field of foreign affairs. Their persistence is a pointed reminder that the historian is involved in much more than art for art's sake. History *does* repeat itself, with variations, and the price seems to go up each time. As trustees of the nation's past, we historians have a special obligation to set the record straight and keep it straight. We cannot muzzle the poets, the playwrights, the pedagogues, the "patrioteers," the press, the politicians, and other muddiers of historical waters; but we can, if we will, control ourselves. The Republic has wrought so many mighty deeds since independence that our people no longer need to be proud of history that never happened.

Notes

1. A historical myth is here defined as an account or belief that is demonstrably untrue, in whole or substantial part. I here exclude fantasies, like Coronado's Seven Cities of Cibola, or the fabrications of hoaxers and charlatans.
2. See Henry Steele Commager, *The Search for a Usable Past and Other Essays in Historiography* (New York, 1967), 3–27.
3. The numerous immigrants also needed the cohesion of legends; many newcomers had little in common except a miserable crossing of the Atlantic Ocean.
4. I am indebted to Dr. Norman E. Tutorow for a number of personal interviews with teachers at various levels in the San Jose area of California.
5. Esther Forbes, *Paul Revere & the World He Lived In* (Boston, 1942), 461, 472. Henry Wadsworth Longfellow also popularized the legends of Miles Standish, Evangeline, and Hiawatha, as John Greenleaf Whittier did the legend of Barbara Fritchie. Ballads have also played an important role in myth-making. The popular song, "The Hunters of Kentucky," for example, left the impression that the riflemen rather than the cannoneers inflicted the heaviest losses at the battle of New Orleans.
6. See Ray Allen Billington and others, *The Historian's Contribution to Anglo-American Misunderstanding* (New York, 1966); Arthur Walworth, *School Histories at War* (Cambridge, 1938).
7. The publication by the Yale University Press in 1965 of a book containing a pre-Columbian map of America stirred up the Italians. See R. A. Skelton and others, *The Vinland Map and the Tartar Relation* (New Haven, 1965).
8. Board of Education, City of New York, *The Negro in American History* (New York, 1964); The Board of Education of the City of Detroit, *The Struggle for Freedom and Rights: Basic Facts about the Negro in American History* (Detroit, 1964).
9. See Kenneth M. Stampp and others, "The Negro in American History Textbooks," *Integrated Education*, II (October–November 1964), 9–13; Howard N. Meyer, "Overcoming the White Man's History," *Massachusetts Review*, VII (Summer 1966), 569–78.
10. E. K. Alden, "Crispus Attucks," Allen Johnson and Dumas Malone, eds., *Dictionary of American Biography* (20 vols., New York, 1928–1936), I, 415. A recent pro-Attucks version is an editorial, "The Boston Massacre and the Martyrdom of Crispus Attucks," *Negro History Bulletin*, XXX (March 1967), 4.
11. See Albert Castel, "Andrew Johnson: His Historiographical Rise and Fall," *Mid-America*, XLV (July 1963), 175–84.
12. This category includes radio and television commentators. Mankind evidently has a natural affinity for both exaggeration and error. Contrary to legend, the Salem witches were hanged (not burned); little George Washington (in the Weems version) only *barked* the tree; and the Liberty Bell was fatally cracked in 1835 (not while proclaiming independence).
13. Drew Pearson and Jack Anderson, *U.S.A.—Second-Class Power?* (New York, 1958), 303.
14. Walter Lippmann, *U.S. Foreign Policy: Shield of the Republic* (Boston, 1943), 17. I was informed by a Harvard historian in 1943 that he had prepared a lengthy critique of the Lippmann manuscript for the publishers, but evidently little heed was taken of his list of errors.
15. Homer Davenport's cartoons of little "Willie" McKinley as a puppet of blowsy Mark Hanna implanted the picture of a wishy-washy President which to this day has not been fully corrected.

16. Lucius Beebe, "Pandemonium at Promontory," *American Heritage*, IX (February 1958), 21.
17. R. F. Adams, *Burrs under the Saddle: A Second Look at Books and Histories of the West* (Norman, 1964); Kent Ladd Steckmesser, *The Western Hero in History and Legend* (Norman, 1965).
18. A related expression is "The verdict of history will be. . . ." History is dead and speechless. Interpreters of history, including historians, return the verdicts.
19. The discredited legend that Marcus Whitman saved Oregon from the British by a hurry-up trip on horseback (or foot) to Washington appealed to President Warren G. Harding as a stirring hero tale, and he preferred to cherish it on the grounds that "it ought to be true." He also endorsed the poetical version of Paul Revere and Barbara Fritchie. *Speeches and Addresses of Warren G. Harding, President of the United States: Delivered During the Course of His Tour from Washington, D.C., to Alaska and Return to San Francisco, June 20 to August 2, 1923* (Washington, D.C., 1923), 256–57.
20. New York *Times*, May 13, 1961; Philip Geyelin, *Lyndon B. Johnson and the World* (New York, 1966), 237; Arthur M. Schlesinger, Jr., *The Bitter Heritage* (Boston, 1967), 32n. President Franklin D. Roosevelt was a frequent user of "managed history." In urging a repeal of the arms embargo upon Congress in 1939, he alleged that Thomas Jefferson's embargo, followed by limited sanctions, had been "the major cause" of the War of 1812. The evidence is strong that such economic pressures came within a few weeks of averting it. See *Department of State Bulletin*, I (September 23, 1939), 277.
21. Quoted in Egon Friedell, *A Cultural History of the Modern Age* (3 vols., New York, 1932), III, 7.
22. The New Englander Edward Channing did not even mention Captain John Smith of Virginia in his six-volume history of the United States. Perhaps he was unduly influenced by Henry Adams' famous attack, which is a classic example of a young historian striving for quick fame by attacking a big name. See Henry Adams, *Historical Essays* (New York, 1891), 42–79. In the light of recent evidence Smith seems somewhat more trustworthy than scholars previously assumed. Consult Philip L. Barbour, *The Three Worlds of Captain John Smith* (Boston, 1964).
23. William E. Dodd, *Woodrow Wilson and His Work* (Garden City, 1920).
24. James R. Mock and Cedric Larson, *Words That Won The War: The Story of the Committee on Public Information, 1917–1919* (Princeton, 1939), 158–86. I knew several of these scholars who, during the 1930s and 1940s, seemed to have a defensive guilt complex regarding their participation.
25. The efforts of the United Nations Educational, Scientific and Cultural Organization (UNESCO) to rewrite national history from the viewpoint of the man on Mars has evoked violent outcries from right-wing patriotic groups in the United States. On the other hand, there is the self-flagellation school of historical writers which evidently takes pleasure in finding the United States preponderantly in the wrong in its international dealings. An example is D. F. Fleming, *The Cold War and Its Origins, 1917–1960* (2 vols., Garden City, 1961).
26. Charles A. Beard, *American Foreign Policy in the Making, 1932–1940: A Study in Responsibilities* (New Haven, 1946); Charles A. Beard, *President Roosevelt and the Coming of the War, 1941: A Study in Appearances and Realities* (New Haven, 1948).
27. Edward Waldo Emerson and Waldo Emerson Forbes, eds., *Journals of Ralph Waldo Emerson, with Annotations, 1820–1872* (10 vols., Boston, 1909–1914), IV, 160.

28. Slogans have contributed richly to the mythology of American history. "He Kept Us Out of War" is often cited as a pledge by Wilson in 1916. He did not devise it, did not use it, and did not really approve of its use as a tacit promise.
29. See Harry Elmer Barnes, ed., *Perpetual War for Perpetual Peace: A Critical Examination of the Foreign Policy of Franklin Delano Roosevelt and Its Aftermath* (Caldwell, Idaho, 1953), 1–78.
30. W. E. Woodward and Rupert Hughes (the novelist) were in the forefront of a move to debunk Washington. Hughes' unfinished work stopped with volume three (1930), and reveals the conversion of a man who came to scoff and remained to worship.
31. Edgar Lee Masters, the poet, wrote a debunking life of Abraham Lincoln, *Lincoln, the Man* (New York, 1931); but it fell flat. For evidence that the editors of the *Encyclopaedia Britannica* softened an exposure of the Weemsian cherry tree myth, presumably in response to patriotic pressure, see Harvey Einbinder, *The Myth of the Britannica* (New York, 1964), 173–74.
32. Arthur M. Schlesinger, Jr., in his pre-publication series in *Life,* gives an account of John F. Kennedy's tearful breakdown after the Bay of Pigs botch. More tastefully, it does not appear in his later book, *Life,* 59 (July 23, 1965), 75; Arthur M. Schlesinger, Jr., *A Thousand Days* (Boston, 1965). For a revelation of some of the pressures brought to bear on William Manchester—*The Death of a President* (New York, 1967)—to put the Kennedys in a better light, see John Corry, *The Manchester Affair* (New York, 1967).
33. See Irwin Unger, "The 'New Left' and American History: Some Recent Trends in United States Historiography," *American Historical Review,* LXXII (July 1967), 1237–63.
34. Julius W. Pratt's *Expansionists of 1812* (New York, 1925) quite legitimately focused on the West, but Marxists have out-Pratted Pratt in their emphasis on economic determinism.
35. After observing the conduct of trained historians in two world wars, I fear that they do not keep their heads much better than other scholars in times of great emotional stress.
36. William E. Dodd, Jr., and Martha Dodd, eds., *Ambassador Dodd's Diary, 1933–1938* (New York, 1941). Internal and circumstantial evidence suggests that the Dodd diary was largely put together in some fashion by Dodd's son and daughter, the joint editors. Charles A. Beard was asked to write the introduction, and Martha Dodd inserted some hyperbole on her own. When Beard saw the galley proofs, he insisted on restoring his own prose, and demanded not only the page proofs but also the plate proofs. Declaring that he had seen only a typescript copy of what purported to be the original diary, he insisted that, in view of this experience, he would not believe a word of it. From the author's notes of a conversation with Beard at The Johns Hopkins University, in the spring of 1941.
37. Bernard Mayo, *Myths and Men: Patrick Henry, George Washington, Thomas Jefferson* (Athens, Ga., 1959), 4.
38. Thomas C. Cochran, "The Legend of the Robber Barons," *Pennsylvania Magazine of History and Biography,* LXXIV (July 1950), 307–21; Edward C. Kirkland, "The Robber Barons Revisited," *American Historical Review,* LXVI (October 1960), 68–73.
39. Following the desegregation decision of the Supreme Court in 1954, some publishers brought out editions of books with integrated or non-integrated pictures, in an effort to cater to local prejudices.

40. Daniel H. Thomas, "Pre-Whitney Cotton Gins in French Louisiana," *Journal of Southern History*, XXXI (May 1965), 135–48.
41. Thomas A. Bailey, "Dewey and the Germans at Manila Bay," *American Historical Review*, XLV (October 1939), 59–81. The Russian fleet myth of 1863 has also been useful during those periods when Americans were interested in promoting a hands-across-the-Volga policy. See Thomas A. Bailey, "The Russian Fleet Myth Re-Examined," *Mississippi Valley Historical Review*, XXXVIII (June 1951), 81–90.
42. A promising beginning in abstracting has been made by the American Bibliographical Center, Santa Barbara, California, in its quarterly publication, launched in 1964, and entitled *America, History and Life: A Guide to Periodical Literature.*
43. In addition to those hereinafter discussed, one may mention the Lafayette myth (that nations help others primarily for sentimental reasons); the immutability myth (that a policy enunciated by Washington is good for all circumstances and ages); the Yalta myth (we cannot negotiate with the Russians); and the Marshall Plan myth (what will work industrially in sophisticated Europe will work in backward Latin America or Vietnam). For the dangers inherent in myths like the Jewish stab in the back, see Dietrich Orlow, "The Conversion of Myths into Political Power: The Case of the Nazi Party," *American Historical Review*, LXXII (April 1967), 906–24.
44. Robert D. Heinl, Jr., comp., *Dictionary of Military and Naval Quotations* (Annapolis, Md., 1966), 240.
45. Mr. James Reston reported this statement on the basis of hearsay testimony, but it is in character. New York *Times*, Oct. 1, 1967. Related to the myth of invincibility is that of "free security," which allegedly was provided in the nineteenth century by the oceans and defense in depth. "Free security" is like free love, which can be extremely costly in the end. This concept proved to be expensive in wars that we might have avoided with adequate preparedness, and in wasteful expenditures involved in trying to prepare, after war was declared. Moreover, many Americans felt quite insecure during much of the nineteenth century, especially during the recurrent Anglo-American crises, which posed the threat of the British navy. For a contrary view, see C. Vann Woodward, "The Age of Reinterpretation," *American Historical Review*, LXVI (October 1960), 1–19.
46. The history of the United States is one of the great success stories of all time, and Americans have let success go to their heads. A slogan in World War II used by a branch of the United States forces was: "The difficult we do immediately. The impossible takes a little longer."
47. This inconsistency seems all the more curious in view of President Kennedy's willingness to risk a nuclear holocaust rather than agree to withdraw from Turkey the obsolescent Jupiter missiles which he had ordered removed some two months earlier. Elie Abel, *The Missile Crisis* (Philadelphia, 1966), 191. The withdrawal had been recommended in 1961 by both the Congressional Committee on Atomic Energy and the Secretary of Defense. Schlesinger, *A Thousand Days*, 807. The Jupiter missiles were removed from Turkey, April 15–26, 1963, some six months later. Assistant Secretary of Defense Warnke to Representative Charles S. Gubser, January 8, 1968 (letter in possession of author).
48. Secretary of State Dean Rusk, publicly defending his Vietnam policy, repeated in classic form the Hitler appeasement analogy. New York *Times*, December 9, 1967.

But how do they spend their time, think you? Faith, in imagining and framing fictions to themselves of things never done nor never likely to be done, in believing these their fictions, and in following these beliefs. This is the reason why they . . . hate to be interrupted in their airy castle-buildings.

Joseph Hall
The Discovery of a New World, 1605

1

MYTHS OF EARLY AMERICA

Mezzo-tint after G. H. Boughton. Reproduced from the collection of the Library of Congress.

Puritans at home: visible saints.

John Greenwood, "Sea Captains Carousing in Surinam" (1785). The St. Louis Art Museum.

Puritans away from home: sea captains carousing in Surinam.

Introduction

According to some reports, Sir Humphrey Gilbert was sitting on the deck of his ship reading a copy of Sir Thomas More's *Utopia* just prior to his demise in 1583 somewhere in the North Atlantic. Whether he was reading *Utopia* or (as some suggest) the *Bible*, or whether the account is sheer hyperbole, is unimportant. The point is that Gilbert, rough-hewn as he might have been, was representative of the breed of Englishmen who early dreamed of New World possibilities and then attempted to realize them. Many of this group, including Gilbert, the Hakluyts, and Sir Walter Raleigh, indeed had read the *Utopia* (published in Latin, 1516; English translation, 1551), as they were generally well-educated, as well as being soldiers and courtiers (and, in the younger Hakluyt's case, clergyman and publicist). These men reflected the English Renaissance, one of the most stimulating, productive, and expansive eras in all of English history—the age of Jonson, Marlowe, Shakespeare, Byrd, Morley, and Bacon. Thomas More, a precursor of the English Renaissance, is supposed to have been enough influenced by some of Amerigo Vespucci's crewmen to set his *Utopia* somewhere in the New World.

Thus, inspiration for England's colonial beginnings, while in many respects similar to that of Portugal, Spain, and France, differed in that it generally reflected a broader utopian vision of the New World. This vision as it was practically worked out in English settlement of North America in the seventeenth and eighteenth centuries would indeed provide fertile ground for the development of myth as contemporaries and later historians attempted to tell the story of early America.

This story—a mixture of aspirations and the hard realities of actual settlement in the New World—many times resulted in frustration, whether that of the "gentlemen" of early Jamestown, or of John Winthrop. Another book could be written about frustrated utopias, but their development and many of their results have contributed heavily to the building of myth in American history.

Historians bring their own age to bear on the history they write—myths included. It should come as no surprise that faced with a two-front attack, early American history has succumbed to the onslaught of mythmakers—its own and that of future historians.

The readings in this chapter will introduce and demonstrate the viability of a myth-oriented approach to the study of American history generally, and to early American history in particular. This perspective can direct the reader to new and exciting encounters in American history—perhaps involve him in a total revision of his ideas on the subject.

Myths that Hide the American Indian

Oliver La Farge

It seems that Americans have only recently become aware of a glaring omission in their history—an adequate appreciation of the role of the American Indian. To the present, any measure of "understanding" achieved has seldom transcended the level of myth. Oliver La Farge, a novelist and professional anthropologist, has made an important attempt to redress the balance. In a telling selection distilled from years of study and observation, La Farge speaks to three levels of myth that hide the American Indian—Noble Red Man, Bloodthirsty Savage, Indolent Drunk. Myth serves to reinforce stereotypes; La Farge attempts to counter such distortion by conveying a sensitivity for the complexity and distinctiveness of the Indian past.

Ever since the white men first fell upon them, the Indians of what is now the United States have been hidden from white men's view by a number of conflicting myths. The oldest of these is the myth of the Noble Red Man or the Child of Nature, who is credited either with a habit of flowery oratory of implacable dullness or else with an imbecilic inability to converse in anything more than grunts and monosyllables.

That first myth was inconvenient. White men soon found their purposes better served by the myth of ruthless, faithless savages, and later, when the "savages" had been broken, of drunken, lazy good-for-nothings. All three myths coexist today, sometimes curiously blended in a schizophrenic confusion such as one often sees in the moving pictures. Through the centuries the mythical figure has been variously equipped; today he wears a feather headdress, is clothed in beaded buckskin, dwells in a tepee, and all but lives on horseback.

It was in the earliest period of the Noble Red Man concept that the Indians probably exerted their most important influence upon Western civilization. The theory has been best formulated by the late Felix S. Cohen, who, as a profound student of law concerning Indians, delved into early white-Indian relations, Indian political economy, and the white men's view of it. According to this theory, with which the present writer agrees, the French and English of the early seventeenth century encountered, along the East Coast of North America from Virginia southward, fairly advanced tribes whose semi-hereditary rulers depended upon the acquiescence of their people

From "Myths that Hide the American Indian," by Oliver La Farge, in American Heritage 7 (October 1956); reprinted by permission of Consuelo La Farge;

for the continuance of their rule. The explorers and first settlers interpreted these rulers as kings, their people as subjects. They found that even the commonest subjects were endowed with many rights and freedoms, that the nobility was fluid, and that commoners existed in a state of remarkable equality.

Constitutional monarchy was coming into being in England, but the divine right of kings remained firm doctrine. All European society was stratified in many classes. A somewhat romanticized observation of Indian society and government, coupled with the idea of the Child of Nature, led to the formulation, especially by French philosophers, of the theories of inherent rights in all men, and of the people as the source of the sovereign's authority. The latter was stated in the phrase, "consent of the governed." Both were carried over by Jefferson into our Declaration of Independence in the statement that "all men are created equal, that they are endowed by their Creator with certain unalienable Rights" and that governments derive "their just powers from the consent of the governed. . . ."

Thus, early observations of the rather simple, democratic organization of the more advanced coastal tribes, filtered through and enlarged by the minds of European philosophers whose thinking was ripe for just such material, at least influenced the formulation of a doctrine, or pair of doctrines, that furnished the intellectual base for two great revolutions and profoundly affected the history of mankind.

In the last paragraph I speak of "the more advanced" tribes. Part of the myth about the first Americans is that all of them, or most of them, had one culture and were at the same stage of advancement. The tribes and nations that occupied North America varied enormously, and their condition was anything but static. The advent of the white men put a sudden end to a phase of increasingly rapid cultural evolution, much as if a race of people, vastly superior in numbers, in civilization, and above all in weapons, had overrun and conquered all of Europe in Minoan times. Had that happened, also, the conquerors would undoubtedly have concluded, as so many white men like to conclude about Indians, that that peculiar race of light-skinned people was obviously inferior to their own.

Human beings had been in the New World for at least 15,000 years. During much of that time, as was the case in the beginning everywhere, they advanced but little from a Paleolithic hunting culture. Somewhere around 2,500 B.C. farming began with the domestication of corn either in Peru or in Meso-America* in the vicinity of western Guatemala. Farming brought about the sedentary life and the increased food supply necessary for cultural progress. By the time of the birth of Christ, the influence of the high cultures,

*Meso-America denotes the area in which the highest civilizations north of Peru developed, extending from a little north of Mexico City into Honduras.

soon to become true civilizations, in Meso-America was beginning to reach into the present United States. Within the next 1,500 years the Indians of parts of North America progressed dramatically. When the white men first landed, there were three major centers of high culture: the Southeast-Mississippi Valley, the Southwest, and the Northwest Coast. None of the peoples of these regions, incidentally, knew about war bonnets or lived in tepees.

The Southeast-Mississippi Valley peoples (for brevity, I shall refer to the area hereafter simply as "Southeast") seem to have had the strongest influences from Meso-America, probably in part by land along the coast of Texas, in part by sea across the Gulf of Mexico, whether direct from Mexico or secondhand through the peoples of the West Indies. There is a striking resemblance between some of their great earthen mounds, shaped like flat-topped pyramids, with their wood-and-thatch temples on top, and the stone-and-mortar, temple-topped pyramids of Meso-America. Some of their carvings and engravings strongly suggest that the artists had actually seen Meso-American sculptures. The list of similarities is convincingly long.

There grew up along the Mississippi Valley, reaching far to the north, and reaching also eastwards in the far south, the high culture generally called "Mound Builder." It produced a really impressive art, especially in carving and modeling, by far the finest that ever existed in North America. The history of advancing civilization in the New World is like that of the Old—a people develops a high culture, then barbarians come smashing in, set the clock part way back, absorb much of the older culture, and carry it on to new heights. A series of invasions of this sort seems to have struck the Mound Builders in late prehistoric times, when they were overrun by tribes mainly of Muskhogean and Iroquoian linguistic stock. Chief among these were the ancestors of the well-known Five Civilized Tribes—the Seminoles, Creeks, Choctaws, Chickasaws, and Cherokees. When white men first met them, their culture was somewhat lower than that of the earlier period in the land they occupied. Nonetheless, they maintained, in Florida, Alabama, Mississippi, Louisiana, and Georgia, the highest level east of the Rockies. A late movement of Iroquoian tribes, close relatives of the Cherokees, among them the Iroquois themselves, carried a simpler form of the same culture into Pennsylvania, New York, Ohio, and into the edge of Canada.

All of these people farmed heavily, their fields stretching for miles. They were few in a vast land—the whole population of the present United States was probably not over a million. Hunting and fishing, therefore, were excellent, and no reasonable people would drop an easy source of abundant meat. The development of their farming was held in check quantitatively by the supply of fish and game. They farmed the choice land, and if the fields began to be exhausted, they could move. They moved their habitations somewhat more freely than do we, but they were anything but nomadic. The southern tribesmen lived neither in wigwams nor tepees, but in houses with thatched roofs, which in the extreme south often had no walls. They had an elaborate social structure with class distinctions. Because of their size, the white men called their settlements "towns." The state of their high chiefs was kingly. They were a people well on the road toward civilization.

The Natchez of Mississippi had a true king, and a curious, elaborate social system. The king had absolute power and was known as the Sun. No ordinary man could speak to him except from a distance, shouting and making obeisances. When he went out, he was carried on a litter, as the royal and sacred foot could not be allowed to touch the ground. The Natchez nation was divided into two groups, or moieties: the aristocracy and the common people. The higher group was subdivided into Suns (the royal family), Nobles, and Honored Ones. The common people were known simply as Stinkers. A Stinker could marry anyone he pleased, but all the aristocrats had to marry out of their moiety, that is, marry Stinkers. When a female aristocrat married a Stinker man, her children belonged to her class; thus, when a Sun woman married a Stinker, her children were Suns. The children of the men, however, were lowered one class, so that the children of a Sun man, even of the Sun himself, became Nobles, while the children of an Honored One became lowly Stinkers.

This system in time, if nothing intervened, would lead to an overwhelming preponderance of aristocrats. The Natchez, however, for all their near-civilization, their temples, their fine crafts and arts, were chronically warlike. Those captives they did not torture to death they adopted, thus constantly replenishing the supply of Stinkers (a foreigner could become nothing else, but his grandchildren, if his son struck a royal fancy, might be Suns).

The Indians of the Southeast knew the Mexican-West Indian art of feather weaving, by means of which they made brilliant, soft cloaks. The Sun also wore a crown of an elaborate arrangement of feathers, quite unlike a war bonnet. In cloak and crown, carried shoulder-high on a litter, surrounded by his retainers, his majesty looked far more like something out of the Orient than anything we think of ordinarily when we hear the word "Indian."

The Natchez were warlike. All of the southeasterners were warlike. War was a man's proper occupation. Their fighting was deadly, ferocious, stealthy if possible, for the purpose of killing—men, women, or children, so long as one killed—and taking captives, especially strong males whom one could enjoy torturing to death. It is among these tribes and their simpler relatives, the Iroquois, that we find the bloodthirsty savage of fiction, but the trouble is that he is not a savage. He is a man well on the road toward civilization.

With the Iroquois, they shared a curious pattern of cruelty. A warrior expected to be tortured if captured, although he could, instead, be adopted, before torture or at any time before he had been crippled. He entered into it as if it were a contest, which he would win if his captors failed to wring a sign of pain from him and if he kept taunting them so long as he was conscious. Some of the accounts of such torture among the Iroquois, when the victim was a member of a tribe speaking the same language and holding to the same customs, are filled with a quality of mutual affection. In at least one case, when a noted enemy proved to have been too badly wounded before his capture to be eligible for adoption, the chief, who had hoped that the man would replace his own son, killed in battle, wept as he assigned him to his fate. At intervals between torments so sickening that one can hardly make one's self read through the tale of them, prisoner and captors exchanged news of friends and expressions of mutual esteem. Naturally, when tribes who did not hold to these customs, including white men, were subjected to this treatment it was not well received.

This pattern may have come into North America from a yet more advanced, truly civilized source. The Mexicans—the Aztecs and their neighbors—expected to be sacrificed if they were captured, and on occasion might insist upon it if their captors were inclined to spare them. They were not tortured, properly speaking, as a general rule, but some of the methods of putting them to death were not quick. What we find in North America may have been a debasement of the Mexican practices developed into an almost psychopathic pleasure among people otherwise just as capable of love, of kindness, of nobility, and of lofty thought as any anywhere—or what the conquistadores found in Mexico may have been a civilized softening of earlier, yet more fearful ways. The Aztecs tore fantastic numbers of hearts from living victims, and like the people of the Southeast, when not at war said "We are idle." They were artists, singers, dancers, poets, and great lovers of flowers and birds.

The Iroquois and Muskhogeans had a real mental sophistication. We observe it chiefly in their social order and what we know of their religions. The Iroquois did not have the royalty and marked divisions of classes that we find farther south, but their well-organized, firmly knit tribes were what enabled them, although few in numbers, to dominate the Algonkians who surrounded them. The Iroquois came nearer to having the matriarchy that popular fable looks for among primitive people than any other American tribe. Actual office was held by the men, but the women's power was great, and strongly influenced the selection of the officers.

Five of the Iroquois tribes achieved something unique in North America, rare anywhere, when in the sixteenth century they formed the League of the Five Nations—Senecas, Onondagas, Mohawks, Cayugas, and Oneidas—to which, later, the Tuscaroras were added. The league remained united and powerful until after the American Revolution, and exists in shadowy form to this day. It struck a neat balance between sovereignty retained by each tribe and sovereignty sacrificed to the league, and as so durable and effective a union was studied by the authors of our Constitution.

The league was founded by the great leader Hiawatha. Any resemblance between the fictional hero of Longfellow's poem and this real, dead person is purely coincidental. Longfellow got hold of the name and applied it to some Chippewa legends, which he rewrote thoroughly to produce some of the purest rot and the most heavy-footed verse ever to be inflicted upon a school child.

The Iroquois lived in "long houses," which looked like extended Quonset huts sheathed in bark. Smaller versions of these, and similarly covered, domed or conical structures, are "wigwams," the typical housing of the Northeast. Many people use the word "wigwam" as synonymous with "tepee," which is incorrect. A tepee, the typical dwelling of the Plains Indians of a later period, is a functional tent, usually covered with hides or, in recent years, canvas, and one of its essential features is that it is the shelter of constantly mobile people. A tepee, incidentally, is about the most comfortable tent ever invented, winter or summer—provided you have two or three strong, competent women to attend to setting it up and striking it.

The great tribes we have been discussing showed their sophistication in a new way in their response to contact with Europeans. Their tribal organizations became tighter and firmer. From south to north they held the balance of power. The British success in establishing good relations with many of them was the key to driving the French out of the Mississippi area; to win the Revolution, the Americans had to defeat the Iroquois, whose favor up to then had determined who should dominate the Northeast. The southern tribes radically changed their costume, and quickly took over cattle, slaves, and many arts. By the time Andrew Jackson was ready to force their removal, the Cherokees had a stable government under a written constitution, with a bicameral parliament, an alphabet for writing their language, printing presses, a newspaper, schools, and churches.

Had it not been for the white men's insatiable greed and utter lawlessness, this remarkable nation would have ended with a unique demonstration of how, without being conquered, a "primitive" people could adapt itself to a new civilization on its own initiative. They would have become a very rare example of how aborigines could receive solid profit from the coming of the white men.

After the five Civilized Tribes were driven to Oklahoma, they formed a union and once again set up their governments and their public schools. Of course we could not let them have what we had promised them; it turned out that we ourselves wanted that part of Oklahoma after all, so once again we tore up the treaties and destroyed their system. Nonetheless, to this day they are a political power in the state, and when one of their principal chiefs speaks up, the congressmen do well to listen.

The tribes discussed until now and their predecessors in the same general area formed a means of transmission of higher culture to others, east and west. Their influence reached hardly at all to the northwards, as north of the Iroquois farming with native plants was difficult or impossible. On the Atlantic Coast of the United States the tribes were all more or less affected. Farming was of great importance. Even in New England, the status of chiefs was definite and fairly high. Confederacies and hegemonies, such as that of the Narragansetts over many of the Massachusetts tribes, occurred, of which more primitive people are incapable. Farther south, the state of such a chief as Powhatan was royal enough for Europeans to regard him as a king and his daughter as a true princess.

To the westward, the pattern of farming and sedentary villages extended roughly to the line that runs irregularly through Nebraska and Kansas, west of which the mean annual rainfall is below twenty inches. In wet cycles, there were prehistoric attempts to farm farther west, and in historic times the Apaches raised fair crops in the eastern foothills of the southern tip of the Rockies, but only the white men combined the mechanical equipment and the stupidity to break the turf and exhaust the soil of the dry, high plains.

An essay as short as this on so large a subject is inevitably filled with almost indefensible generalizations. I am stressing similarities, as in the case of the Iroquois-Southeast tribes, ignoring great unlikenesses. Generalizing again, we may say that the western farmers, whose cultures in fact differed enormously, also lived in fairly fixed villages. In the southern part, they built large houses covered with grass thatch. At the northwestern tip of the farming zone we find the Mandans, Hidatsa, and Crows, who lived in semi-subterranean lodges of heavy poles covered with earth, so big that later, when horses came to them, they kept their choice mounts inside. These three related, Siouan-speaking tribes living on the edge of the Plains are the first we have come to whose native costume, when white men first observed them, included the war bonnet. That was in the early nineteenth century; what they wore in 1600, no one knows.

The western farmers had their permanent lodges; they also had tepees. Immediately at hand was the country of the bison, awkward game for men on foot to hunt with lance and bow, but too fine a source of meat to ignore. On their hunting expeditions they took the conical tents. The size of the tepees was limited, for the heavy covers and the long poles had to be dragged either by the women or by dogs. Tepee life at that time was desirable only for a short time, when one roughed it.

The second area of Meso-American influence was the Southwest, as anthropologists define it—the present states of New Mexico and Arizona, a little of the adjacent part of Mexico, and various extensions at different times to the north, west, and east. We do not find here the striking resemblances to Meso-America in numbers of culture traits we find in the Southeast; the influence must have been much more indirect, ideas and objects passing in the course of trade from tribe to tribe over the thousand miles or so of desert northern Mexico.

In the last few thousand years the Southwest has been pretty dry, although not as dry as it is today. A dry climate and a sandy soil make an archaeologist's paradise. We can trace to some extent the actual transition from hunting and gathering to hunting plus farming, the appearance of the first permanent dwellings, the beginning of pottery-making, at least the latter part of the transition from twining and basketry to true weaving. Anthropologists argue over the very use of the term "Southwest" to denote a single area, because of the enormous variety of the cultures found within it. There is a certain unity, nonetheless, centering around beans, corn, squashes, tobacco, cotton, democracy, and a preference for peace. Admitting the diversity, the vast differences between, say, the Hopi and Pima farmers, we can still think of it as a single area, and for purposes of this essay concentrate on the best-studied of its cultures, the Pueblos.

The name "Pueblo" is the Spanish for "village," and was given to that people because they lived—and live—in compact, defensible settlements of houses with walls of stone laid up with adobe mortar or entirely of adobe. Since the Spanish taught them how to make rectangular bricks, pure adobe construction has become the commoner type. They already had worked out the same roofing as was usual in Asia Minor and around the Mediterranean in ancient times. A modern Pueblo house corresponds almost exactly to the construction of buildings dating back at least as far as 600 B.C. in Asia Minor.

The Pueblos, and their neighbors, the Navahos, have become well enough known in recent years to create some exception to the popular stereotype of Indians. It is generally recognized that they do not wear feathers and that they possess many arts, and that the Pueblos are sedentary farmers.

Farming has long been large in their pattern of living, and hunting perhaps less important than with any people outside the Southwest. Their society is genuinely classless, in contrast to that of the Southeast. Before the Spanish conquest, they were governed by a theocracy. Each tribe was tightly organized, every individual placed in his niche. The power of the theocracy was, and in some Pueblos still is, tyrannical in appearance. Physical punishment was used to suppress the rebellious; now more often a dissident member is subjected to a form of being sent to Coventry. If he be a member of the tribal council, anything he says at meetings is pointedly ignored. If he has some ceremonial function, he performs it, but otherwise he is left in isolation. I have seen a once self-assertive man, who for a time had been a strong leader in his tribe, subjected to this treatment for several years. By my estimation, he lost some thirty pounds, and he became a quiet conformist.

The power of the theocracy was great, but it rested on the consent of the government. No man could overstep his authority, no one man had final authority. It went hard with the individual dissident, but the will of the people controlled all.

The Pueblos had many arts, most of which still continue. They wove cotton, made handsome pottery, did fine work in shell. Their ceremonies were spectacular and beautiful. They had no system of torture and no cult of warfare. A good warrior was respected, but what they wanted was peace.

The tight organization of the Pueblo tribes and the absolute authority over individuals continues now among only a few of them. The loosening is in part the result of contact with whites, in part for the reason that more and more they are building their houses outside of the old, solid blocks of the villages, simply because they are no longer under constant, urgent need for defense.

It is irony that the peace-loving southwestern farmers were surrounded by the worst raiders of all the wild tribes of North America. Around A.D. 1100 or 1200 there began filtering in among them bands of primitives, possessors of a very simple culture, who spoke languages of the Athabascan stock. These people had drifted down from western Canada. In the course of time they became the Navahos and the Apaches. For all their poverty, they possessed a sinew-backed bow of Asiatic type that was superior to any missile weapon known to the Southwest. They traded with the Pueblos, learned from them, stole from them, raided them. As they grew stronger, they became pests. The Navahos and the northeastern branch of the Apaches, called Jicarilla Apaches, learned farming. The Navahos in time became artists, above all the finest of weavers, but they did not give up their raiding habits.

These Athabascans did not glorify war. They made a business of it. Killing enemies was incidental; in fact, a man who killed an enemy had to be purified afterwards. They fought for profit, and they were about the only North Americans whose attitude toward war resembled professional soldiers'. This did not make them any less troublesome.

The last high culture area occupied a narrow strip along the Pacific Coast, from northern California across British Columbia to southern Alaska, the Northwest Coast culture. There was no Meso-American influence here, nor was there any farming. The hunting and fishing were so rich, the supply of edible wild plants so adequate, that there was no need for farming—for which in any case the climate was unfavorable. The prerequisite for cultural progress is a food supply so lavish that either all men have spare time, or some men can specialize in non-food-producing activities while others feed them. This condition obtained on the Northwest Coast, where men caught the water creatures from whales to salmon, and hunted deer, mountain sheep, and other game animals.

The area was heavily forested with the most desirable kinds of lumber. Hence wood and bark entered largely into the culture. Bark was shredded and woven into clothing, twined into nets, used for padding. Houses, chests, dishes, spoons, canoes, and boats were made of wood. The people became carvers and woodworkers, then carried their carving over onto bone and horn. They painted their houses, boats, chests, and their elaborate wooden masks. They made wooden armor, including visored helmets, and deadly wooden clubs. In a wet climate, they made raincloaks of bark and wore basketry hats, on the top of which could be placed one or more cylinders, according to the wearer's rank. The chiefs placed carvings in front of their houses that related their lineage, tracing back ultimately to some sacred being such as Raven or Bear—the famous, so-called totem poles.

I have said that the finest prehistoric art of North America was that of the Mound Builders; in fact, no Indian work since has quite equaled it—but that is, of course, a matter of taste. The greatest historic Indian art was that of the Northwest Coast. Their carvings, like the Mound Builder sculptures, demand comparison with our own work. Their art was highly stylized, but vigorous and fresh. As for all Indians, the coming of the white men meant ruin in the end, but at first it meant metal tools, the possession of which resulted in a great artistic outburst.

Socially they were divided into chiefs, commoners, and slaves. Slaves were obtained by capture, and slave-raiding was one of the principal causes of war. Generosity was the pattern with most Indians, although in the dry, Southwest we find some who made a virtue of thrift. In the main, a man was respected because he gave, not because he possessed. The Northwest Coast chiefs patterned generosity into an ugliness. A chief would invite a rival to a great feast, the famous potlatch. At the feast he would shower his rival and other guests with gifts, especially copper disks and blankets woven of mountain sheep wool, which were the highest units of value. He might further show his lavishness by burning some possessions, even partially destroy a copper disk, and, as like as not, kill a few slaves.

If within a reasonable time the other chief did not reply with an even larger feast, at which he gave away or destroyed double what his rival had got rid of, he was finished as a chief—but if he did respond in proper form, he might be beggared, and also finished. That was the purpose of the show. Potlatches were given for other purposes, such as to authenticate the accession of the heir to a former chief, or to buy a higher status, but ruinous rivalry was constant. They seem to have been a rather disagreeable, invidious, touchy people. The cruelty of the southeasterners is revolting, but there is something especially unpleasant about proving one's generosity and carelessness of possessions by killing a slave—with a club made for that special purpose and known as a "slave-killer."

The Meso-American culture could spread, changing beyond recognition as it did so, because it carried its food supply with it. The Northwest Coast culture could not, because its food supply was restricted to its place of origin.

North and east of the Northwest Coast area stretched the sub-Arctic and the plains of Canada, areas incapable of primitive farming. To the south and east were mountains and the region between the Rockies and the Coastal ranges called the Great Basin. Within it are large stretches of true desert; most of it is arid. Early on, Pueblo influences reached into the southern part, in Utah and Nevada, but as the climate grew drier, they died away. It was a land to be occupied by little bands of simple hunters and gatherers of seeds and roots, not strong enough to force their way into anywhere richer.

In only one other area was there a natural food supply to compare with the Northwest Coast's, and that was in the bison range of the Great Plains. But, as already noted, for men without horses or rifles, hunting bison was a tricky and hazardous business. Take the year 1600, when the Spanish were already established in New Mexico and the English and French almost ready to make settlements on the East Coast, and look for the famous Plains tribes. They are not there. Some are in the mountains, some in the woodlands to the northeast, some farming to the eastward, within the zone of ample rainfall.

Instead we find scattered bands of Athabascans occupying an area no one else wanted.

Then the white men turned everything upside down. Three elements were most important in the early influence: the dislodgment of eastern tribes, the introduction of the horse, and metal tools and firearms. Let us look first at the impact on the centers of high culture.

White men came late to the Northwest Coast, and at first only as traders. As already noted, early contact with them enriched the life of the Indians and brought about a cultural spurt. Then came settlers. The most advanced, best organized tribes stood up fairly well against them for a time, and they are by no means extinct, but of their old culture there are now only remnants, with the strongest survivals being in the arts. Today, those Indians who are in the "Indian business," making money from tourists, dress in fringed buckskin and war bonnets, because otherwise the tourists will not accept them as genuine.

The tribes of the Atlantic Coast were quickly dislodged or wiped out. The more advanced groups farther inland held out all through colonial times and on into the 1830's, making fairly successful adjustments to the changed situation, retaining their sovereignty, and enriching their culture with wholesale taking over of European elements, including, in the South, the ownership of Negro slaves. Finally, as already noted, they were forcibly removed to Oklahoma, and in the end their sovereignty was destroyed. They remain numerous, and although some are extremely poor and backward, others, still holding to their tribal affiliations, have merged successfully into the general life of the state, holding positions as high as chief justice of the state supreme court. The Iroquois still hold out in New York and in Canada on remnants of their original reservations. Many of them have had remarkable success in adapting themselves to white American life while retaining considerable elements of their old culture. Adherents to the old religion are many, and the rituals continue vigorously.

The British invaders of the New World, and to a lesser degree the French, came to colonize. They came in thousands, to occupy the land. They were, therefore, in direct competition with the Indians and acted accordingly, despite their verbal adherence to fine principles of justice and fair dealing. The Spanish came quite frankly to conquer, to Christianize, and to exploit, all by force of arms. They did not shilly-shally about Indian title to the land or Indian sovereignty, they simply took over, then granted the Indians titles deriving from the Spanish crown. They came in small numbers—only around 3,000 settled in the Southwest—and the Indian labor force was essential to their aims. Therefore they did not dislodge or exterminate the Indians, and they had notable success in modifying Indian culture for survival within their regime and contribution to it.

In the Southwest the few Spaniards, cut off from the main body in Mexico by many miles of difficult, wild country, could not have survived alone against the wild tribes that shortly began to harry them. They needed the Pueblo Indians and the Pueblos needed them. The Christian Pueblos were made secure in their lands and in their local self-government. They approached social and political equality. During the period when New Mexico was under the Mexican Republic, for two years a Taos Indian, braids, blanket, and all, was governor of the territory. Eighteen pueblos survive to this day, with a population now approaching 19,000, in addition to nearly 4,000 Hopis, whose culture is Pueblo, in Arizona. They are conservative progressives, prosperous on the whole, with an excellent chance of surviving as a distinctive group for many generations to come. It was in the house of a Pueblo priest, a man deeply versed in the old religion as well as a devout Catholic, that I first saw color television.

The Spanish, then, did not set populations in motion. That was done chiefly from the east. The great Spanish contribution was loosing the horses. They did not intend to; in fact, they made every possible effort to prevent Indians from acquiring horses or learning to ride. But the animals multiplied and ran wild; they spread north from California into Oregon; they spread into the wonderful grazing land of the high Plains, a country beautifully suited to horses.

From the east, the tribes were pressing against the tribes farther west. Everything was in unhappy motion, and the tribes nearest to the white men had firearms. So the Chippewas, carrying muskets, pushed westward into Minnesota, driving the reluctant Dakotas, the Sioux tribes, out of the wooded country into the Plains as the horses spread north. At first the Dakotas hunted and ate the strange animals, then they learned to ride them, and they were off.

The Sioux were mounted. So were the Blackfeet. The semi-civilized Cheyennes swung into the saddle and moved out of the farming country onto the bison range. The Kiowas moved from near the Yellowstone to the Panhandle; the Comanches came down out of the Rocky Mountains; the Arapahos, the Crows, abandoning their cornfields, and the Piegans, the great fighting names, all followed the bison. They built their life around the great animals. They ate meat lavishly all year round; their tepees, carried or dragged now by horses, became commodious. A new culture, a horse-and-bison culture, sprang up overnight. The participants in it had a wonderful time. They feasted, they roved, they hunted, they played. Over a serious issue, such as the invasion of one tribe's territory by another, they could fight deadly battles, but otherwise even war was a game in which shooting an enemy was an act earning but little esteem, but touching one with one's bare hand or with a stick was the height of military achievement.

This influx of powerful tribes drove the last of the Athabascans into the Southwest. There the Apaches and the Navahos were also mounted and on the go, developing their special, deadly pattern of war as a business. In the Panhandle country, the Kiowas and Comanches looked westward to the

Spanish and Pueblo settlements, where totally alien peoples offered rich plunder. The Pueblos, as we have seen, desired to live at peace. The original Spanish came to conquer; their descendants, becoming Spanish-Americans, were content to hold what they had, farm their fields, and graze their flocks. To the north of the two groups were Apaches and Utes; to the east, Kiowas and Comanches; to the south, what seemed like unlimited Apaches; and to the west the Navahos, of whom there were several thousands by the middle of the seventeenth century.

The tribes named above, other than the Kiowas and Comanches, did not share in the Plains efflorescence. The Navahos staged a different cultural spurt of their own, combining extensive farming with constant horseback plundering, which in turn enabled them to become herdsmen, and from the captured wool develop their remarkable weaving industry. The sheep, of course, which became important in their economy, also derived from the white men. Their prosperity and their arts were superimposed on a simple camp life. With this prosperity, they also developed elaborate rituals and an astoundingly rich, poetic mythology.

The Dakotas first saw horses in 1722, which makes a convenient peg date for the beginning of the great Plains culture. A little over a hundred years later, when Catlin visited the Mandans, it was going full blast. The memory of a time before horses had grown dim. By 1860 the Plains tribes were hard-pressed to stand the white men off; by 1880 the whole pattern was broken and the bison were gone. At its height, Plains Indian culture was brittle. Materially, it depended absolutely on a single source of food and skins; in other aspects, it required the absolute independence of the various tribes. When these two factors were eliminated, the content was destroyed. Some Indians may still live in tepees, wear at times their traditional clothing, maintain here and there their arts and some of their rituals, but these are little more than fringe survivals.

While the Plains culture died, the myth of it spread and grew to become embedded in our folklore. Not only the Northwest Coast Indians but many others as unlikely wear imitations of Plains Indian costume and put on "war dances," to satisfy the believers in the myth. As it exists today in the public mind, it still contains the mutually incongruous elements of the Noble Red Man and the Bloodthirsty Savage that first came into being three centuries and a half ago, before any white man had ever seen a war bonnet or a tepee, or any Indian had ridden a horse.

Captain John Smith's Image of America

Edwin C. Rozwenc

Many early American historians and their works fell victim to the onslaught of the late nineteenth-century "scientific" historians. It seemed necessary not only to expose exaggerations and errors, but to discredit them completely as useful contributors to American history—they had not written history as it actually happened. John Smith was one of these discredited historians. In this article Edwin Rozwenc, Professor of History at Amherst College, attacks the myth that Smith was not a credible historian. If Smith did elaborate and expand and exhibit egotism, he was also one of the first to see the real promise and vision of America, as well as to write much very credible history.

Nearly a hundred years ago, John Gorham Palfrey, a devoted student of New England's antiquities, remarked to Henry Adams that he had certain historic doubts as to the story of Captain John Smith and Pocahontas. An article in the *North American Review* on that subject, he suggested, "would attract as much attention, and probably break as much glass, as any other stone that could be thrown by a beginner."[1] Adams' essay on Captain John Smith in the *North American Review* was a full-scale attack on Smith's veracity as a historian. He centered his attack on the Pocahontas story as it appears in *The Generall Historie of Virginia, New England and the Summer Isles* published more than a decade after Smith had written his first brief account of his adventures in the New World. Adams frankly stated that his purpose was "nothing less than the entire erasure of one of the more attractive portions of American history."[2]

For a generation or more after Henry Adams' famous essay, Smith became the subject of one of the most celebrated controversies in American history. To a certain extent, the quarrel over Smith's reputation as a historian became a sectional battle in which Southern writers, particularly Virginians, sought to defend Smith against a Yankee conspiracy to defame him.[3] More recent scholarship, however, demonstrates that there is substantial truth in Smith's historical writings, even in the fantastic European adventures recorded in *The True Travels, Adventures, and Observations of Captain John Smith.*[4]

The interminable debate as to whether the dramatic Pocahontas story can be preserved as part of a true record of the American historical experience

From "Captain John Smith's Image of America," by Edwin C. Rozwenc, in *William and Mary Quarterly,* Ser. 3, XVI (January 1959), reprinted by permission of the author and publisher.

has diverted attention from other important questions about Captain John Smith. Those we raise must be concerned with more than the truthfulness of his historical accounts, important—and fascinating—as such questions may be. The redoubtable Captain's accounts of the settlement of Virginia lie athwart the starting point of our history and in one way or another we must come to terms with them. His writings, indeed, are one of the first attempts to make an imaginative reconstruction of the origins and meaning of the American experience.

Every man's vision is directed by the metaphors which rule his mind. We must, therefore, seek to discover how Captain Smith chose to give order and meaning to his experiences in the New World: what models of historical reporting were available to him and what resources could he draw upon out of the imaginative experience of Europeans to construct his own narrative? In the light of these questions, we begin to see how a spirit of knight-errantry and the yearnings of a self-made man are interwoven in his conception of America and its possibilities.

The *Generall Historie,* which contains the fullest account of Smith's experiences in America, adds new dimensions to the literary conventions of the chivalric romance. The third and fourth books, particularly, have a dramatic rhythm and an exciting vividness that charmed Americans for generations until Henry Adams began to throw his stones. Excitement and suspense are at high pitch throughout the *Generall Historie;* surprise attacks and ambuscades, spectacular Indian fights in boats and canoes as well as in the forest, colorful Indian feasts, dances and ceremonies fill its pages. The creation of tension prior to the deliverance by Pocahontas is a little masterpiece of dramatic preparation. Our hero is tied to a tree, and Indian braves dance around him, painted in a fearful manner, shaking rattles and shouting; there are orations, with the chief priest speaking in a "hellish voyce," and the pitting of white man's magic against Indian magic. Throughout the narrative, Captain Smith looms above all other men, matching wits with a wily and resourceful Powhatan, issuing commands, performing acts of individual heroism when personal bravery was the last resource.[5]

The *Generall Historie,* indeed, breathes a spirit that we associate with the popular romances of the Elizabethan Age. As Smith grew to manhood on a Lincolnshire farm, the vogue of the medieval chivalric romance was at its height in England. Popular versions of the knightly deeds of Guy of Warwick, Tom of Lincoln, and Palmerin of England fell from the presses like autumn leaves and fed the imaginations of middle-class readers for generations.

Although little is known of Smith's reading habits, Bradford Smith has reminded us that the Captain's imagination was fired by the heroic models of the knightly romance.[6] In the autobiographical *True Travels* written a few years after the *Generall Historie,* Smith chooses to recall that, when a young man, he left his home for a time and retired to a wooded area. "Here by a faire brook he built a Pavillon of boughes, where only in his cloaths he lay. His study was *Machiavills* Art of warre and *Marcus Aurelius;* his exercise a good horse, with his lance and Ring; his food was thought to be more of venison than anything else. . . ." His life as a knightly hermit attracted notice and he was soon invited to Tattersall Castle, the seat of Henry, Earl of Lincoln, where he was taught the finer arts of horsemanship by an Italian riding master. Afterwards, he went to the Low Countries to begin his series of "brave adventures" across Europe.[7]

The romantic hermitage in the forest by "a faire brook" smacks of a Robin Hood without followers. There are resemblances, too, to certain familiar patterns in the Arthurian romances. Tom of Lincoln and Bevis of Hampton lived in fields and forests as shepherd boys until their true nobility could be put to the test before the princes and ladies of the world.

As for Smith's later adventures in Europe, we are reminded of Guy of Warwick who "enjoyned" his ladylove to watch and wait while he proved himself by "deeds." He then set sail for Normandy and fought his way through Flanders, Spain, and Lombardy, eventually to fight the Saracens at Constantinople. Smith followed a similar pattern of great deeds from the Low Countries across Europe to the Hungarian plains. There, in single combats before the eyes of the two armies, "the Rampiers all beset with fair Dames," Smith slew three Turkish champions with lance, pistol, and battle-ax. Their decapitated heads were mounted on lances at the subsequent ceremony, and the General of the army bestowed on Smith a promotion, "a faire Horse richly furnished," and a "Semitere and belt worth three hundred ducats."[8]

Like many a knight of old, Smith was rescued by a fair lady at the moment of direst peril—not once, but three times. The beauteous Lady Tragabigzanda aided him when he was a captive of the Turks; the Lady Callamata gave him succor after he arrived half dead from his fearful flight from Turkish captivity across the Russian steppes to the Don; and Pocahontas saved his life in the New World whence he had gone to add new deeds to the brave adventures already accomplished in the Old. Unlike the heroes of knightly romances however, Smith never had affairs of love with his rescuers. They were stage deities who intervened at the proper moments, and always women of high rank—an aid no doubt to Smith's pretensions to being a gentleman, coat of arms and all.

The fantastic adventures recorded in the *True Travels* were regarded by Henry Adams as partly fictitious and as a further reason for impugning the reliability of Smith's writings. More recent investigations have shown us that the inconsistencies and seeming inventions in Smith's writings are greatly outnumbered by reports and observations that have successfully passed the critical scrutiny of geographers, anthropologists, and historians. Henry Adams' generation was enthralled by the possibilities of scientific history, and Adams himself sought to discover whether history could be written "by the severest process of stating, with the least possible comment, such facts as seemed sure." Nevertheless the artist and the scientist are as inseparably connected in all of his historical writing as the two opposite faces of an ancient deity. Perhaps if Henry Adams had not been a mere "beginner" when he wrote his essay on Captain John Smith, he might have been able to appreciate that Smith's historical writing was affected by the popular literary attitudes of Elizabethan and Jacobean England.

Yet the influence of popular literary taste alone cannot account for the character of Smith's historical writing. We must remember also that the conceptions of the nature of history and of the office of the historian as it was held in Smith's day differ greatly from our own. When Smith's *Generall Historie* was written, one of the most widely read historians in England was Sir Walter Raleigh. In a panegyric on history prefixed to his own *History of the World,* Raleigh wrote:

> True it is, that among other benefits, for which History hath been honoured, in this one it triumpheth over all human knowledge–that it hath given us life in our understanding, Since the world itself and life and beginning, even to this day: yea it hath triumphed over time, which besides it, nothing but eternity hath triumphed over. . . . And it is not the least debt we owe to History, that it hath made us acquainted with our dead ancestors and out of the depth and darkness of the earth, delivered us of their memory and fame.

The end and scope of history, Raleigh wrote, was to "teach by example of times past such wisdom as may guide our desires and actions"; the memory and the fame of the great deeds of men were the best examples.[9]

No less was Captain John Smith a child of the Elizabethan Age. In 1630, he wrote, "Seeing honour is our lives ambition, and our ambition after death, to have an honourable memory of our life: and seeing by no meanes we would be abated of the dignitie and glory of our predecessors, let us imitate their vertues to be worthily their successors. . . ."[10] His opening lines in the third book of the *Generall Historie,* which relates the dramatic story of the founding of Virginia, express his desire for the "eternizing of the memory of those that effected it." [11]

Smith's concept of history and his literary imagination gave him the proper dress with which to clothe his image of America. The deeds of Englishmen in Virginia were as worthy of being eternized as those of the Spaniards in Peru and Mexico. Although no gold and silver were discovered in Virginia, Smith saw much that was wonderous in the accomplishments of "those that the three first yeares began this Plantation; notwithstanding all their factions, mutinies, and miseries, so gently corrected, and well prevented. . . ." He challenged his readers to "peruse the *Spanish Decades,* the Relations of Master *Hackluit,* and tell me how many ever with such small meanes as a Barge of 22 (*or rather two*) tuns, sometimes with seaven, eight, or nine, or but at most, twelve or sixteene men, did ever so discover so many fayre and navigable Rivers, subject so many severall Kings, people, and Nations, to obedience and contribution, with so little bloudshed."[12]

We can understand, therefore, why so much is related about Smith's explorations and Indian fights, and so little is told us of the day-by-day events at Jamestown. Whatever his motives to puff up his personal reputation, history was a matter of the glories and great deeds of men—not their prosaic daily affairs.

Yet we must not be led into a mistaken idea of John Smith's conception of America by the romantic glitter of many of the narrative passages in the *Generall Historie.* America was not simply another field of action for a bold knight. America was a land of opportunity—where men of enterprise might create a flourishing social order. The idea of America that is revealed in other portions of Smith's writing is filled with expectations of great opportunity for the individual even if the society of the New World does not change all of the distinctions of the English social order. John Smith was a self-made gentleman and the impulses that made for social mobility in Elizabethan England are writ large in his estimate of the New World's possibilities.

In the sixth book of the *Generall Historie* dealing with the prospects of New England, Smith asks:

> Who can desire more content that hath small meanes, or but onely his merit to advance his fortunes, than to tread and plant that ground he hath purchased by the hazard of his life; if hee have but the taste of vertue and magnanimity, what to such a minde can bee more pleasant than planting and building a foundation for his posterity, got from rude earth by Gods blessing and his owne industry without prejudice to any. . . .

America is not primarily a place for the soldier-knight; it beckons to the industrious who are willing to build a fortune for themselves and their posterity. But America offers more than a good chance for fortune hunters; it presents the opportunity for creating a happier and more enlightened society. In the same passage, he asks further:

> What so truly sutes with honour and honesty, as the discovering things unknowne, erecting Townes, peopling Countries, informing the ignorant, reforming things unjust, teaching vertue . . . finde imploiment for those that are idle, because they know not what to do: so farre from wronging any, as to cause posterity to remember thee; and remembering thee, ever honour that remembrance with praise.[13]

This is a magnificent dream of America's possibilities, one which drew thousands of Englishmen to America's shores and is still with us in many respects. But we must remember that this vision of social opportunity is not one of a society of yeoman farmers each relatively equal to the other in his station in life. Much has been made of Captain Smith's effort to organize the labor of the Jamestown settlers when he was president by laying down the rule that "he that will not worke, shall not eate." Yet we must not assume that he was responding to the wilderness environment by instituting a rough-and-ready frontier equalitarianism. This was the order of a military captain seeking to maintain discipline, not that of a social visionary seeking to create a new social order in which manual labor was to have the highest value. Elsewhere, when Smith recounts the story of how he made "two gallants . . . both proper Gentlemen" cut down trees till their tender fingers were blistered, he hastens to add: "By this, let no man thinke that the President, and these Gentlemen spent their times as common Woodhaggers at felling of trees, or such other like labours; or that they were pressed to it as hirelings, or common slaves; for what they did, after they were but once a little inured, it seemed, and some conceited it, onely as a pleasure and recreation."[14] Smith was too proud of his coat of arms acquired by valorous exploits in Transylvania to war upon a social system based on honor and distinction.

Nevertheless, something in Captain Smith, perhaps the hard core of common sense of a man who makes his own way, made him realize that the destiny of North America would not lie with gold and silver treasure. One cause of his quarrels with other leaders in Jamestown had been his opposition to vain searches after fool's gold; he preferred to direct the energies of the men at Jamestown into hacking trees, cutting clapboards, and making pitch and potash for shipment to England. Smith's vision of America is closer to that of Richard Hakluyt and Sir Humphrey Gilbert who thought of America as a place where a balanced English society would grow, producing commodities of use to the mother country and serving as a market for the profit of English merchants and manufacturers.[15]

America was more than a land of profit and contentment, even more than a land of honor and virtue; it was a presence of great natural beauty. A tireless explorer and map-maker whose observations in Virginia and New England contributed much to the geographical knowledge of the time, Smith was also a man who felt the power and the charm of Nature in the New World. Often his descriptions have the obvious purpose of advertising the New World to prospective immigrants—the climate is temperate, the soil fertile, the woods abound with wild fruits and game, the waters swim with fish in plenty—but there are also frequent flashes of subjective responses to "glistering tinctures" of water rushing over the rocks in a mountain stream, "sweet brookes and christall springs," the awesome, craggy "clifty rocks" of the Maine coast near Penobscot, the "high sandy clifts" and "large long ledges" along the coast of Massachusetts Bay. By 1616, Smith had become a convinced "northern man" among those in England who were seeking to promote other colonial ventures in America. He speaks of Massachusetts as the "Paradice of all those parts" and declares "of all the foure parts of the world that I have yet seene not inhabited . . . I would rather live here than any where."[16] To be sure, any honest New Englander will grant that Smith often exaggerates the fertility of the soil in New England and the moderateness of the climate, but no one can doubt that the natural beauty of the land had cast a spell on the Captain that exceeded the requirements of seventeenth-century advertising!

Aside from short voyages made to New England, Smith's experience with America was limited to the two years he lived in Virginia; yet to the end of his days his heart and mind were bewitched by America, as it was and as he dreamed it; and Americans in turn have been bewitched by him ever since. In the words of the poet:

> He is one of the first Americans we know,
> And we can claim him, though not by bond of birth,
> For we've always bred chimeras.[17]

In a very compelling sense, John Smith is an American historian—one who tried to express the meaning of events in the origins of American experience. By the modern canons of history, a man who writes of events in which he is a participant is already suspect, but, when he does so with zestful attention to his personal exploits, we are tempted to dismiss him as a braggart and a liar. Nevertheless, there is an intractable worth in John Smith's historical writings that will not allow us to cast them aside. Wesley Frank Craven says of him: "Allowing for the exaggeration of his own importance, it must be recognized that his works contain much reliable information and that he himself was a man of real courage and strength. . . . His judgment of the conditions of the colony and their causes in the maladministration of the company through the years immediately preceding its fall are supported in the main by a careful study of the sources now at hand."[18]

By and large, the discrepancies of fact in his historical writing, involving as they often do such questions as the number of Indians who guarded him or the quantities of food served to him, are really trivial matters—the peccadillos of an amateur historian over which we need not blush any more than we do for the peccadillos of a historian of any age. The greater amount of data in Smith's historical writings has survived tests of credibility in every generation since they were published. The Pocahontas story may be an invention of Smith's mind, or of many minds in the taverns of seventeenth-century London, but on the basis of recent reexaminations of the evidence, the critical historian can admit the likelihood of Smith's deliverance by "the Indian princess" with fewer doubts than he might have had a generation ago.[19]

Smith's historical imagination is one key to our understanding of the approach of Englishmen to the New World. He wrote of a brief moment only in the minuscule beginnings of Anglo-Saxon culture in North America. But he brought to his relation of events in Virginia the spirit of knight-errantry which still had a hold upon the imaginations of men in Elizabethan and Jacobean England and gave to Englishmen a vision of America as a place in which to achieve personal honor and glory. When we remember W. J. Cash's penetrating analysis of the aristocratic ideals of the South, we can understand readily that the chivalric spirit of the *Generall Historie* makes the defense of John Smith's reputation by Southerners something of an automatic reflex. The *Generall Historie* points to social attitudes and styles of life that actually became fundamental social traits in Virginia and much of the South.

But Captain John Smith is more than a totem in the Southern tradition of chivalry. After his brief trials and encounters in Virginia, he understood well that America was destiny and possibility—that America's history lay in the future. He saw that destiny in terms of opportunity for improvement. America would be a place where men might find economic betterment, not by plunderings of gold and other treasure, but in a balanced society of husbandmen, tradesmen, and merchants. The New World, withal, would be a place where men might teach virtue and establish a morality free of the encumbrances of the Old. John Smith's *Generall Historie* is an important part of the deeper cultural consciousness which has sustained this perennial faith in the promise of American life.

Notes

1. Henry Adams, *The Education of Henry Adams* (New York, 1931), p. 222. Henry Adams' account of the genesis of his essay on Captain John Smith makes the episode briefer than it really was. Actually, Adams began his investigations in the British Museum in 1861 and the article in the *North American Review* was not published until 1867. See letters to Palfrey and Charles Deane in Harold Cater, *Henry Adams and His Friends* (Boston, 1947), pp. 8–23, 29–36.
2. Henry Adams, "Captain John Smith," in *Chapters of Erie and other Essays* (Boston, 1871), p. 193. The original article appeared in the *North American Review*, CIV (January 1867), 1–30.
3. See Jarvis M. Morse, "John Smith and his Critics . . . ," *Journal of Southern History*, I (1935), 124. Edward Channing was certain that the controversy was used "to stimulate Southern hatred of New England scholars." *A History of the United States*, I (New York, 1905), 174.
4. See Bradford Smith, *Captain John Smith: His Life and Legend* (Philadelphia, New York, 1953). The author attempts a full-scale defense of the truth of the *True Travels* as well as Smith's other historical writings. See chap. 2 and especially appended essay by Laura Palonyi Striker, pp. 311–342. See also Philip L. Barbour, "Captain John Smith's Route through Turkey and Russia," *William and Mary Quarterly*, 3d Ser., XIV (July 1957), 358–369, and prefatory essay by Laura Polanyi Striker in the new edition of Henry Wharton's *The Life of John Smith, English Soldier* (Chapel Hill, 1957), pp. 1–31.
5. *Travels and Works of Captain John Smith*, ed. Edward Arber (Edinburgh, 1910), II, 395–400. Hereafter cited as Smith, *Works*.
6. Bradford Smith, *Captain John Smith*, pp. 26–27, 36–39.
7. Smith, *Works*, II, 823.
8. *Ibid.*, 838–840.

9. See Charles H. Firth's "Sir Walter Raleigh's History of the World," *Proceeding of the British Academy*, 1917–18, pp. 427–446. Quotations taken from pp. 432–433.
10. Smith, *Works*, II, 936.
11. *Ibid.*, 385.
12. *Ibid.*, 465.
13. *Ibid.*, 722–723.
14. *Ibid.*, 439.
15. *Cf.* George B. Parks, *Richard Hakluyt and the English Voyages* (New York, 1928), pp. 89–98; also David B. Quinn, *Raleigh and the British Empire* (New York, 1949), pp. 16–17.
16. Smith, *Works*, II, 719, I, 193–194.
17. Stephen Vincent Benet, *Western Star* (New York, 1943), p. 72.
18. Wesley Frank Craven, *Dissolution of the Virginia Company* (New York, 1932), p. 5.
19. The best recent examination of the literary legend of Pocahontas is Jay B. Hubbell's "The Smith-Pocahontas Story in Literature," *Virginia Magazine of History and Biography*, LXV (July 1957), 275–300.

Were the Puritans "Puritanical"?

Carl N. Degler

Few groups in history have suffered more from a "bad press" than have the seventeenth-century Puritans of the Massachusetts Bay Colony. The word *Puritan* immediately resurrects images of a dour and drab society populated by prigs and "moral athletes." This popular image of the Puritans as premature Victorians needs definite readjustment. In the essay that follows, Carl Degler, formerly of Vassar and now Professor of History at Stanford, challenges many of the stock notions so long associated with Puritan New England. He concludes that the Puritans were both more humane and more complex than we might formerly have imagined.

To most Americans—and to most Europeans, for that matter—the core of the Puritan social heritage has been summed up in Macaulay's well-known witticism that the Puritans prohibited bearbaiting not because of torture to the bear, but because of the pleasure it afforded the spectators. And as late as 1925, H. L. Mencken defined Puritanism as "the haunting fear that someone, somewhere, may be happy." Before this chapter is out, much will be said about the somber and even grim nature of the Puritan view of life, but quips like those of Macaulay and Mencken distort rather than illumine the essential character of the Puritans. Simply because the word "Puritan" has become encrusted with a good many barnacles, it is worth while to try to scrape them off if we wish to gain an understanding of the Puritan heritage. Though this process is essentially a negative one, sometimes it is clarifying to set forth what an influence is *not* as well as what it is.

Fundamental to any appreciation of the Puritan mind on matters of pleasure must be the recognition that the typical, godly Puritan was a worker in the world. Puritanism, like Protestantism in general, resolutely and definitely rejected the ascetic and monastic ideals of medieval Catholicism. Pleasures of the body were not to be eschewed by the Puritan, for, as Calvin reasoned, God "intended to provide not only for our necessity, but likewise for our pleasure and delight." It is obvious, he wrote in his famous *Institutes*, that "the Lord have endowed flowers with such beauty . . . with such sweetness of smell" in order to impress our senses; therefore, to enjoy them is not contrary to God's intentions. "In a word," he concluded, "hath He not made many things worthy of our estimation independent of any necessary use?"

It was against excess of enjoyment that the Puritans cautioned and legislated. "The wine is from God," Increase Mather warned, "but the Drunkard is from the Devil." The Cambridge Platform of the Church of 1680 prohibited games of cards or dice because of the amount of time they consumed and the encouragement they offered to idleness, but the ministers of Boston in 1699 found no difficulty in condoning public lotteries. They were like a public tax, the ministers said, since they took only what the "government might have demanded, with a more *general imposition* . . . and it employes for the welfare of the publick, all that is raised by the *lottery*." Though Cotton Mather at the end of the century condemned mixed dancing, he did not object to dancing as such; and his grandfather, John Cotton, at the beginning saw little to object to in dancing between the sexes so long as it did not become lascivious. It was this same John Cotton, incidentally, who successfully contended against Roger Williams' argument that women should wear veils in church.

In matters of dress, it is true that the Massachusetts colony endeavored to restrict the wearing of "some new and immodest fashions" that were coming in from England, but often these efforts were frustrated by the pillars of the church themselves. Winthrop reported in his *History,* for example, that though the General Court instructed the elders of the various churches to reduce the ostentation in dress by "urging it upon the consciences of their people," little change was effected, "for divers of the elders' wives, etc., were in some measure partners in this general disorder."

We also know now that Puritan dress—not that made "historical" by Saint-Gaudens' celebrated statue—was the opposite of severe, being rather in the English Renaissance style. Most restrictions on dress which were imposed were for purposes of class differentiation rather than for ascetic reasons. Thus long hair was acceptable on an upper-class Puritan like Cromwell or Winthrop, but it was a sign of vanity on the head of a person of lower social status. In 1651 the legislature of Massachusetts called attention to that "excess in Apparell" which has "crept in upon us, and especially amongst people of mean condition, to the dishonor of God, the scandall of our profession, the consumption of Estates, and altogether unsuitable to our poverty." The law declared "our utter detestation and dislike, that men or women of mean condition, should take upon them the garb of Gentlemen, by wearing Gold or Silver Lace, or Buttons, or Points at their knees, or to walk in great Boots; or Women of the same rank to wear Silk or Tiffany hoods, or Scarfes, which tho allowable to persons of greater Estates, or more liberal education, is intolerable in people of low condition." By implication, this law affords a clear description of what the well-dressed Puritan of good estate would wear.

If the Puritans are to be saved from the canard of severity of dress, it is also worth while to soften the charge that they were opposed to music and art. It is perfectly true that the Puritans insisted that organs be removed from the churches and that in England some church organs were smashed by zealots. But it was not music or organs as such which they opposed, only music in the meetinghouse. Well-known American and English Puritans, like Samuel Sewell, John Milton, and Cromwell, were sincere lovers of music. Moreover, it should be remembered that it was under Puritan rule that opera was introduced into England—and without protest, either. The first English dramatic production entirely in music—*The Siege of Rhodes*—was presented in 1656, four years before the Restoration. Just before the end of Puritan rule, John Evelyn noted in his diary that he went "to see a new opera, after the Italian way, in recitative music and scenes. . . ." Furthermore, as Percy Scholes points out, in all the voluminous contemporary literature attacking the Puritans for every conceivable narrow-mindedness, none asserts that they opposed music, so long as it was performed outside the church.

The weight of the evidence is much the same in the realm of art. Though King Charles' art collection was dispersed by the incoming Commonwealth, it is significant that Cromwell and other Puritans bought several of the items. We also know that the Protector's garden at Hampton Court was beautified by nude statues. Furthermore, it is now possible to say that the Puritan closing of the theaters was as much a matter of objection to their degenerate lewdness by the 1640's as an objection to the drama as such. As far as American Puritans are concerned, it is not possible to say very much about their interest in art since there was so little in the seventeenth century. At least it can be said that the Puritans, unlike the Quakers, had no objection to portrait painting.

Some modern writers have professed to find in Puritanism, particularly the New England brand, evidence of sexual repression and inhibition. Though it would certainly be false to suggest that the Puritans did not subscribe to the canon of simple chastity, it is equally erroneous to think that their sexual lives were crabbed or that sex was abhorrent to them. Marriage to the Puritan was something more than an alternative to "burning," as the Pauline doctrine of the Catholic Church would have it. Marriage was enjoined upon the righteous Christian; celibacy was not a sign of merit. With unconcealed disapprobation, John Cotton told a recently married couple the story of a pair "who immediately upon marriage, without ever approaching the *Nuptial* Bed," agreed to live apart from the rest of the world, "and afterwards from one another, too. . . ." But, Cotton advised, such behavior was "no other than an effort of blind zeal, for they are the dictates of a blind mind they follow therein and not of the Holy Spirit which saith, *It is not good that man should be alone.*" Cotton set himself against not only Catholic asceticism but also the view that women were the "unclean vessel," the tempters of men. Women, rather than being "a necessary Evil are a necessary Good," he wrote. "Without them there is no comfortable Living for Man. . . ."

Because, as another divine said, "the Use of the Marriage Bed" is "founded in man's Nature" the realistic Puritans required that married men unaccompanied by wives should leave the colony or bring their wives over forthwith. The Puritan settlements encouraged marriages satisfactory to the participants by permitting divorces for those whose spouses were impotent, too long absent, or cruel. Indeed, the divorce laws of New England were the easiest in Christendom at a time when the eloquence of a Milton was unable to loosen the bonds of matrimony in England.

Samuel Eliot Morison in his history of Harvard has collected a number of examples of the healthy interest of Puritan boys in the opposite sex. Commonplace books, for example, indicate that Herrick's poem beginning "Gather ye rosebuds while ye may" and amorous lines from Shakespeare, as well as more erotic and even scatological verse, were esteemed by young Puritan men. For a gentleman to present his affianced with a pair of garters, one letter of a Harvard graduate tells us, was considered neither immoral nor improper.

It is also difficult to reconcile the usual view of the stuffiness of Puritans with the literally hundreds of confessions to premarital sexual relations in the extant church records. It should be understood, moreover, that these confessions were made by the saints or saints-to-be, not by the unregenerate. That the common practice of the congregation was to accept such sinners into church membership without further punishment is in itself revealing. The civil law, it is true, punished such transgressions when detected among the regenerate or among the nonchurch members, but this was also true of contemporary non-Puritan Virginia. "It will be seen," writes historian Philip A. Bruce regarding Virginia, "from the various instances given relating to the profanation of Sunday, drunkenness, swearing, defamation, and sexual immorality, that, not only were the grand juries and vestries extremely vigilant in reporting these offenses, but the courts were equally prompt in inflicting punishment; and that the penalty ranged from a heavy fine to a shameful exposure in the stocks . . . and from such an exposure to a very severe flogging at the county whipping post." In short, strict moral surveillance by the public authorities was a seventeenth-century rather than a Puritan attitude.

Relations between the sexes in Puritan society were often much more loving and tender than the mythmakers would have us believe. Since it was the Puritan view that marriage was eminently desirable in the sight of God and man, it is not difficult to find evidence of deep and abiding love between a husband and wife. John Cotton, it is true, sometimes used the Biblical phrase "comfortable yoke mate" in addressing his wife, but other Puritan husbands come closer to our romantic conventions. Certainly John Winthrop's letters to his beloved Margaret indicate the depth of attachment of which the good Puritan was capable. "My good wife . . . My sweet wife," he called her. Anticipating his return home, he writes, "So . . . we shall now enjoy each other again, as we desire. . . . It is now bed time; but I must lie alone; therefore I make less haste. Yet I must kiss my sweet wife; and so, with my blessing to our children . . . I commend thee to the grace and blessing of the lord, and rest. . . ."

Anne Bradstreet wrote a number of poems devoted to her love for her husband in which the sentiments and figures are distinctly romantic.

> To my Dear and loving Husband
> I prize thy love more than whole Mines of gold
> Or all the riches that the East doth hold.
> My love is such that Rivers cannot quench,
> Nor aught but love from thee give recompense.

In another poem her spouse is apostrophized as

> My head, my heart, mine Eyes, my life, nay more
> My joy, my Magazine of earthly store

and she asks:

> If two be one, as surely thou and I,
> How stayest thou there, whilst I at Ipswich lye?

Addressing John as "my most sweet Husband," Margaret Winthrop perhaps epitomized the Puritan marital ideal when she wrote, "I have many reasons to make me love thee, whereof I will name two: First, because thou lovest God and, secondly, because thou lovest me. If these two were wanting," she added, "all the rest would be eclipsed."

It would be a mistake, however, to try to make these serious, dedicated men and women into rakes of the Renaissance. They were sober if human folk, deeply concerned about their ultimate salvation and intent upon living up to God's commands as they understood them, despite their acknowledgment of complete depravity and unworthiness. "God sent you not into this world as a Play-House, but a Work-house," one minister told his congregation. To the Puritan this was a world drenched in evil, and, because it truly is, they were essentially realistic in their judgments. Because the Puritan expected nothing, Perry Miller has remarked, a disillusioned one was almost impossible to find. This is probably an exaggeration, for they were also human beings; when the Commonwealth fell, it was a Puritan, after all, who said, "God has spit in our faces." But Professor Miller's generalization has much truth in it. Only a man convinced of the inevitable and eternal character of evil could fight it so hard and so unceasingly.

The Puritan at his best, Ralph Barton Perry has said, was a "moral athlete." More than most men, the Puritan strove with himself and with his fellow man to attain a moral standard higher than was rightfully to be expected of so depraved a creature. Hence the diaries and autobiographies of Puritans are filled with the most torturous probing of the soul and inward seeking. Convinced of the utter desirability of salvation on the one hand, and equally cognizant of the total depravity of man's nature on the other, the Puritan was caught in an impossible dilemma which permitted him no rest short of the grave. Yet with such a spring coiled within him, the Puritan drove himself and his society to tremendous heights of achievement both material and spiritual.

Such intense concern for the actualization of the will of God had a less pleasant side to it, also. If the belief that "I am my brother's keeper" is the breeding ground of heightened social conscience and expresses itself in the reform movements so indigenous to Boston and its environs, it also could and did lead to self-righteousness, intolerance and narrow-mindedness, as exemplified in another product of Boston: Anthony Comstock. But this fruit of the loins of Puritanism is less typical of the earthy seventeenth-century New Englander than H. L. Mencken would have us think. The Sabbatarian, antiliquor, and antisex attitudes usually attributed to the Puritans are a nineteenth-century addition to the much more moderate and essentially wholesome view of life's evils held by the early settlers of New England.

To realize how different Puritans could be, one needs only to contrast Roger Williams and his unwearying opponent John Cotton. But despite the range of differences among Puritans, they all were linked by at least one characteristic. That was their belief in themselves, in their morality and in their mission to the world. For this reason, Puritanism was intellectual and social dynamite in the seventeenth century; its power could behead kings, overthrow governments, defy tyrants, and disrupt churches.

The Reformation laid an awesome burden on the souls of those who broke with the Roman Church. Proclaiming the priesthood of all believers, Protestantism made each man's relationship to God his own terrifying responsibility. No one else could save him; therefore no one must presume to try. More concerned about his salvation than about any mundane matter, the Puritan was compelled, for the sake of his immortal soul, to be a fearless individualist.

It was the force of this conviction which produced the Great Migration of 1630–40 and made Massachusetts a flourishing colony in the span of a decade. It was also, ironically, the force which impelled Roger Williams to threaten the very legal and social foundations of the Puritan Commonwealth in Massachusetts because he thought the oligarchy wrong and himself right. And so it would always be. For try as the rulers of Massachusetts might to make men conform to their dogma, their own rebellious example always stood as a guide to those who felt the truth was being denied. Such individualism, we would call it today, was flesh and bone of the religion which the Puritans passed on. Though the theocracy soon withered and died, its harsh voice softened down to the balmy breath of Unitarianism, the belief in self and the dogged resistance to suppression or untruth which Puritanism taught never died. Insofar as Americans today can be said to be individualistic, it is to the Puritan heritage that we must look for one of the principal sources.

In his ceaseless striving for signs of salvation and knowledge of God's intentions for man, the Puritan placed great reliance upon the human intellect, even though for him, as for all Christians, faith was the bedrock of his belief. "Faith doth not relinquish or cast out reason," wrote the American Puritan Samuel Willard, "for there is nothing in Religion contrary to it, tho' there are many things that do transcend and must captivate it." Richard Baxter, the English Puritan, insisted that "the *most Religious*, are the *most* truly, and *nobly rational*." Religion and reason were complementary to the Puritan, not antithetical as they were to many evangelical sects of the time.

Always the mere emotion of religion was to be controlled by reason. Because of this, the university-trained Puritan clergy prided themselves on the lucidity and rationality of their sermons. Almost rigorously their sermons followed the logical sequence of "doctrine," "reasons," and "uses." Conscientiously they shunned the meandering and rhetorical flourishes so beloved by Laudian preachers like John Donne, and in the process facilitated the taking of notes by their eager listeners. One of the unforgivable crimes of Mistress Anne Hutchinson was her assertion that one could "feel" one's salvation, that one was "filled with God" after conversion, that it was unnecessary, in order to be saved, to be learned in the Bible or in the Puritan writers. It was not that the Puritans were cold to the Word—far from it. A saint was required to testify to an intense religious experience—almost by definition emotional in character—before he could attain full membership in the Church. But it was always important to the Puritans that mere emotion—whether it be the anarchistic activities of the Anabaptists or the quaking of the Friends—should not be mistaken for righteousness or proper religious conduct. Here, as in so many things, the Puritans attempted to walk the middle path—in this instance, between the excessive legalism and formalism of the Catholics and Episcopalians and the flaming, intuitive evangelism of the Baptists and Quakers.

Convinced of reason's great worth, it was natural that the Puritans should also value education. "Ignorance is the mother (not of Devotion but) of Heresy," one Puritan divine declared. And a remarkably well-educated ministry testified to the Puritan belief that learning and scholarship were necessary for a proper understanding of the Word of God. More than a hundred graduates of Cambridge and Oxford Universities settled in New England before 1640, most of them ministers. At the same date not five men in all of Virginia could lay claim to such an educational background. Since Cambridge University, situated on the edge of Puritan East Anglia, supplied most of the graduates in America, it was natural that Newtown, the site of New England's own college, would soon be renamed in honor of the Alma Mater. "After God had carried us safe to New-England," said a well-known tract, some of its words now immortalized in metal in Harvard Yard, "one of the next things we longed and looked after, was to advance learning, and perpetuate it to posterity; dreading to leave an illiterate ministry to the churches, when the present ministers shall lie in the dust." "The College," founded in 1636, soon to be named Harvard, was destined to remain the only institution of higher learning in America during almost all the years of the seventeenth century. Though it attracted students from as far away as Virginia, it remained, as it began, the fountainhead of Puritan learning in the New World.

Doubt as one may Samuel Eliot Morison's claims for the secular origins of Harvard, his evidence of the typically Renaissance secular education which was available at the Puritan college in New England is both impressive and convincing. The Latin and Greek secular writers of antiquity dominated the curriculum, for this was a liberal arts training such as the leaders had received at Cambridge in England. To the Puritans the education of ministers could be nothing less than the best learning of the day. So important did education at Harvard seem to the New Haven colony in 1644 that the legislature ordered each town to appoint two men to be responsible for the collection of contributions from each family for "the mayntenaunce of scolars at Cambridge. . . ."

If there was to be a college, preparatory schools had to be provided for the training of those who were expected to enter the university. Furthermore, in a society dedicated to the reading of the Bible, elementary education was indispensable. "It being one chief project of that old deluder Satan to keep men from the knowledge of the Scriptures" began the first school laws of Massachusetts (1647) and Connecticut (1650). But the Puritans supported education for secular as well as religious reasons. The Massachusetts Code of 1648, for instance, required children to be taught to read inasmuch "as the good education of children is of singular behoof and benefit to any Commonwealth."

The early New England school laws provided that each town of fifty families or more was to hire a teacher for the instruction of its young; towns of one hundred families or more were also directed to provide grammar schools, "the master thereof being able to instruct youths so far as they may be fitted for the University." Though parents were not obliged to send their children to these schools, if they did not they were required to teach their children to read. From the evidence of court cases and the high level of literacy in seventeenth-century New England, it would appear that these first attempts at public-supported and public-controlled education were both enforced and fruitful.

No other colony in the seventeenth century imposed such a high educational standard upon its simple farming people as the Puritans did. It is true, of course, that Old England in this period could boast of grammar schools, some of which were free. But primary schools were almost nonexistent there, and toward the end of the seventeenth century the free schools in England became increasingly tuition schools. Moreover, it was not until well into the nineteenth century that the English government did anything to support schools. Primary and secondary education in England, in contrast with the New England example, was a private or church affair.

Unlike the Puritans, the Quakers exhibited little impulse toward popular education in the seventeenth and early eighteenth centuries. Because of their accent on the Inner Light and the doctrine of universal salvation, the religious motivation of the Puritans for learning was wanting. Furthermore, the Quakers did not look to education, as such, with the same reverence as the Puritans. William Penn, for example, advised his children that "reading many books is but a taking off the mind too much from meditation." No Puritan would have said that.

Virginia in the seventeenth century, it should be said, was also interested in education. Several times in the course of the century, plans were well advanced for establishing a university in the colony. Free schools also existed in Virginia during the seventeenth century, though the lack of village communities made them inaccessible for any great numbers of children. But, in contrast with New England, there were no publicly supported schools in Virginia; the funds for the field schools of Virginia, like those for free schools in contemporary England, came from private or ecclesiastical endowment. Nor was Virginia able to bring its several plans for a college into reality until William and Mary was founded at the very end of the century.

Though the line which runs from the early New England schools to the distinctly American system of free public schools today is not always progressively upward or uniformly clear, the connection is undeniable. The Puritan innovation of public support and control on a local level was the American prototype of a proper system of popular education.

American higher education in particular owes much to religion, for out of the various churches' concern for their faiths sprang a number of colleges, after the example of the Puritans' founding of Harvard. At the time of the Revolution, there were eight colleges besides Harvard in the English colonies, of which all but one were founded under the auspices of a church. William and Mary (1693) and King's College, later Columbia (1754), were the work of the Episcopalians; Yale (1701) and Dartmouth (1769) were set up by Congregationalists not comforted by Harvard; the College of New Jersey, later Princeton (1747), was founded by the Presbyterians; Queens College, later Rutgers (1766), by the Dutch Reformed Church; the College of Rhode Island, later Brown (1764), by the Baptists. Only the Academy of Philadelphia, later the University of Pennsylvania (1749), was secular in origin.

The overwhelming importance of the churches in the expansion of American higher education during the colonial period set a pattern which continued well into the nineteenth century and to a limited extent is still followed. Well-known colleges like Oberlin, Wesleyan, Haverford, Wittenberg, Moravian, Muhlenberg, and Notre Dame were all founded by churches in the years before the Civil War. By providing a large number of colleges (recall that England did not enjoy a third university until the nineteenth century), the religious impulses and diversity of the American people very early encouraged that peculiarly American faith in the efficacy and desirability of education for all.

When dwelling on the seminal qualities of the seventeenth century, it is tempting to locate the source of the later American doctrine of the separation of Church and State and religious freedom in the writings of Roger Williams and in the practices of provinces like New York, Maryland and Pennsylvania. Actually, however, such a line of development is illusory. At the time of the Revolution all the colonies, including Rhode Island, imposed restrictions and disabilities upon some sects, thus practicing at best only a limited form of toleration, not freedom of religion—much less separation of Church and State. Moreover, Roger Williams' cogent and prophetic arguments in behalf of religious freedom were forgotten in the eighteenth century; they could not exert any influence on those who finally worked out the doctrine of religious freedom enshrined in the national Constitution. In any case, it would have been exceedingly difficult for Williams to have spoken to Jefferson and the other Virginians who fought for religious freedom. To Williams the Puritan, the great justification for freedom of religion was the preservation of the purity of the Church; to the deistic Virginians, the important goal was the removal of a religious threat to the purity and freedom of the State.

The Locus of Authority in Colonial Massachusetts

Clifford K. Shipton

The specter of an authoritarian theocracy directing the political and religious destinies of the Massachusetts Bay Colony still sustains a measure of both popular and academic currency. It is the prevailing "Puritan myth" that supports the triangular view of Puritan existence as having been anti-sexual, anti-intellectual, and anti-democratic. Clifford K. Shipton, of the American Antiquarian Society, isolates the major deficiencies of such a view. Shipton's reply to the charge of Puritan theocratic control is pointed—"nonsense." He points to the town and congregational structure as having been one that cultivated local involvement. In the end, it was the Puritans who staged the New World commitment to "freedom of the mind" and established a society in which authority rested, in so far as was practicable for the time, on the conscience of the individual.

We of the western world generally agree that the purpose of life is the realization of a set of values which in their political form we call democracy, by which we mean that they rest authority in the people. The course of the evolution of these principles is clearly marked from the Magna Carta, through the Massachusetts Civil Code of 1648, to the Bill of Rights in the Federal Constitution. The century and a half during which the Colony and Province of Massachusetts Bay were trying to adjust law and authority in order to realize these principles are critical ones in this long period of their evolution. But what went on in these years has been quite generally misunderstood by historians, particularly by those who have not realized that in the period and the group with which we are concerned, religious and civil life were an integrated whole. Religious values were not segregated out and discriminated against as they are today when members of the Massachusetts legislature demand of anyone who would testify on social problems, "Do you take your stand on moral grounds," and deny him a hearing if he pleads guilty. The Puritan's preoccupation with moral values made him keenly aware that he should keep an eye out for the fallen sparrow, and should temper the law to the shorn lamb, or to the debtor. This is why Massachusetts passed the first statute forbidding cruelty to animals, and, for their day, the most liberal

From "The Locus of Authority in Colonial Massachusetts," by Clifford K. Shipton, in George Billias (ed.), *Law and Authority in Colonial America,* Barre Publishers, 1965. Reprinted by permission of the publisher.

laws for the protection of debtors. With the concern for the physical well-being of the individual went a certain amount of respect for his opinions.

The last generation of writers on colonial New England were cynical of the Puritan professions, and saw the Bay Colony as a self-centered autocracy devoted to the perpetuation of a particular theological orthodoxy. According to this interpretation, the significance of the evolution of law, authority, and democracy in Massachusetts was in the liberation of the colony from a theocracy by the extension of the franchise. One would have thought that this thesis had been entirely disproved by the research of this generation, but the recent publication of Emery Battis' excellent biography of Anne Hutchinson contains the following utterly irrelevant conclusion to describe the situation in the Bay Colony after Mrs. Hutchinson's exile: "the established church was the sole repository of religious truth, with full scope to determine who had erred against that truth in matters of doctrine and morals." Nonsense. There never was an established church in Massachusetts, there was no agreed-upon body of dogma, and serious moral deviation was punished by the state, not by the church.

In spite of the integration of civil and religious life in the seventeenth century, the government of Massachusetts never was a theocracy in any normal sense of the term. There was no unitary church, and many of the normal functions of the established churches in Europe were here transferred to the state. This was true at the local level as well. For most of the settlers, the accustomed instrument of local government had been the oligarchic Church of England parish; in New England its functions passed to the town, and were exercised by the inhabitants in open town meeting. Today, the established churches in England, Scandinavia, and the Latin countries exercise authority in what were purely civil fields in colonial Massachusetts. The Bay Colony never had an established church which could have exercised these civil powers; it had only individual and independent churches. The law required that every town maintain a minister and a schoolmaster, both of its own selection; but beyond that point the Colony and Province exercised no authority. Taxation of non-members of the church by the town to support the ministers was defended on the same ground as taxation of childless people to support the schools. Many towns were cited by the General Court for failing to maintain a school, but I cannot recollect a case in which a town was taken to task for failing to maintain a minister, though many did for years on end. The town, acting with the concurrence of an ecclesiastical council of its own choosing, formed the local church, which possessed no funds or property, and was independent of all other churches and of any outside authority. The town did not legally participate in the call of subsequent ministers until 1692, but inasmuch as the minister's contract was with the town, he was never called by the church without previous assurance of the concurrence of the town. Since all inhabitants, regardless of denominational preference, participated in these transactions, the minister's theological views had to be acceptable to the majority. Quakers, Baptists, and Presbyterians were vocal in these town and parish meetings, with the result that the minister's theological difficulties were usually with the civil body rather than with the church.

Unlike the Scottish presbyteries, the Massachusetts associations of ministers exercised no authority over the individual churches or their members. Their powers, like those of the occasional synods, were purely advisory. Their consent was not required for either the ordination or the dismissal of a minister, these functions being exercised by ad hoc councils chosen jointly by town and church with an eye to getting their own decisions ratified quietly. Ordaining councils heard any opponents of a call, and never proceeded to settle a minister who was opposed by a majority or even a large minority of the inhabitants of a town, knowing that he would be denied adequate financial support. Technically, the consent of such a council, chosen jointly by the disputants, was necessary for the dismissal of a minister. But even where the minister was clearly in the right, all that the council could do to protect him was to arbitrate the best possible terms of separation for him; for the town could refuse to pay the settlement and could go on calling other councils until it obtained a decision which it considered suitable. Where there was recourse to the courts, and it was frequent, the decision was almost always on the terms of the financial contract; rarely was cognizance taken of theological questions which might have been the reason for the dismissal.

It has been argued, however, that although there was no legal authority for a theocracy in Massachusetts, one existed because of the influence of the clergy. This is amply disproved by the legislative history of the Colony, and by the contrasts between the suggestions of the synods and the subsequent legislation by the General Court. The tradition that a Black Regiment of the clergy led the American Revolution in New England has little substance. Many individual Congregational ministers were neutral or Tory, and ministerial associations usually avoided even expressions of opinion on political matters. Robert E. Brown in his *Middle-Class Democracy and the Revolution in Massachusetts 1691–1780* exaggerates the political influence of the clergy, as when he mistakenly makes the Reverend Charles Chauncy a member of the upper house of legislature. Brown was unaware of the existence of an absolutely fundamental principle of separation of church and state in Massachusetts, which forbade the election of clergymen to the General Court in Colony or Province time. So clearly understood was this principle that the clergy were not to participate in government that when the Province asked a missionary to the Eastern Indians to negotiate a treaty, a wise old Roman Catholic chief pointed out to the minister the fact that his profession disqualified him from any such participation in government.

The clergyman was excluded from office in the civil government in the Bay Colony, but the meanest inhabitant was invited to participate in the legislative process. From the first, Massachusetts law provided that "Every man whether inhabitant or Forreiner, free or not free" had the right "to come to any publique Court, Council or Town Meeting" and there either by speech or writing to initiate and advocate action. The radical nature of this system is apparent when one realizes that through most of the world today legislation can be introduced only by the executive or by the ministry.

The great majority of the early settlers in the Bay Colony had held their English property not in what we would call fee simple, but by some type of feudal tenure or grant, and all of them had lived under local governments which were self-perpetuating oligarchies. In the Southern colonies, the English practice of local government by a self-perpetuating oligarchy of vestrymen remained. In New England, a few of the first town meetings had oligarchic tendencies, but within a decade the legislative and executive processes had passed into the hands of the body of inhabitants. In Massachusetts, the settler owned his land in fee simple, voted the taxes upon it in town meeting, and disposed of it at will. Liberty 12 of the Massachusetts Code of 1648 had guaranteed to everyone the right of a voice in town meeting, and, as Thomas Hutchinson later put it, "anything in the semblance of a man" was permitted to vote in spite of property qualifications established by law. In consequence, all of the functions of the English parish vestries, borough councils, and similar local bodies, passed into the hands of the body of inhabitants, who thus had control of most of the matters which affected their daily lives. The only cases I have found where votes have been challenged on the ground of voting by unqualified individuals have occurred when the minority has included the church members and more substantial people, while the majority has consisted of Baptists, Quakers, and small farmers, some of whom pretty obviously could not have met the property qualifications established by law. In no case which I have seen did the court which heard the appeal base its decision on the legal qualifications of the voters. So far as one can determine from the colonial record, the situation in town meeting was then precisely what it is today, when the chairman of the finance committee tries in vain to get the moderator to exclude unqualified persons from voting. The colonial statutes in regard to voting qualifications had little to do with actual practice, and give no substantial evidence as to the degree of democracy prevailing. Far better evidence, but quite impossible to evaluate, are such pictures as Governor Winthrop laboring in the fields with his servants, and Governor Endicott taking his turn in the saw pit.

One of the best criteria of the degree of democracy in any state is the amount of protection afforded by its laws to the individual; protection against the state itself, against other individuals, and against economic adversity. In this regard, the Massachusetts Code of 1648 was centuries ahead of the greater part of the world. The compilers, whetting their consciences to discover the will of God, selecting wisely, innovating when necessary, drew a document which is a milestone in the history of individual liberty. Their successors, a century and a half later, put forth the essence of these principles at the price of Massachusetts' ratification of the Federal Constitution, and they became the substance of the Bill of Rights.

Guarantees of freedom of the person and of property of the type afforded by the Massachusetts Code of 1648 are, we of western tradition believe, essential to a life worth living. Even more important, however, is freedom of the mind. It is the attitude toward this freedom which is the critical difference between the East and West today. Indeed, it has been a problem in every civilized society. To the Massachusetts Puritans of 1630, the whole good of man, which was the end of society, required freedom for every man to live according to his conscience. What, then, was the actual place of this most crucial freedom, the freedom of the mind, in the legal system and in the society, of the Colony and Province of Massachusetts Bay? This is a point on which historians are still confused, and which even Perry Miller and George L. Haskins did not think through. The statement of the Cambridge Platform of 1648 is this:

> Idolatry, Blasphemy, Heresy, venting corrupt & pernicious opinions, that destroy the foundations, open contempt of the word preached, prophanation of the Lords day, disturbing the peaceable administration of the worship & holy things of God, the like, are to be restrayned & punished by civil authority.

Today every state will use the civil authority against those who disturb "the peaceable administration & Exercise of the worship" of God, or of the doctrines of Karl Marx; and every state has certain ground rules beyond which lie blasphemy and heresy, or intolerable indecency. Becoming a citizen of a state has always involved joining in a compact and accepting the local ground rules. North Americans who today live in other parts of the world may not like the local ground rules, but they must recognize the fact that the world respects the right of every state to make its own rules and to enforce them against those who have accepted its citizenship.

The Massachusetts Code of 1648 states explicitly that all who settle in the colony are assumed "totally to submit to this government." Massachusetts authorities, like those of any other state, used the civil power against individuals who "vented corrupt and vicious opinions" which tended to "destroy the foundations" of the City upon a Hill. Liberty of mind was limited to matters of "faith and conscience." This was the reason, however mistaken as a matter of policy, for the civil action taken against Roger Williams, Anne Hutchinson, and the Quakers. These Antinomians held that authority was vested in the conscience of the individual, not in the state, the church, nor in the consensus of the people. While accepting this principle, the Bay authorities believed that the venting of the views which Mrs. Hutchinson held was a danger sufficient to require the disarming of her followers. Note that the authorities did not claim jurisdiction over the beliefs of the Antinomians, but only over the promulgation of them.

The Bay government never sought out intellectual deviates. The great majority of Antinomians, Baptists, and Quakers in the Bay Colony lived in good relations with their neighbors who adhered to the majority view, and even Cotton Mather welcomed such dissenters at the Communion Table of his church. By contrast, the Book of Common Prayer of the Church of England forbade such unconfirmed persons to approach the Communion Table, and Blackstone declared that by the laws of the kingdom, all dissenters were criminals.

The New England respect for freedom of conscience eventually carried over into the political field. In the American Revolution, New England Tories suffered less than the losing side in perhaps any other civil war. There were no purges, no executions, and no lynchings. The right of Tories to their opinion was respected so long as they were not a menace to the state. Our yearning for freedom of the mind is not satisfied with mere tolerance; we insist that our beliefs must be accorded the dignity of reasonable truth. When the suggestions of the Cambridge Synod were incorporated into the legal code as adopted by the Colony in the same year, they were qualified by a provision that "No human power [is] Lord over the Faith and Conscience of men, and therefore may not constrain them to believe or profess against their Consciences." That this was fundamental to the thinking of New England Puritans is indicated by the corresponding clause in the New Haven laws of 1656, asserting that "no Creature be Lord, or have any power over the faith and consciences of men, nor constreyn them to believe or profess, against their consciences."

After this doctrine had been tried in the fires of controversy with the New Haven Quakers for a century, William Livingston in *The Independent Reflector* for August 2, 1753, rephrased the Puritan principle thus: "The civil Power hath no jurisdiction over the [religious] Sentiments or Opinions of the subject, till such Opinions break out into Actions prejudicial to the Community, and then it is not the Opinion but the Action that is the Object of our Punishment." It has been recently asserted that this principle of freedom of thought was first expressed as state policy in the Virginia statutes of January 16, 1786, but it may well be that this is another case where the Virginians were deliberately drawing on Puritan documents.

What were the heresies which could not be vented without danger to the Bay community? In 1646 the General Court enumerated a number of theological errors the promulgation of which should be punished by banishment. All of these, it pointed out, were recognized as dangerous errors in most contemporary societies; the Puritans were not peculiar in dreading them. Neither the General Court, nor any ecclesiastical body in Massachusetts attempted to define heresy in any way other than by pointing out European consensus. Since there was no theological code in the Bay Colony, it is not surprising that there was no civil trial for heresy in Colony or Province. Of the literally hundreds of ecclesiastical councils before which ministers were charged with, among other things, theological deviations, there was only one which was clearly a heresy trial, and in that the foolish young defendant was out of bounds by most standards.

Modern historians are fond of using the word "orthodoxy" in connection with the Puritans, although the latter rarely employed the word themselves. Haskins uses the term "Puritan Orthodoxy" without defining it, and other historians use it with the terms "Baptist Orthodoxy" and "Quaker Orthodoxy" as if these were clearly stated theological positions. If by "Puritan Orthodoxy" you mean loyalty to the community, the term has cohesion, but once you try to prod its theological implications, you are in trouble. The fact is that orthodoxy was incompatible with the Puritan faith in reason. Orthodoxy is static. The Reverend John Robinson's parting words to the Pilgrims leaving Leyden included an admonition not to close their minds, as the Lutherans and Calvinists had done, to the progress of the knowledge of the nature of God. The minority in the Westminster Assembly of Divines took this same attitude, and they represented the Independent element which provided the leadership for the settlement of Massachusetts. Oliver Cromwell was probably the only head of state ever to beseech his followers to believe that they might be mistaken. The Puritans, recognizing that they were the children of an intellectual reformation resulting from individual examination of orthodoxy, thought of themselves as in a current sweeping toward a better knowledge of God, a knowledge to be reached by learning and study, not by the unpredictable personal revelations of the Antinomians.

To map the theological beliefs of a few Puritan theologians and to call the result "Puritan Orthodoxy" is to ignore one of the chief tenets of that community. The favorite Biblical text of the New England ministers was that which enjoins us to call no man father; and the improvement which they made of it was to point out that they, the clergy, had no authority to enjoin upon laymen any particular interpretation of doctrine. Even some of the most conservative of the Massachusetts ministers, themselves completely Calvinistic in doctrine, told the members of their congregations that the layman's chief duty toward God was to arrive at an understanding of Him by an examination of the validity of every tenet of Christian doctrine. The Calvinistic and Lutheran churches of Europe required that their members accept certain theological dogmas, but in Massachusetts the primary requirement for church membership was an individual experience of God's Grace, described by the individual in his own words.

This emphasis on freedom of the mind was then unique, and today is far from universal. Most of the early settlers of Massachusetts had been members of Church of England parishes, which were by definition agencies of an external power which dictated doctrine and practice, and discouraged criticism of it. Today the Roman Catholic Church denies liberty of conscience in matters of orthodoxy and morals, and the Protestant Episcopal Church requires its members to accept its doctrines and discipline. The colonial New England churches, like the Church of England, required the consent of the individual members to their moral discipline, but each offender was heard by his peers in open church meeting, instead of being tried by the clergy according to a fixed external standard. Instead of an established Congregational Church with power to enforce conformity in doctrine and morals, we have only individual churches which could punish what they determined to be heresy or sin only by denying the sinners fellowship until they repented. Actually, they rarely excommunicated anyone for heresy. The General Court submitted the Platform of 1648 to the local churches for their approval, but no ratification was called for, for it would not have been binding. The General Court printed the result of the Boston Synod of 1662, and "commended" it "unto the churches and people." In 1680 it ordered the Savoy Confession printed "for the benefit of the churches," but its use was optional. In 1708 Connecticut "commended" the Saybrook Platform to the churches.

Puritan orthodoxy, then, was a consensus of the views of the whole community, most members of which did not feel that they were authorized to cast stones at any man who held other theological opinions. Let's see how this worked out in practice. The one significant employment of the term "orthodoxy" in Massachusetts law was that requiring every town to maintain a learned and orthodox minister. Under this law, a few towns or parishes called Baptist ministers and used the power of civil taxation to support them, but there never was a case, so far as I can find, in which the town's choice of a minister was challenged in the courts on the basis of his orthodoxy.

After a town had chosen a minister, a group of neighboring churches was invited to send lay and clerical delegates to ordain him. In eighteenth-century ordinations there were frequently minority protests to the effect that the candidate was not sound on certain points of Calvinistic theology, but in few if any cases was a candidate rejected on primarily theological grounds. The council sometimes advised a candidate to decline a call because his theological views would cause trouble in that particular town, but I cannot remember the record of a case in which he was denied ordination because the council disagreed with his theology. The general custom was for the council to ask the candidate to state his religious convictions in his own words, although there were some ministers who would never permit a council of which they were members to require any theological statements. If the candidate said that he agreed with the Westminster Assembly of Divines, his orthodoxy was questioned no further; but candidates were never required to subscribe to the Westminster Catechism, or to accept any creed, or any other prearranged theological formulation. The minister who delivered the charge to the candidate commonly took the opportunity to disclaim any authority over his beliefs, or teachings.

The candidate would accept the covenant of the church over which he was ordained, but this document usually contained no theology, being a general statement of pious intent which any good man of the present generation could accept. Among the Massachusetts churches, the confession of faith was a late and limited development. When, in the Calvinistic reaction of the eighteenth century, some of the churches adopted detailed theological covenants, they also, commonly, adopted simple and untheological "forms of admission" so that people with "tender consciences" would not be excluded from communion. Some of these churches thus had a kind of theological "Half Way Covenant" which permitted Arminians and Unitarians to be members of Calvinistic town churches. In any case, the covenant or confession of faith was not dictated by any external authority, but was arrived at by mutual consent of its members and was subject to frequent revision. No Puritan church used any of the creeds in its services, much less required the acceptance of them as proof of orthodoxy. The creeds were, the ministers said, worthy of respect as the beliefs of pious men, but they were formulated by men, and therefore no other man could be required to accept them. Ministers who were Calvinists held to their beliefs because to them they seemed logically sound, not because they were received from authority. Revelation was confined strictly to the Bible, and if a colleague could find no proof of the Trinity in it, this personal idiosyncracy did not disqualify him as a minister in good standing.

Since there was no Congregational Church, but only individual churches, each with a doctrine arrived at by a consensus of the opinions of the inhabitants of town or parish, there could be no Congregational orthodoxy except of the vaguest and most general sort. There was no clear-cut theological difference between Congregationalists, Baptists, and Episcopalians. So far as the Baptists were concerned, the Congregationalists admitted that they were right as to baptism. The dread which the early Puritans had of Baptist Antinomianism had proved unfounded, and their chief criticism of that denomination was the lack of college-educated clergy among them. The Baptists tended to attack the Congregational ministers as not being sound Calvinists, but some of their own ministers were overt Arminians. The Baptist churches were congregational in polity, each with its own consensus of theological beliefs, so a Baptist orthodoxy would be as hard to find as a Congregational one.

The Puritans made the Thirty-Nine Articles the shibboleth which divided Dissenter from Anglican, but their objection was not to the theological content of the Articles but the fact that they were a limitation on freedom of conscience. The liberal bishops were as Arminian as Charles Chauncy could wish, while the American converts to the Church of England tended to be as Calvinistic as any New-Light whose noisy conduct they deplored. The American converts to Anglicanism to a large degree represented a reaction against the democratic theological polity of the Congregationalists. One of the reasons for the founding of King's College was to have an institution in which the students were not, as at Harvard and Yale, encouraged to get intellectual exercise by playing battledore and shuttlecock with the axioms of Christian dogma. Thus the difference between Anglican and Congregationalist was not in theology, but in the locus of authority.

Massachusetts in her first century and a half was an ideal proving ground for the principles on which our democratic way of life rests. Fortunate choice of settlers, happy isolation which afforded freedom to experiment, a basic philosophical faith in the reason of the common man, and freedom from the shackles of orthodoxy, make this a critical period in the growth of the democratic doctrine which we today regard as fundamental. The critical moment of the American Revolution came in the first decade of settlement, when the individual settlers took into their own hands and managed, through democratic town and church machinery, all of the matters of property, civil government, and religion which could be handled at that level. They made what was perhaps the most remarkable effort in the history of civilization to establish a society in which authority rested, in so far as possible, on the conscience of the individual. The rest of the colonial period in New England is the story of the adjustments in law and authority which that revolution made necessary.

The Virginia Gentry and the Democratic Myth

D. Alan Williams

One of the thrusts of post World War II "consensus" conservative historians has been to demonstrate that democracy was indeed widespread and deep during the colonial period, particularly during the eighteenth century. In the case of Virginia it was argued that political, economic, and social democracy existed for all. According to this view, a political minority, the gentry, had to defer to the wishes of the majority—the small and the middle-sized farmers. D. Alan Williams, Professor of History at the University of Virginia, calls that view fallacious. He demonstrates here that it was in fact the landed gentry—a tight-knit group—that dominated Virginia's political, economic, and social life, with the support and good wishes of the lesser groups. The important positions were controlled and filled by the gentry; the "people" could only vote for members of the House of Burgesses, but even then their choices came from among the privileged classes.

Colonial Virginia invariably provides the model for the typical southern colony—an aristocratic, staple-producing, agrarian society, divided geographically, economically, and socially into a coastal tidewater and an upcountry piedmont and valley. Originally conceived as a home for free laborers, craftsmen, and small farmers, Virginia by the eighteenth century exploited slave labor, nearly destroyed its yeoman farmer class, and turned over its government to a planter gentry. Landownership was a prerequisite for voting and essential for political advancement and social prestige, and though many were landowners, government remained a monopoly of the wealthy and well born. The Anglican church was more firmly established in law than New England Congregationalism. All political officials were appointed, except members of the House of Burgesses. In sum, Virginia possessed most of the classic ingredients for social and political conflict.

Yet, in fact, sectional and social controversy were at a minimum in eighteenth-century Virginia. Some historians have even proclaimed the colony a democratic society with power in the hands of the people rather than the gentry. They have duly noted the presence of such Virginia revolutionaries, republicans, and libertarians as George Washington, Patrick Henry, George

Reprinted with permission from D. Alan Williams, "The Virginia Gentry and the Democratic Myth," in *Main Problems of American History*, No. 103, Quint, Albertson, Cantor, eds. (Rev. Ed.; Homewood, Ill.: The Dorsey Press), pp. 25–33.

Mason, Thomas Jefferson, and James Madison. Indeed, they have seen in Virginia's golden age (1720–70) the symbol of the ideal agrarian society whose monuments have been preserved in Williamsburg, Mount Vernon, Monticello, and the great James River plantations.

Clearly, Virginia presents us with contradictions. How do we explain them? Are historical appearances deceiving? Or is it a matter of semantics? Does government led by the wealthy necessarily mean aristocracy? Does democracy exist just because a majority of the populace has the right to vote?

Essentially, seventeeth-century Virginia society was a small-farmer society. Although some large landholders existed, most settlers themselves cultivated the fields with the aid of an occasional indentured servant. Even the large farmers were self-made men who had attained their positions by hard work. Small farmer and large planter sat together on the county courts, the vestries, and in the assembly. Class distinctions were blurred in a society made up entirely of struggling farmers, most of whom found life crude and precarious.

Three major developments between 1660 and 1720 changed the kind of society and government Virginia would have: (1) establishment of the English imperial system, (2) Bacon's Rebellion, (3) introduction of slavery and the large plantation.

The great test of whether Virginia would manage her own affairs came between 1660 and 1720. From the collapse of the London Company until the restoration of Charles II in 1660, Virginia, an isolated and insignificant royal colony, had been virtually free from English control. After 1660, the English formulated a uniform policy for their expanding empire. Political economists, royal officials, merchants, and parliamentary leaders were confident they could construct a thoroughly planned and integrated economy by fitting all parts into the whole and enforcing mercantilistic principles through the navigation acts. The Crown would manage the operation. Charles II and James II appointed governors loyal to them, and issued orders making the royal colonies responsive to their wishes. No longer could Virginia act without recourse to the motherland; the colony must fit the pattern.

In Virginia, it fell to popular Governor William Berkeley (1642–52, 1660–77) to reconstitute royal government after the Civil War and to enforce imperial policies with which he frequently disagreed. These were years of poverty, turmoil, and upheaval. The navigation acts, naval wars with the Dutch, and overproduction almost ruined the tobacco trade and plunged Virginia into a prolonged depression. King Charles not only granted the Carolinas, the Jerseys, and Pennsylvania to his favorites, but also gave away valuable Virginia lands. All colonists suffered, but none more than the small farmers and the older colonial leaders. The result was Bacon's Rebellion.

Bacon's Rebellion of 1676 has been called the forerunner of the American Revolution, a class war between small farmers and planter aristocrats, a struggle for self-government against a despotic governor, and a typical encounter between irresponsible frontiersmen and ill-treated Indians. Some have contended that the revolutionary generation, eager to find precedents for its own rebellion, created a myth out of a minor incident little different from numerous rural disturbances in North Carolina, New Jersey, Maryland, and in England itself.

An Indian war was the immediate cause of the rebellion. The obvious sources of upheaval were economic—depression, high taxes, war, and the destruction of the Dutch tobacco trade by the navigation acts. The underlying source was social—the old leaders' loss of status to new migrants coming into the colony after 1650.

For several years, both large landholders and small farmers had been gradually moving westward in search of rich tobacco land. They paid scant attention to Indian treaty rights or possible reprisals. Although settlement had reached only fifty miles beyond Jamestown and had barely penetrated inland from the rivers, incidents along the frontier mounted, with both whites and Indians committing raids and atrocities. The frontiersmen were no more restrained than the half-savage Indians. Though undeclared war raged, by early 1676 Governor Berkeley vacillated. He feared to touch off a general Indian war, which would bring needless bloodshed, as in King Philip's War in New England, and would upset the Indian trade that several of his friends were engaged in. The harassed settlers, some large landholders among them, rallied behind Nathaniel Bacon, a financially embarrassed young councilor whose overseer had been killed by roving Indians. Against Berkeley's express orders, Bacon attacked and slaughtered two tribes allied with Virginia. He contended that they were hostile Indians, but some cynics noted that these same Indians also held choice lands and large caches of furs. The governor promptly proclaimed the attackers in rebellion.

Bacon's forces, fully aroused and armed, turned from Indian problems to redress their political grievances, thereby revealing the social facet of the conflict. During the English Civil War, Virginians had had a taste of the independent local government they long savored. In the early part of the war, Berkeley set up efficient county and parish governments. After Cromwell triumphed in England, he abolished royal government in the colony and replaced Berkeley with powerless governors elected by the assembly. In the absence of effective central leadership, county justices of the peace, parish vestrymen, and local burgesses became Virginia's political leaders.

However, when the Restoration came in 1660, Berkeley regained his office and attempted to reestablish the central government in Jamestown. In the spirit of Stuart politics, he appointed favorites to the county courts and supported local cliques, which established property qualifications for voting and replaced popularly elected vestries with self-perpetuating vestries.

Berkeley consolidated his position by keeping the same loyal assembly in session for fifteen years. To the chagrin of the early colonial leaders, his favorites were new men who had come to Virginia during and after the Civil War. They were frequently well trained, and had political and economic connections in England. Bacon's chief lieutenants were older, established planters, disgruntled at losing their former power and prestige. These frustrated colonists seized on the unsettled Indian conditions to voice political protests. At a hastily called assembly in June, 1676, they passed laws, "democratical" in nature, aimed at breaking the power of Berkeley's county oligarchies and reasserting the position of the old settlers. What ultimately was intended is unknown. Bacon died; the rebellion collapsed; and Berkeley, going berserk, executed twenty men in what was the only political blood purge in American history.

Bacon's Rebellion produced no great Virginia victory over royal authority. Crown restraints in Virginia and other colonies grew greater in the 1680's. Governor Thomas Lord Culpeper (1677–83) and Lord Howard of Effingham (1684–88) both were selected representatives of Stuart imperial policies. Lord Howard, in particular, was a persistent, obedient servant of the Stuarts, a confirmed believer in the divine right of kings, and completely unsympathetic toward representative government. The assembly, he asserted, should meet only when called by the king, should consider business previously approved by the Crown, and should execute only those laws that had been scrutinized by royal attorneys. Had such a policy been carried out, colonial self-government would have been squelched. But this did not happen, because bitter opponents of the 1670's joined forces to isolate and neutralize the governors, thereby depriving them of the loyalty of a proroyalist political faction in Virginia.

The Stuart threat to representative government ended with the Glorious Revolution of 1688. Englishmen thrust James II from the throne and called William and Mary to be their monarchs. This bloodless coup brought significant changes to Virginia. Howard left the colony, and his able successors, if they did not always appreciate the assembly, respected its right to speak for the colony and relied heavily on it for direction. The Virginia Assembly, sensitive to the growing powers of Parliament, sought the same for itself. From stubbornly resisting direct royal influence in the 1680's, Virginia after 1690 waged a subdued, unspectacular, and highly effective campaign to neutralize the governor's influence in domestic politics. By 1720, the campaign had succeeded.

Social and economic changes understandably paralleled and interacted with political change. By the early eighteenth century, the Indian threat had vanished, expansion without fear was possible, altered marketing conditions in Europe created new demands, and English and Scottish merchants turned to the Virginia market with new vigor. The colony was looked on as an economically underdeveloped area in need of credit. British merchants who controlled the tobacco trades extended credit with reasonable assurance of recovering their investment. Most of this credit went to the larger planters and their friends, who, in turn, acquired more land, expanded operations, upgraded their standard of living, and built the great plantations for which the colony became known.

The slave was the decisive difference between mid-seventeenth-century and mid-eighteenth-century Virginia. Before 1680, slavery on a large scale was rare, but it was commonplace thereafter. Slavery and mass-production methods characterized the tobacco plantation economy after 1720. Virginians condoned slavery as an established fact, though few defended it. The real sufferers they thought, were not the slaves but the small planters and yeoman farmers who worked the fields with their families and with an occasional indentured servant. The yeoman might draw some satisfaction from knowing that the slave was permanently tied to the bottom rung of the social scale, but he also knew that his position was not much higher because of that same slave. While the small planter might buy a few slaves, he lacked the resources to match his more affluent neighbors, and he lost economic power and social position to the growing number of large slaveholding, landed gentry.

One major change came after 1720, when thousands of Scots-Irish and German immigrants pushed down from Pennsylvania into the fertile Shenandoah Valley and into the western piedmont. Socially and religiously, these new settlers differed from those to the east. They were Presbyterians, Lutherans, Quakers, and German pietists—all dissenters from the established Church of England. Highly individualistic, they were alien to eastern traditions. Tobacco was not their king, since it could not be grown in the hilly back country. Yet, there was no sectionalism in colonial Virginia, no regulator uprisings similar to those of the Carolinas, no Paxton boys marching on Williamsburg as they did on Philadelphia, no tenant riots like those in New York and New Jersey. Unlike the Carolina frontier, the Virginia frontier was an overlay of new immigrants and old Virginians. At the same time that Germans and Scots-Irish were drifting south into the valley, settlers from eastern Virginia were moving west onto the piedmont, and speculators were making bold plans to sell their western lands. Acting with dispatch, the Virginia General Assembly wisely established counties and extended representation to the new areas, leaving the settlers with none of the complaints about governmental inequities that upset inhabitants in the Carolinas and Pennsylvania. In an earlier day, the influx of dissenters might have caused serious problems, but religious fanaticism (never strong in Virginia) was on the wane by the eighteenth century, and toleration was on the rise. Some dissenters were harassed, but most were left free to worship as they pleased, provided they paid their tithes to the Anglican church. Moreover, the colony's political leaders were also its leading land speculators. To sell land, they had to have settlers; to get settlers, they had to provide attractions. Their attractions were cheap land, available government, religious toleration, and a minimum of interference by spiritual and secular authorities. Most immigrants wanted no more than that. There was no sectionalism, for there were no sectional grievances. Sectionalism as a divisive force was not apparent until after the Revolution.

The golden age of the Virginia plantation society ran from about 1720 to the eve of the Revolution. The populace—free and slave, native and immigrant—doubled, tripled, and then quadrupled in number. Tobacco was king, land was wealth. With the widest coastal plain in the colonies and fertile valleys just beyond the first mountain ridge, Virginians, unlike South Carolinians, had little difficulty in acquiring land. Dominating this society were the planter gentry—the first aristocracy of the rural south, the counterparts of Charleston's planter-merchants, the equals of Philadelphia and Boston merchants.

The first planter gentry of Virginia had been a score or so of men, primarily members of the council—the Carters, Randolphs, Byrds, Lees, Custises, Pages, and Ludwells—whose families in Virginia had found positions denied them in England, and who had risen to the top through shrewd business practices and the accumulation of vast tracts of land. They had helped carve a civilization out of the wilderness with little help from the Crown; consequently, they often thought royal governors were interlopers gathering spoils after the labor had been done. By intermarriage, they had created a tight coterie of leaders that no governor could break. Sensitive to insult and quick to anger, they zealously guarded their interests through the distribution of Crown land, a function of the council. Generous in parceling land to themselves and their friends, they were equally generous in granting the king's land to all Virginians.

By the mid-eighteenth century, as the colony grew and tobacco trading flourished, the number of affluent planter families reached several hundred. The council could no longer contain all the gentry families. Many burgesses not only were as wealthy as councilors but also were their social equals. As the lower house gained ascendancy over the upper house, the new generation of Randolphs, Harrisons, Lees, and Pages preferred to sit in the House of Burgesses alongside other rising gentry. No longer did small planters gain election to this "tobacco club." Neither did small farmers serve as justices or vestrymen, for offices at all levels were taken up by the gentry and their sons. Distinctions between classes, blurred in the seventeenth century, were much clearer in the eighteenth.

Even though well-defined class lines existed in colonial Virginia, government by the gentry was not necessarily detrimental to the popular interests or so difficult to perform objectively as it would be in a more diverse and complex social order. First, the common bond of land and farming gave the large and small cultivators similar economic interests and made the society homogeneous, at least east of the Blue Ridge Mountains. Second, the lesser farmer naturally elected his more affluent neighbors to the House of Burgesses, since the poorly run plantation was no recommendation for a public office whose main trust was promoting agricultural prosperity. Third, the hard-working small farmers lacked the time to serve in political offices. Finally, since social mobility was fairly fluid in a fast-growing society, the independent farmers and small slaveholders saw no reason to oust or destroy the larger planters. They wanted to join them.

The liberal humanism of the planter gentry did much to assure the people that they had little to fear from planter leadership. The gentry willingly served in government because they believed in noblesse oblige—with power and privilege went responsibility. Honor, duty, and devotion to class interest had called them to office, and they took the call seriously. Not without a certain amount of condescension, they thought that government would be run by those less qualified if they refused to serve. They alone had the time, the financial resources, and the education necessary for public office. Moreover, they were the social leaders, and were therefore expected to set an example in manners and morals, to uphold the church, to be generous with benevolences, to serve the government with enlightened self-interest, and in general to be paragons of duty and dignity.

Not surprisingly, they enjoyed the prestige that came with office. To be in a position of authority, to control government, to enact laws, to have the power of life and death over men are intangibles for which there can be no financial compensation. Not that such compensations were omitted from the scheme of things. The real advantage of political service to most officeholders came from the opportunity to acquire land and to extend their business acquaintances. It would not be remiss to say that the gentry had a split personality—one side governed by duty, the other side by lust for land. Perhaps this is what is meant by "enlightened self-interest."

Trained for public duties on their self-contained plantations, the gentry brought to office well-developed talents and tastes for wielding power. Though they remembered their own interests, they nevertheless believed that they were bound to respect and protect those of others. They held that sovereignty was vested in the people, who delegated certain powers to government. They extolled republicanism and willingly enfranchised the people. Their humanism was a product of experience, common sense, and the common law. Liberal humanism not only seemed the right and just attitude; equally important, it worked. Of course, the Virginia gentry were in a position to be charitable. They trusted the people because the people trusted them. One may speculate whether their view of individual liberties would have been so liberal had Virginia been less homogeneous in character or had the lower classes challenged their leadership.

The small farmers and slaveholders had one protection against gentry oligarchy: they were in the majority and they had the right to vote. True, they elected only the burgesses, but that single choice was an important guarantee of their rights, since the House of Burgesses was the strongest political body in Virginia. Thomas Jefferson once remarked that the election process itself tended to eliminate class conflicts and extremism; the aristocrat with no concern for the small farmer was not apt to be elected, and the man who demagogically courted the popular vote was ostracized by the gentry. Therefore, the House of Burgesses became, at the same time, the center of planter rule and of popular government. It operated as a restraint on oligarchy.

Recently, historians Robert and B. Kathryn Brown have gone one step further and argued that Virginia, like Massachusetts, was a democratic society. Economic, social, and political opportunity, they say, existed for all. Far from the genty's dominating the society, while the small- and middle-sized farmers and slaveholders deferred to their judgment, the reverse was actually the case. Since the gentry were in a minority, they had to defer to the wishes of the majority—the small landholders—if they wanted to retain the reins of office. So say the Browns.

A comparison of the relative positions of the small landowners in the seventeenth and eighteenth centuries shows that without doubt they had immeasurably improved their economic lot at the same time they were being socially outstripped by their more affluent neighbors. Politically, they shifted from holders of office to a check on officeholders.

Yet, was this democracy? What good, indeed, was majority vote when the majority had so little to vote for? Choosing a burgess to sit at the occasional meetings of the General Assembly in Williamsburg was not nearly so important as having a voice in county affairs, where most matters affecting small farmers were decided. Could a society be democratic when every single official except one was appointed by self-perpetuating justices, vestrymen, councilors, and the royal governor, none of whom was responsible to the electorate? Could it be democratic when only men of means held office and when advancement seemed more dependent on wealth and birth than on talent? To a large extent, the small farmers were effectively separated from the power structure, with little means of uniting in a rural society.

The gentry, a minority, were a group of like-minded men working in close alliance, careful not to disturb the social equilibrium. When they contested each other for a seat in the assembly, they offered the electorate only a choice between planter A and planter B, between Tweedledum and Tweedledee. They were the perfect example of what has been consistently true in American society: a cohesive minority dominating an amorphous majority. Perhaps the question that ought to be asked about this planter gentry government is not whether it was democratic but whether it was effective. William Penn once wrote, "governments depend on men rather than men upon governments, let them be good and government cannot be bad." If this is the primary question, then must not one say that the planter gentry, with their own type of consensus politics, provided eighteenth-century Virginia with enlightened and dynamic leadership?

Or is the half-century of the golden age a period too short to judge the gentry society? After the Revolution, Virginia declined as the soil lost its richness, tobacco lacked foreign markets, and the younger generations moved west and south to more promising opportunities. When the planter aristocracy ceased to be infused and refreshed with the rising gentry, it became inert, lacking in insight, inbred, and distrustful of progress elsewhere. In the place of a masculine Washington or a visionary Jefferson, nineteenth-century leadership could offer as its spokesmen only an effete Edmund Randolph and a myopic John Tyler. Equally significant, the lower class, having deferred so long to the excellent leadership of the eighteenth century, could not recapture what it had let atrophy—its political consciousness. Not until the 1960's did Virginia voters exercise their voting privileges in proportions equaling those of their colonial ancestors.

Suggested Further Reading for Chapter 1

Loren Baritz, *City on a Hill: A History of Ideas and Myths in America* (New York: John Wiley & Sons, Inc., 1964).
Carl Bridenbaugh, *Cities in the Wilderness: The First Century of Urban Life In America, 1625–1742* (New York: Capricorn Books, 1964).
Carl Bridenbaugh, *Myth and Realities: Societies of the Colonial South* (New York: Atheneum Publishers, 1963).
Wesley F. Craven, *The Legend of the Founding Fathers* (Ithaca: Cornell University Press, 1965).
David D. Hall (ed.), *Puritanism in Seventeenth-Century Massachusetts* (New York: Holt, Rinehart & Winston, Inc., 1968).
Edmund S. Morgan, "The Puritans and Sex," *New England Quarterly*, 15 (1942).
Samuel Eliot Morison, *The Intellectual Life of Colonial New England* (Ithaca: Cornell University Press, 1963).
Warren C. Scoville, "Did Colonial Farmers 'Waste' Our Land?," *The Southern Economic Journal*, 20 (1953).
Page Smith, *As a City Upon a Hill* (New York: Alfred A. Knopf, Inc., 1966).
Louis B. Wright, *The Dream of Prosperity in Colonial America* (New York: New York University Press, 1965).

We are now to detail the causes of events, the most interesting of any in the history of the world; the overthrow of tyranny and despotism in the United Colonies, and the erection there of an altar, sacred to liberty.

Egbert Guernsey—
History of the United States Designed for Schools, 1848

2

MYTHS OF THE REVOLUTIONARY ERA

Grant Wood "Daughters of Revolution"; reproduction courtesy of the Cincinnati Art Museum and Associated American Artists.

Daughters of Revolution: Spirit of '76.

Tisdale engraving reproduced from the collection of the Library of Congress.

The Tory's day of judgment: neglected underside of the American Revolution.

Introduction

The American colonial scholar Alan Simpson once counseled students of America's past to be especially aware of what he called the "special character of American history"—its "deceptive resemblance to a short story with a simple plot." Although initially suggested within the context of our colonial past, Simpson's concerns have come to be shared by students and scholars of America's revolutionary era as well. Perhaps for too long, as the historiographical article contained in this chapter will suggest, the Whig interpretation of the revolutionary era was dominant. According to Whig historians, of whom George Bancroft was the most accomplished practitioner, American history was told rather simply as the "story of liberty." To Bancroft's mind, the great dynamic of the revolution and its aftermath was clearly the engagement of the principle of freedom and the instrument of tyranny. Simply put, America symbolized the forces of liberty and progress—Great Britain, those of despotism and reaction.

Whig historians were perhaps the first to systematically construct a usable past from America's revolutionary experiences. And although the Whig interpretation has been largely modified if not preempted, the spirit of nationalism and patriotism which the Whig historians inspired continues. Ever since, the era of the American revolution has served as the touchstone of American institutions and traditions. The rhetoric of this period has at various times served to justify the designs of social and political movements from the radical left to the reactionary right. Both Black Nationalists and the Daughters of the American Revolution have found the revolution "as American as apple pie." Not surprisingly, because of some rather blatant disregard for historical accuracy, the revolutionary era has remained all things to all men—and a rather grand mythology has followed in its wake. This chapter seeks to isolate some of the cherished historical myths that have continued to surround leading personalities and events of the revolutionary period. Historians have taken us far beyond merely questioning the historical accuracy of Paul Revere's ride or Washington's crossing the Delaware. Myths reside here, but they are of little consequence. Rather, twentieth-century historians in particular have forced us to reexamine our standard emphasis upon the heroic qualities of America's revolutionary leadership, the tyrannical nature of the British empire in general and George III in particular, the unity of revolutionary sentiment amongst the colonists, the failures of the Confederation period, and the almost-divine qualities of the Founding Fathers. The following selections present some significant challenges to viewing the revolutionary era in such simplistic and mythical terms.

The American Revolution: The Critical Issues

Robert F. Berkhofer, Jr.

Much that might be construed as historical myth is the byproduct of historical study itself. In their quest for certitude and "truth," historians themselves have often overstated their argument so as to create a biased or distorted image of the past. For this reason, we have felt it advisable to include historiographical selections, particularly when dealing with the major wars of American history. The discrepancies that can emerge between history as actuality and history as perceived seem to be most apparent within this context. The inherent complexity of the war-time environment seems to trigger the intellectual energy of its commentators so that myth-constructing is more likely to occur. Robert F. Berkhofer, Jr., formerly of the University of Minnesota and of late the University of Wisconsin, provides this perspective as regards the critical issues of the American Revolution. By emphasizing the "mental climate" in vogue as historians forwarded their differing interpretations, Professor Berkhofer stresses the importance of theory, as well as evidence, as a determinant in historical judgment. Mr. Berkhofer suggests that historians seek a new level of historical understanding —one based more on evidence than theory, perhaps more on reality than myth.

Before a historian can explain the whys of the American Revolution, he must figure out what it was; and its nature is as perplexing and controversial a problem in historical circles as the explanation of its causes. To professional historians, the phrase "American Revolution" means more than the hostilities between England and thirteen of her colonies. It refers also to the social, economic, and political changes in the colonies that they presume caused, accompanied, or resulted from the conflict. Historians, therefore, usually have grouped their questions about the nature, causes, and consequences of the Revolution around three images:

1. *A war of independence between colonies and a mother country.* Who initiated the hostilities? When and where did the conflict start? What were the issues? Did the conflict result from the grievances voiced shortly before the war broke out, or did it result from long-term trends? Who were the individuals involved upon both sides and why? What was the rebels' aim? Was it independence or some accommodation within the empire? Why were just thirteen of England's North American colonies involved? Why was it a war of rebellion rather than a guerrilla war or a palace revolution?

2. *A political revolution.* Did the colonies revolt to preserve the basic political system they had or to establish a new kind of government? Why? Were there political innovations despite the aims of the revolutionaries, and, if so, why? What was new about the political results of the Revolution? Was it a new type of revolution at the time? Can it be compared to other revolutions at the time, such as the French Revolution? Can it be compared to the revolutions to establish new nations today?

3. *A social revolution.* Was the American Revolution a social revolution as well as a political revolution? If so, why; if not, why not? What is the model for the meaning of the word "revolution"? How do we judge a set of events to be a revolution? Is the American Revolution comparable to other full-scale revolutions or not? What is the relationship between the social structure of a country and a revolution in general and the social structure of the American colonies and the American Revolution in particular?

These questions suggest the whole problem of comparability as an important way of describing what the American Revolution was and explaining why it was what it was. In other words, we must try to determine what was "American" about the American Revolution and what was revolutionary about it in order to discuss its nature, causes, and consequences.

Answers to all these questions depend as much upon the historian's theories about human behavior as upon the evidence he discovers about past human actions. In fact, he cannot interpret the evidence about the past without employing his theories about the nature of man and society to make sense of it. The credence the historian gives the multitude of pamphlets, newspapers, and letters written by the participants in the Revolution directly reflects his belief whether professed ideals or something else better explains why men did what they did. For example, should the rhetoric of the Declaration of Independence be taken at face value in explaining why the colonists went to war with England? In other words, is there a difference between rationale and motivation, and how do we differentiate between them? Are there deeper causes for human behavior than men of the time say or even understand fully? How do we know whether to trust words or deeds more in seeking to understand the American Revolution? How does the historian know the real reasons for such a complex occurrence as the Revolution? Ultimately each student of history must combine the evidence from the past with his theories of how men act and societies operate in order to derive the "facts" he says happened and that he calls history.

The historian must use his theories of man and society to interpret his evidence in another way also, for he asserts facts about a whole society upon the basis of documents produced by a few of its members. How representative of the people of their time were Thomas Jefferson, Patrick Henry, or John and Sam Adams? Were their aims also the goals of all segments of the population? Or, did they desire some end quite different from what they told the public? What is the role of leaders in a revolution, and what relationship do they bear to the society of their day? Were some groups of people quite unrepresented by any of the spokesmen for the Revolution? Did most colonists support the war? Did they even care about it? How do we know when so little evidence about their thoughts remains? Should the analyst presume a societal consensus on Revolutionary goals, excepting Tories of course, in order to interpret his evidence? Or, should he assume agreement on goals was due to majority compromise, or public apathy, or coerced submission, or all of these in combination? Again the historian resorts as much to his theories of culture and society as he does to his evidence in constructing the synthesis of facts that he calls history.

So fundamental are these questions about theoretical orientations and so complex the set of events called the Revolution that historians today are no more in agreement upon the answers about the nature, causes, and consequences of the Revolution than were contemporary observers. Now as then some historians focus their attention on the battle of ideas and ideals expressed in the polemical literature of the period. For them the Revolution was fought for political and constitutional ends and the society as a whole subscribed to these aims. Still other observers, then as now, picture the Revolutionary leaders as seeking only selfish political and economic ends behind their propaganda of ideals. To these analysts, the Revolution was perpetrated by an elite which sought to retain or gain political office and social status denied to them by the British imperial system. To attain their economic and political goals, according to this view, the Revolutionary leaders not only challenged English sovereignty and control but also repressed the demands of the masses for the very rights and ideals the leaders proclaimed they were denied in their polemics against England.

Although these two interpretations have existed since the Revolution, their fullest formulation has come in the twentieth century. One group of historians, led by Charles McLean Andrews in the 1920s and Lawrence Henry Gipson more recently, sought to place the colonists' aims and activities in the larger context of the British Empire. Hence, they are called the imperial school. In looking at the colonial struggle in terms of the imperial system, they generally took at face value the importance of the debates over political representation and the constitutional issues of empire. Opposing this approach were such historians as Carl Becker, Charles Beard, Arthur Schlesinger, Sr., and, more recently, Merrill Jensen. They portrayed the Revolution as a struggle among different colonial classes for economic and political hegemony in addition to the fight for independence from England. Since this interpretation arose during the Progressive period and featured an economic interpretation of people's motives, it has been named the progressive or economic interpretation school.

According to the progressive school, the Revolution became an internal or class conflict as well as a rebellion against an external power. As one of the chief formulators of this approach, Carl Becker, stated in *History of Political Parties in the Province of New York, 1760–1776*,[1]

> The American Revolution was the result of two general movements; the contest for home-rule and independence, and the democratization of American politics and society. Of these movements, the latter was fundamental; it began before the contest for home-rule, and was not completed until after the achievement of independence. From 1765 to 1776, therefore, two questions, about equally prominent, determined party history. The first was whether essential colonial rights should be maintained; the second was by whom and by what methods they should be maintained. The first was the question of home-rule; the second was the question, if we may so put it, of who should rule at home.

Arthur M. Schlesinger, Sr., bolstered this view with *The Colonial Merchants and the American Revolution*,[2] in which he found that merchants in all the colonies spearheaded the opposition at first against the Stamp and Trade Acts. When, however, they discovered their movement encouraged men lower in the social hierarchy to question their leadership, they drew back from such bold opposition to English control. Only the Tea and Coercive Acts, in Schlesinger's opinion, provided sufficient provocation to reunite the merchants with the more radical elements of society in favor of open rebellion against British rule. As the capstone of this interpretation, Charles Beard in *An Economic Interpretation of the Constitution*[3] portrayed the foundation document of the federal union as the work of conservative upper-class men to foster their own economic welfare by inventing a system of government directly benefitting their own economic interests at the expense of the bulk of small farmers and tradesmen and by forcing this document through ratifying conventions before the majority of Americans understood what was happening.

According to these historians and others who followed their lead, the course of the Revolution moved from conservatives demanding colonial rights, to radicals seeking the rights of men as opposed to property in the Declaration of Independence, to a counter-revolution of the conservatives culminating in the adoption of the Constitution and the temporary repression of the lower classes. It remained for Merrill Jensen to finish this picture by showing in *Articles of Confederation*[4] and *New Nation*[5] that the history of the whole Revolutionary era resulted from the struggle for power between two continuous and consistently opposed groups based upon socioeconomic cleavages fundamental in the American society of the time. On one side were most members of the colonial upper classes and nouveau riche of the Revolution who favored stronger central government always as means to check lower-class democracy and to regulate trade and pass taxes in their interest. In opposition to these "nationalists" were the "federalists," or the democratic radicals, who favored decentralization of government in the interests of the agrarian democratic views of the majority of the population. For Jensen, as for the others of this school, the ideals expressed in the polemics of the period determined less the actual behavior of the Founding Fathers than their economic interests, and the significant story of the Revolution was found more in the internal conflict of social classes based upon economic power than in the external struggle with England.

After World War II, the progressive version of the causes, nature, and consequences of the Revolution was denied by such writers as Daniel Boorstin, Louis Hartz, Benjamin Wright, and most important, Edmund Morgan, who synthesized his research and their outlook in his influential little book, *Birth of the Republic, 1763–89*[6]. As the title of Benjamin Wright's *Consensus and Continuity, 1776–1787*[7] suggests, these men find neither class conflict nor swings between radical and conservative leadership during the course of the Revolution. Rather they see a consensus upon ideals and aims among the whole non-Tory population. For them, as for nineteenth-century interpreters, the fight was over constitutional principles expressed in the rhetoric of the period, and they minimize the internal divisions among the people. Robert E. Brown in *Middle-Class Democracy and the Revolution in Massachusetts, 1691–1780*,[8] in fact, reversed the progressive or social conflict school by arguing that the colonists were primarily middle-class property owners, making conflict as unnecessary as it was absent. According to these historians, the revolutionaries went to war to conserve or preserve the rights and class structure they already possessed against England's efforts to change the system rather than to gain new rights and new institutions. As a result of their approach, these men have been denominated the conservative or the consensus school. Later observers think they reflect the conservative ideology of the post-war Eisenhower years.

The consensus school approach continued into the decade of the 1960s and formed the focus of much of the discussion upon the nature of the Revolution. The inclusive term, consensus school, hides the difference between those concerned about the ideas of the revolutionists and those interested in the nature of social stratification and political power. The former analyzed the ideology said to be shared by all, while the latter reconstructed the statistics of class and leadership. During the 1960s Robert E. Brown extended his research to Virginia as a crucial example of his thesis on middle-class democracy and found the Old Dominion relatively equalitarian in class structure and open in economic opportunity. Jackson Turner Main came to the same conclusion in *The Social Structure of Revolutionary America*.[9] However, in a study of legislative membership he found a trend toward greater democratization during the course of the Revolution. The major contributor to the analysis of ideology during the 1960s was Bernard Bailyn. By taking all of the rhetoric of the revolutionaries seriously, he reconstructed their world-view of political ideals, history, and social hierarchy. He also converted the previous static view of Revolutionary ideals and principles into one that was dynamic and evolving. Thus, he calls his introduction to *Pamphlets of the American Revo-*

lution,[10] "The Transforming Radicalism of the American Revolution." In these ways, both he and Main subtly but nevertheless definitely shifted the emphasis upon ideas and class of the consensus school into a new path stressing change and new developments.

Although the consensus school dominated the interpretation of the Revolution during most of the 1960s, it never held the field uncontested. Not only did older men such as Merrill Jensen continue to write vigorously in refutation of the consensus view, but younger men once again found class conflict a key to Revolutionary history. Chief among these was Staughton Lynd, who employed New York State, just as Becker did, to study the effects of class division upon Revolutionary politics. Parallel to this reemphasis upon class conflict and the internal struggle for political power has been the attempt of the "New Left" school, as it is called, to determine the actual views of the inarticulate masses, or to produce the history of "The American Revolution Seen From the Bottom Up," as Jesse Lemisch, the most vociferous advocate of this approach, phrased it in Barton Bernstein, ed., *Towards a New Past: Dissenting Essays in American History.*[11]

By the end of the 1960s, a new mood was evident among historians of the Revolution. Even younger historians trained by consensus or idealist historians questioned the exclusive stress upon ideas, no matter how dynamic. Bailyn's student, Gordon Wood . . . wonders whether attention to rhetoric alone answers the question why the colonists acted as they did as opposed to what they said. Though his book, *The Creation of the American Republic, 1776–1787*[12] mainly examines the public ideology of Revolutionary leaders in the tradition of his mentor, he asserts in passing that the leaders' words were motivated by reasons other than those that appeared in their public pronouncements—by anxieties grounded in changing social realities of the time. Bailyn himself in *The Origins of American Politics*[13] moved to place the ideology he had uncovered into a political context. Other historians reassessed their own and newer work upon the nature of political factions and conflict before, during, and after the Revolution. In short, the conflict and consensus schools seem to be combining to create a new synthesis that acknowledges the existence of social classes but also points out that conflict, except in certain conspicuous cases, was confined to fights among the elites in the colonies. Similarly this emerging synthesis says the majority of the population shared the same ideology although Tories and certain radicals formed a strong minority. Thus, neither conflict nor consensus, neither ideas nor action is stressed to the exclusion of the other. Rather, further research is needed to determine the role of each element.

So far we have discussed only the ideological and other behavior of the American side of the Revolution without giving any attention to the conflict between Britain and her colonies. A discussion of when and who began the Revolution and why must include consideration of both sides in the controversy, leading directly to the problem of overall causation. Again the historian must resort to some theoretical framework of how he explains revolution or "internal wars" in the words of one analyst. Some patriot historians, inspired by the indictment in Jefferson's Declaration of Independence, blamed the war on English selfishness in general and the stupidity of George III in particular. Some loyalist historians, on the other hand, condemned the stubborn colonists and the shrewd demagogues who duped the people into disloyalty to Crown and mother country. On the whole, however, observers then and historians of this century agree that the factors that produced the hostilities were diverse and the causes for independence extend beyond the battles of Lexington and Concord or even the Sugar and Stamp Acts. No matter which side the imperial school historians took on the constitutionality of the English and colonial views of the empire and sovereignty, they placed the perspective of causation where it belonged: on the changing relations between both sides in the conflict. Though many books have been published on this phase of the Revolution, the relationships were so complex that still more research is needed. The imperial school also questioned whether the imperial economic regulations were unfair to colonial capitalists. In other words, did the colonists have legitimate grievances against trade regulation, or was the English government only requesting the colonists to pay their fair share of the empire's expenses? Today we study this issue on two levels: (1) what the actors said and believed regardless of what the true balance of payments may have been, and (2) what the historian reconstructs that true balance of payments to have been using statistics and economic theory. In this debate, as in preceding ones, we see historians seeking resolution of issues through greater precision in specifying what questions the problem involves and what theories and evidence are needed to produce answers to these questions. . . .

From this hasty survey of the history of the history (called historiography) of the Revolution, the student can see the importance of theory as well as evidence in seeking to understand the nature, causes, and consequences of it. Equally obvious is the need for a good set of questions about what has to be known and what we seek to and can know from the evidence. The student should therefore compare the questions historians ask and the questions that he wants to ask. . . .

The American Revolution created American history by creating a new nation. Thus, Americans study the history surrounding the American Revolution for clues to American identity and character. At the same time their beliefs about themselves as a people influence what they perceive to be the nature, causes, and consequences of the Revolution. What the Revolution was, then, depends to a large extent upon what Americans think they are or ought to be. Thus, as the attitudes Americans hold about themselves change, so too does the history of the Revolution and especially the meaning of the Revolution for American history. . . .

As a result of this changing compound of morality, theory, and the search for national identity, each generation interprets and reinterprets the

American Revolution. Is this the ultimate, and perhaps the only, truth about the Revolution, or can we determine the facts about it independently of the mental climate of our times?

Notes

1. Carl Becker, *History of Political Parties in the Province of New York, 1760–1776* (Madison: University of Wisconsin, 1909).
2. Arthur M. Schlesinger, Sr., *The Colonial Merchants and the American Revolution* (New York: Longmans, 1918).
3. Charles Beard, *An Economic Interpretation of the Constitution* (New York: The Macmillan Company, 1913).
4. Merrill Jensen, *Articles of Confederation* (Madison: University of Wisconsin Press, 1940).
5. Merrill Jensen, *New Nation* (New York: Alfred A. Knopf, Inc., 1950).
6. Edmund Morgan, *Birth of the Republic, 1763–89* (Chicago: University of Chicago Press, 1956).
7. Benjamin Wright, *Consensus and Continuity, 1776–1787* (Boston: Boston University Press, 1958).
8. Robert E. Brown, *Middle-Class Democracy and the Revolution in Massachusetts, 1691–1780* (Ithaca: Cornell University Press, 1955).
9. Jackson Turner Main, *The Social Structure of Revolutionary America* (Princeton: Princeton University Press, 1965).
10. Bernard Bailyn, *Pamphlets of the American Revolution* (Cambridge, Mass.: Harvard University Press, 1965).
11. Barton Bernstein, ed., *Towards a New Past: Dissenting Essays in American History* (New York: Pantheon Books, Inc., 1968).
12. Gordon Wood, *The Creation of the American Republic, 1776–1787* (Chapel Hill: University of North Carolina Press, 1969).
13. Bernard Bailyn, *The Origins of American Politics* (New York: Alfred A. Knopf, Inc., 1968).

George III: The Myth of a Tyrannical King

Darrett B. Rutman

The name of George III of England and the word *tyranny* have become synonymous in the American mind. With the accumulation of new evidence, however, many historians challenge the legendary war guilt of King George. Representative of those who have contributed to rehabilitating his tarnished image is Darrett B. Rutman of the University of New Hampshire. One of the premier scholars of colonial America, Professor Rutman here speaks to the seminal importance of Thomas Paine in redirecting the colonists' revolutionary sentiment from Parliament to king. As Rutman argues the case, before the appearance of Paine's pamphlet *Common Sense* of January, 1776, the colonists had sustained their loyalty to the Crown and sought "home rule under the king" and a redress of grievances from the British Parliament, not independence.

What the colonists considered an effort to change the governance of the empire by depriving their little parliaments of the exclusive right to legislate in local affairs—an effort increasingly discerned as a conspiracy of tyrants against man's innate liberty—had led to open war. Through all of this, however, the colonists had remained loyal subjects of George III. Stamp distributors, customs commissioners, lobsterbacks, the intolerable acts—all symbolized a confrontation with Parliament and ministers, not king. Indeed, during the early years of argument, the king's governors were obeyed, even to the extent of the Virginians going unrepresented in the Stamp Act Congress because their governor dissolved the House of Burgesses just as it was about to name representatives. As late as 1775 the same crowd which "huzzahed" for George Washington as he crossed Manhattan Island on his way to take command of the colonial forces around Boston rushed to the Battery to "huzzah" for a newly-arrived royal governor. Anglicans in the colonies prayed for the health of the king in conformity with the Book of Common Prayer, while in the taverns men drank the health of George and wished him the best of fortune.

> This bumper I crown for our sovereign's health,
> And this for Britannia's glory and wealth.

So went the last verse of "The Liberty Song," almost the national anthem of pre-independence days. Petitions and remonstrances directed to the king professed in all sincerity the loyalty of the colonists. And as the confrontation with Parliament and the king's ministers continued in time, as the colonists came to the position of denying Parliament any authority whatsoever over them, the king, to an ever increasing extent, symbolized the colonists' attachment to an empire which they had not yet considered leaving. "Allegiance to Parliament?" the Second Continental Congress asked rhetorically in 1775; "we never owed—we never owned it. Allegiance to our king? Our words have ever avowed it—our conduct has ever been consistent with it."

Allegiance could be stretched so far, however, before it would break. And colonial allegiance to king and empire was brought almost to the breaking point by Lexington and Concord. In New York and Georgia, militiamen seized control of the ports; in Williamsburg, militiamen (including students at William and Mary College) patrolled the streets to prevent the royal governor from seizing the arms in the public magazine. Extra-legal governments began making their appearance, in some cases extensions of the committees of correspondence, more usually the old lower houses of the legislatures sitting independently of the governor and council. Thus in Virginia, when the governor attempted to stop certain activities of the House of Burgesses by dissolving the House as had been done in Stamp Act days, the House, rather than meekly obeying him, trooped across the street to a tavern and went about its business, subsequently setting itself up as a supreme Virginia Convention. Soon after the governor fled to the safety of a British warship. By December 1775, royal governments had been swept away in all but New Jersey, although the proprietary governments of Pennsylvania and Maryland remained. By July 1776 these too were gone.

On an inter-colonial level, the Second Continental Congress met in May 1775 to remain in session throughout the remainder of the controversy and through the war years ahead. The delegates from the various colonies to the Congress immediately accepted the war situation which existed. In June an organization for war was created, the Congress assuming control of the forces besieging Boston and appointing Virginia's George Washington to command. To pay for the war effort, the Congress authorized the issuance of two million dollars in paper money. In July a "Declaration of the Reasons for Taking up Arms" was issued.

Yet war and independence were not synonymous, a fact which the members of the Congress pressed in their "Declaration." Their quarrel was still with corrupt ministers and a Parliament which had sought "all the easy emoluments of statutable plunder" by undertaking "to give and grant our money without our consent, though we have ever exercised an exclusive right to dispose of our own property." They were resisting only the "intemperate rage for unlimited domination" on the part of ministers and Parliament. This had led to war, but for their part military activities would cease "when hostilities shall cease on the part of the aggressors, and all danger of their being renewed shall be removed." They were not seeking to break with their "friends and fellow subjects in any part of the empire." "We assure them that we mean not to dissolve that union which has so long and so happily subsisted between us, and which we sincerely wish to see restored." In a petition to the king approved at the same time—the so-called "Olive Branch Petition"—their loyalty to George III was expressed in fervent terms, and that good monarch was humbly requested to intercede for them with Parliament and the ministry to obtain a repeal of the intolerable acts, the withdrawal of the troops, and a renunciation of Parliament's assertion of authority over the colonies. Some objected to what seemed a craven appeal. Massachusetts' John Adams, a delegate to the Congress, considered that the outbreak of war signified the end of such petitions and denounced the Olive Branch as putting "a silly cast on all our doings." But undoubtedly it represented the feelings of most of the colonial leaders. They were fighting to preserve their liberty within the empire as it had been prior to 1763 and as they had come to define it formally during the long controversy: Home rule under the king.

For over a year the Continental Congress remained in this anomalous position of leading a fight against the king's troops for liberty under the king. In July 1775, the Congress hinted at the possibility of looking for foreign aid against the king's army and shortly after set up a five-man "Committee of Secret Correspondence" for the purpose of corresponding with "friends in Great Britain, Ireland, and other parts of the world"—the last phrase ominously portending the future alliance with France. War supplies were purchased abroad and a navy provided under Commodore Esek Hopkins. To the north, Fort Ticonderoga was taken by "rebels" commanded by Ethan Allen and Benedict Arnold; the Battle of Bunker Hill (more accurately Breed's Hill) was fought June 17, 1775 and the siege of Boston went on; an unsuccessful march on Canada was set underway. All in the name of the king.

But the king would not accept the role assigned him by the colonists. He would not be their father and protector. Firm in his support of Parliament and his ministers, he curtly rejected the Olive Branch Petition in August 1775. Subsequently he proclaimed that the Americans were in a state of rebellion to his person.

In the situation the position of the colonists was somewhat unique and certainly difficult. The king was the only link to England and empire which they were prepared by this time to admit, yet the king refused to serve as such a link. As a consequence this last link had to be severed.

It was not easy to do. The colonial leaders were Englishmen. Their professions of loyalty to the monarch were and had always been sincere. If they discerned—and wrote of—a conspiracy to tyrannize in London, the king was no part of it, only his ministers and the Parliament they dominated. Moreover, the king over the years of argument had always been well presented. There was, in effect, little if any animosity toward him.

Still, the last link was severed. Gradually the person of the king began losing some of the sanctity attached to him. The action of the monarch in bluntly and personally refusing the Olive Branch tarnished his reputation, as did the hiring of German mercenary soldiers for the war in America. The various actions of royal officials "in the name of the king" rubbed off on the monarch—Falmouth, Maine, shelled; Norfolk, Virginia, shelled and burned. Then, in January 1776, an outright attack on the king appeared, the first of importance since the start of the troubles. This was *Common Sense*, a little pamphlet by Thomas Paine, an English radical newly arrived in Philadelphia.

Here the very institution of monarchy was attacked, and the English monarchy in particular:

> Government by kings was first introduced into the world by the heathens, from whom the children of Israel copied the custom. It was the most prosperous invention the devil ever set on foot for the promotion of idolatry. The heathens paid divine honors to their deceased kings, and the Christian world has improved on the plan by doing the same to their living ones. How impious is the title of sacred majesty applied to a worm, who in the midst of his splendor is crumbling into dust!
>
> England since the conquest hath known some few good monarchs but groaned beneath a much larger number of bad ones; yet no man in his senses can say that their claim under William the Conqueror is a very honorable one. A French bastard landing with an armed banditti and establishing himself king of England against the consent of the natives is in plain terms a very paltry rascally original. It certainly hath no divinity in it.
>
> In England a king hath little more to do than to make war and give away places, which in plain terms is to impoverish the nation and set it together by the ears. A pretty business indeed for a man to be allowed eight hundred thousand sterling a year for and worshipped into the bargain! Of more worth is one honest man to society, and in the sight of God, than all the crowned ruffians that ever lived.
>
> But the king, you'll say, has a negative in England; the people there can make no laws without his consent. In point of right and good order, it is something very ridiculous that a youth of twenty-one (which hath often happened) shall say to several millions of people older and wiser than himself, 'I forbid this or that act of yours to be law.'

George III himself was castigated as "the royal brute." Aristocracy was castigated for its continual exploitation of the people for the support of luxuries. All the difficulties of the last years were laid not merely to Parliament or the ministers, but to the king as the very leader of their conspiracy against liberty and the thought of reconciliation under the king was dismissed as ridiculous. Independence and a republican government were, to Paine, the common sense solution to the preservation of liberty in America. Sold in record numbers, passed from hand to hand and from tavern to tavern, the pamphlet was vital in creating a tyrant of George III.

The Loyalists and the American Revolution

Wallace Brown

History is particularly harsh with losers. It chooses to recall the triumphs and achievements of only the victors. In this sense the Loyalists or Tories—those who remained faithful to England and king during the course of the American Revolution—represent the forgotten Americans of the revolutionary period. If for no other reason than their numbers, however, they bear closer attention. On the eve of the conflict with England, by far the majority of Americans could be justly described as "reluctant revolutionaries," and by most estimates clearly one-third of colonial society harbored loyalist sentiments and thought the thrust to revolution ill-advised. In the following essay, Wallace Brown, of the University of New Brunswick, explores the attitudes and motives of the Loyalists, a forgotten dimension of the American Revolution.

The exile of the Loyalists represented the removal of the crust of increasing aristocratic pretensions that was forming on Colonial society.

In the numerous celebrations of the American Civil War centenary now taking place, Northerners usually honor and respect the Southern rebels. But the losers of an earlier civil war, the War for Independence, are practically forgotten outside academic circles, and even there the only general study of the Loyalists, or Tories, is sixty years old; hence this article must be rather tentative in its conclusions.[1] The Loyalists, those American colonists who opposed independence and wished to remain in the Empire, although often condemned out of hand during the nineteenth century, have since been more fairly treated by historians; but the present neo-Bancroftian interpretations of the Revolution, which minimize social conflict within the colonies, apparently forget them.[2]

In Great Britain the Loyalists, perhaps an embarrassment to the Whig school of historiography, have been snubbed, just as they often were as refugees at the time. In Canada, however, where many emigrated and were officially named the United Empire Loyalists, they are venerated as founding fathers, which helps to explain the surprising differences—to many Americans, at least—between the Dominion and the United States.

Any discussion of the American Revolution that neglects the Loyalists is distorted. For a start, there is their sheer number. In 1814 Thomas McKean, the Pennsylvanian Patriot and statesman, agreed with ex-President John

From "The Loyalists and the American Revolution," by Wallace Brown, in *History Today*, 12 (March 1962); reprinted by permission of the author and publisher.

Adams that about one-third of the colonists had been opposed to the Revolution. The usual estimate of the number of Loyalist exiles is 100,000 out of a population of 2,500,000, and Professor R. R. Palmer has recently suggested, on the basis of a lower estimate, that the American Revolution produced twenty-four émigrés per thousand of the population compared with only five per thousand in the French Revolution. He also calculated that the American confiscation of property was proportionally almost as great as the French.[3] Between 30,000 and 50,000 Loyalists fought on a regular basis for the King, and many more served in the militia or engaged in guerilla warfare. In 1780 8,000 Loyalists were in the regular army at a time when Washington's army numbered only about 9,000. All these figures represent only hard-core Loyalists. Most escaped exile and confiscation, or were quietist, biding their time, merely expressing their loyalty with a secret prayer for the King or a muted curse for the Congress.

The strength of the Loyalists varied from state to state. John Adams believed that New York and Pennsylvania would have joined the British if strongly patriotic Virginia and New England on either side "had not kept them in awe," and he agreed with Chief Justice Marshall that the Southern States were "nearly equally divided." Timothy Pickering referred to eastern Pennsylvania as "enemies' country," and in 1776 Washington, who had many harsh words for the Tories, considered them "our great danger." Modern scholarship agrees that the Loyalists were very strong in the Middle States, the Carolinas and Georgia, and weakest in New England, Virginia and Maryland. But they were a force to be reckoned with everywhere.

John Adams has left contradictory estimates of the number of Loyalists; not surprisingly, because they are impossible to count and difficult to define. Many changed sides, sometimes more than once, and usually according to variations in the fortunes of war. Before the Declaration of Independence numerous Loyalists, such as Joseph Galloway of Pennsylvania and William Smith, last royal Chief Justice of New York, took a Whig position. Also it must be remembered that up to one-third of the population probably remained neutral during the struggle. Contemporary definitions of the Loyalists include, "A Tory is a thing whose head is in England, and its body in America, and its neck ought to be stretched," and "Every fool is not a Tory, yet every Tory is a fool," but basically a Tory was simply someone who remained loyal to George III and opposed the Declaration of Independence.

There are, as yet, no statistics with which to answer the question, who were the Loyalists? As with Whigs, Loyalists can be found in every class, race, occupation, religion and geographical area in the colonies. But some very speculative classification can be made.

Office-holders, from royal Governors to humble customs officials, were usually loyal, even when descended from old colonial families. William Franklin, Governor of New Jersey and illegitimate son of Benjamin Franklin, is a representative of this group. It has been estimated that between one-half and two-thirds of the members of the colonial councils remained loyal.[4] So did many lawyers, like Jonathan Sewall of Massachusetts or Peter Van Schaak of New York, who often did well out of Crown fees. Professional people in general, particularly doctors and teachers, contributed heavily to the Loyalist ranks. The leading physician of Charleston, South Carolina, was the loyal Alexander Garden, while Myles Cooper and John Camm, respectively heads of King's College, New York and the College of William and Mary, Virginia, shared this outlook.

Two classes usually loyal were the large land-owners, especially proprietors like the Penns, or the Granville heirs in North Carolina, and the merchants (a list of proscribed Boston Tories in 1778 included thirty-six merchants).

Religion was sometimes important. Dissent tended to be patriotic, identifying Anglicanism with the setting up of a dreaded bishopric, missionaries and foreign domination. Anglicanism was often the religion of the conservative classes, and a revolt against King George was a revolt against the head of the Church. Thus the whole congregation of Trinity Church, New York, and their minister went to Nova Scotia to escape the Republican government. In Virginia, on the other hand, where the Church of England was in many ways independent, Anglicanism was not particularly associated with loyalism. Jefferson and Washington were at least nominal Anglicans. The pacifist religious sects, mainly the Quakers, were usually branded as Tories, not always fairly because they opposed violence by *both* sides, and their refusal to take oaths of allegiance to the new states was not necessarily political.

Some special categories of Loyalists should be mentioned. Political expediency could be the deciding factor; in New York the De Lanceys took the Tory side against the Whig Livingstons. Some loyalist groups perchance saw Great Britain as an ally against their own more immediate enemies; the small farmers of New York who had rebelled under Prendergast against their Whig landlords; the Baptists of Ashfield, Massachusetts who were struggling against the established patriotic Congregational Church; the back-country Regulators of North Carolina defeated at the battle of Alamance by the dominating Whiggish seaboard; the Highlanders, sent to the Carolinas after the '45, who had been leniently treated and feared a Whig attack on their land titles. A number of Indians and Negroes can be classed as Loyalists. Dunmore, Clinton and Cornwallis offered Negroes their freedom in return for military service, and Joseph Brant led what was left of the Six Nations for the British.

Most Loyalists had, or thought they had, something material or spiritual to lose by the break with Britain. This fear is the great unifying factor. Officials had their jobs to lose, lawyers their fees, merchants their trade, land-owners their proprietorship, Anglicans their dream of a bishop, King-worshippers their idol, Anglophiles their membership of the Empire, Regulators and Massachusetts Baptists their hope of royal help, Negroes their freedom, Indians the British alliance against the frontiersmen. Conservatives and the better-off in general had most to lose in a revolutionary upheaval; the timid became loyalist in areas occupied by British troops; some office-holders, and perhaps the Highlanders, were loath to break their oaths of allegiance.

It is a great mistake to imagine that the Loyalists were always or even usually of high social standing. Most of those who settled in modern Canada were of humble origins, many signing their names with a cross. A recent study of New Brunswick Loyalists by Esther Clark Wright reveals that ninety per cent were American born and that the majority were farmers, tradesmen and artisans.[5] Canada attracted the poorer classes because it was much more cheaply reached than England. Every colony abounds with examples of humble Loyalists, and the conclusion must be that the Loyalists were a complete cross-section of the population.

The example of a single state will illustrate this. In June 1778 Delaware listed forty-six particularly obnoxious Tories excepted from a general pardon. The list included: two captains, three physicians, one lawyer, and seven described as assemblymen, office-holders and wealthy citizens; then lower down the social scale, nine husbandmen and two yeomen; lower still, two labourers, one weaver, three coopers, one cordwainer, one coppersmith, one tailor, one saddler, one bricklayer, one hatter, two innkeepers, two mariners, three shallopmen and three pilots.

The Whigs, of course, had few good words for the Tories. Thomas McKean called them "the timid and those who believed the colonies would be conquered . . . also the discontented and capricious of all grades," while Tom Paine added "Interested men, who are not to be trusted; weak men who *cannot* see; prejudiced men who *will not* see; and a certain set of moderate men who think better of the European world than it deserves."

No doubt many Loyalists were weak and timid, but it took courage to face social ostracism, mob violence and finally, in some cases, banishment and confiscation. Tenacity was required to start a new life in the frozen wastes of Canada. It was the Whigs who were "discontented and capricious" as they continually shifted their argument from one stand to another, disavowing independence until almost the last moment.

In 1775 the *Massachusetts Spy* described a Tory as "one who is a maintainer of the infernal doctrine of arbitrary power, and indefeasible right on the part of the sovereign, and of passive obedience and non-resistance on the part of the subject." This was true only of extremists. Many Loyalists such as Thomas Hutchinson, the distinguished descendant of the seventeenth-century heretic, Anne Hutchinson, Daniel Dulany, the native-born Maryland lawyer, and Samuel Seabury, the Connecticut-born future first Episcopalian American bishop, vigorously opposed the Stamp Act and most of the "new" legislation after 1760. For example, Dulany had vehemently denied the right of Parliament to tax the colonies. The Declaration of Independence precipitated the genuine Loyalists, and in Hobbesian terms, at least, they became the rebels while the Whigs became the loyalists. The quarrel continued to be not over colonial rights or "passive obedience," but rather over whether the colonies' future well-being could be best assured within the Empire or without. The Loyalists had a fundamental trust in Britain, the Whigs a fundamental distrust.

Sometimes only very subtle differences might separate a Loyalist from a Whig. John Jay and Peter Van Schaak, both successful New York lawyers, came from similar aristocratic backgrounds. Jay became a reluctant Patriot, bowing before the *fait accompli;* Van Schaak became a reluctant Tory by following his conscience; both had opposed British policy, and both remained firm friends even after Jay had served on the committee which exiled Van Schaak.

That personal reasons often determined a man's allegiance is shown by the number of split families. As in every revolution, brother fought brother. General Timothy Ruggles, a leading Massachusetts Loyalist, was opposed by his wife, brothers and some of his children. David Ogden, a Loyalist judge from New Jersey, had three sons of the same persuasion, but two others were patriots. Two of the sons of John Lovell, the eminent Loyalist teacher at the Boston Latin School, followed their father while a third was a patriot.

Usually the younger generation in split families was Whig, such as John Randolph of Virginia, the Loyalist father of patriotic Edmund Randolph, but the Loyalist Governor of New Hampshire, John Wentworth, had a Whig father, and the Franklins offer a similar example.

Some split families were even accused of keeping a foot in both camps in order to be on the winning side whatever happened. Benjamin Pickman fled from Salem, Massachusetts, in 1775, but left his wife behind to look after their property to which he returned ten years later. The Dulanys of Maryland were charged with a similar subterfuge.

But kinship and intermarriage were often potent forces in deciding allegiance. In Petersham, Massachusetts, the Whig schoolmaster, Ensign Man, opposed the Loyalist minister, Aaron Whitney until he married Whitney's daughter and became a Tory. Elizabeth Gray was of sterner stuff. From a Tory background she married into the patriotic Otis family which isolated her from her own relatives. Rightly, she remained with her husband, but her letters reveal her unhappiness and continuing loyalty.

It is now necessary to explain the comparative ineffectiveness of the Loyalists, in spite of their number and talent. They were at an initial disadvantage because so many were in basic agreement with the Whigs until the Declaration of Independence. Because they were conservatives, the Loyalists failed to organize themselves and had nothing to compare with the Sons of Liberty or Committees of Correspondence. It was thought that the revolt would soon peter out, and many agreed with Lord Dunmore, Governor of Virginia, that the Patriots should be given enough rope to hang themselves. This attitude, combined with a belief in British invincibility, produced apathy. Many Loyalists neglected to vote for delegates to the first Continental Congress where the Loyalist Joseph Galloway's plan for reconciliation was narrowly defeated. Meanwhile, the revolutionary Whigs perfected their machinery and the Loyalists were not able to control a single state government.

Unfortunately, the Loyalist faith in the power of the redcoats was shared, especially in the early stages of the war, by the British authorities who failed to use the Loyalist support effectively. The British officers, true to perennial form, looked down on the colonials. Thus Colonel Timothy Ruggles, who raised a Loyalist Massachusetts regiment, was very badly treated, and Edward Winslow, the Master-Muster-General of the Loyalist Provincial Forces, testified to British neglect and contempt.

As an additional discouragement, there were the activities of the British and Hessian troops which must have alienated many Loyalists and made Patriots of many more. The Reverend Leonard Cutting wrote from a strongly Loyalist area, Hempstead, Long Island, in 1781, complaining: "We have nothing we can call our own, and the door to redress is inaccessible. The army has done more essential injury to the King's cause than the utmost efforts of his enemies." Even Judge Thomas Jones, a leading New York Loyalist, devoted a whole chapter in his partisan history of the state to the "Illegal and Cruel Treatment of Loyalists by the British Military during the War!" It was reported that the British army was even driving the Quakers to take up arms.

But, of course, the worst persecution, both legal and illegal, came from the Whigs. The states passed test acts and finally acts of banishment and confiscation. Many Loyalists lost their civil liberties and political rights. At the same time they faced ostracism and the danger of mob violence. A Newport toast of 1775, "A cobweb pair of breeches, a hedge-hog saddle, a hard-trotting horse, and a continual riding to all enemies of America," was only too easily translated into destruction of property, tarring and feathering, or the horrible riding on a rail. Deaths, however, were rare. Loyalists were frequently imprisoned; one famous prison, which housed such distinguished inmates as William Franklin, was the "Newgate of Connecticut," the Simsbury copper mines transformed into dungeons.

Too much sympathy must not be lavished on the persecuted Loyalists. Where they were able, they dealt with the Whigs in similar fashion and, in spite of the British shortcomings, they did contribute to the war effort which naturally led to the bitterness of civil war. Several famous Loyalist regiments fought with distinction, such as Robert Rogers' Queen's Rangers, Patrick Ferguson's American Riflemen, Cortlandt Skinner's New Jersey Volunteers and John Butler's Loyal Rangers whose activities in New York state made Butler, possibly unfairly, a sort of folk-villain. (D. W. Griffith cast him for this role in his last great spectacle, *America*.)

The Loyalists were also used as civilian workers at army camps, as spies and as counterfeiters of Continental currency. Jonathan Bush of Shrewsbury, Worcester County, Massachusetts owned an hotel which was the centre for making and distributing counterfeit, but the Continental currency needed little encouragement to depreciate!

If the Loyalists had much talent, the Patriots had more. The Loyalists had no great leaders to compare with Washington, Jefferson, Franklin, or John Adams. They had only one really effective newspaper, James Rivington's *New York Gazetteer*, and no propagandist to compare with Samuel Adams. There were some outstanding Loyalist writers such as Jonathan Odell, the Tory satirist, and Joseph Stansbury, the song-writer, but Moses Coit Tyler, the literary historian of the Revolution, concluded that they were generally inferior to the Patriots. In the field of propaganda another scholar has reached a similar conclusion.

The exodus of the Loyalists began in 1776, when over 1,000 left Boston with the retreating British, and it continued throughout the war. In 1783 the evacuation of New York and Charleston resulted in the departure of 9,000 Loyalists from each city. The final total was probably 100,000 scattered around Great Britain, modern Canada, Florida and the British West Indies.

In London, the haven of the wealthier, the émigrés stuck together. In 1775 Samuel Curwen, of Salem, Massachusetts, founded a New England Club, meeting at the Adelphi Tavern for a weekly dinner, which was attended by such prominent New Englanders as ex-Governor Hutchinson, John Singleton Copley, the artist, Robert Auchmuty, the Boston lawyer, and Samuel Quincy, another lawyer, related to John Adams by marriage. The New England Coffee House in Threadneedle Street and the Old Jewry meeting-house were also habitual gathering-places. For most of them, separated from their homeland and often from their families, it was an unhappy time and sometimes one of real poverty. Furthermore, the exiles were the victims of English snobbery and patronage. Curwen was stung to write in his Journal for December 1776, after having heard the colonists described as "cowards" and "poltroons":

> It is my earnest wish the despised Americans may convince these conceited islanders, that without regular standing armies our continent can furnish brave soldiers and judicious and expert commanders, by some knock-down, irrefragable argument; for then, and not till then, may we expect generous or fair treatment. It piques my pride, I confess, to hear us called *"our colonies, our plantations,"* in such terms and with such airs as if our property and persons were absolutely theirs, like the "villains" and their cottages in the old feudal system, so long since abolished, though the spirit or leaven is not totally gone, it seems.

Curwen, like so many American visitors since, complained of the inadequate heating in London. On January 28th, 1776, he wrote: "Almost as cold as ever I felt in New England," and the next day, "The fires here not to be compared to our large American ones of oak and walnut, nor near so comfortable; would that I was away!" It is not surprising that Curwen returned home at the end of the war.

Thomas Hutchinson, the loving historian of Massachusetts, wrote, "I had rather die in a little county farm-house in New England than in the best nobleman's seat in old England." There was also disillusionment with Nova Scotia. One writer reported plaintively in 1784:

> All our golden promises are vanished in smoke. We were taught to believe this place was not barren and foggy as had been represented, but we find it ten times worse. We have nothing but his Majesty's rotten pork and unbaked flour to subsist on.... It is the most inhospitable clime that ever mortal set foot on.

This was the Loyalists' tragedy; they were Americans without a home.

The Loyalists felt betrayed by the Peace Treaty of 1783. The British negotiators, Oswald and Shelburne, had tried to get them a complete amnesty and return of all rights and property, but the only American concession was that Congress would "earnestly recommend" to the various states that the Loyalists be allowed to return for twelve months "unmolested in their endeavours to obtain the restitution of their estates, rights, and property." Further confiscation of property was to cease. In fact, confiscation continued and Loyalists found it practically impossible to regain their possessions, and active Loyalists often found it unfeasible even to visit their native states. The Loyalists were abandoned by the Treaty. But short of re-opening the war, the British were impotent, nor had Congress the power to enforce its pledge.

Some conservative elements in the United States deplored the loss of the Loyalists and wished to encourage the exiles to return. Alexander Hamilton complained, "We have already lost too large a number of valuable citizens." As early as May 1783, John Rutherford of New Jersey argued that wealthy Loyalist merchants would aid the state commercially if they returned; in 1784 a New Haven town meeting voted that the Loyalists be allowed to return for similar reasons; and this was typical of the attitude of the business community. It is common to find former Tories in positions of social and political trust in the decade following the end of the war. Hatred was reserved for active Loyalists who had helped the British. One such was a South Carolinian named Love, a participator in a massacre, who was lynched after a court had discharged him. Generally speaking, bitterness depended on the degree of civil war there had been in an area.

Although they felt betrayed by the Peace Treaty, the Loyalists were handled quite well by the British government. Throughout the war several pensions were paid out which reached an annual bill of £70,000 by 1782, and in July 1783, a Compensation Act was passed appointing a commission of five to enquire into the claims of the Loyalists for losses of property and income sustained during the war. Claims were heard in London and various Canadian locations, and after several years the final tally was: 5,072 claims presented for a total sum of £10,358,413. About one thousand of these were for various reasons not proceeded with; the remainder were paid over £3 million out of a total claim of £8,216,126. This represented property losses. In addition, about £26,000 was granted annually in pensions for losses of salaries, and a further sum in annual allowances to such people as widows and orphans. Beyond all this an equal amount was spent to help the Loyalists settle in Canada, while many received offices in the colonies or commissions in the British army. One interesting footnote is that certain humble Loyalists who had emigrated to America, made good, and then returned to England for political reasons, found that their treatment by the Claims Commission was unfair because of prejudice and class attitudes—a rather sad reward for loyalty.

Finally, what is the importance of the Loyalist exiles? By creating New Brunswick and Nova Scotia, and by injecting a large English-speaking element into French Quebec, they helped assure the future of Canada within the British Empire. The break-up and sale of large Loyalist estates probably had a democratizing effect. (This is a moot point that awaits further research.) In some places new men replaced the departed Loyalists, such as the Cabots and Lowells who moved into Boston from Essex County early in the war. In Rhode Island, the war helped to advance Providence and its leading commercial family, the Browns, over Newport which was occupied by the British for a time and became partly loyalist. There certainly were some changes of leadership in parts of the North, but in the South there seems to have been very little social change.

The loss of the Loyalists has been likened to the departure of the French Huguenots and the expulsion of the Moors from Spain. The list of Loyalists banned from Massachusetts has been said to read "almost like a bead-roll of the oldest and noblest families concerned in the founding and the upbuilding of New England civilization."[6] The great ability represented by New England Loyalists in particular cannot be denied, nor can the general cultural mediocrity of the first years of the Republic. The loss of such Loyalists as J. S. Copley, the artist, and Benjamin Thompson (Count Rumford), the scientist, must have had an effect; but against this it must be remembered that, apart from the fact that the United States *gained* certain useful people like Joseph Priestly, the exiled Loyalists represented the removal of the crust of increasing aristocratic pretensions that was forming on colonial society before the Revolution. Had they won, some Loyalists envisaged the setting up of a permanent aristocracy, and a lessening of the power of the lower houses of the colonial Assemblies. Because émigrés did not normally return, the United States was spared the sort of problems that France met after 1815, and it seems credible that the growth of democracy was thus helped considerably.

Against this it has been argued that the youthful financial, diplomatic and political mistakes of the Republic might have been ameliorated if the experience of the Loyalists had not been lost, but the trend of recent research is that the Tory emigration was less of a loss than previously thought; at any rate, the whole question is essentially speculative.

That it is probably fortunate that hard-core Loyalists generally left the United States is illustrated by considering two who did not—Catherine and Mary Byles. These two game old ladies, descended from the famous New England families, the Mathers and the Cottons, are perhaps a fitting subject on which to end this essay. They dwelt on in their old Boston house until the mid-1830's, reliving such memories as walking arm-in-arm with General Howe during the siege of Boston, frigidly putting up with the new régime, writing incessantly to their far-flung Loyalist family as they sipped "loyal tea" and complained of the "Yankees" maintaining their quarters as a permanent Loyalist museum (with themselves as chief exhibits), celebrating George III's birthday each year, and finally (Catherine) writing to congratulate George IV on his accession (the King never replied). They ensured that on their deaths their property all left the United States for more congenial loyal resting places. In 1835 the Boston authorities pulled down part of the sisters' home to make way for a road. They were outraged, but hardly surprised—it was simply "one of the consequences of living in a Republic."

John Eardley-Wilmot, one of the Claims Commissioners, began his enquiry with no particular liking for the Loyalists, but long familiarity with their misfortunes produced in him considerable admiration so that his account of the Claims Commission proceedings, published in 1815, was prefaced, rather appropriately, with the following lines from Milton

> Their Loyalty they kept, their love, their zeal,
> Nor number, nor example with them wrought
> To swerve from truth, or change their constant mind.

Notes

1. Claude H. Van Tyne, *The Loyalists in the American Revolution* (New York, 1902).
2. I am thinking of such historians as Robert E. Brown and Edmund S. Morgan.
3. Robert R. Palmer, *The Age of the Democratic Revolution* (Princeton, 1959), 188.
4. Leonard W. Labaree, "Nature of American Loyalism," *Proceedings of the American Antiquarian Society* (April, 1944), LIV, 19n.
5. Esther Clark Wright, *The Loyalists of New Brunswick* (Fredericton, 1955), 155–159.
6. Moses C. Tyler, "The Party of the Loyalists in the American Revolution," *American Historical Review* (October, 1895), I, 31. See also, E. A. Jones, *The Loyalists of Massachusetts* (London, 1930), ix; Lee N. Newcomer, *The Embattled Farmers* (New York, 1953), 78 and Lawrence S. Mayo, "The Massachusetts Loyalists," *Commonwealth History of Massachusetts*, ed. A. B. Hart (New York, 1929), 275–76 disagree with Tyler.

The Myth of the Critical Period

Merrill Jensen

The 1780's witnessed the institution of the Articles of Confederation as the first instrument of government, the first constitution for the new nation. Given the document's life span—the Articles prevailed from 1781 until the ratification of the Constitution in 1789—it has often been seen as an unfortunate interlude in the development of American democracy. Though the Articles were from a later perspective imperfect instruments of federal control, they were not, as has been argued, grotesquely inadequate. Merrill Jensen, the foremost historical scholar of the Confederation period and Professor of History at the University of Wisconsin, has sought to mitigate the stereotypes and deal sympathetically with the 1780's. Taking issue with the fashionable argument that the Articles represented the "critical period of American history," Jensen contends that such a view is a "phantom of the imagination," and that "some semblance of reality" can be achieved if one rather attempts to see the period from the perspective of those who lived it.

This book is an account of the first years of the new nation that was born of the American Revolution. Like every other segment of time, the history of the United States from 1781 to 1789 was an integral part of the past in which it was rooted and of the future into which it was growing. It was a time when men believed they could shape the future of the new nation, and since it was also a time in which they disagreed as to what that future should be, they discussed great issues with a forthrightness and realism seldom equalled in political debates. The history of the Confederation is therefore one of great inherent importance for the study of human society if for no other reason than that during it men debated publicly and even violently the question of whether or not people could govern themselves.

Aside from its inherent importance, the history of the Confederation has been of enormous significance to one generation of Americans after another in the years since then. Repeatedly Americans have turned to that history in the course of innumerable social and political struggles. They have done so because it was during those years that the Articles of Confederation were replaced by the Constitution of 1787. In order to explain their Constitution, Americans have appealed to the history of the period out of which it came. In the course of such appeals, sometimes honestly for light and guidance and sometimes only for support of partisan arguments, Americans have usually found what they sought. As a result the "history" has been obscured in a haze of ideas, quotations, and assumptions torn bodily from the context of fact that alone gives them meaning. Again and again political opponents have asserted that the founding fathers stood for this or that, while their writings have stood idly and helplessly in volumes on shelves or have lain buried in yellowed manuscripts and newspapers.

Since the founding fathers themselves disagreed as to the nature of the history of the period and as to the best kind of government for the new nation, it is possible to find arguments to support almost any interpretation one chooses. It is not surprising therefore that conflicting interpretations have filled thousands of pages and that all this effort has never produced any final answers and probably never will, for men have ever interpreted the two constitutions of the United States in terms of their hopes, interests, and beliefs rather than in terms of knowable facts.

The conflict of interpretation has been continuous ever since the first debates over the Articles of Confederation in the summer of 1776. Men then differed as to the kind of government which should be created for the new nation. They continued to debate the issue during the 1780's. The members of the Convention of 1787 differed as to the need for and the amount of constitutional change. When the Constitution was submitted to the public in October 1787 the controversy rose to new heights. Men talked in public meetings and wrote private letters and public essays in an effort to explain, justify, or denounce what the Convention had done. They disagreed as to what had happened since the war. Some said there had been chaos; others said there had been peace and prosperity. Some said there would be chaos without the new Constitution; others that there would be chaos if it were adopted.

Once it was adopted Thomas Jefferson and Alexander Hamilton, with two opposed ideals of what the United States should be, laid down two classic and contradictory opinions of the nature of the Constitution. These two basic interpretations may be simply stated. Jefferson held that the central government was sharply limited by the letter of the Constitution; that in effect the states retained their sovereign powers except where they were specifically delegated. Hamilton argued in effect that the central government was a national government which could not be restrained by a strict interpretation of the Constitution or by ideas of state sovereignty. These rival interpretations did not originate with Hamilton and Jefferson, for they had been the very core of constitutional debate ever since the Declaration of Independence, and even before it, for that matter.

Jefferson and his followers used the states rights idea to oppose the plans of the Federalists when they passed the Alien and Sedition Acts in 1798. But when Jefferson became President and purchased Louisiana, he justified his actions by constitutional theories that even Hamilton hardly dared use. Meanwhile Jefferson's opponents seized upon his earlier theories in a vain attempt to block the expansion of the United States. They did so again during the War of 1812 when the Federalists of New England became out-and-out exponents of "states rights" and threatened secession because they were opposed to the war.

In the decades before the Civil War, Daniel Webster and John C. Calhoun carried on the dispute, each having changed sides since his youthful years in politics. Webster, who had been a states rights spokesman during the War of 1812, became the high priest of nationalism, while Calhoun, a leading nationalist in 1812, became the high priest of the states rights idea which he elaborated to defend the slave-owning aristocracy of the South.

The Civil War itself was the bloody climax of a social conflict in which the ultimate nature of the Constitution was argued again and again in seeking support for and arguments against antagonistic programs. But even the Civil War did not finally settle the constitutional issue. The stresses and strains that came with the rise of industrial and finance capitalism produced demands for social and regulatory legislation. The passage of such legislation by the states involved the interpretation of the nature of the Constitution, for business interests regulated by state governments denied their authority and appealed to the national courts. Those courts soon denied the power of regulation to state legislatures. Then, when regulatory laws were passed by the national government, the regulated interests evolved a "states rights" theory that limited the power of the central government, and the national courts once more agreed.

Throughout American history the courts have drawn boundary lines between state and national authority. The pose of judicial impartiality and finality assumed by the courts cannot hide the fact that they have shifted those boundary lines with the shifting winds of politics, and always with sufficient precedents, if not with adequate grace. As a result they had created by 1900 a legal and constitutional no man's land in which all sorts of activity could be carried on without effective regulation by either state or national governments.

The crash of American economy in 1929 once more posed in imperative terms the problem of the nature of the Constitution. How should it, how could it deal with the potentiality of chaos inherent in unemployment, starvation, and bankruptcy, and ultimately, the loss of faith in the utility of the economic and political foundation of the society itself?

As the national government began to act where, plainly, state and local governments had failed to or were unable to act, the question of constitutionality was raised. For a time the courts once more listened to and heeded states rights constitutional theories which were expounded by opponents of the New Deal. New Deal lawyers, in turn, adopted as weapons John Marshall's nationalistic interpretations of the Constitution for ends which Marshall himself would have fought to the death. President Roosevelt, in his fight on the Supreme Court, declared that the Constitution was not a lawyer's document; yet some of the ablest lawyers who ever lived in America wrote it. New Deal publicists wrote tracts in the guise of history to prove that there had been a "national sovereignty" in the United States from the beginning of the Revolution. Therefore, they argued, the courts could not stop the New Deal from doing what needed doing by following a strict interpretation of the Constitution. Both the New Dealers and the Republicans insisted that they were the sole heirs of the legacy of Thomas Jefferson, while Alexander Hamilton went into an eclipse from which he has not yet emerged.

The most recent appeal to the history of the Confederation Period has come from those who support some form of world government. Adequate arguments for such a government can be found in twentieth-century experience, but, like most men, its backers turn to history for analogies and lessons.

When the League of Nations was set up at the end of the First World War men turned to American history after the American Revolution as a parallel experience. At that time books were written to show the "chaos" of the Confederation Period and the happy solution that came with the Constitution of 1787. Among them was a book by a great authority on international law with the title *James Madison's Notes of Debates in the Federal Convention of 1787 and their Relation to a More Perfect Society of Nations.* The book was widely distributed by the Carnegie Endowment for International Peace. This and other books like it had little relation to the realities of world politics in the 1920's and 1930's, but despite this supporters of the United Nations and of various plans of world government have again turned to the history of the American states after the American Revolution.

The most notable appeal has been that of Clarence Streit. In his book *Union Now* he analyzes the history of our past as he sees it. He calls the Articles of Confederation a "league of friendship." He says, paraphrasing John Fiske, that by 1786 there was universal depression, trade had wellnigh stopped, and political quackery with cheap and dirty remedies had full control of the field. Trade disputes promised to end in war between states. Territorial disputes led to bloodshed. War with Spain threatened. The "league" could not coerce its members. Secession was threatened by some states. Congress had no money and could borrow none. Courts were broken up by armed mobs. When Shays' Rebellion came, state sovereignty was so strong that Massachusetts would not allow "league" troops to enter the state, even to guard the "league's" own arsenal. Streit goes on to say that the idea of turning a league into a union was not even seriously proposed until the Convention opened in May 1787. And then, he says, within two years the freedom-loving American democracies decided to try out this invention for themselves. Streit goes on to argue that it would be just as easy to secure union of the democracies now as it was for the American democracies to achieve a union then. Some things made it difficult then; some make it so now. Some made it easy then; some make it easy now. . . .

Even if it can be granted that most appeals to the history of the Confederation have been sincere, let it also be said that they have seldom been infused with any knowledge of the period or its problems. The result has been the drawing of lessons the past does not have to teach. This is a luxury too expensive in an age when men have discovered how to unhinge the very force that holds matter itself together but have advanced very little beyond cave men in their notions of how to live peacefully with one another.

Yet it is little wonder that such false lessons have been drawn in the twentieth century because most of them have come from John Fiske's *The Critical Period of American History,* a book of vast influence but of no value as either history or example. Fiske, a philosopher and popular lecturer, wrote the book "without fear and without research," to use the words of Charles A. Beard. As long ago as 1905, Andrew C. McLaughlin, an impeccably conservative historian of the Constitution who wrote a far better book on the same period, said that Fiske's book was "altogether without scientific standing, because it is little more than a remarkably skilful adaptation of a very few secondary authorities showing almost no evidence of first hand acquaintance with the sources."

The story told by Fiske and repeated by publicists and scholars who have not worked in the field—and some who have, for that matter—is based on the assumption that this was *the* "critical period" of American history during which unselfish patriots rescued the new nation from impending anarchy, if not from chaos itself. The picture is one of stagnation, ineptitude, bankruptcy, corruption, and disintegration. Such a picture is at worst false and at best grossly distorted. It is therefore important to attempt a history which makes an effort to examine the sources, which is concerned with the nature of political and economic problems rather than with proving that one side or another in the innumerable political battles of the period was "right" or "wrong." Nothing is to be gained by following a "chaos and patriots to the rescue" interpretation. We have too long ignored the fact that thoroughly patriotic Americans during the 1780's did not believe there was chaos and emphatically denied that their supposed rescuers were patriotic. The point is that there were patriots on both sides of the issue, but that they differed as to desirable goals for the new nation. At the same time, of course, there were men as narrow and selfish on both sides as their political enemies said they were.

If one approaches the history of the Confederation in this way, if one tries to see it as men who lived in it saw it and to write of it in their terms, one may achieve some semblance of reality. It is not the task of the historian to defend or attack the various groups of men whose conflicts were the essence of the period, but to set forth what they believed and what they tried to achieve. This can be illustrated no better than in the definition of terms. Throughout this book the words "federalist" and "nationalist" are used to describe two opposed bodies of opinion as to the best kind of central government for the United States. In so doing I have followed the members of the Convention of 1787. Those men believed that the Articles of Confederation provided for a "federal" government and the majority of them wanted to replace it with a "national" government. The fact that the men who wanted a national government called themselves Federalists after their work was submitted to the public is relevant to the history of politics after 1787, not to the discussion of the nature of the central government prior to and during the Convention of 1787.

Whatever the confusion since then, there was none at the time. Gouverneur Morris stated the issue concisely in the Convention when he "explained the distinction between a federal and a national, supreme government; the former being a mere compact resting on the good faith of the parties; the latter having a complete and compulsive operation." This explanation was in answer to those members of the Convention who wanted to know what Edmund Randolph meant in his opening speech when he spoke of the "defects of the federal system, the necessity of transforming it into a national efficient government. . . ."

The issue was not, as has been argued from time to time, whether there was a "nation" before the adoption of the Constitution of 1787. That was not the question at all during the 1780's. There was a new nation, as the men of the time agreed: they disagreed as to whether the new nation should have a federal or a national government. They did so from the outset of the Revolution and men have continued to do so ever since. The Constitution of 1787 was, as Madison said, both national and federal. And while this fact has led to innumerable conflicts of interpretation, it has also been a source of strength; for as one political group after another has gotten control of the central government it has been able to shape the Constitution to its needs and desires. Thus with the single exception of the Civil War, peaceful change has always been possible, and as long as Americans are willing to accept the decisions of ballot boxes, legislatures, and courts, the Constitution will continue to change with changing needs and pressures. . . .

The foregoing pages indicate that the Confederation Period was one of great significance, but not of the kind that tradition has led us to believe. The "critical period" idea was the result of an uncritical acceptance of the arguments of the victorious party in a long political battle, of a failure to face the fact that partisan propaganda is not history but only historical evidence. What emerges instead is a much more complex and important story in which several themes are interwoven. It was a period of what we would call post-war demobilization, of sudden economic change, dislocation, and expansion, and of fundamental conflict over the nature of the Constitution of the United States. Each of these themes is so interwoven with the others that any separation is arbitrary but, taken separately or together, they are better keys to an understanding of the period than the traditional one.

At the end of the war Americans faced innumerable problems arising from it. What should be done with war veterans? Should the Loyalists return to their homes? What should be our relations with foreign friends and foes?

Should commerce be free or should there be discrimination, and if so, against whom and for whose benefit? How would peace affect the economy? How should the war debt be paid? What kind of taxes should be levied to pay it, and who should pay them? When the war-boom collapsed, why did it? What should the state or central governments, or both, do about it? Should government encourage one form of economic enterprise over another or should it keep hands off? What about discontented groups: should government ignore them, cater to them, or forcibly suppress those who might revolt?

Such questions or others like them have probably been asked after every great war in history. They were asked, debated, and given various solutions during the 1780's. The significance of those debates and solutions has often been misunderstood. This is no better illustrated than in the case of the national debt during the 1780's which is usually discussed only in terms of depreciation and nonpayment of interest. Actually much more was involved than this. The debt was fantastically low compared with the national debt of today—about twelve dollars per capita as compared with seventeen hundred—and the nation had vast untouched natural resources with which to pay it. Multitudes of accounts had to be reduced to simple forms so that they could be paid, and this the Confederation government managed to do. But even more important than the economics of the national debt was its politics: should it be paid by the states or the central government? A fundamental assumption of every political leader was that the political agency which paid the debt would hold the balance of power in the new nation. Hence, the supporters of a strong central government insisted that the national debt must be paid by Congress while their opponents insisted that it should be divided among the states and paid by them. The latter group was on the way to victory by the end of the 1780's, for they were supported by clamoring creditors. The result was that one state after another assumed portions of the national debt owing to its citizens. Thus the traditional story is so out of context as to be virtually meaningless. This is true of other traditions as well. Most of the ports of the world were open, not closed, to American citizens. Reciprocity and equal treatment of all United States citizens was the rule in the tonnage and tariff acts of the states, not trade barriers.

To say that many of the pessimistic traditions are false is not to say that all Americans were peaceful and satisfied. The holders of national and state debts wanted bigger payments than they got. The merchants wanted more government aid than was given them. The farmers, hit by high taxes and rigid collection of both taxes and private debts, demanded relief in the form of lower taxes and government loans from state legislatures. Such demands kept state politics in an uproar during the 1780's. However, the often violent expression of such discontents in politics should not blind us to the fact that the period was one of extraordinary economic growth. Merchants owned more ships at the end of the 1780's than they had at the beginning of the Revolution, and they carried a greater share of American produce. By

1790 the export of agricultural produce was double what it had been before the war. American cities grew rapidly, with the result that housing was scarce and building booms produced a labor shortage. Tens of thousands of farmers spread outwards to the frontiers. There can be no question but that freedom from the British Empire resulted in a surge of activity in all phases of American life. Of course not all the problems of the new nation were solved by 1789—all have not yet been solved—but there is no evidence of stagnation and decay in the 1780's. Instead the story is one of a newly free people who seized upon every means to improve and enrich themselves in a nation which they believed had a golden destiny.

Politically the dominating fact of the Confederation Period was the struggle between two groups of leaders to shape the character of the state and central governments. The revolutionary constitutions of the states placed final power in the legislatures and made the executive and judicial branches subservient to them. The members of the colonial aristocracy who became Patriots, and new men who gained economic power during the Revolution deplored this fact, but they were unable to alter the state constitutions during the 1780's. Meanwhile they tried persistently to strengthen the central government. These men were the nationalists of the 1780's.

On the other hand the men who were the true federalists believed that the greatest gain of the Revolution was the independence of the several states and the creation of a central government subservient to them. The leaders of this group from the Declaration of Independence to the Convention of 1787 were Samuel Adams, Patrick Henry, Richard Henry Lee, George Clinton, James Warren, Samuel Bryan, George Bryan, Elbridge Gerry, George Mason and a host of less well known but no less important men in each of the states. Most of these men believed, as a result of their experience with Great Britain before 1776 and of their reading of history, that the states could be best governed without the intervention of a powerful central government. Some of them had programs of political and social reform; others had none at all. Some had a vision of democracy; others had no desire except to control their states for whatever satisfactions such control might offer. Some were in fact as narrow and provincial as their opponents said they were. However, the best of them agreed that the central government needed more power, but they wanted that power given so as not to alter the basic character of the Articles of Confederation. Here is where they were in fundamental disagreement with the nationalists who wanted to remove the central government from the control of the state legislatures.

The nationalist leaders from the Declaration of Independence to the Philadelphia convention were men like Robert Morris, John Jay, Gouverneur Morris, James Wilson, Alexander Hamilton, Henry Knox, James Duane, George Washington, James Madison, and many lesser men. Most of these men were by temperament or economic interest believers in executive and judicial rather than legislative control of state and central governments, in the rigorous collection of taxes, and, as creditors, in strict payment of public and private debts. They declared that national honor and prestige could be maintained only by a powerful central government. Naturally, not all men who used such language used it sincerely, for some were as selfish and greedy as their opponents said they were. The nationalists frankly disliked the political heritage of the Revolution. They deplored the fact there was no check upon the actions of majorities in state legislatures; that there was no central government to which minorities could appeal from the decisions of such majorities, as they had done before the Revolution.

There were men who veered from side to side, but their number is relatively small and their veering is of little significance as compared with the fact that from the outset of the Revolution there were two consistently opposed bodies of opinion as to the nature of the central government. There was, of course, a wide variation of belief among adherents of both points of view. There were extremists who wanted no central government at all and others who wanted to wipe out the states entirely. There were some who wanted a monarchy and others who would have welcomed dictatorship. But such extremists are not representative of the two great bodies of men whose conflict was the essence of the years both before and after 1789.

While the federalist leaders gradually moved to a position where they were willing to add specific powers to the Articles of Confederation, the nationalist leaders campaigned steadily for the kind of government they wanted. During the war they argued that it could not be won without creating a powerful central government. After the war they insisted that such a government was necessary to do justice to public creditors, solve the problems of post-war trade, bring about recovery from depression, and win the respect of the world for the new nation. Meanwhile their experience with majorities in state legislatures merely intensified their desire. They became desperate as state after state in 1785 and 1786 adopted some form of paper money that could be loaned on farm mortgages and be used to pay taxes, and in some cases private debts as well. When they were able to hold off such demands and farmers revolted, as in Massachusetts, they were thoroughly frightened.

They looked upon such events as evidence of the horrors of unchecked democracy and they said so in poetry, private letters, newspaper essays, and public speeches. The problem, they said, was to find some refuge from democracy. They worked hard to control state legislatures and they were often successful, but such control was uncertain at best, for annual elections meant a constant threat of overturn and the threat was realized repeatedly.

We may not call it democracy, but they did. Edmund Randolph put their case bluntly in his opening speech in the Convention of 1787. He said, "our chief danger arises from the democratic parts of our constitutions . . . None of the [state] constitutions have provided a sufficient check against the democracy. The feeble senate of Virginia is a phantom. Maryland has a more powerful senate, but the late distractions in that state, have discovered that it is not powerful enough. The check established in the constitutions of New York and Massachusetts is yet a stronger barrier against democracy, but they all seem insufficient." Outside the Convention General Knox was saying that a "mad democracy sweeps away every moral trait from the human character" and that the Convention would "clip the wings of a mad democracy." James Madison in the *Federalist Papers* argued that the new Constitution should be adopted because a "republican" form of government was better than a "democracy."

The debate was white-hot and was carried on with utter frankness. It was white-hot because for a moment in history self-government by majorities within particular political boundaries was possible. Those majorities could do what they wanted, and some of them knew what they wanted. Democracy was no vague ideal, but a concrete program: it meant definite things in politics, economics, and religion. Whatever side of the controversy we take, whether we think the majorities in state legislatures governed badly or well—the fact to face is that men of the 1780's believed that the issue was democracy as a way of government for the United States of those days.

They faced the issue squarely. They thought hard and realistically about the problems of government. They understood that society is complex and that the truth about it is multifold rather than simple. James Madison summed it up as well as it has ever been done. There are, he said, many passions and interests in society and these will ever clash for control of government and will ever interpret their own desires as the good of the whole. Men like Madison and John Adams believed, as Madison said, that the "great desideratum which has not yet been found for Republican governments seems to be some disinterested and dispassionate umpire in disputes between different passions and interests in the state." In the tenth number of *The Federalist*, after citing various origins of political parties, Madison said that "the most durable source of factions [parties] has been the various and unequal distribution of property. Those who hold and those who are without property have ever formed distinct interests in society. Those who are creditors and those who are debtors, fall under a like discrimination. A landed interest, a manufacturing interest, a mercantile interest, a monied interest, with many lesser interests, grow up of necessity in civilized nations, and divide them into different classes, actuated by different sentiments and views. The regulation of these various and interfering interests forms the principal task of modern legislation, and involves the spirit of party and faction in the necessary and ordinary operations of the government."

The constitutional debate of the 1780's was thus carried on by men with a realistic appreciation of the social forces lying behind constitutional forms and theories, by men who were aware of the relationship between economic and political power. This realistic approach was lost sight of in the nineteenth century by romantic democrats who believed that once every man had the right to vote the problems of society could be solved. It was lost sight of too by those who came to believe in an oversimplified economic interpretation of history. In a sense they were as romantic as the democrats, for they assumed a rationality in the historic process that is not always supported by the evidence.

If the history of the Confederation has anything to offer us it is the realistic approach to politics so widely held by the political leaders of the time, however much they might differ as to forms of government and desirable goals for the new nation. Throughout the Confederation men with rival goals pushed two programs simultaneously. The federalists tried to strengthen the Articles of Confederation; the nationalists tried to create a new constitution by means of a convention, and thus avoid the method of change prescribed by the Articles of Confederation. The movement to strengthen the Articles failed on the verge of success; the movement to call a convention succeeded on the verge of failure. The failure of one movement and the success of the other, however we may interpret them, is one of the dramatic stories in the history of politics.

The Founding Fathers: Young Men of the Revolution

Stanley Elkins and Eric McKitrick

According to Stanley Elkins, Professor of History at Smith College in Northampton, Massachusetts, and Eric McKitrick, a historian at Columbia, the American Constitution operated as "the central myth" of our political culture during the nineteenth century. The reverence accorded both the document and its formulators—the Founding Fathers—was pervasive indeed. In the twentieth century the motives of those who met at Philadelphia in May of 1787 have come in for questioning and reexamination. As the ensuing article suggests, this reevaluation has developed in three rather distinct stages. According to Elkins and McKitrick, new perspectives on "the central myth" of the Constitution have resulted because of changing definitions as to what constitutes historical "reality."

The intelligent American of today may know a great deal about his history, but the chances are that he feels none too secure about the Founding Fathers and the framing and ratification of the Federal Constitution. He is no longer certain what the "enlightened" version of that story is, or even whether there is one. This is because, in the century and three quarters since the Constitution was written, our best thinking on that subject has gone through two dramatically different phases and is at this moment about to enter a third.

Americans in the nineteenth century, whenever they reviewed the events of the founding, made reference to an Olympian gathering of wise and virtuous men who stood splendidly above all faction, ignored petty self-interest, and concerned themselves only with the freedom and well-being of their fellow-countrymen. This attitude toward the Fathers has actually never died out; it still tends to prevail in American history curricula right up through most of the secondary schools. But bright young people arriving at college have been regularly discovering, for nearly the last fifty years, that in the innermost circle this was regarded as an old-fashioned, immensely oversimplified, and rather dewy-eyed view of the Founding Fathers and their work. Ever since J. Allen Smith and Charles Beard wrote in the early years of the twentieth century, the "educated" picture of the Fathers has been that of a group not of disinterested patriots but of hard-fisted conservatives who were looking out for their own interests and those of their class. According

From "The Founding Fathers: Young Men of the Revolution," by Stanley Elkins and Eric McKitrick, in *Political Science Quarterly*, Vol. LXXVI, No. 1 (June 1961). Reprinted by permission of the authors.

to this worldlier view, the document which they wrote—and in which they embodied these interests—was hardly intended as a thrust toward popular and democratic government. On the contrary, its centralizing tendencies all reflected the Fathers' distrust of the local and popular rule which had been too little restrained under the Articles of Confederation. The authors of the Constitution represented the privileged part of society. Naturally, then, their desire for a strong central government was, among other things, an effort to achieve solid national guarantees for the rights of property—rights not adequately protected under the Articles—and to obtain for the propertied class (their own) a favored position under the new government.

This "revisionist" point of view—that of the Founding Fathers as self-interested conservatives—has had immeasurable influence in the upper reaches of American historical thought. Much of what at first seemed audacious to the point of *lèse majesté* came ultimately to be taken as commonplace. The Tory-like, almost backward-turning quality which this approach has imparted to the picture of constitution-making even renders it plausible to think of the Philadelphia Convention of 1787 as a counter-revolutionary conspiracy, which is just the way a number of writers have actually described it. That is, since the Articles of Confederation were the product of the Revolution, to overthrow the Articles was—at least symbolically—to repudiate the Revolution. The Declaration of Independence and the Constitution represented two very different, and in some ways opposing, sets of aspirations; and (so the reasoning goes) the Philadelphia Convention was thus a significant turning-away from, rather than an adherence to, the spirit of the Declaration.

In very recent years, however, a whole new cycle of writing and thinking and research has been under way; the revisionists of the previous generation are themselves being revised. The economic ideas of the late Professor Beard, which dominated this field for so long, have been partially if not wholly discredited. And yet many of the old impressions, intermingled with still older ones, persist. Much of the new work, moreover, though excellent and systematic, is still in progress. Consequently the entire subject of the Constitution and its creation has become a little murky; new notions having the clarity and assuredness of the old have not as yet fully emerged; and meanwhile one is not altogether certain what to think.

Before the significance of all this new work can be justly assessed, and before consistent themes in it may be identified with any assurance, an effort should be made to retrace somewhat the psychology of previous conceptions. At the same time, it should be recognized that any amount of fresh writing on this subject will continue to lack something until it can present us with a clear new symbolic image of the Fathers themselves. The importance of this point lies in the function that symbols have for organizing the historical imagination, and the old ones are a little tired. The "father" image is well and good, and so also in certain respects is the "conservative" one. But we may suppose that these men saw themselves at the time as playing other rôles too, rôles that did not partake so much of retrospection, age, and restraint as those which would come to be assigned to them in after years. The Republic is now very old, as republics go, yet it *was* young once, and so were its founders. With youth goes energy, and the "energy" principle may be more suggestive now, in reviewing the experience of the founding, than the principle of paternal conservatism.

I

Charles A. Beard, who in 1913 published *An Economic Interpretation of the Constitution of the United States,* did more than any single figure to make of the Constitution something other than a topic for ceremonial praise. By calling it a product of economic forces, Beard established an alternative position and enabled the entire subject to become one for serious historical debate. He thus created the first real dialectic on the Constitution and Founding Fathers, and for that reason Beard's work must still be taken as the point of departure for any historical treatment of that subject.

For Beard, the reality behind the movement for a constitution in the 1780's was economic interest. The animating surge came from holders of depreciated Continental securities who were demanding that their bonds be paid at par, and from conservative elements throughout the Confederation who wanted a national bulwark against agrarian-debtor radicalism. Beard thus identified the Federalists as those who wanted protection for property, especially personal property. The Anti-Federalists, on the other hand, were the great mass of agrarian debtors agitating for schemes of confiscation and paper money inflation in the state legislatures. Their hard-earned taxes would go to support any new bonds that a stronger United States government might issue; conversely, further fiscal experimentation on their part would be checked by national power. The Anti-Federalists, those who opposed a new constitution, were therefore the radicals; the Federalists, who favored it, were the conservatives.

Beard's argument was immediately challenged and kept on being challenged, which helped it to retain the fresh attractiveness of an *avant-garde* position for many years. But the man's influence grew, and his work played a vital part in historical thinking until well after the Second World War. Historical thinking, however, has its own historical setting. Why should such a statement as Beard's not have been made until the twentieth century, more than 125 years after the event?

In the nineteenth century the American Constitution had operated as the central myth of an entire political culture. While that culture was still in the tentative stages of its growth, still subject to all manner of unforeseen menaces, and with very little that was nationally sacred, there reigned everywhere the tacit understanding that here was the one unifying abstraction, the one symbol that might command all loyalties and survive all strife. The Constitution thus served multiple functions for a society that lacked tradition, folk-memory, a sovereign, and a body of legend. The need to keep the symbol inviolate seems to have been felt more instinctively during its earlier history than later on. Public controversy of the bitterest kind might occur over the charter's true meaning; enemies might accuse each other of misconstruing the document; but one did not challenge the myth itself. Americans even fought a civil war with both sides claiming to be the true upholders of the Constitution. Thus it was natural that when the historians of the nineteenth century—Bancroft, Hildreth, Frothingham, Fiske, McMaster—came to describe the origins of the Constitution, they should reach for the non-controversial idiom and imagery of a Golden Age. The Supreme Law had been fashioned and given to the people by a race of classic heroes.

America's veneration for its Constitution became steadily more intense in the years that followed the Civil War. Now it was the symbol not only of the Union, for which that generation had made such heavy sacrifices, but also of the unfettered capitalism which was turning the United States into one of the richest and most powerful nations in the world. The new material order—wasteful, disorderly, already acquainted with labor disturbances, yet immensely productive—was watched over by the benevolent and solicitous eye of the Constitution.

In 1888, in a setting darkened by portents of industrial warfare, John Fiske published *The Critical Period of American History,* an account of the events leading to the Philadelphia Convention of 1787. It was an instant success; the notion of the Confederation interlude as a "critical period" was dramatically perfect. A time of trouble, political drift, threatening disunity, and irresponsible agitation provided the occasion at Philadelphia for a supreme act of disinterested statesmanship. There, an intrepid conclave of Old Romans rose above personal and local concerns and presented their countrymen with an instrument of vigorous and effective government.

By the opening of the twentieth century, the state of mind in which men could uncritically ascribe a sort of immaculateness to their political and legal arrangements had altered sharply. By then a profound economic and social crisis had been met and overcome, but with remnants of psychological crisis left unresolved in its wake. The ending of the depression and hard times of the 1890's, the defeat of Populism and Bryanism, the election of McKinley and return of Republican rule—these things were not enough to restore the old complacent innocence. The American public, now full of guilty misgivings, had begun to ask itself searching questions about the evils of the existing order and about the price it had allowed itself to pay for material progress. The answer which was hit upon by publicists and civic spokesmen was *vested interest.* The formula was not exactly new, but after the experience of the 1890's, when public rhetoric had abounded in sinister allusions to "Wall Street" and "the monopolies," it was no more than natural that the "vested interest" concept should have taken on an immensely new and widened range of application. The "interests" were the shadowy powers that manipulated things and made them run the way they did. Thus vested interest came to be seen in the Progressive Era—those years roughly from the turn of the century through the First World War—as the ultimate reality behind the life of affairs.

It was in that era, moreover, that "reality" itself first came to be a synonym for all the equivocal, seamy, and downright evil facts of life from which innocent and respectable people are normally sheltered. Few periods in American history have been so strikingly noted for civic awareness and the reforming spirit—and reform meant getting to the bottom of things. The most efficacious step in exorcising an evil was exposing it. Thus the literature of exposure, which claimed an enormous amount of journalistic and literary energy, did much to whet and sustain that generation's relish for reform. "Muckraking" meant dredging up heaps of grubby "reality" for all to behold. "Reality," as Richard Hofstadter has said,

> was the bribe, the rebate, the bought franchise, the sale of adulterated food. It was what one found in *The Jungle, The Octopus, Wealth against Commonwealth,* or *The Shame of the Cities.* . . . Reality was a series of unspeakable plots, personal iniquities, moral failures, which, in their totality, had come to govern American society. . . .

The sheer excitement of discovery tended to leave people's perceptions of appearance and reality somewhat unbalanced. It is perhaps too much to say that anything hidden was taken as bad (though there were certainly strong presumptions); yet one of the great unspoken dogmas of American thought, implanted in this period, was that the "facts of life" had to be hidden in order to qualify as "real."

In academic precincts, meanwhile, such thinkers as Roscoe Pound, John Dewey, Thorstein Veblen, Arthur Bentley, and J. Allen Smith had begun to challenge the older static and formalist theories of law, philosophy, economics, and government. They were no longer so interested in the formal outlines which enclosed, say, government or the law; they were much more concerned to locate the dynamic forces inside these realms—to identify the powers that made them really work. Thus "economic interest" as a kind of *élan vital,* a basic prime mover, came to be given greater and greater emphasis. "Wherever we turn," wrote E. R. A. Seligman as early as 1902, ". . . we are confronted by the overwhelming importance attached by the younger and abler scholars to the economic factor in political and social progress." Here was "reality" being given an intellectual and scholarly sanction.

In view of this mounting preoccupation with "interests," one might be led to conclude that significant numbers of intelligent people were approaching a "class" theory of society not unlike that of Marx—a theory in which classes and class interests contended more or less frankly with each other for advantage. Yet by and large this did not happen; these were not the terms in which most people thought about society. For one reason, there was very little evidence to support such a theory. But a more important reason was that, to a people saturated in democratic prejudices, "class" habits of thought were fantastically difficult to understand, let alone imitate. To the Progressive mind, the way vested interest worked was not so much through class as through *conspiracy.*

Vested interest and conspiracy were concepts so closely related that they were almost synonymous. The interests worked in secret; their power rested on stealthy understandings and was exercised through the pulling of invisible strings. Hidden from view, they might freely circumvent the law and gain their ends by corrupting and manipulating the agencies of government. . . . Such a mode of conceiving reality would even be brought to bear upon the origins of the United States Constitution.

Two of Charles Beard's immediate precursors in that realm were J. Allen Smith and Algie Simons. They were, for their own purposes, innovators; yet in a broader sense their minds followed a typical Progressive pattern. [For example] in J. Allen Smith's *Spirit of American Government, A Study of the Constitution* (1907), the myth of the Philadelphia convention as a forum of disinterested statesmen came under sharp attack. . . .

But it was Charles A. Beard, taking up the "class interest" formula in his famous *Economic Interpretation* the following year, who succeeded to all intents and purposes in making it stick. Whereas neither Smith nor Simons had made any secret of their reforming passions (they denied that the Constitution was a sacred document, so their fellow-citizens should feel free to change it if they wished), Beard disclaimed any intention of writing a political tract. He would simply be the observer of historical events, impassively examining the facts. All he wanted to do was discover whether in fact economic forces had played a significant part in the drafting and ratification of the Constitution. Early in his book Beard insisted that it was not his purpose "to show that the Constitution was made for the personal benefit of the members of the Convention," but merely to determine whether the Fathers represented "distinct groups whose economic interests they understood and felt in concrete, definite form, through their own personal experience with identical property rights. . . ." Then, setting in motion an impressive system of scholarly apparatus, he proceeded to answer his own questions.

. . . At any rate, the reason he was able to create his sensation was that the things he showed the Fathers doing were of exactly the sort that the muckraking magazines had, in other connections, made all too familiar.

Beard's basic research materials were a batch of old Treasury records which had never previously been opened ("reality"), and in them he found the names of a number of the Federalist leaders, members of the Philadelphia Convention as well as delegates to ratifying conventions in the various states. These men held substantial amounts of Continental securities which—Beard reasoned from later developments—would rise sharply in value with the establishment of a strong central government. This seemed to explain the energy with which they worked to bring such a government into being, and this was just the sort of evidence that impressed Beard's contemporaries most. Beard himself, for all his disclaimers, sums up his argument in language whose dominant theme is *direct personal interest*. Here, three of his thirteen conclusions are quite explicit:

> (1) The first firm steps toward the formation of the Constitution were taken by a small and active group of men immediately interested through their personal possessions in the outcome of their labors.
>
> (2) The members of the Philadelphia Convention who drafted the Constitution were, with a few exceptions, immediately, directly, and personally interested in, and derived economic advantages from, the establishment of the new system.
>
> (3) The leaders who supported the Constitution in the ratifying conventions represented the same economic groups as the members of the Philadelphia Convention; and in a large number of instances they were also directly and personally interested in the outcome of their efforts.

Accompanying the principal theme of personal interest were several subthemes:

> (1) The Constitution was essentially an economic document based upon the concept that the fundamental private rights of property are anterior to government and morally beyond the reach of popular majorities.
>
> (2) [The entire process, from the calling of the Philadelphia Convention to the ratifying of the Constitution, was unrepresentative and undemocratic; there was no popular vote on calling the convention; a large propertyless (and therefore disfranchised) mass was not represented at Philadelphia; and only a small minority in each state voted for delegates to the ratifying conventions.]
>
> (3) [Where battles did occur over ratification], the line of cleavage . . . was between substantial personalty interests on the one hand and the small farmers and debtors interests on the other.

. . . Beard himself was nothing if not a Progressive, fully immersed in his times. It was the interests and their inside doings that caught the Progressive imagination; it was this that the Progressives longed to befool and discomfit by public exposure. If Beard was to show that the Federal Constitution was not a product of abstract political theory but of concrete economic drives, there was no happier way of doing it than to paint the Founding Fathers in the familiar image of the vested interests—the small group of wealthy conspirators hostile to, even contemptuous of, the majority will, and acting for clear, "practical" reasons such as rigging the value of public securities.

Despite the bursts of pained protests which *An Economic Interpretation* initially drew from many older academics (who either thought that Beard could comprehend no motives other than base ones, or else concluded that he must be a socialist), it also drew plenty of praise from academic as well as non-academic quarters. Not only did the book do well for a scholarly monograph, it did better and better as time went on. . . .

. . . At the same time Beard had bequeathed to American historical method something far more pervasive, a technique of explanation which could take "class" interpretations or leave them alone. This was the "reality" technique, which assumes that the most significant aspects of any event are those concealed from the eye. Men's true intentions are to be judged neither from the words we hear them speak nor the deeds we see them do, and the "real" forces behind historical change will turn out, more often than not, to be those of conspiracy.

II

In 1940 certain new and interesting corollaries were added to the mode of approach which, due so largely to Beard's example, had come to influence historical thinking on the formation of the Constitution. In that year Merrill Jensen published *The Articles of Confederation: An Interpretation of the Social-Constitutional History of the American Revolution, 1774–1781*. Jensen's own approach was consistent with most of the general principles which had been laid down by Beard. . . .

In a second book, *The New Nation* (1950), Jensen considered the accomplishments of the Confederation, together with the social and economic conditions of the period from 1781 to 1789. He concluded that the "critical period" was really not so critical after all. American ships were not excluded from many foreign ports; tariff wars between states were the exception rather than the rule; the Confederation government had solved the problem of western lands and was well on the way to settling the outstanding boundary disputes. By 1786 the economic depression which had struck the country in 1784 was coming to an end. Even the problem of national credit was not so serious as the Federalists wanted people to believe, since a number of the states had assumed responsibility for portions of the Continental debt held by their own citizens. Had the states been brought to accept a national impost—a tariff duty on incoming foreign goods levied solely and exclusively by Congress, the revenue of which would be reserved for the support of the government—the Confederation would have been fully capable of surviving and functioning as a true federal establishment.

The collapse of the Confederation, Jensen argued, was not the logical outcome of weakness or inefficiency. It was the result of a determined effort by a small but tightly-organized group of nationalists to impose a centralized government upon the entire country despite the contrary desires of great majorities everywhere:

> Most of these men were by temperament or economic interest believers in executive and judicial rather than legislative control of state and central governments, in the rigorous collection of taxes, and, as creditors, in strict payment of public and private debts. . . . They deplored the fact that there was no check upon the actions of majorities in state legislatures; that there was no central government to which minorities could appeal from the decisions of such majorities, as they had done before the Revolution.

These were the men who conspired to overthrow the Confederation and who masterminded the triumph of the Constitution.

There were points at which Jensen had not seen eye to eye with Beard. He was more impressed, for instance, by the Fathers' general outlook and ideology than by their property holdings; unlike Beard, moreover, he denied that the Confederation era was a time of serious economic difficulty. Yet he had actually strengthened the Beardian logic at more than one point, and the differences were minor in the light of the convictions which united the two in spirit and intention. The work of Merrill Jensen, like that of Beard and Parrington and J. Allen Smith before him, still balanced on the assumption that the energy behind the American Constitution was conspiratorial energy, and that the Constitution came into being by means of a *coup d'état*—through the plotting of a well-disciplined Toryish few against the interests of an unvigilant democratic majority.

Indeed, Merrill Jensen's *The New Nation*—published two years after the death of Charles Beard—was the last major piece of Constitution scholarship to be done in the Progressive tradition, and represented the end of an era. By that time, 1950, Beard's own notions had begun to arouse not the admiration, but the suspicion, of a new generation of postwar intellectuals.

III

. . . By 1956, Beard's *Economic Interpretation* had been set up for the *coup de grâce*. The executioner was Robert E. Brown, a professor at Michigan State who had been at work for some time implacably compiling a catalogue of the Master's offenses. In his *Charles Beard and the Constitution*, published that year, Brown tracked Beard through every page of the latter's masterpiece and laid the ax to virtually every statement of importance that Beard had made in it. There was absolutely no correlation between the Philadelphia delegates' property holdings and the way they behaved on the question of a constitution. It was not true that large numbers of adult males were disfranchised; the suffrage was remarkably liberal everywhere. Farmers as a class were by no means chronically debtors; many were creditors and many others were both. The supporters of Shays' Rebellion (the debtors' uprising in western Massachusetts which occurred during the fall and winter of 1786-1787) were certainly not united against the Constitution; if they had been, it could never have been ratified, since the Shaysites had a clear majority at the time of the Massachusetts convention. . . .

Not only was Beard's evidence inconclusive at all points, Brown insisted, but there were even occasions when the Master had not been above doctoring it. He edited Madison's *Federalist* No. 10 to eliminate all but its economic emphasis; he quoted only those passages of the Philadelphia debates that made the Fathers look least democratic; he arranged his treatment of the ratification process in an order that violated chronology, centered unjustified attention on states where hard struggles did occur, overlooked the ease with which ratification was achieved in other states, and thus created a wildly exaggerated picture of the opposition at large.

Brown's book was respectfully received; there was little inclination to dispute his arguments; no champions arose to do serious battle for the departed Beard. Some of the reviewers were a little dismayed at Brown's tone; they thought it need not have been quite so ferocious. And the book did seem to bear out the principle that any work of destruction in the realm of discourse, however necessary, must be executed within restrictions that make for a certain stultification. Richard Hofstadter remarked in this connection that Brown was "locked in such intimate embrace with his adversary that his categories are entirely dictated by Beard's assertions." Even Brown, in his way, had toyed with the "reality" theme. He had exonerated the Fathers of conspiratorial intentions but convicted Charles Beard in their place: Beard had cooked the evidence, had conspired to hide the truth.

The first effort in recent years to view the Constitution all over again in a major way, shaking off the Beardian categories and starting as it were from scratch, has been undertaken by Forrest McDonald. *We The People*, published in 1958, was the first of a planned trilogy whose design was to survey anew the entire story of how the Constitution was brought into existence. Although McDonald, like Brown, felt it necessary to show the inadequacy of Beard's conclusions, his strategy was quite different from Brown's; it was undertaken less to discredit Beard than to clear the way for his own projected treatment of the great subject. In *An Economic Interpretation*, Beard had made a number of proposals for research which he himself had not performed—and never did perform—but which would, Beard felt, further corroborate his own "frankly fragmentary" work. McDonald began by undertaking the very research which Beard had suggested, and its results convinced him that Beard had simply asked all the wrong questions.

One of the things McDonald investigated in *We The People* was an assumption upon which Beard had put a great deal of stress, the notion of a fundamental antagonism between "personalty" and "realty" interests at the time of the Philadelphia Convention. ("Personalty" was wealth based on securities, money, commerce, or manufacturing; "realty" was landed property whose owners' outlook tended to be primarily agrarian.) He found that there was no such split in the Convention. The seven men who either walked out of the Convention or else refused to sign the completed document were among the heaviest security-holders there, and represented "an all-star team of personalty interests." In state after state, moreover, there was no appreciable difference between the property holdings of Federalists and Anti-Federalists. Finally, the three states that ratified the Constitution unanimously—Delaware, New Jersey, and Georgia—were overwhelmingly dominated by agrarian interests.

Unlike Brown, McDonald was quite unwilling to write off the possibility of an economic analysis (his book's subtitle was *The Economic Origins of the Constitution*); it was just that Beard's particular economic categories led nowhere. Beard's sweeping "personalty" and "realty" classifications were meaningless, and he had deceived himself profoundly in supposing that the Federalists' property interests "knew no state boundaries" but were "truly national in scope." On these two points of difference McDonald set up an entirely new and original research scheme, and in so doing effected a really impressive conceptual maneuver. He was quite ready, in the first place, to find "economic forces" behind the movement for a constitution, but these must be sought not in "classes" or in broad categories of property but rather in the specific business interests of specific groups in specific places. The other organizing category would be the individual states themselves. The political framework within which any group had to operate was still that imposed by the state; the states were, after all, still sovereign units, and the precise relationship between economic forces and political action depended almost entirely on the special conditions within those states, conditions which varied from one to the other.

By abandoning Beard's "national" framework and recasting the entire problem on a state-by-state basis, McDonald made it possible to see with a sudden clarity things which ought to have been obvious all along. The states where ratification was achieved most readily were those that were convinced, for one reason or another, that they could not survive and prosper as independent entities; those holding out the longest were the ones most convinced that they could go it alone. The reasons for supporting ratification might vary considerably from state to state. For Georgia, an impending Indian war and the need for military protection could transcend any possible economic issue; New York, at one time imagining for itself an independent political and economic future, would finally ratify for fear of being isolated from a system which already included ten states and which might soon be joined by a seceded New York City. . . .

Recognizing the importance of specific location made it also easier and more natural to appreciate the way in which particular interests in particular places might be affected by the question of a stronger national government. Boston shipping interests, for example, seem to have been less concerned in the 1780's over class ideology or general economic philosophy than over those conditions of the times which were especially bad for business. The British would not let them into the West Indies, the French were excluding their fish, and their large vessels were no longer profitable. A strong national government could create a navy whose very existence would reduce high insurance rates; it could guarantee an orderly tariff system that would remove all pressure for higher and higher state tariffs; and it could counter British and French discrimination by means of an effective navigation act. . . .

Forrest McDonald's work, according to him, has only just begun; years of it still lie ahead. But already a remarkable precision of detail has been brought to the subject, together with a degree of sophistication which makes the older economic approach—"tough-minded" as it once imagined itself—seem now a little wan and misty. The special internal conditions of the several states now seem fully valid as clues to the ratification policies of those states, each in its separate turn. And there is a credibility about the immediate needs and aspirations of particular groups, and the way they varied from place to place, that Beard's "interests" never quite possessed—or if they did, they had long since lost their hold on the modern mind.

And yet there are overtones in McDonald's work—for all its precise excellence, perhaps partly because of it—that have already succeeded in creating a new kind of "reality" spell. McDonald is very open-minded about all the manifold and complex and contradictory forces that converged upon the movement for a constitution. But somehow the ones he takes most seriously—the "real" forces behind the movement—were specific, particular, circumscribed, hard, and immediate. They were to be looked for mostly on the local level, because that is where one really finds things. A state—the largest permissible "reality" unit—was an agglomeration of specific, particular, immediate localities. There were interests to be served, political or economic, and they were *hard*. They were pursued rationally and without sentimentality; men came down where they did because their hard, immediate, specific interests brought them there. But are we prepared to say that the final result was just the sum—or extension—of these interests? . . .

The new approach is extremely enlightening and useful. But has it yet taken on life? When will it fully engage the question of initiative and energy? How do we account for the dedication, the force and *éclat*, of Federalist leadership? When all is said and done, we do not exactly refer to the "interests" of a James Madison. We wonder, instead, about the terms in which he conceives of personal fulfillment, which is not at all the same. What animates him? The nationalist movement *did* have a mystique that somehow transfigured a substantial number of its leaders. What was it like, what were its origins?

IV

The work of Merrill Jensen, done in the 1930's and 1940's, has suffered somewhat in reputation due to the sweep and vehemence of the anti-Beardian reaction. Yet that work contains perceptions which ought not to be written off in the general shuffle. They derive not so much from the overall Beardian traditions and influences amid which Jensen wrote, as from that particular sector of the subject which he marked off and preëmpted for his own. Simply by committing himself—alone among Beardians and non-Beardians—to presenting the Confederation era as a legitimate phase of American history, entitled to be taken seriously like any other and having a positive side as well as a negative one, he has forced upon us a peculiar point of view which, by the same token, yields its own special budget of insights. For example, Jensen has been profoundly impressed by the sheer force, determination, and drive of such nationalist leaders as Hamilton, Madison, Jay, Knox, and the Morrises. This energy, he feels, created the central problem of the Confederation and was the major cause of its collapse. He deplores this, seeing in the Confederation "democratic" virtues which it probably never had, finding in the Federalists an "aristocratic" character which in actual fact was as much or more to be found in the Anti-Federalists, smelling plots everywhere, and in general shaping his nomenclature to fit his own values and preferences. But if Professor Jensen seems to have called everything by the wrong name, it is well to remember that nomenclature is not everything. The important thing —what does ring true—is that this driving "nationalist" energy was, in all probability, central to the movement that gave the United States a new government.

The other side of the picture, which does not seem to have engaged Jensen's mind half so much, was the peculiar sloth and inertia of the Anti-Federalists. Cecelia Kenyon, in a brilliant essay on these men, has shown them as an amazingly reactionary lot. They were transfixed by the specter of power. It was not the power of the aristocracy that they feared, but power of any kind, democratic or otherwise, that they could not control for themselves. Their chief concern was to keep governments as limited and as closely tied to local interests as possible. Their minds could not embrace the concept of a national interest which they themselves might share and which could transcend their own parochial concerns. Republican government that went beyond the compass of state boundaries was something they could not imagine. Thus the chief difference between Federalists and Anti-Federalists had little to do with "democracy" (George Clinton and Patrick Henry were no more willing than Gouverneur Morris to trust the innate virtue of the people), but rather in the Federalists' conviction that there was such a thing as national interest and that a government could be established to care for it which was fully in keeping with republican principles. To the Federalists this was not only possible but absolutely necessary, if the nation was to avoid a future of political impotence, internal discord, and in the end foreign intervention. So far so good. But still, exactly how did such convictions get themselves generated?

Merrill Jensen has argued that the Federalists, by and large, were reluctant revolutionaries who had feared the consequences of a break with England and had joined the Revolution only when it was clear that independence was inevitable. The argument is plausible; few of the men most prominent later on as Federalists had been quite so hot for revolution in the very beginning as Patrick Henry and Samuel Adams. But this may not be altogether fair; Adams and Henry were already veteran political campaigners at the outbreak of hostilities, while the most vigorous of the future Federalists were still mere youngsters. The argument, indeed, could be turned entirely around: the source of Federalist, or nationalist, energy was not any "distaste" for the Revolution on these men's part, but rather their profound and growing involvement in it.

Much depends here on the way one pictures the Revolution. In the beginning it simply consisted of a number of state revolts loosely directed by the Continental Congress; and for many men, absorbed in their effort to preserve the independence of their own states, it never progressed much beyond that stage even in the face of invasion. But the Revolution had another aspect, one which developed with time and left a deep imprint on those connected with it, and this was its character as a continental war effort. If there is any one feature that most unites the future leading supporters of the Constitution, it was their close engagement with this continental aspect of the Revolution. A remarkably large number of these someday Federalists were in the Continental Army, served as diplomats or key administrative officers of the Confederation government, or, as members of Congress, played leading rôles on those committees primarily responsible for the conduct of the war.

Merrill Jensen has compiled two lists, with nine names in each, of the men whom he considers to have been the leading spirits of the Federalists and Anti-Federalists respectively. It would be well to have a good look at this sample. The Federalists—Jensen calls them "nationalists"—were Robert Morris, John Jay, James Wilson, Alexander Hamilton, Henry Knox, James Duane, George Washington, James Madison, and Gouverneur Morris. Washington, Knox, and Hamilton were deeply involved in Continental military affairs; Robert Morris was Superintendent of Finance; Jay was president of the Continental Congress and minister plenipotentiary to Spain (he would later be appointed Secretary for Foreign Affairs); Wilson, Duane, and Gouverneur Morris were members of Congress, all three being active members of the war committees. The Anti-Federalist group presents a very different picture. It consisted of Samuel Adams, Patrick Henry, Richard Henry Lee, George Clinton, James Warren, Samuel Bryan, George Bryan, George Mason, and Elbridge Gerry. Only three of these—Gerry, Lee, and Adams—served in Congress, and the latter two fought consistently against any effort to give Congress executive powers. Their constant preoccupation was state sovereignty rather than national efficiency. Henry and Clinton were active war governors, concerned primarily with state rather than national problems, while Warren, Mason, and the two Bryans were essentially state politicians.

The age difference between these two groups is especially striking. The Federalists were on the average ten to twelve years younger than the Anti-Federalists. At the outbreak of the Revolution George Washington, at 44, was the oldest of the lot; six were under 35 and four were in their twenties. Of the Anti-Federalists, only three were under 40 in 1776, and one of these, Samuel Bryan, the son of George Bryan, was a boy of 16.

This age differential takes on a special significance when it is related to the career profiles of the men concerned. Nearly half of the Federalist group—Gouverneur Morris, Madison, Hamilton, and Knox—quite literally saw their careers launched in the Revolution. The remaining five—Washington, Jay, Duane, Wilson, and Robert Morris—though established in public affairs beforehand, became nationally known after 1776 and the wide public recognition which they subsequently achieved came first and foremost through their identification with the continental war effort. All of them had been united in an experience, and had formed commitments, which dissolved provincial boundaries; they had come to full public maturity in a setting which enabled ambition, public service, leadership, and self-fulfillment to be conceived, for each in his way, with a grandeur of scope unknown to any previous generation. The careers of the Anti-Federalists, on the other hand, were not only state-centered but—aside from those of Clinton, Gerry, and the young Bryan—rested heavily on events that preceded rather than followed 1776. . . .

. . . A significant proportion of relative newcomers, with prospects initially modest, happened to have their careers opened up at a particular time and in such a way that their very public personalities came to be staked upon the national quality of the experience which had formed them. In a number of outstanding cases energy, initiative, talent, and ambition had combined with a conception of affairs which had grown immense in scope and promise by the close of the Revolution. There is every reason to think that a contraction of this scope, in the years that immediately followed, operated as a powerful challenge.

V

The stages through which the constitutional movement proceeded in the 1780's add up to a fascinating story in political management, marked by no little *élan* and dash. That movement, viewed in the light of the Federalist leaders' commitment to the Revolution, raises some nice points as to who were the "conservatives" and who were the "radicals." The spirit of unity generated by the struggle for independence had, in the eyes of those most closely involved in coordinating the effort, lapsed; provincial factions were reverting to the old provincial ways. The impulse to arrest disorder and to revive the flame of revolutionary unity may be pictured in "conservative" terms, but this becomes quite awkward when we look for terms with which to picture the other impulse, so different in nature: the urge to rest, to drift, to turn back the clock. . . .

The revolutionary verve and ardor of the Federalists, their resources of will and energy, their willingness to scheme tirelessly, campaign everywhere, and sweat and agonize over every vote meant in effect that despite all the hairbreadth squeezes and rigors of the struggle, the Anti-Federalists would lose every crucial test. There was, to be sure, an Anti-Federalist effort. But with no program, no really viable commitments, and little purposeful organization, the Anti-Federalists somehow always managed to move too late and with too little. They would sit and watch their great stronghold, New York, being snatched away from them despite a two-to-one Anti-Federalist majority in a convention presided over by their own chief, George Clinton. . . . By the time the New York convention was ready to act, ten others had ratified, and at the final moment Hamilton and his allies spread the chilling rumor that New York City was about to secede from the state. The Anti-Federalists, who had had enough, directed a chosen number of their delegates to cross over, and solemnly capitulated.

In the end, of course, everyone "crossed over." The speed with which this occurred once the continental revolutionists had made their point, and the ease with which the Constitution so soon became an object of universal veneration, still stands as one of the minor marvels of American history. But the document did contain certain implications, of a quasi-philosophical nature, that make the reasons for this ready consensus not so very difficult to find. It established a national government whose basic outlines were sufficiently congenial to the underlying commitments of the whole culture—republicanism and capitalism—that the likelihood of its being the subject of a true ideological clash was never very real. That the Constitution should mount guard over the rights of property—"realty," "personalty," or any other kind —was questioned by nobody. There had certainly been a struggle, a long and exhausting one, but we should not be deceived as to its nature. It was not fought on economic grounds; it was not a matter of ideology; it was not, in the fullest and most fundamental sense, even a struggle between nationalism and localism. The key struggle was between inertia and energy; with inertia overcome, everything changed.

There were, of course, lingering objections and misgivings; many of the problems involved had been genuinely puzzling and difficult; and there remained doubters who had to be converted. But then the perfect bridge whereby all could become Federalists within a year was the addition of a Bill of Rights. After the French Revolution, anti-constitutionalism in France would be a burning issue for generations; in America, an anti-constitutional party was undreamed of after 1789. With the Bill of Rights, the remaining opponents of the new system could say that, ever watchful of tyranny, they had now got what they wanted. Moreover, the Young Men of the Revolution might at last imagine, after a dozen years of anxiety, that *their* Revolution had been a success.

Suggested Further Reading for Chapter 2

Douglas G. Adair, "'Experience Must Be Our Only Guide': History, Democratic Theory, and the United States Constitution," in *The Reinterpretation of Early American History*, Ray A. Billington (ed.) (San Marino: Huntington Library, 1966).

George A. Billias (ed.), *The American Revolution: How Revolutionary Was It?* (New York: Holt, Rinehart & Winston, Inc., 1970).

Wallace Brown, *The King's Friends: The Composition and Motives of the American Loyalist Claimants* (Providence: Brown University Press, 1965).

Sidney G. Fisher, "The Legendary and Myth-Making Process in Histories of the American Revolution," American Philosophical Society, *Proceedings*, 51 (1912).

Cecelia Kenyon, "Men of Little Faith: The Anti-Federalists on the Nature of Representative Government," *William and Mary Quarterly*, 12 (1955).

Richard B. Morris, "The Diplomats and the Mythmakers," in *The American Revolution Reconsidered* (New York: Harper & Row, Publishers, 1967).

This people is the hope of the human race. It may become the model. It ought to show the world, by facts, that men can be free and yet peaceful, and may dispense with the chains in which tyrants and knaves of every colour have presumed to bind them, under the pretext of the public good. The Americans should be an example of political, religious, commercial and industrial liberty. The asylum they offer to the oppressed of every nation, the avenue of escape they open, will compel governments to be just and enlightened; and the rest of the world in due time will see through the empty illusions in which policy is conceived. But to obtain these ends for us, America must secure them to herself; and must not become, as so many of your ministerial writers have predicted, a mass of divided powers, contending for territory and trade, cementing the slavery of peoples by their own blood.

Turgot, 1778

3

MYTHS OF THE NATIONAL PERIOD

Chinese painting (c. 1800), artist unknown. Courtesy, the Henry Francis du Pont Winterthur Museum.

The legendary Washington: the apotheosis.

Kemmelmeyer, "General George Washington Receiving the Western Army at Fort Cumberland the 18th of October 1794." Courtesy, the Henry Francis du Pont Winterthur Museum.

The "Father of His Country" prepares to smite the people: the Whiskey Rebellion, 1794.

Introduction

As reflected in the chapter's opening quote from the French statesman Turgot, foreign expectations ran high as the United States launched a government in 1789 under the auspices of its new Constitution. America's own goals and aspirations, as manifested in the documents of the Revolutionary era and the Constitution, matched those prevailing on the Continent. Throughout the National Period, as Americans strove to live up to the high standards set for them both from without and within, the temptation to mythologize proved insurmountable. Later, historians would prove as susceptible as contemporaries to myth-building. As Henry Steele Commager demonstrates in this chapter's first article, Americans attempted to live up to this ideal image by displaying a tremendous urge to create a hurried, "usable past." The results only contributed further to the American propensity for mythmaking.

There was an abundance of material, and conditions were ripe for the creation of a usable past as the National Period began to unfold. Getting the nation started under the new Constitution was important in itself, but to be led by the nation's most famous hero, George Washington, further heightened the level of excitement and expectation. If Washington's popularity waned during his second presidential term, his death in 1799 set him on the road to immortality, aided of course by the amiable Parson Weems.

The beginnings of American foreign policy formed another area of national concern rich with mythic possibilities. Based on Washington's "Neutrality Proclamation" and his "Farewell Address," contemporaries, and later historians, developed what can only be described as a paradox —a foreign policy of simultaneous involvement and noninvolvement. A closer look at some of the underlying assumptions of American foreign policy help at least to neutralize some of the myths.

As the National Period progressed, America witnessed the early development of political parties from factions that had polarized around Alexander Hamilton and Thomas Jefferson. This led to the so-called Jeffersonian "Revolution of 1800." Perhaps a key to understanding the nature of this "revolution" is a de-mythologized picture of the central figure in the phenomenon—Thomas Jefferson.

The anomalous War of 1812, its causes dating back at least to the opening of English-French hostilities in 1793, also demands attention from a myth-oriented approach to American history. The causes of the war and President Madison's role in its coming continue to be debated. No doubt some myth has been generated as historical consensus has tended to place much blame on the President for our involvement, and then to accuse him of a lack of wartime leadership. Does he deserve the rather harsh treatment that history has accorded him?

After the War of 1812, during the presidency of James Monroe, America's foreign policy had decided nationalistic overtones. For many, the Monroe Doctrine of 1823 epitomized this spirit of nationalism. Were they correct, or was the policy merely a measure which later conveniently fitted America's view of its foreign policy?

These are the topics drawn from the National Period to which a myth-oriented approach seems most viable, and to which the articles in this chapter address themselves.

The Search for a Usable Past

Henry Steele Commager

It seems tenable that Americans have found the material for myth-making more readily at hand than have Europeans. Henry Steele Commager, distinguished historian at Amherst, and a well-known public lecturer, explores the historical and psychological conditions that served to evoke a national consciousness in Americans during the period from the Revolution to the Civil War. Arguing that American self-consciousness was deliberately created and fostered, Commager sees that American nationalism, myths included, was "to an extraordinary degree, a literary creation. . . ." It was poets and storytellers who "created" the fund of culture, tradition, and experience so necessary to bind national sentiment. As such, the growth of the American Republic has surely witnessed a merging of fact and fancy unique in modern history.

The United States was the first of the "new" nations. As the American colonies were the first to rebel against a European "mother country," so the American states were the first to create—we can use Lincoln's term, to bring forth—a new nation. Modern nationalism was inaugurated by the American, not the French, Revolution. But the new United States faced problems unknown to the new nations of nineteenth-century Europe—and twentieth. For in the Old World the nation came before the state; in America the state came before the nation. In the Old World nations grew out of well-prepared soil, built upon a foundation of history and traditions; in America the foundations were still to be laid, the seeds still to be planted, the traditions still to be formed.

The problem which confronted the new United States then was radically different from that which confronted, let us say, Belgium, Italy, Greece, or Germany in the nineteenth century, or Norway, Finland, Iceland, and Israel in the twentieth. These "new" states were already amply equipped with history, tradition, and memory—as well as with many of the other essential ingredients of nationalism except political independence. Of them it can be said that the nation was a product of history. But with the United States, history was rather a creation of the nation, and it is suggestive that in the New World the self-made nation was as familiar as the self-made man.

It is unnecessary to emphasize anything as familiar as the importance of history, tradition, and memory to successful nationalism. On this matter

From "The Search for a Usable Past," by Henry Steele Commager, in *American Heritage Magazine* (February 1965). Reprinted by permission of the author.

statesmen, historians, and philosophers of nationalism are all agreed. It was the very core of Edmund Burke's philosophy: the nation—society itself—is a partnership of past, present, and future; we (the English) "derive all we possess as an inheritance from our forefathers." It is indeed not merely the course of history but of nature itself. Thus Friedrich von Schlegel, trying to quicken a sense of nationalism in the Germans, urged that "nothing is so important as that the Germans . . . return to the course of their own language and poetry, and liberate from the old documents of their ancestral past that power of old, that noble spirit which . . . is sleeping in them." And Mazzini, in his struggle for the unification of Italy, was ever conscious that "the most important inspiration for nationalism is the awareness of past glories and past sufferings."

So, too, with the philosophers of nationalism, and the historians as well. Listen to Ernest Renan. In that famous lecture "What Is a Nation?" he emphasized "the common memories, sacrifices, glories, afflictions, and regrets," and submitted that the worthiest of all cults was "the cult of ancestors." So, too, with the hard-headed John Stuart Mill, across the Channel. "The strongest cause [for the feeling of nationality] is identity of political antecedents, the possession of a national history, and consequent community of recollections, collective pride and humiliation, pleasure and regret."

But if a historical past and a historical memory are indeed essential ingredients for a viable nationalism, what was the new United States to do in 1776, or in 1789, or for that matter at almost any time before the Civil War? How does a country without a past of her own acquire one, or how does she provide a substitute for it? Where could such a nation find the stuff for patriotism, for sentiment, for pride, for memory, for collective character? It was a question that came up very early, for Americans have always been somewhat uncomfortable about their lack of history and of antiquity, somewhat embarrassed about being historical *nouveaux riches*.

It was Henry James who put the question in most memorable form. I refer to the famous passage about the historical and intellectual environment in which the young Nathaniel Hawthorne found himself in 1840. It takes a great deal of history to make a little literature, said James, and how could Hawthorne make literature with a history so meager and so thin: "No state, in the European sense of the word, and indeed barely a specific national name. No sovereign, no court, no personal loyalty, no aristocracy, no church, no clergy, no army, no diplomatic service, no country gentlemen, no palaces, no castles, nor manors, nor old country houses, nor parsonages, nor thatched cottages, nor ivied ruins; no cathedrals, nor abbeys, nor little Norman churches; no great Universities, nor public schools, no Oxford nor Eton nor Harrow; no literature, no novels, no museums, no pictures, no political society, no sporting class—no Epsom nor Ascot!"

There is almost too much here; the indictment, as James himself remarked, is a lurid one, and he noted, too, with some satisfaction, that Hawthorne had not been wholly frustrated by the thinness of his materials—how he managed was, said James wryly, our private joke. It is suggestive that James' famous outburst was inspired by Hawthorne himself; he had, so he wrote, delighted in a place—his own dear native land—which had "no shadow, no antiquity, no mystery, no picturesque and gloomy wrong, nor anything but a commonplace prosperity, in broad and simple daylight, as is happily the case with my dear native land." It is worth dwelling on this for a moment, for this is from the author of *The Scarlet Letter*, and of *The House of Seven Gables*, and of a score of stories which did precisely dwell on shadows, antiquities, gloomy wrongs—witchcraft, for example. If a Hawthorne, who all his life felt it necessary to immerse himself in New England antiquities and inherited wrongs, could yet contrast his own dear native land with the Old World in these terms, think how unshadowed were the lives of most Americans—or how empty, if you want to adopt the James point of view.

A host of Americans had anticipated all this, but with different emphasis. Thus the poet Philip Freneau, introducing the abbé Robin's *New Travels in America*: "They who would saunter over half the Globe to copy the inscription on an antique column, to measure the altitude of a pyramid, or describe the ornaments on the Grand Seigneur's State Turban, will scarcely find anything in American Travels to gratify their taste. The works of art are there comparatively trivial and inconsiderable, the splendor of pageantry rather obscure, and consequently few or none but the admirers of simple Nature can either travel with pleasure themselves or read the travels of others with satisfaction, through this country." And half a century later James Fenimore Cooper, caught in that dilemma of New World innocence and Old World corruption so pervasive in the first century of our history, admitted that in America "there are no annals for the historian; no follies beyond the most vulgar and commonplace for the satirist; no manners for the dramatist; no obscure fictions for the writer of romance; no gross and hardy offenses against decorum for the moralist; nor any of the rich artificial auxiliaries of poetry."

But if there were "no annals for the historian," and if a historical past was necessary to nation-making, what were Americans to do?

Americans had, in fact, several courses open to them, and with characteristic self-confidence, took them all.

Over a century before the Revolution it had been observed of the Virginians that they had no need of ancestors, for they themselves were ancestors. The variations on this theme were infinite, but the theme was simple and familiar: that Americans had no need of a past because they were so sure of a future. Goethe had congratulated them on their good fortune in a famous but almost untranslatable poem: *Amerika, du hast es besser*: "no ruined castles, no venerable stones, no useless memories, no vain feuds [he said]. . . . May a kind providence preserve you from tales of knights and robber barons and ghosts."

Americans took up the refrain with enthusiasm. The romantic artist Thomas Cole observed that though American scenery was "destitute of the vestiges of antiquity" it had other features that were reassuring, for "American associations are not so much with the past as of the present and the future, and in looking over the uncultivated scene, the mind may travel far into futurity."

This theme runs like a red thread through early American literature and oratory, and finally connects itself triumphantly with Manifest Destiny. It began, appropriately enough, with Crèvecoeur: "I am sure I cannot be called a partial American when I say that the spectacle afforded by these pleasing scenes must be more entertaining and more philosophical than that which arises from beholding the musty ruins of Rome. Here everything would inspire the reflecting traveller with the most philanthropic ideas; his imagination, instead of submitting to the painful and useless retrospect of revolutions, desolations, and plagues, would, on the contrary, wisely spring forward to the anticipated fields of future cultivation and improvement, to the future extent of those generations which are to replenish and embellish this boundless continent." Washington Irving's friend and collaborator, James Paulding, entertained the same sentiment: "It is for the other nations to boast of what they have been, and, like garrulous age, muse over the history of their youthful exploits that only renders decrepitude more conspicuous. Ours is the more animating sentiment of hope, looking forward with prophetic eye."

Best of all is Cooper's John Cadwallader in *Notions of the Americans*, rebuking his travelling companion, the bachelor Count, for his unmanly longing for antiquity: "You complain of the absence of association to give its secret, and perhaps greatest charm which such a sight is capable of inspiring. You complain unjustly. The moral feeling with which a man of sentiment and knowledge looks upon the plains of your [Eastern] Hemisphere is connected with his recollections; here it should be mingled with his hopes. The same effort of the mind is as equal to the one as to the other."

The habit of looking forward instead of back blended readily enough with Manifest Destiny. Thus John Louis O'Sullivan, who all but invented Manifest Destiny, dismissed the past in favor of the future: "We have no interest in scenes of antiquity, only as lessons of avoidance of nearly all their examples. The expansive future is our arena. We are entering on its untrodden space with the truth of God in our minds, beneficent objects in our hearts, and with a clear conscience unsullied by the past. We are the nation of human progress, and who will, what can, set limits on our onward march? . . . The far-reaching, the boundless future will be the era of American greatness. . . ."

There was nothing surprising in Emerson's conclusion that America had no past. "All," he said, "has an outward and prospective look." For transcendentalism—the first genuine expression of the American temperament in philosophy, or New England's at least—was impatient with origins, put its confidence in inspiration, looked upon each day as a new epoch and each man as an Adam. It is difficult to exaggerate the impatience of the transcendentalists with the past. It was not so much that they were opposed to it as they found it irrelevant. And note that New England's major historians—Bancroft, Prescott, Ticknor, Motley, and Parkman—were all outside the mainstream of transcendentalism.

This was all very well, this confidence in the future. But it was, after all, pretty thin fare for nationalism to feed on at a time when other self-conscious nations were rejoicing in an ancient and romantic past. To be sure, the past became ancient and the future became present more rapidly in America than anywhere else: thus Thomas Jefferson could write from Paris in 1787 that much was to be said for keeping the "good, old, venerable, fabrick" of the six-year-old Articles of Confederation. And thus, too, John Randolph, in the Virginia ratifying convention, could "take farewell of the Confederation, with reverential respect, as an old benefactor."

Happily, there was a second formula to which Americans had recourse, and one no less convenient than the first: that America had, in fact, the most impressive of all pasts; *all* Europe was the American past. After all, we speak the tongue that Shakespeare spake—and for good measure, the tongues of Luther and Racine and Dante and Cervantes as well. Just because Americans had crossed the Atlantic Ocean did not mean that they had forfeited or repudiated their heritage. Americans enjoyed, in fact, the richest and most varied of all heritages. Other benighted peoples had only their past—the Danes a Danish, the Germans a German—but Americans had them all. Were we not in very truth a teeming nation of nations? Edward Everett asserted this as early as 1820: "We suppose that in proportion to our population Lord Byron and Walter Scott are more read in America than in England, nor do we see why we are not entitled to our full share of all that credit which does not rest . . . in the person of the author. . . ." Whitman made this the burden of "Thou Mother With Thy Equal Brood":

> Sail, sail thy best, ship of Democracy,
> Of value is thy freight, 'tis not the Present only,
> The Past is also stored in thee,
> Thou holdest not the venture of thyself alone, not of the Western
>   Continent alone,
> Earth's résumé entire floats on thy keel O ship, is steadied by thy
>   spars, . . .
> Steer then with a good strong hand, and wary eye O helmsman,
>   thou carriest great companions,
> Venerable priestly Asia sails this day with thee,
> And royal feudal Europe sails with thee.

All very well, but a risky business, this assimilation of the Old World past. For could the Old World be trusted? Could the past be trusted? We come here to one of the major themes of American intellectual history, and one of the most troublesome of all the problems in the creation of a usable past.

The theme of New World innocence and Old World corruption emerged early, and persisted all through the nineteenth century: it is a constant of American literature as of American politics, and if it no longer haunts our literature, it still bedevils our politics and diplomacy.

How deeply they were shocked, these innocent Americans, by the goings on in Europe! Benjamin Franklin, after a long residence in England, could deprecate the notion of a reconciliation between the Americans and the mother country on moral grounds: "I have not heard what Objections were made to the Plan in the Congress, nor would I make more than this one, that, when I consider the extreme Corruption prevalent among all Orders of Men in this old rotten State, and the glorious publick Virtue so predominant in our rising Country, I cannot but apprehend more Mischief than Benefit from a closer Union." Dr. Benjamin Rush, who had studied in Edinburgh and in London, never ceased to preach the danger of contamination from abroad. With Jefferson—surely the most cosmopolitan American of his generation—New World innocence and Old World corruption was almost an *idée fixe*. How illuminating, that famous letter to John Banister about the education of his son. "Why send an American youth to Europe for education? . . . Let us view the disadvantages. . . . To enumerate them all, would require a volume. I will select a few. If he goes to England, he learns drinking, horse racing, and boxing. These are the peculiarities of English education. The following circumstances are common to education in that, and the other countries of Europe. He acquires a fondness of European luxury and dissipation, and a contempt for the simplicity of his own country; he is fascinated with the privileges of the European aristocrats and sees, with abhorrence, the lovely equality which the poor enjoy with the rich, in his own country; he contracts a partiality for aristocracy or monarchy; he forms foreign friendships which will never be useful to him . . . he is led, by the strongest of all the human passions, into a spirit for female intrigue, destructive of his own and others' happiness, or a passion for whores, destructive of his health, and, in both cases, learns to consider fidelity to the marriage bed as an ungentlemanly practice. . . . It appears to me, then, that an American coming to Europe for education, loses in his knowledge, in his morals, in his health, in his habits, and in his happiness. . . ."

The theme, and the arguments, persisted. Hezekiah Niles wrote on the eve of the War of 1812 that "the War, dreadful as it is, will not be without its benefits in . . . separating us from the *strumpet governments of Europe.*" It is the most persistent theme in American literature from Crèvecoeur to Tocqueville, from Hawthorne's *Marble Faun* to James' *Daisy Miller* and *Portrait of a Lady,* from *Innocents Abroad* to *The Sun Also Rises*. Something of its complexity and difficulty can be seen in the position of the expatriate.

Here Americans long maintained a double standard; it was taken for granted not only that European immigrants to the United States give up their nationality and identify themselves with their adopted country, but that they do so exuberantly. But for Americans to give up their nationality and identify themselves with a foreign country was another matter.

Needless to say, there are philosophical and psychological implications here which we ignore at our peril. For this concept of New World innocence and Old World corruption encouraged that sense of being a people apart which nature herself had already sufficiently dramatized. How characteristic that Jefferson should have combined nature and morality in his first inaugural: "Kindly separated by nature from one quarter of the globe; too high-minded to endure the degradations of the others. . . ." To this day Americans are inclined to think that they are outside the stream of history, exempt from its burden.

But quite aside from the theme of Old World corruption, the availability of the European past was not a simple matter of chronological assimilation or absorption. It was available, to be sure, but only on limited terms. It was there more for purposes of contrast than for enrichment; it pointed the moral of American superiority, and adorned the tale of American escape from contamination. It was there, too, as a museum, a curio shop, and a moral playground. But for practical purposes it contributed little to the juices of American Life.

Americans had a third choice: They could use what they had. "We have not, like England and France, centuries of achievements and calamities to look back on," wrote the indefatigable diarist George Templeton Strong, "but being without the eras that belong to older nationalities—Anglo-Saxon, Carolingian, Hohenstaufen, Ghibelline, and so forth—we dwell on the details of our little all of historic life and venerate every trivial fact about our first settlers and colonial governors and revolutionary heroes." Not all Americans struck so modest a pose. All their past lacked, after all, was antiquity, and antiquity was relative; in any event, this meant that the American past was better authenticated than the European.

Nothing in the history of American nationalism is more impressive than the speed and the lavishness with which Americans provided themselves with a usable past: history, legends, symbols, paintings, sculpture, monuments, shrines, holy days, ballads, patriotic songs, heroes, and—with some difficulty—villains. Henry James speaks of Emerson dwelling for fifty years "within the undecorated walls of his youth." To Emerson they did not seem undecorated, for he embellished them with a profusion of historical association and of memory: the author of "Concord Hymn" was not unaware of the past.

Not every American, to be sure, was as deeply rooted as Emerson, but even to newcomers America soon ceased to be undecorated. Uncle Sam was quite as good as John Bull, and certainly more democratic. The bald eagle (Franklin sensibly preferred the turkey, but was overruled) did not compare badly with the British lion and was at least somewhat more at home in America than the lion in Britain. The Stars and Stripes, if it did not fall straight out of heaven like Denmark's *Dannebrog*, soon had its own mythology, and it had, besides, one inestimable advantage over all other flags, in that it provided an adjustable key to geography and a visible evidence of growth. Soon it provided the stuff for one of the greatest of all national songs—the tune difficult but the sentiments elevated—and one becoming to a free people. The Declaration of Independence was easier to understand than Magna Carta, and parts of it could be memorized and recited—as Magna Carta could not. In addition it had a Liberty Bell to toll its fame, which was something the British never thought of. There were no less than two national mottoes—*E pluribus unum*, selected, so appropriately, by Franklin, Jefferson, and John Adams, and *Novus ordo seclorum*, with their classical origins. There were no antiquities, but there were shrines: Plymouth Rock, of course, and Independence Hall and Bunker Hill and Mount Vernon and Monticello; eventually there was to be the Log Cabin in which Lincoln was born, as indestructible as the hull of the *Mayflower*.

These were some of the insignia, as it were, the ostentatious manifestations of the possession of a historical past. The stuff of that past was crowded and rich; it is still astonishing that Americans managed to fill their historical canvas so elaborately in so short a time. The colonial era provided a remote past: Pocahontas saving John Smith; the Pilgrims landing on the sandy coast of Plymouth, and celebrating the first Thanksgiving; Roger Williams fleeing through the wintry storms to Narragansett Bay; William Penn treating with the Indians; Deerfield going up in flames, its captives trekking through the snow to Canada; Franklin walking the streets of Philadelphia, munching those "three great puffy rolls" that came to be permanent props.

The Revolution proved a veritable cornucopia of heroic episodes and memories: Washington crossing the Delaware; Washington dwelling at Valley Forge; the signing of the Declaration; Captain Parker at Lexington Common: "If they mean to have a war, let it begin here!"; Prescott at Bunker Hill: "Don't fire until you see the whites of their eyes!"; John Paul Jones closing with the *Serapis*: "I have not yet begun to fight!"; Nathan Hale on the gallows: "I only regret that I have but one life to lose for my country"; Tom Paine writing the first *Crisis* on the flat of a drum, by the flickering light of campfires; George Rogers Clark wading through the flooded Wabash bottom lands to capture Vincennes; Washington at Yorktown: "The World Turned Upside Down"; Washington, again, fumbling for his glasses at Newburgh: "I have grown gray in your service, and now find myself growing blind"; Washington even in Heaven, not a pagan Valhalla but a Christian Heaven, doubly authenticated by a parson and a historian—one person to be sure—the incomparable Parson Weems.

The War of 1812, for all its humiliations, made its own contributions to national pride. Americans conveniently forgot the humiliations and recalled the glories: Captain Lawrence off Boston Harbor: "Don't give up the ship"; the *Constitution* riddling the *Guerrière*; Francis Scott Key peering through the night and the smoke to see if the flag was still there; Perry at Put-in-Bay: "We have met the enemy and they are ours"; the hunters of Kentucky repulsing Pakenham—

> There stood John Bull in Martial pomp
> But here was old Kentucky.

No wonder Old Hickory went straight to the White House.

The West, too—not one West but many—provided a continuous flow of memories and experiences and came to be, especially for immigrants, a great common denominator. There was the West of the Indian; of Washington at Fort Necessity; the West of Daniel Boone; of Lewis and Clark; of the Santa Fe Trail and the Oregon Trail and the California Gold Rush; the West of the miner and the cowboy; the West of the Union Pacific trail and the other transcontinentals. "If it be romance, if it be contrast, if it be heroism that we require," asked Robert Louis Stevenson, "what was Troytown to this?" What indeed?

And richest of all in its contribution to the storehouse of American memory was the Civil War, with its hero, Lincoln: it produced the best literature and the best songs of any modern war; it was packed with drama and with heroism. To one part of America it gave the common bond of defeat and tragedy, but a defeat that fed sentiment so powerful that it was metamorphosed into victory. It gave to the whole of America a dramatic sense of unity; to Negroes it associated national unity with freedom; and to all it gave the most appealing of national heroes, probably the only modern hero to rank with Alfred and Barbarossa and Joan of Arc. Certainly, of all modern heroes it is Lincoln who lends himself most readily to mythology; his birth humble and even mysterious; his youth gentle and simple; his speech pithy and wise; his wit homely and earthy; his counsels benign. He emerged briefly to save his nation and free the slaves, and died tragically as the lilacs bloomed; no wonder the poets and the mythmakers have exhausted themselves on this theme.

No less remarkable was the speed and comprehensiveness with which the new nation provided itself with an artistic record. From the beginning, to be sure, Americans had been fortunate in this realm; no other nation, it is safe to say, has had its entire history so abundantly recorded as the American, from the first contributions by Le Moyne and De Bry and John White to the realism of the Ash Can school of the early twentieth century. Never before in recorded history had anything excited the imagination like the discovery of the New World—O brave new world, O strange new world, new world that was Utopia and Paradise. Everything about it excited the explorers and conquerors: the Patagonian giants and the Amazons of Brazil and the pygmies of the Far North; the mountains that soared fifty miles into the clouds and the lakes as vast as continents and the caves of solid gold; the natives who were descended from the Chinese or the Jews or the Norwegians or the Welsh; the flora and fauna so strange they all but defied description. How to make clear the wonder and the terror of it all?

All the explorers were historians, to be sure; almost all of them were artists as well, and soon all Europe could share the wonder of those who had seen what men had never seen before. It was as if cartographers had given us maps of the voyages of the Phoenicians or of the Vikings; it was as if artists had pictured Hector and Agamemnon before the walls of Troy or Romulus founding the city that would bear his name, or Hengist and Horsa on the shores of Ebbsfleet!

Political independence brought with it artistic freedom, and an ardent preoccupation with the birth of the nation created the stirring political drama; the scenes of battle, lurid and triumphant; the Founding Fathers, grave, as became men occupying a sure place in history. In a generation when Franklin doubted the possibility and John Adams the propriety of art, a host of artists emerged, as if in defiance of counsels too sober; if they were not Rembrandts or Turners, they were better than anyone had any right to expect. It is not, however, their artistic merits that interest us, but their historical function. John Singleton Copley gave us a rich and crowded portrait gallery of colonial society in the process of becoming American—the merchants, the statesmen, the captains, and their ladies as well. John Trumbull regarded himself as the official painter of the Revolution and covered that chapter of history systematically though not comprehensively. Scarcely less impressive was the contribution of the versatile Charles Willson Peale, who left us a whole gallery of Founding Fathers as well as an academy of artistic sons, while the achievement of Gilbert Stuart in impressing on future generations his image of the Father of His Country is almost without parallel in the history of art. This school of artistic historians came to an end when its work was done, when it had provided posterity with artistic archives and monuments of its birth and its youth. Then the new nation, secure in the possession of an artistic record, could afford to indulge the romanticism of an Allston or a Cole, of the Hudson River school, or of genre painters like the puckish John Quidor—worthy companion to Washington Irving—or William Sidney Mount.

The celebration of independence and the founding of the republic was but one chapter in the history of the creation of an artistic image of the American past. Another school seized, almost instinctively, on the inexhaustible theme of the Indian and the winning of the West. Thus, while scores of American artists sailed for the Italian Arcadia, others, untrained, or trained in the irrelevant school of Düsseldorf, moved quite as confidently across the Alleghenies and on to the prairies and the plains and the mountains of the West. What a romantic group they were: the Swiss Carl Bodmer, who went with Prince Maximilian of Wied up the Missouri River in the early 1830's, and who gave us a crowded gallery of Sioux, Crees, Assiniboins, and Mandans; the indefatigable George Catlin with his hundreds of Indian portraits—surely the fullest artistic re-creation of the West before photography; Alfred Jacob Miller, who was the artist for Captain Stewart's explorations in the Far West and who sketched not only Indians but the landscape—Chimney Rock and Independence Rock and the Tetons and the Wind River Mountains; the luckless John Mix Stanley, who was ubiquitous, from the lead mines of Galena to the Cherokee country, with Kearny on the Santa Fe Trail, one thousand miles by canoe up the Columbia, even to distant Hawaii—the work of a lifetime lost in the great Smithsonian fire of 1865.

Not all of these artists of the early West re-created the past for their own generation. Miller, for example, was not really known in his own day, nor was Stanley. Far more important in the creation of the popular image of America were two artist-ornithologists, Alexander Wilson and John James Audubon, who captured for all time the flora and fauna of America in its pastoral age. Wilson's nine-volume *American Ornithology* was perhaps the most ambitious work of science in the early republic. Soon came Audubon's *Birds of America,* less scientific than Wilson's *Ornithology* but more splendid, "the most magnificent monument" said Cuvier, "which art has ever raised to ornithology." And Audubon, of course, contributed more: his own extraordinary life and legend.

The sumptuous paintings of Wilson and Audubon reached the public only gradually, and in cheap reproductions. More effective was the impact of the almost forgotten school of panoramists. The hapless John Vanderlyn, who had dared display his nude *Ariadne* to an outraged public, introduced the panorama, in a specially built rotunda in New York's City Hall Park. But it was Versailles and Athens and Mexico which he chose to display; perhaps that is why he failed. His successors preferred to reveal America, and particularly the Father of Waters, which had the advantage of being almost the only object of nature longer than their paintings. One John Rowson Smith did a panorama of the Mississippi as early as 1844; when he displayed it at Saratoga Springs, New York, he took in twenty thousand dollars in six weeks. Soon there were a dozen rivals in the field: John Banvard, for example, who claimed that his Mississippi panorama was three miles long (actually it was only a quarter of a mile—a bad calculation, that). Poor John Stanley, who had so little luck with his Indian paintings, scored a tremendous success with a panorama of the *Western Wilds,* forty-two episodes, no less, requiring a minimum of two hours to view! Greatest of all the panoramists was Henry Lewis, who managed to cover almost three quarters of a mile of canvas with his paintings; his earnings from his great panorama enabled him to settle in Düsseldorf and learn to paint. Whatever their artistic merits, or demerits, the panoramas helped give a whole generation of Americans some feeling for the spaciousness and the beauty of the early West.

Writing in 1841, Emerson had lamented that "banks and tariffs, the newspaper and caucus, Methodism and Unitarianism, are flat and dull to dull people but rest on the same foundations of wonder as the town of Troy and the temple of Delphi. . . . Our logrolling, our stumps and their politics, our fisheries, our Negroes and Indians, our boasts and our repudiations . . . the northern trade, the southern planting, the western clearing, Oregon and Texas, are yet unsung. Yet America is a poem in our eyes; its ample geography dazzles the imagination." Poets and artists had responded, but none had quite encompassed American nature. Even Whitman and Winslow Homer could not quite do that. For nature played a special role in American history and in the process of creating a sense of history and a national consciousness. Since the seventeenth century, Europeans have not had to concern themselves energetically with the conquest of nature, for nature, like history, was given. For Americans, on the other hand, the relationship to nature was more personal, and more complex. They had an empty continent to settle and successive frontiers to conquer, and for them nature had always played a twofold role: her ruggedness was a challenge, and her richness a manifestation of divine favor. How suggestive it is that for over two hundred years Europeans could not make up their minds whether the New World was Paradise or an accursed place, whether its natives were Noble Savages or degenerate men without souls. But however nature was to be interpreted—and by the nineteenth century the paradisiacal interpretation had triumphed—it was, in a peculiar way, the great common denominator and the great common experience. Virginians, Pilgrims, and Quakers alike could rejoice in the abundance of nature, and generations of pioneers, even those who were not *Mayflower* descendants or FFV's, could cherish the common memory of hardship endured and overcome.

Because they had conquered nature, Americans came in time to think that they had created it and to display toward it a proprietary interest. The stupendous flow of Niagara, the luxuriance of the Bluegrass, the power and majesty of the Father of Waters, the limitless expanse of prairie and plain, the glory of the Rockies—all of these came to be regarded as national attributes, and failure to appreciate them, like failure to appreciate political attributes, an affront. How interesting that from "Swanee River" to "Ol' Man River" songs celebrating nature have usurped the place of formal patriotic music—"Dixie," for example, or "My Old Kentucky Home," or "On the Banks of the Wabash," or "Home on the Range," or best of all, "America, the Beautiful."

And how interesting, too, that where in other countries topography is local, in America it is national. In the Old World, plains, valleys, and mountains belong to the people who happen to inhabit them, but in America the whole country, "from sea to shining sea," belongs to the whole people. The Italians and Germans traditionally celebrate their own cities, their particular churches or bridges; the English write two-volume works on Fly-casting in the Dart, or Cricket in Lower Slaughter, but until recently there has been little of this local possessiveness about Americans. "We have so much country that we have no country at all," Hawthorne lamented back in 1837, but Hawthorne was far from typical, and newcomers who could find little satisfaction in the slums of New York or the coal mines of Pennsylvania or the steel mills of Gary might yet rejoice in the Great Lakes and Yosemite. Movement, especially westward movement, is an essential ingredient in the American memory. When John F. Kennedy hit on the slogan, "Get America moving," he touched a responsive chord.

The task of providing themselves with a historical past was peculiarly difficult for Americans because it was not something that could be taken for granted, as with most peoples, or arranged once and for all. It was something that had to be done over and over again, for each new wave of newcomers, and that had to be kept up to date, as it were, continually reinvigorated and modernized. Above all, it had to be a past which contained an ample supply of easily grasped common denominators for a heterogeneous people, English and German, Irish and Norse, white and black, gentile and Jew, Protestant, Mormon, and Catholic, old stock and newcomer. Almost inevitably the common denominators tended to be pictorial and symbolic: the Pilgrims and Valley Forge, Washington and Lincoln, cowboy and Indian, and along with them ideas and institutions like Democracy, Liberty, Equality, the American Dream, and the American Way of Life.

One consequence of this emphasis on the simple, the symbolic, and the ideological is that American patriotism tended to be more artificial, labored, and ostentatious than that of most Old World peoples. It was almost inevitably calculated and artificial: after all, the process of drawing the juices of tradition for a German boy newly arrived in America was very different from that for a French or an English lad at home, where everything could be taken for granted, or left to nature. Tradition in America had to be labored, for it was not born into the young; it did not fill the horizon, as the glory of Joan of Arc or the fame of Nelson filled the horizons of French and English boys and girls. The American past could not be absorbed from childhood on in the art and architecture of every town and village, in song and story and nursery rhyme, in novel and history, in the names of streets and squares and towns. Growing up in Pittsburgh or Chicago was a very different experience, historically, from growing up in London or Edinburgh, Paris or Rome. And patriotism probably had to be ostentatious; in any event, it is. Ostentation characterizes new wealth, and new loyalties as well. This is doubtless one reason there is so much emphasis on the overt observance of patriotism in America. Americans dedicate a large number of days to ceremonial patriotism: the Fourth of July, Memorial Day, Confederate Memorial Day, Veterans Day, Washington's Birthday, Lincoln's Birthday, Columbus Day, Loyalty Day, and many others, and for good measure many states have their own special holidays—Patriots' Day in Massachusetts or Texas Independence Day. Americans require children to "pledge allegiance to the flag," impose loyalty oaths for every conceivable occasion, and march in "I Am an American Day" parades, and there is no W. S. Gilbert to satirize what so many take with passionate seriousness. Perhaps nowhere else in the Western world is loyalty such a touchstone as in the United States, perhaps nowhere else are there so many organizations dedicated to fostering patriotism: the Daughters of the American Revolution, the Sons of the American Revolution, the Colonial Dames, the United Daughters of the Confederacy, the Americanism committees of the great veterans' organizations, and, more recently, the Minute Women.

The process of acquiring a usable past was immensely facilitated by two extraordinary circumstances. The first was the eagerness of almost all newcomers from every part of the globe to slough off their pasts and take on an American habit, an eagerness so avid and so pervasive that it made nonsense of the compunctions and fears of native Americans from Fisher Ames to Thomas Bailey Aldrich a century later. Perhaps no other society in the process of transforming itself into a nation had more co-operative material to work with. The American newcomer, as he told us over and over again, was under both moral and practical compulsions to achieve acceptance for himself and for his children by becoming completely American as rapidly and as thoroughly as possible. Crèvecoeur, who saw so much, saw this, and so too the magisterial Tocqueville, but it is a lesson that has had to be relearned in every generation.

That is was *possible* for newcomers to become American overnight was the second circumstance. The explanation here lies in large part in the high degree of literacy that obtained in America, even in the eighteenth century, and the tradition of literacy and of education that flourished in that and the next century. Schools proved, in the long run, the most effective agencies for the creation and the transmission of an American memory. If they did not deliberately inculcate Americanism, that was because they did not need to: Noah Webster's Spellers, McGuffey's many Readers, Jedidiah Morse's Geographies and Peter Parley's Histories—these and scores of books like them conjured up an American past and provided, for generations of children, the common denominators, the stories and songs and poems, the memories and symbols. And it was the children, in turn, who educated the parents, for America is the only country where, as a matter of course, it is assumed that each new generation is wiser and more sophisticated than the old, and where parents adopt the standards of their children rather than children adopting those of their parents. For newcomers too old for school, and too inflexible to learn from their children, the work of providing an American past was carried on by voluntary organizations which have always performed the most miscellaneous of social tasks: churches, political parties, labor unions, lyceums, fraternal and filiopietistic organizations, and so forth.

What this meant was that the sentiment of American nationalism was, to an extraordinary degree, a literary creation, and that the national memory was a literary and, in a sense, a contrived memory. The contrast here with the Old World is sharp. There the image of the past was conjured up and sustained by a thousand testimonials: folklore and folk song, the vernacular and the patois, church music and architecture, monuments, paintings and murals, the pageantry of the court and of popular feasts and holidays. To be sure, literature—poetry and drama and formal histories—came to play a role, but only when it was quarried from cultural foundations that went deep. In America the image of the past was largely the creation of the poets and the storytellers, and chiefly of the New England–New York group who flourished between the War of 1812 and the War for the Union, that group familiar to an earlier generation through the amiable game of Authors: Irving, Cooper, and Bryant; Longfellow, Hawthorne, and Whittier; Emerson, Lowell, and Holmes. These were the Founding Fathers of American literary nationalism, and their achievement was scarcely less remarkable than that of the Founding Fathers of political nationalism.

In a single generation these men of letters gave Americans the dramas, the characters, the settings, which were to instruct and delight succeeding generations: Uncas and Deerslayer and Long Tom Coffin; Rip Van Winkle and the Headless Horseman; Miles Standish, Paul Revere, Evangeline, and Hiawatha; Goodman Brown, the Grey Champion, and Hester Prynne, as well as the Salem Customs House, the House of Seven Gables, the Old Manse, and the Great Stone Face; Skipper Ireson and Concord Bridge and Old Ironsides and the One-Hoss Shay and Hosea Biglow with all his Yankee company.

Note that this image of the past which the literary Founding Fathers created and imposed upon Americans was very largely a New England image, and much that was most distinctive about American nationalism was to be conditioned by this circumstance. It meant that Americans on Iowa prairies or the plains of Texas would sing "*I love thy rocks and rills, thy woods and templed hills*" with no sense of incongruity; that Plymouth would supplant Jamestown as the birthplace of America; that Thanksgiving Day would be a New England holiday; that Paul Revere would be the winged horseman of American history and Concord Bridge the American equivalent of the Rubicon; that Boston's Statehouse would vindicate its claim—or Holmes'—to be the "hub of the solar system." If all this was hard on the South, southerners had only themselves to blame for their indifference to their own men of letters. The most familiar of southern symbols came from the North: Harriet Beecher Stowe of New England gave us Uncle Tom and Little Eva and Topsy and Eliza, while it was Stephen Foster of Pittsburgh who sentimentalized the Old South, and even "Dixie" had northern origins.

The literary task of creating a usable past was largely performed by 1865; after that date perhaps only Mark Twain, Bret Harte, and Louisa May Alcott added anything substantial to the treasure house of historical memories. This was, in perspective, the most significant achievement of American literature and one almost without parallel in the literature of any other country in a comparable period. How interesting that a people supposed to be indifferent to literature—supposed by some to have no literature—should depend so largely upon literature for the nourishment of its historical self-consciousness. Certainly the speed and effectiveness with which Americans rallied their resources to supply themselves with a historical past cannot but excite astonishment. And what a past it was—splendid, varied, romantic, and all but blameless, in which there were heroes but no villains, victories but no defeats—a past that was all prologue to the Rising Glory of America.

Parson Weems, the Cherry Tree and the Patriotic Tradition

Nicholas Cords

Richard Hofstadter has argued that the Abraham Lincoln myth was self-made and self-perpetuated. While George Washington had some part in the creation of the myths concerning him—subjects usually do—one man, more than any other, was responsible for a vast proportion of his mythic monument. Mason Locke Weems was such a successful mythmaker that, as Marcus Cunliffe has suggested, he too has passed into folklore. This article by Nicholas Cords, one of this work's editors, briefly discusses Parson Weems, his times, the genesis and development of his *Life of Washington*, some of his techniques, and the strong emphasis on patriotism which was common throughout the National Period. No attempt is made to destroy either the parson or his myths; late nineteenth-century "scientific historians" attempted that, without much success. Indeed, the consensus now seems to be that, regardless of fabrication, one can learn a lot—even about Washington—from the "father" of the Father of Our Country.

American historical writing after the Revolution came to be dominated by the Federalist–Whig tradition. This tradition, while socially conservative, was consumed with liberal nationalism. Its proponents were of the upper-middle-class leisured group, and were highly selective in the materials they included in their histories. They accepted the view of the Revolution as put forth in the Whig publication, the *Annual Register,* and were anti-Jeffersonian. The providential approach to historical writing was on the wane, and this development continued as clergymen lost more and more of their influence. Local loyalties continued but were overshadowed by nationalistic fervor.

The new national spirit demanded of the historian that he express the ideals of the Republic and affirm its virtues and destiny. As the Revolution was the foundation stone of this new national spirit, its men and events provided the subject matter for most patriotic writing. Authors from Warren and Ramsay through Bancroft and Hildreth played heavily on the Whig-influenced patriotic theme. Even literary figures such as Barlow and Irving sang the refrain. The man who is the subject of this article, however, did more to enhance the patriotic tradition than any of the others. If he did not exactly fit into the Federalist–Whig mold, it was probably because he was the type of person who did not fit well into any fixed category. What he lacked in social conservatism and selectivity, he made up for in patriotism. Who was this figure? "I can't tell a lie"; it was Parson Weems.

Mason Locke Weems was born on October 11, 1759 at Marshes Seat, Herring Bay, Anne Arundel County, Maryland. His father was of a Scottish noble family (Wemyss) and had emigrated sometime before 1722. Little is known of Weems' early life, although legends abound. He is said to have made some voyages on his brothers' ships, and he studied medicine at Edinburgh or London.

By 1783 Weems was back in London where he studied for the Episcopal ministry. He was ordained in 1784 by the Archbishop of Canterbury, only after the oath of allegiance law had been abrogated (he had refused to take the oath). While in London he had correspondence with John Adams and Benjamin Franklin. On his return to Maryland he was rector of the All Hallows Parish (1785-89) and St. Margaret's (1791-94).

In 1794 Weems left the permanent ministry and pursued what was to become part of his life's work—bookselling. Striking up a relationship with Mathew Carey, a young Philadelphia publisher, Weems acted as his selling agent for practically the remainder of his life. His bookselling career was accompanied by one of editing and writing. He edited a series of improving books and wrote political pamphlets, biographies and tracts. He travelled between New York and Savannah, and became a well-known figure throughout the entire area.

It has already been stated that Mason Weems did not exactly belong to the Federalist–Whig historical tradition; this was mainly because of his attraction to, and constant dealings with, the common people. Although he got along well with people of all classes, he was more at home and more successful with those of the lower groups. The upper class tended to resent his crusading zeal, breadth of view in matters of dogma, outbursts of liberalism and lack of dignity. Also, his affinity for the Negro did not suit upper-class taste in the South. He conducted services for them every other Friday and once said concerning preaching to them, "Oh, it is sweet preaching, when people are desirous of hearing. Sweet feeding the flock of Christ, when they have so good an appetite." Bishop Meade referred to Weems as a "curious oddity," and to his family as "interesting and pious." What really irked Meade was the fact that Weems sold books in taverns on election and Court-House days, and extolled Tom Paine from the pulpit. Weems had once said concerning Paine, "divinity, for this climate, sh'd be very rational and liberal. . . ."

If Weems did not represent the socially conservative aspect of the Federalist–Whig tradition, he certainly had the patriotic line well in hand. His writings exude patriotism, embroidered with religion and morality. Concerning the Revolution, the Whig theory was easy for him to accept. The war had been cruelly made on the American people and its cause was simple to ascertain—"the king wanted money for his hungry relations and the ministers stakes for their gaming tables or diamond necklaces for their mistresses." Thus armed with these views, Weems, a merrily disposed white-haired individual, preached, prayed and sold his way back and forth across the southern half of the country. His saddlebags always contained a manuscript on which he was working, and he was constantly ready to dance or play the violin (Weems' family disclaimed that he ever played his violin on the road).

Weems' patriotic historical writing—as well as his talent for myth-building—is best typified by his biography of George Washington. The first known meeting between the two men occurred in 1787 and is recorded in Washington's diary for March 3rd of that year. Correspondence between them continued until Washington's death and Weems, always a businessman, used the acquaintanceship to his own advantage. Washington wrote a testimonial to an improving book edited by Weems, *The Immortal Mentor* (1796); the Parson immediately had it printed on the back of the title page. In 1799 Weems published *The Philanthropist; or A Good Twenty-five cents worth of Political Love Powder, for Honest Adamsites and Jeffersonians.* In this book Weems, brandishing his nationalism, pleaded for toleration in politics and recognition of what true equality meant. He defended John Adams and even Jefferson, of whom he was not particularly enamored. Washington's written praise of the effort appeared on the title page under the heading: "With the Following Recommendation by George Washington."

Upon Washington's death in 1799, the floodgates were released on the already swelling tide of legend concerning him. Here was an opportunity for Mason L. Weems and a torrent of other authors to expound the traditions, values and goals of the new nation in terms of the life and character of its most important citizen.

Parson Weems preached a eulogy at Pohick Church in Truro Parish, seven miles from Mount Vernon. This eulogy was expanded to eighty pages and published as a pamphlet under the title: *A History of the Life and Death, Virtues and Exploits of General George Washington.* The good Parson spent much of the remainder of his life expanding this work and bringing out new editions (twenty-nine before his death). The second edition added to the title: "faithfully taken from authentic documents." The fifth edition (1806) contained the cherry tree story and claimed that Weems was the "former rector of Mount Vernon Parish." Later the author went all out and called himself "former rector of General Washington's parish"—based on the fact that on a few occasions he had preached at the church Washington attended before the Revolution.

Weems is quite clear as to his purposes in the *Life of Washington.* The title of a later edition is helpful: *The Life of George Washington, with curious anecdotes equally honorable to himself and exemplary to his young countrymen. . . .* In a letter to a publisher (1800) Weems said he wanted to bring out "his [Washington's] Great Virtues. 1 His Veneration for the Diety [*sic*], or Religious Principles. 2 His Patriotism. 3*d* His Magninimity [*sic*]. 4 his Industry. 5 his Temperance and Sobriety. 6 his Justice, &^{c} &^{c}." Another goal of Weems, interesting in light of criticism levelled at him for creating much of the Washington myth, was to get at the real Washington. He stated: "In most of the elegant orations pronounced to his praise, you see nothing of Washington below *the clouds* . . . 'tis only Washington the HERO, and the Demigod . . . Washington the *sun beam* in council, or the *storm* in war." The actual result of his effort, of course, was that Weems created a Washington which all research scholars have been unable to erase and with whom they must come to grips—"a figure of truly terrifying piosities and incredible perfections." According to Senator Albert Beveridge, at times this Washington was an "impossible and intolerable prig."

Washington's characteristics and accomplishments, as put forth by the Parson, are exhausting just to contemplate. He had the old-fashioned virtues, loved his parents, loved and feared God, was a leader, a good student and was born to be a soldier. He proved that duty leads to advantage, he did not drink or gamble, he was talented and a case of smallpox marked him agreeably. He had a great sense of patriotism and duty combined with religiosity, he had intuitive perception, was a good writer, was benevolent, industrious and a gentleman. After all this—and more—Weems' readers were probably not surprised to find Washington, upon his death, ascending to heaven amidst choirs of angels to meet, among others, Benjamin Franklin and General Wolfe.

Reading two hundred and twenty-five pages of such material would not be too rewarding if it were not for Parson Weems' racy style, vivid descriptions and ever-present sense of humor. Throughout it all his delightful ability to adorn a tale keeps the narrative alive and interesting. One is tempted to agree with Sidney Fisher who said: "Reckless in statement, indifferent to facts and research, his books are full of popular heroism, religion and morality, which you at first call trash and cant and then, finding it extremely entertaining, you declare with a laugh, as you lay down the book, what a clever rogue."

Weems used the anecdotal method extensively. Considering the general literacy level of the day and the fact that his reading public consisted mainly of lower-class southern people, this seems a wise choice. Besides, the anecdotal method gave Weems a better chance to moralize and inspire; it also sold more books. The *Life of Washington* was laden with these anecdotes, the most famous of which is the one concerning the cherry tree incident.

George was blessed with a kindly old homily-laden father who, although not intellectually endowed, was a wonderful man and a great teacher. He early had told little George that he would rather see him dead than to see him become a liar:

> Hard, indeed, would it be to me to give up my son, whose little feet are always so ready to run about with me, and whose fondly looking eyes, and sweet prattle make so large a part of my happiness. But still I would give him up, rather than see him a common liar.

When George was six years old, he was given a hatchet with which he blithely tripped around chopping everything that came in his way—including his mother's pea-sticks. One day, in Weems' words, "he unluckily tried the edge of his hatchet on the body of a beautiful young English cherry tree, which he barked so terribly, that I don't believe the tree ever got the better of it." When asked by his father if he knew who had done it, George gave the reply which every schoolchild knows:

> "I can't tell a lie, Pa; you know I can't tell a lie. I did cut it with my hatchet."—"Run to my arms, you dearest boy," cried his father in transports, "run to my arms; glad am I, George, that you killed my tree; for you have paid me for it a thousand fold. Such an act of heroism in my son is more worth than a thousand trees, though blossomed with silver, and their fruits of purest gold."

The documentation for this and other of the anecdotes was "an aged lady, who was a distant relative, and, when a girl, spent much of her time in the family." Although the consensus of opinion seems to be that the incident originated with Weems in 1806, Emily Ford Skeel, in her work on the Parson, shows an illustration of a pottery mug with the incident depicted on it; the mug is dated 1776 and believed to have been made in Germany. Irrespective of this, certainly it was Weems who popularized the tale.

As to Washington's patriotism, Weems left no doubt. He quotes the general on his death-bed:

> Your government claims your utmost confidence and support. Respect for its authority, compliance with its laws, acquiescence in its measures, are duties enjoined by the fundamental maxims of true liberty. The basis of our political system is the right of the people to make and alter their constitution of government. But the constitution, which at any time exists, until changed by an explicit and authentic act of the whole people, is sacredly obligatory upon all.

Again Washington is quoted upon hearing that his plantation manager had given supplies to a British frigate commander in order to avert the destruction of Mount Vernon:

> Sir—It gives me extreme concern to hear that you furnished the enemy with refreshments. It would have been a less painful circumstance to me, to have heard that, in consequence of your non-compliance with their request, they had laid my plantation in ruins.

Weems was also concerned with the relationship of patriotism and religion, and thus Washington was. The book informed the reader that in the "Farewell to the People of the United States," Washington dwelled chiefly on the union and brotherly love. For Washington, in Weems' words, this combination appeared as "the one thing needful, the spring of political life, and bond of perfection."

The author outdid himself when it came to discussing the death of Washington. No normal death for the father of the country; after the rest of the book this would have been an anticlimax. After seeking the face of God (like Moses) and hesitating to quit the earth, Washington humbled himself (like Christ) and submitted to his fate. After death the following came to pass:

> Swift on angels' wings the brightening saint ascended; while voices more than human were warbling through the happy regions, and hymning the great procession towards the gates of heaven. His glorious coming was seen afar off; and myriads of mighty angels hastened forth, with golden harps, to welcome the honoured stranger.

Weems' second biography was of General Francis Marion, the Swamp Fox. This work, although not as popular as the Washington biography, sold well and again shows Weems' ability to expound patriotism through his writing. The Parson got the material from General P. Horry, an old fighting mate and friend of Marion's. Horry wanted to write the book himself but lack of prose ability forced him to seek another author. Weems extracted the material from him on the promise that it would in no way be embellished or changed. In a statement of fact, Weems wrote to Horry on August 3, 1808: "I beg you to indulge no fears that Marion will ever die; while I can say or write anything to immortalize him. . . ." General Horry began to worry. Ten months later Weems wrote:

> It gives me great pleasure to inform you, by our mutual friend Dr. Blythe, that your ever honored and beloved Marion lives in History. . . . I have endeavored to throw your ideas and facts about General Marion into the garb and dress of a military romance.

Horry panicked. After taking to his sickbed he wrote a rather apt critique to Weems:

> You have carved and mutilated it [the book] with so many erroneous statements, that your embellishments, observations and remarks must necessarily be erroneous as proceeding from false grounds. Most certainly 'tis not my history, but your romance.

Perhaps an example of this "romance" is in order. Marion and his men surprised several score of Tory partisans who had been feasting, dancing and playing cards; the fight virtually ended with the first volley. Weems describes the post-battle scene thus:

> Even their fiddles and fiddle bows, and playing cards, were all left strewed around their fires. One of the gamblers (it is a serious truth) though shot dead, still held the cards hard griped [*sic*] in his hands. Led by curiosity to inspect this sight, a dead gambler, we found that the cards which he held were ace, deuce and jack. Clubs were trumps. Holding high, low, jack and the game in his own hand, he seemed in a fair way to do well; but Marion came down on him with a trump that spoiled his sport, and non-suited him forever.

Weems also wrote tracts. These were against a variety of things—bachelorhood, adultery, gambling, infidelity. They fit into the patriotic theme because of Weems' connection of good government with religion and morality. An uplifted and improved people would be more patriotic. Lack of time and space does not permit a discussion of the tracts here; however, the full title of one tells a great deal about this aspect of the Parson's literary efforts.

> The Drunkard's Looking Glass—Reflecting a faithful likeness of the drunkard, in sundry very interesting attitudes, with lively representations of the many strange capers which he cuts at different stages of his disease:
>
> At first, when he has only "a drop in his eye;" second, when he is "half shaved;" third, when he is getting "a little on the staggers or so;" and fourth and fifth, and so on, till he is quite capsized;" or "snug under the table with the dogs," and can "stick to the floor without holding on."
>
> By Mason L. Weems

Mason Locke Weems has escaped relatively unscathed from over a century and a half of criticism. His acceptance by writers during the past fifty years has usually run the range from apathy to captivation.

Marcus Cunliffe refers to Weems as a Victorian before the Victorian era because he fitted Washington into the nineteenth-century mold. Thus Washington had all the nineteenth-century virtues from courage to punctuality, from modesty to thrift.

Lawrence C. Wroth claims that Weems was successful because Americans wanted an exciting vagabond writer—an American Marlowe or Villon. Wroth goes on to say that the Parson's influence on American youth has been good, citing the influence on Lincoln as an example. Besides, the anecdotes are good and are the only ones extant about Washington.

Harold Kellock sees Weems as the first American salesman, combining an indefatigable pushing ability with the instinct for giving the public what it wants. Weems did once say: "God knows there is nothing I so dread as Dead stock, dull sales, back loads, and blank looks. But the Joy of my soul is quick & clear sales—Heavy pockets, and light hearts."

Sidney G. Fisher claimed that Weems was a mixture of Scriptures, Homer, Virgil and backwoods. His history was all wrong but then so were all the other histories of the Revolutionary period. They were incorrect because they were based on the *Annual Register* and ignored the true documents. Bancroft was nothing more than a scholarly Weems. The Parson at least helped religion and youth.

Walter B. Norris evidently, or hopefully, has come under the influence of Weems' sense of humor. He wrote of a hypothetical S.P.P.C.T. (Society for the Protection and Preservation of *Cherished* Traditions) with Weems as chief *preserver*. He went on to say that the cherry tree incident could have taken place, offering as proof the known colonial regard for fruit trees and the fact that Virginia passed laws to protect them. He also suggested that, if the incident were false, the people living in Washington's home area would have disclaimed it.

There are other ways to judge the importance of an historian than to study his critics. Assuming success in sales and number of readers are valid criteria, perhaps we must agree with Sidney Fisher who viewed Weems as "a writer of the highest order of popularity, and in that sense and influence the ablest historian we have ever produced. Prescott, Motley and Parkman are mere children when compared with him."

Weems' contribution to American historical mythology is considerable; on the subject of George Washington he is without peer. Attempts to destroy his credibility generally have proved to be exercises in futility—perhaps they are even superfluous; ignoring him is impossible. This article has discussed the Parson, his times, some of his works, his "creative" techniques and his strong concern for patriotism, religion and morality, in the belief that, particularly in this case, understanding is the most viable approach to the subject; certainly it is the most enjoyable.

Washington's Farewell, the French Alliance, and the Election of 1796

Alexander DeConde

Largely because of services rendered during the war of the revolution, American enthusiasms for France found friendly expression in the foreign policy of the postwar decades. Thus, the military marriage of France and the United States, itself the subject of considerable myth, bears strategic importance to the presidential administrations of George Washington—most particularly his famous "Farewell," and the election of 1796. In addition to the fact that the "Farewell Address" was not an address at all but rather a position paper disseminated by Washington through the press, it was not the "wise, timeless, and unbiased warning to the nation" that it has traditionally been thought to be. As argued by Alexander DeConde of the University of California at Santa Barbara, the "Farewell Address" was rather an important political manifesto critical to the election of 1796. It was only "posterity" that gave the piece a meaning it neither deserved nor intended.

When in 1789 George Washington became the nation's first president the French alliance was the cornerstone of American foreign policy. It largely had made possible American independence and had established American foreign policy orientation. At the end of Washington's second term, in fact as he prepared his farewell to public life, the life-giving alliance was practically dead and the United States was virtually at war with France. Why, in eight formative years, did such a drastic reversal in foreign policy take place? A full answer to this question would be long and complex; yet by looking closely at the election of 1796 and by reviewing the Farewell Address in its political context we may find a partial answer as to how the alliance received its mortal wound. We may also find additional reason for revising the traditional interpretation of the Farewell Address as a wise, timeless, and unbiased warning to the nation.

The blow from which the alliance never recovered was the Jay Treaty of 1794. While this Federalist-negotiated treaty averted a war with England, a war which Federalists feared, the major objectives which John Jay had been expected to win were not realized. Because it failed to obtain specific concessions on impressments, ship seizures, and Indian raids on the frontier,

From "Washington's Farewell, the French Alliance, and the Election of 1796," by Alexander DeConde, in *Mississippi Valley Historical Review* (March 1957). Reprinted by permission of *The Journal of American History*.

the treaty infuriated Republicans and others who still nurtured a Revolution-bred hatred of England. At the same time it blighted Franco-American relations. Successive French revolutionary governments were convinced that the Jay Treaty violated the Franco-American treaties of 1778 and that the American government had accepted it against the will of an overwhelming public sentiment. Believing that the bulk of the American people were pro-French even though Washington's Federalist government was pro-English, the French sought to arouse their allies, the American people, to their true interest. This true interest was alliance with France and disassociation with England, America's natural enemy and France's major antagonist in war since February, 1793.

To arouse the American people in defense of the 1778 alliance the French Directory in June, 1795, sent to the United States a new minister, a young man in his early thirties, Pierre Auguste Adet. To the French the Jay Treaty created an intimate alliance between the United States and France's worst enemy. In Adet's instructions, therefore, the idea that the treaty violated the French alliance stood out as the foremost grievance against the Washington administration.

Despite French anger, and despite Adet's attempts to prevent ratification, the Senate approved the Jay Treaty eleven days after Adet had landed in Philadelphia. Two months later, while Adet continued his efforts to kill it, Washington ratified the treaty. England accepted the ratified treaty and in April, 1796, after a long, last-ditch battle in which Adet used all the influence he could muster against the treaty, the House of Representatives voted funds to implement it. To Adet as to other Frenchmen this meant the end of the 1778 alliance and another triumph for England and English gold.

Not knowing that Washington already had decided to retire from the presidency, Adet now saw the overthrow of Washington and his Federalist administration as the only salvation for the 1778 alliance. Adet and the French Directory viewed the Washington administration as the captive of English policy; to save the alliance it had to be replaced by a pro-French Republican administration. Charles Delacroix, French foreign minister, advocated inciting an uprising against Washington to break the Jay Treaty and to invigorate the alliance. Thomas Jefferson, he believed, would replace Washington and thus France would command the influence in the United States which she deserved. Prospects for the defeat of Washington were good, he believed, since the President, once the idol of the American people, had become to some an object of scorn and even hatred as the result of the Jay Treaty; already the journals attacked him, his principles, and his conduct.

Taking into account what it conceived to be the temper of American popular opinion, and with the objective of destroying English influence in the United States and salvaging the 1778 alliance, the French government intervened actively in the presidential election of 1796. Through Adet and other French officials in the United States the Directory openly supported the Republican party and wherever possible attacked the Federalist party. French intervention in the election became, therefore, one of the main issues in the campaign of 1796. The fate of the alliance hung on the outcome of the election.

The decision of the Directory to intervene in the 1796 election, while a decisive factor, contributed but one element to the complex politics of the election. Domestic issues and the Jay Treaty itself contributed others. Final acceptance of the treaty plunged Franco-American relations to their lowest depths since independence and marked a great political triumph for Federalists. Yet to Republicans all hope of ultimately defeating the treaty did not appear lost. Seeing the extent of the Jay Treaty's unpopularity, Republican leaders believed that it would make an excellent campaign issue in the 1796 election as an unrivaled party rallying point for national sentiment. Thomas Jefferson, James Madison, and other party leaders believed that popular opinion remained still largely pro-French and anti-British. Being politicians they reacted logically. Their party had ready-made national issues; they had only to exploit them properly and victory would be theirs. Republicans, consequently, carried over into the election of 1796 their campaign against the Jay Treaty and the pro-British "system" of Alexander Hamilton.

Granted the logic and appeal of the Republican campaign plan, a towering obstacle—the person and prestige of George Washington—stood in the way of success, as was clear to the French. So deep was the impression Washington had made on fellow Americans that to attack him would be to risk injuring the attacker. Twice he had been chosen President without a dissenting vote. Had he so desired he could undoubtedly have held office for a third term, for, as a foreign observer remarked, "there is a Magic in his name more powerful in this Country than the Abilities of any other man." No man, moreover, was better aware of this than Jefferson. "Republicanism," he advised, "must lie on it's [*sic*] oars, resign the vessel to it's pilot [Washington], and themselves to the course he thinks best for them."

Despite Washington's great political strength the situation in 1796 was far different from 1789 and 1792; Washington probably could have had a third term, but not by unanimous choice. In political battles over neutrality, the Jay Treaty, and other issues, he had divested himself of nonpartisanship. To Republicans and Francophiles the guise of being above party and of working for the welfare of the nation as a whole, in view of his intimate connections with his Federalist subordinates and his consistent practice of acting in accord with their principles, appeared the sheerest hypocrisy. In town and country some men now spat at the mention of his name, denounced him as a monocrat and an Anglomaniac, and prayed for his removal from office. Washington in 1796 had become a central figure in emerging party politics; he was a principal target for the violent personal politics of the time; and to the French he was the main barrier to reactivation of the 1778 alliance.

So bitter was feeling between English and French partisans that domestic issues drifted into relative insignificance. In their conviction that the Federalist administration did not truly represent the American people, the French were encouraged by pro-French partisans among Republicans who indicated that the Federalist government would topple if only France were to take a strong stand. As the election year of 1796 opened, Republicans intensified their attacks against the Federalist administration. The Jay Treaty and the loud cry of aristocracy, monarchy, and plutocracy aroused deep popular emotions. Mutual hatred characterized the two large political segments of the American public.

With his government under fire on both domestic and foreign policy and with himself the target of unrestrained scurrility, Washington found the demands of his office increasingly difficult to endure. Publicly he maintained a dignified silence, but privately he revealed the strain. Even he had come to see that the myth of nonpartisanship was shattered, and that his concept of an administration above party and the tumult of politics had been illusory. Foreign relations had exploded the myth while serving as a catalyst in the formation of national political parties. This was an issue capable of transforming the opposing local alliances of Federalist and anti-Federalist into integrated national parties—an emotional foreign policy issue capable of capturing public imagination in a way which abstruse problems of finance could not.

Despite his increasing distaste for the office and the increasing speculation about his not wishing to be a candidate for a third term, the President remained silent as to future plans. Leaders of both political parties, however, had little doubt that he would not run. "He gave me intimations enough," asserted John Adams, "that his reign would be very short." Early in 1796, and even before, both parties had laid tentative plans which did not include Washington as a candidate.

The attacks on Washington grew increasingly bitter during the year. Opponents charged that he had betrayed a solemn pledge to France by destroying the French alliance. Personal attacks accused him of taking more salary than was allotted him. His mail was tampered with for political advantage, and forged letters of 1777 were refurbished and printed as genuine. Particularly cutting was Tom Paine's bitter attack from Paris, which city was the source, Federalists were convinced, of the anti-Washington campaign. Jefferson, too, had lost patience with the exalted role of Washington. The President, he wrote, like Samson had had his head "shorn by the harlot England."

Despite pressures to stay and ride out the storm, Washington disclosed in May, 1796, that he intended definitely to retire. If he had nurtured at all the desire to seek a third term it was killed by the acid criticism to which he had been subjected. The President decided not to seek a third term not only because he sought retirement in his old age but also because he was disgusted with the abuse from political opponents. "The true cause of the general's retiring," declared one of his staunchest supporters, "was . . . the *loss of popular-*

ity which he had experienced, and the further loss which he apprehended from the rupture with France, which he looked upon as inevitable."

Once the decision to retire was made, Washington turned to Hamilton, as usual, for advice. When, he asked, would be the best time for publication of his farewell to the nation? Hamilton, with his eye on the coming election, advised that the public announcement be held off as long as possible. "The proper period now for your declaration," wrote Hamilton, "seems to be *Two months* before the time for the Meeting of the Electors. This will be sufficient. The parties will in the meantime electioneer conditionally, that is to say, *if you decline*; for a serious opposition to you will I think hardly be risked."

Three months before the gathering of electors Washington announced to the nation his intention to retire. Although in 1792 he had planned a valedictory to the nation and James Madison had drafted one, the September, 1796, version, in which Hamilton's hand was prominent, became a piece of partisan politics directed specifically against Republicans and Francophiles who had made Washington's last years miserable. At the time, it was recognized for what it was: a political manifesto, a campaign document. The 1792 version, drawn up before popular passions had been stirred by the war in Europe, did not, for example, stress politics nor did it touch on foreign affairs. In the 1796 version partisan politics and foreign affairs were central.

Washington's specific target in foreign affairs, heartily seconded by Hamilton, was the alliance with France. He struck at Adet's partisan activities, at French meddling in American politics (while passing over British meddling), and at the allegedly dangerous implications of the French alliance. Washington told Hamilton that had it not been for the status of "party disputes" and of foreign affairs he would not have considered it necessary to revise his valedictory. He was convinced that a warning to the nation was necessary to combat foreign (French) intrigue "in the internal concerns of our country." It is indeed easy "to foresee," he warned, "that it may involve us in disputes and finally in War, to fulfill political alliances." This was the crux of the matter; Washington believed that the French alliance was no longer an asset to the country.

Washington's valedictory trumpeted the Federalist answer to Republican accusations that the administration had sold the country to the British; it countered the anti-administration furor over the Jay Treaty; it was a justification and defense of his policies. As such it was designed and as such it became the opening blast in the presidential campaign, contrived to prevent the election of Thomas Jefferson. The Farewell laid the basis for Federalist strategy of using Washington's great prestige to appeal to patriotism, as against the evil of foreign machinations, to make "Federalist" and "patriot" synonyms in the minds of the electorate. Under the banner of patriotism the Farewell spearheaded the attack on the opposition party and on French diplomacy.

In the address Washington opened with the announcement that he would not be a candidate for a third term and then stressed the advantages of union and the evils of political parties. Having in mind, undoubtedly, the French Republic, he advised against "a passionate attachment of one Nation for another." Such "sympathy for the favourite nation," he warned, leads to wars and quarrels "without adequate inducement or justification." Then followed the oft-quoted "Great rule of conduct" that with foreign nations we should have "as little *political* connection as possible." While stressing fidelity to "already formed engagements," he announced that " 'tis our true policy to steer clear of permanent Alliances with any portion of the foreign world." Washington deplored the growth of political opposition, chastised the public for its attachment to France, and concluded with a defense of his foreign policy, particularly his much criticized policy of neutrality which was based on the Proclamation of April 22, 1793. He called this the "index" to his plan or policy.

Although cloaked in phrases of universal or timeless application, the objectives of the address were practical, immediate, and partisan. Men often attempt to rationalize their partisan political views in pronouncements studded with timeless patriotic appeals; so it was with Washington and Hamilton. The valedictory bore directly on the coming election, on the French alliance, and on the status of Franco-American relations in general.

While expressed cogently and linked forever with Washington's name, the main ideas and foreign policy principles of the Farewell were not unique with either Hamilton or Washington. They were prevalent Federalist ideas on current foreign policy and politics, and can be found expressed in various ways in the polemical literature of the time. The concept of no entanglement with Europe, for instance, was a common one among Federalists and others. More often than not it was a universalized reaction against a specific annoyance—the French alliance. Stated as non-involvement with Europe an attack against the alliance had great psychological appeal. In time this specific meaning was lost and only the generalization remained.

As partisans had expected, Washington's words stoked an already hot political situation. "It will serve as a signal," exclaimed New England Federalist Fisher Ames, "like dropping a hat, for the party racers to start." The Farewell was indeed soon under partisan attack. Washington's advice for the future, taunted William Duane, "is but a defence for the past." Referring to the warning against "permanent alliances," he exclaimed, "this extraordinary advice is fully exemplified in your departure from the spirit and principle of the treaty with France, which was declared to be permanent, and exhibits this very infidelity you reprobate in a most striking and lamentable light." The President had not, Duane continued, "adhered to that rigid and neutral justice which you profess—every concession to Britain in prejudice of France was a deviation from neutrality." Much of the evil which Washington attributed to faction, he claimed, came from the Federalist party. "Your examples of party influence are uniformly drawn from occasions wherein your personal opinions, your pride and passions, have been involved." As to Washington's advice to steer clear of permanent alliances, why, critics asked, was it unwise to extend the nation's political engagements? Was not the Jay Treaty a political connection, practically an alliance with England?

To James Madison—who earlier had feared that under Hamilton's influence the address would become a campaign document—the valedictory confirmed his assumptions; it was all politics. Under the complete influence of the British faction, Madison wrote, Washington obviously sought to destroy the French alliance. "It has been known," he continued, "that every channel has been latterly opened that could convey to his mind a rancor against that country [France] and suspicion of all who are thought to sympathize with its revolution and who support the policy of extending our commerce and in general of standing well with it. But it was not easy to suppose his mind wrought up to the tone that could dictate or rather adopt some parts of the performance."

Minister Adet believed wrongly that the address would arouse the indignation of pro-French "patriots" and would not have the effect on the people that the British faction hoped it would. He consequently plunged into the campaign to see to it that the address would not have its intended effect. Looking upon John Adams as an enemy of France and a friend of England, he electioneered brazenly for Jefferson. The future conduct of France toward America, he made clear to Americans, would be governed by the election's outcome.

Beginning at the end of October and timing himself carefully, Adet began publication of a series of public manifestoes designed to influence the electorate. He conjured up the prospect of war with France, stressing that Jefferson's election would eliminate such a possibility. With the Quakers of Pennsylvania, Federalists lamented, Adet's strategy of fear worked. Fearing a Federalist-sponsored war against France, Quakers cast their votes for Republicans. "French influence never appeared so open and unmasked as at this city [Philadelphia] election," cried William Loughton Smith, Hamilton's congressional mouthpiece. "French flags, French cockades were displayed by the Jefferson party and there is no doubt that French money was not spared. . . . In short there never was so barefaced and disgraceful an interference of a foreign power in any free country."

Adet's procedure was to write an official note to the Secretary of State and then to send a copy for publication to Benjamin Bache's Philadelphia *Aurora*. In his note of October 27, for example, he protested against American foreign policy and appealed to the people to renew their friendship with France by disavowing the Jay Treaty and honoring the French alliance. A few days later (November 5) the pages of the *Aurora* carried Adet's second manifesto, dubbed by Federalists the "cockade proclamation." In the name of the

Directory it called on all Frenchmen in the United States—in the land of an ally—to mount the tricolored cockade, symbol of liberty. Those who did not so give public evidence of their support of the French Republic were to be denied the services of French consuls and the protection of the French flag. Immediately the tricolored cockade blossomed in the streets. Americans as well as Frenchmen wore it as a badge of devotion to the French cause. It became, in short, a symbol of republicanism.

Ten days later Adet followed the "cockade proclamation" with his last and most florid note, which he again sent simultaneously to the Secretary of State and to Bache's *Aurora*. In it he announced that as a result of the Jay Treaty his function as minister had been suspended and that he was returning to France. Adet had timed his announcement so that it might have a maximum political influence, particularly on the electors who were soon to meet to choose Washington's successor.

Adet's notes and Secretary of State Timothy Pickering's replies were used as campaign ammunition by both sides. Federalists, of course, were furious. They denounced Adet's pronouncements for what they were—brazen electioneering maneuvers by a foreign agent. John Adams, against whom the last note was directed, found "it an instrument well calculated to reconcile me to private life. It will purify me from all envy of Mr. Jefferson, or Mr. Pinckney, or Mr. Burr, or Mr. any body who may be chosen President or Vice President." William Cobbett, violent Francophobe and anti-Jeffersonian, published Adet's note under the title of *The Gros Mousqueton Diplomatique; or Diplomatic Blunderbuss*. He ran with it, of course, an adverse commentary.

Friends of France, according to Adet, were delighted. Republican leaders were willing and even eager to use the issue of the French alliance to gain votes. But, contrary to Adet's opinion, they were not happy with the French minister's personal interference. Madison, for instance, maintained that Adet's note announcing his return to France worked "all the evil with which it is pregnant." Its indiscretions, he added, gave comfort to Federalists who had the "impudence" to point out that it was "an electioneering maneuver," and that "the French government had been led into it by the opponents of the British treaty."

Adet did not realize that his activities worked mainly to injure the cause he sought to aid. French popularity, according to competent observers, decreased as a result. Disgusted by Adet's conduct, Washington drew even closer to the British. One piqued New England writer went so far as to declare that since Adet's electioneering on behalf of Jefferson "there is not an elector on this side of the Delaware that would not be sooner shot than vote for him." And Philip Key maintained that Adet's meddling "irretrievably diminished that good will felt for his Government & the people of France by most people here."

Unaware of any adverse reaction, Adet and his intimates believed that his actions and the Directory's measures would influence the presidential electors decisively in favor of Jefferson. What Adet and the Directory had not taken into account was that invariably when a foreign diplomat takes sides openly in the domestic politics of the nation to which he is accredited he makes the party leader he seeks to aid appear to be the pawn of a foreign government. Such a charge, whether or not true, gives the opposition the opportunity of patriotically denouncing foreign interference and of posing as the defender of national honor against foreign subversives. So it was with the Adet case. His activities seemed to confirm the very warnings of foreign interference that were stressed in Washington's Farewell Address.

Sensing the opportunity, Federalists attacked the French alliance, denounced French domestic interference, and pitted the patriotism of Washington and Adams against the Jacobin-tainted Republican campaign. Voters were importuned to beware of foreign influence; to "decide between the address of the President and the [French]"; to follow Washington's counsel. Adet and the Directory, they were told, wished to draw the nation into war and to sever the western from the Atlantic states. No doubt clouded the Federalist mind; the Union was in danger.

Federalist warnings, persistent though they were, did not stop French interference in American politics; nor did the interference end with the choosing of electors in November. Few of the electors were pledged to a specific candidate, so the campaign continued with increasing tumult until December 7, when the electors cast their ballots. Adet, having suspended his diplomatic functions, remained in Philadelphia to continue his anti-administration campaign. He and the Republicans hammered at similar themes, stressing that if Adams were elected the errors of the Washington administration would be continued, since Adams was committed to Washington's tragic policies; and that such policies would lead to war with France.

Candidate Adams, on the other hand, believed that only time would tell whether "the French Directory have only been drawn in to favor the election of a favorite, or whether in their trances and delirium of victory they think to terrify America, or whether in their sallies they may not venture on hostilities." He advised that under the circumstances "Americans must be cool and steady if they can."

But Americans were not cool and steady. In newspapers and elsewhere they debated the French alliance, the mounting crisis with France, and the possibility of war. Hamilton, as was his practice in time of crisis, wrote articles for the press to reply to Adet's manifestoes, to defend administration foreign policy, and to attack the French alliance. Another prominent Federalist, Noah Webster, editor of the *American Minerva*, wrote a series of articles in which he also attacked the alliance. His articles were reprinted and widely circulated. In the Federalist press, in fact, attacks on the alliance now became common. Webster in his article stressed that France had equated the term ally with that of vassal; "an *open* enemy," he declared, "is less dangerous than an *insidious friend*." Although the British, too, had injured the United

States, Webster maintained that the American connection with Great Britain was stronger than the French alliance because "our connection with her is solely *an alliance of interest*. This is the true basis of all national connections. We are therefore in no danger from Great Britain."

In the first week of February, 1797, the American people finally learned the results of the election. Although the Federalist victory was narrow, it was enough to sink French hopes for a revived alliance. By "three votes" John Adams, who wisely had perceived that he was "not enough of an Englishman, nor little enough of a Frenchman, for some people," was elected second president of the United States.

Jefferson, however, captured the second highest electoral total and became vice-president. America's first contested presidential election therefore, although a clear-cut Federalist victory, gave some comfort to Republicans and struck fear into Federalist ranks. But Republican strength had not been sufficient to overturn the government and hence to reverse the course of Franco-American relations. To staunch Hamiltonian Federalists this aspect of the election was indeed sweet. In various election post-mortems, in New England in particular, such Federalists rejoiced that the "French party is fallen," and that the French alliance was at last valueless. Even Adet, one of them pointed out, "avows, and it is rather a tough point to avow, that our treaty is disadvantageous." Now he might inform the Directory that it has "been deceived by the revolutionary Americans in Paris; that we (at least the Yankees) have not been traitors, and have ceased to be dupes."

With the Federalist victory, narrow though it was, the Farewell Address had done its work. The French alliance which had been drawn to last "forever" and which had been the core of American foreign policy when Washington launched the federal government was practically dead as he prepared to leave office. Despite French and Republican efforts to the contrary, and in large part because of the impact of Washington's Farewell, the basic foreign policy orientation of the United States remained pro-British. The Farewell Address now belonged to posterity and posterity has given it meanings to fit its own problems.

Mr. Jefferson in 1801

Marshall Smelser

Thomas Jefferson—author of the Virginia statute on religious freedom, founder of the University of Virginia, and architect of the Declaration of Independence—was in many ways a political philosopher without a doctrine. Despite what Marshall Smelser of the University of Notre Dame calls "a monumental Jeffersonian mythology which makes him out a doctrinaire democrat," the essential Jefferson was of adaptable thought and character. As Mr. Smelser would have it, our understanding of Mr. Jefferson has been too much drawn in terms of Alexander Hamilton. Jefferson has traditionally served as a convenient "liberal" foil for the "conservative" dogmas of Hamilton. Thomas Jefferson was more moderate than radical, and motivated more by what he saw as the public good than by any set of political ideas.

At least we know what he looked like.[1] He was tall and slender, framed of large, loosely shackled bones. His clothes, including a cherished scarlet vest and a pair of run-over slippers, never seemed quite to fit. He struck one observer as a man who was all ends and angles. A Federalist senator, William Plumer of New Hampshire, on calling at the White House, mistook him for "a servant" and carefully noted that he wore a dirty shirt. The senator was fair-minded enough to record the wearing of a clean shirt at a dinner some time later.

Mr. Jefferson's usual manner was good-humored, even sunny, although occasionally abstracted or cynical. His disposition fitted a country squire whose excellent health and enviable digestion gave him a lifelong euphoria, interrupted only by periodic headaches and occasional rheumatic twinges. He had the typical complexion of the freckled gray-eyed Celt. His hair was cut short and powdered. Its color we know, because a correspondent saluted him in a letter, carefully preserved by the recipient, as "You red-headed son of a bitch."[2]

His small talk was built as loosely as his lounging body. Although often brilliant, his conversation was usually rambling and diffuse. It might range from weather and crops to the ingenuity of the Senate in finding excuses to recess during the local race meetings. Following the ponies was a lesser vice than dice; it gave the gentlemen "time for reflection," as he put it, between investments of their risk capital.[3]

That was the exterior Jefferson as seen by the casual caller, but his personality had layers like an onion. His intimate friends knew the next layer, his family knew the third, but no one except God and Thomas Jefferson knew what lay farther inside this sensitive, unsentimental violinist, bird watcher, and horticulturist. We do know that forgiveness of his enemies did not come to him easily.

He broke the precedent of delivering messages orally to the Congress, which was set by George Washington and carried on by John Adams. Jefferson sent his messages to Capitol Hill to be read by a clerk. He said it was to save time, but we know he hated to speak in public, and he was only entirely at ease in the company of kinfolk, artists, savants, and a few Republican leaders.[4] Margaret Bayard Smith, daughter of a warm Federalist and wife of the Republican editor of the new *National Intelligencer*, expected to meet a fanatical boor. To her surprise he was "so meek and mild, yet dignified in his manners, with a voice so soft and low, with a countenance so benignant and intelligent. . . ."[5] But Anthony Merry, the British minister, and his wife did not think the President so dignified and benignant. When Jefferson, lacking a hostess, disregarded all protocol at state dinners, saying "pele-mele is our law," they felt literally degraded and quit coming to the White House. The Spanish minister joined the banquet boycott.[6]

The absence of the diplomatic corps was not of first importance. To Jefferson the dinner party—particularly the stag dinner party—was a principal domestic political tool. Inviting not more than a dozen legislators at a time, he managed to get through the whole list more than once a session. The groups were chosen for compatibility. He seated them at a round table where he would be only first among equals and where private conversations would be difficult. He served his guests himself from a dumb-waiter to preclude the presence of eavesdropping servants. His French chef has been rated highly and his cellar must have been superb. Never dominating the conversation, he guided it away from the shoptalk in which congressmen found themselves already too much immersed, and planted the seeds of his political philosophy by indirection, letting his charm and his menu carry things along. The diplomatic corps knew well enough what he was doing, since it was the customary procedure of European courts, but to the political community in the raw new capital it seems to have been dazzling, and it showed Thomas Jefferson at his guileful best in the tactics of politics.[7]

The contrast between his manner with Mrs. Smith across a tea table and his treatment of the diplomatic corps makes clear the split between his private life and his public bearing as the chief of state of a democratic republic. In private, the gentle introvert; in public matters, the incarnation of a stormy nation of freemen, willing to provoke contention, even though he found controversy painful.[8] When relaxed with friends or family, his simple carriage was obviously not the way of a clod, but was more the manner of a negligent, self-assured nobleman, correctly confident of his status and of his own good taste. Yet, in a conference on the public's business, a senator could notice his "stiff gentility or lofty gravity."[9]

It seems very unlikely that such an undramatic and diffident man, whose charm was felt only in private, could have reached the White House in any later generation. His merits were publicized only by his friends. Not for him was the alley fighting of ballot politics. Once he warned his grandson to avoid two kinds of disputants: self-assured young intellectuals with more confidence than knowledge, and bad-tempered, passionate politicians—these latter needed "medical more than moral counsel."[10]

Now peel down to the third layer. There one sees a homesick widower with chronic money troubles, yearning for his children and his grandchildren. His was a great career but rarely a happy life. Between 1772 and 1782, four of his six children died. In 1781 a British army devastated his farm, and the difficulties of his term as governor of Virginia left a faint smear on his reputation. Then in 1782 Mrs. Jefferson died. At the age of forty his life had become a vacuum. It is almost enough to explain his later career to say that political, scientific, and intellectual projects rushed into his vacant soul to fill that vacuum and to make him the man we remember instead of the reclusive squire he wished to be. His two surviving daughters married young. One, Polly Jefferson Eppes, died in childbirth. He had a brief hope of something approaching normal family life when both of his sons-in-law were elected to the House of Representatives, but each of the girls was advanced in pregnancy and dared not risk the rigors of travel to Washington.[11]

After assuming the debts of his father-in-law, his personal finances were forever out of control. In old age he owed $107,000. When his daughters married, there was nothing left for him to take pleasure in except the talk of his intellectual friends, and the forty years of building and rebuilding Palladian Monticello. What he liked about Washington was that it lay between Monticello[12] and "The American Philosophical Society Held at Philadelphia for the Diffusion of Useful Knowledge."

II

All men claim to be Jeffersonians today. It is doubtful whether the study of any other public man in our national story has been equally absorbing to so many minds. Jefferson's popularity has reached its zenith since 1920. The published evaluations differ so widely that they tell us more about their writers than about Jefferson.[13] There is so much to see, so much to understand about this man of many flashing facets that it requires more self-discipline than most students have been willing to exercise in order to get the emphases in the right places.[14] He would, perhaps, be easier to understand except for the monument of literary evidence he left us—fifty thousand items, dated from 1760 to 1826, one of the richest left by any man.[15] It has not yet been completely mastered.

Thomas Jefferson's work has been scrutinized and searched not so much for understanding as to justify positions which often contradict each other. As the pendulum of public favor swings from generation to generation, he and Alexander Hamilton exchange the roles of Saint Michael and Lucifer. Laissez faire, states' rights, isolationism, agrarianism, rationalism, civil liberty, and constitutional democracy have all been fiercely defended by the use of quotations from Jefferson's writings, regardless of context. On a more sophisticated level of scholarship, professors drub each other with Jeffersonian tags to prove mutually exclusive generalizations. To get all of the academic theorizers under Jefferson's roof, we must label him the Agrarian Commercial Industrial Democratic Federalist. Fortunately for the history of the republic, the Jeffersonian administration, because of its optimistic evaluation of the public's common sense, was keen on explaining everything to the people. The wholly public business, despite the inner personal subtleties and complexities of the leaders, was very well documented, although one must read the public statements with the usual disciplined skepticism.[16]

III

Nothing that promised the ultimate physical or moral improvement of mankind was alien to the polygonal mind of Thomas Jefferson. With the Adamses and Woodrow Wilson he was one of the four most intellectual of the Presidents of the United States, and he and Wilson are still the objects of hero worship by some Americans. His own heroes were Francis Bacon, Isaac Newton, and John Locke, a "trinity of the three greatest men the world had ever produced." His nominal occupations were farmer and lawyer. He was close to being a true scientist of agriculture, and he was a much more active and successful lawyer, at least up to 1771, when public affairs began to take more and more of his time, than has been generally known.[17]

He mastered Greek and Latin before he was eighteen. Thereafter his reading revolved around the classical authors like a wheel around its hub. Because so few of us nowadays know the classics, we miss much in his mind. He not only knew Greek but he tried to reform its pronunciation by an essay in which he leaned more toward eighteenth-century Greek pronunciation than toward the Italian style then in vogue. He spoke French and Italian, although not fluently, and he had looked into, and had some acquaintance with, forty Indian languages. He also tried to reform the spelling of English. Although he was surely a first-rate writer of his own language, he thought of himself only as a discriminating reader. Omnivorous would be as good an adjective as discriminating. By 1794 he could honestly say he had the best library in the United States. Its 6,500 volumes, all of them collected since a fire destroyed his first library in 1770, formed the nucleus of the Library of Congress.[18]

He must have been a pretty fair violinist or he could not have endured to practice as much as he did, and he certainly has won praise as an architect,[19] but his attitude toward the arts was the attitude of his age. Artists were craftsmen who succeeded if their works pleasantly filled the leisure of the connoisseur by giving him something animating, interesting, attractive to contemplate.[20] Jefferson would not have understood the phrase "art for art's sake," nor could he have approved of the self-appointed Great Tormented Souls who floridly dominated the next generation's lush romanticism.

Thomas Jefferson was more inclined toward science than toward politics. He knew more of applied science, and he knew more scientists, than any of his American contemporaries. He was *the* American agricultural student of his day. For forty-seven years he belonged to the American Philosophical Society; for nearly twenty years he was its president and may have contributed more to its greatness than Benjamin Franklin.[21] Not only was his *Notes on the State of Virginia (1784–85)* a respectable contribution, but his stimulation of the researches of other men, for example, Lewis and Clark, is an influence still felt.[22] His scientific methods will still pass close scrutiny.[23] If the Revolution had failed, and if he had escaped the gallows, he would probably have been barred from public life; in the seclusion of Albemarle County, Virginia, he likely would have become the father of American agricultural chemistry.

Early in life he lost his faith, but not his morals; nevertheless, he had his children baptized in the Anglican Church, attended Anglican services, and had all of his relatives buried according to the Anglican rites. In Pennsylvania, he was Unitarian; in Virginia, Episcopalian; and in the District of Columbia, who-knows-what. He ended as a deist after enduring a lifetime of fierce, intemperate, even slanderous attacks on his infidelity from many who became Unitarians, that is, deists, themselves. According to his home-made theology, Saint Paul corrupted Christianity to prove Christ divine. Better, he said, that men should apply reason to the Book of Nature in order to discover the laws of God.[24]

This remarkable virtuoso, nationally honored for the virtues of the intellect before the time of the establishment of the federal government, was a talented connoisseur of all the arts. In some he had a taste and dexterity which approached professional standards. He was neither pure scientist nor pure philosopher.[25]

IV

Thomas Jefferson's prefederal political career was the career of a man who hated contention, who was better at counsel than at execution, who was better in committee than on the floor. As the scribe of Independence he had drawn together the feelings of his fellow countrymen into superb but prudently circumscribed prose. He gained no glory as revolutionary governor of Virginia and, indeed, barely escaped the censure of the Virginia legislature at the end of his term. The famous legislative reforms in Virginia, which were enacted under his leadership, were merely reforms of the squirearchy.

His mild and conversationally uncontentious liberalism, and his diplomatic experience as minister to France, made him seem the natural choice for Secretary of State in President George Washington's new administration. Jefferson accepted the appointment reluctantly and assumed the office in March, 1790. At that moment in the story, the President and the Secretary were cordial friends, but their relations chilled in the late 1790's. When the new Secretary of State came to New York, he was walking on to a political battlefield. He did not take a place in the array immediately. Indeed, as late as 1792, he still recoiled from direct political action.

An opposition had emerged in the Congress, led by Representative James Madison of Virginia. It was hotly opposed to the Treasury policies of Alexander Hamilton. Madison and John Beckley, the Clerk of the House, carried the anti-administration banner. From early 1791 they had Jefferson's sympathy, but he did not create their faction. It recognized and claimed him as its leader. Not until 1796, during the fierce wrangle over the Jay Treaty, did Jefferson become the public partisan head of anti-federalism. The notion that Jefferson founded the opposition was an invention of the Hamiltonians, to suit their short-range vote-getting purposes.[26]

True, Jefferson disapproved of Hamilton's policies because Hamilton influenced the Congress to favor finance and commerce over farming. By late 1792 he was so stirred that he could describe Hamilton's career to the uneasy Washington as "a tissue of machinations against the liberty of the country," but the explanation of the history of the Federalist period as a struggle between Jefferson and Hamilton is useful only as what Broadus Mitchell called "a sociological shorthand." It was Madison and Beckley who organized the group that later made Jefferson its idol. The squire of Monticello has been sketched as a shadowy *provocateur* from 1790 to 1795, holding other men's coats while they smote the enemy in the public prints, but this picture too is a Hamiltonian caricature. Only twice did Jefferson urge men to take up their quills and stab Hamilton, and in each instance it was in a public debate on a question of deep importance. Jefferson was always available at the elbows of the front-rank anti-Hamiltonians, but he did not march in public. The famous liberal sentiments which are so venerated by modern democrats were —after 1776—all written in private letters, not for publication. Even during the campaign of 1800 he stayed at Monticello to supervise the baking of bricks, while letting his political views filter out to the public through letters to his friends.[27]

Thomas Jefferson was never a flaming radical. His environment made it impossible, although there is a monumental Jeffersonian mythology which makes him out a doctrinaire democrat. In truth, he believed in getting what seemed best for the public good with as little painful acrimony and criticism as possible. He had no oratorical talent as a crowd pleaser and he never made a speech that brought cheers. The energy and admiration of his friends, not his own qualities of leadership, put him in the White House.

If the French Revolution had not caused a recanvass of fundamental libertarian principles, he and his supporters probably could not have pulled off the electoral coup of 1800. Nor was his election a victory for infidel rationalism. It was the counterattack of theologically conservative farmers against the Federalists' aristocratic contempt for America's sunburned agricultural drudges. They thought they were voting for electors, or assemblymen who would choose electors, who would favor Thomas Jefferson, a Whiggish moderate, whose only controversial publications had been the Declaration of Independence and the Virginia Statute for Religious Freedom long, long before. And they were right.

Notes

1. This description is compounded from William Maclay, *Journal*, ed. E. S. Maclay (New York, 1890), p. 272; Dumas Malone, "Thomas Jefferson," *Dictionary of American Biography* (11 vols., New York, 1927–58), hereafter cited as Malone, *DAB*; Dumas Malone, *Jefferson the Virginian* (New York, 1948), p. xviii; an unsigned review of the unpublished Augustus Foster, "Notes on the United States," *The Quarterly Review*, CXXXVI (1841), p. 24; and William Plumer, quoted in Lynn W. Turner, *William Plumer of New Hampshire, 1759–1850* (Chapel Hill, 1962), p. 94.
2. E. Millicent Sowerby, "Thomas Jefferson and His Library," Bibliographical Society of America, *Papers*, L (1956), 221–222.
3. Lynn W. Turner, "Thomas Jefferson Through the Eyes of a New Hampshire Politician," *Mississippi Valley Historical Review*, XXX (1943), 205. The politician was William Plumer.
4. Henry Adams, *History of the United States During the Administrations of Jefferson and Madison* (9 vols., New York, 1889–91), I, 143–146. Hereafter cited as Adams, *United States.*
5. Gaillard Hunt (ed.), *The First Forty Years of Washington Society Portrayed by the Family Letters of Mrs. Samuel Harrison Smith (Margaret Bayard) from the Collection of Her Grandson J. Henley Smith* (New York, 1906), p. 6.
6. "Jefferson to William Short on Mr. and Mrs. Merry, 1804," *American Historical Review*, XXXIII (1928), 832–833; Joel Larus, "Pell Mell Along the Potomac," *William and Mary Quarterly*, Third Series, XVII (1960), 349–357.
7. James Sterling Young, *The Washington Community, 1800–1828* (New York, 1966), pp. 168–170. Mr. Young's perspicacious book is a study of the ruling group in Washington by the methods we call behavioral science.
8. Adams, *United States*, I, 143–145.
9. Maclay, *Journal*, p. 310.
10. Malone, *DAB*; Charles A. Beard, "Thomas Jefferson: A Civilized Man," *Mississippi Valley Historical Review*, XXX (1943), 160.
11. Sarah N. Randolph, *The Domestic Life of Thomas Jefferson* (New York, 1871); Julian P. Boyd *et al.* (eds.), *The Papers of Thomas Jefferson* (15 vols., Princeton, 1950-61), VI, VII; Dumas Malone, "Polly Jefferson and Her Father," *Virginia Quarterly Review*, VII (1931), 81–95.

12. Rayford W. Logan (ed.), "Memoirs of a Monticello Slave, As Dictated to Charles Campbell in the 1840's by Isaac, One of Thomas Jefferson's Slaves," *William and Mary Quarterly*, Third Series, VIII (1951), 561–582.
13. Malone, *Jefferson the Virginian*, pp. viii–xi; H. Hale Bellot, "Thomas Jefferson in American Historiography," Royal Historical Society, *Transactions*, IV (1954).
14. Vernon Louis Parrington, *Main Currents in American Thought* (3 vols., New York, 1927–30), I, 342–356, an idolatrous portrait, is a fine thing, but not done from life; evidence is used frugally and predilections govern.
15. Jeffersonian bibliography is a career in itself: "If I may say so, I think one of his really outstanding achievements and contributions to humanity is the number of people, including of course myself, whom he has helped to support since his death." Sowerby, "Jefferson and His Library," p. 213.
16. Bernard Mayo, *Myths and Men: Patrick Henry, George Washington, Thomas Jefferson* (Athens, Ga., 1959), pp. 49–71; Clinton Rossiter, "Which Jefferson Do You Quote?" *The Reporter*, XIII, No. 10 (December 15, 1955), pp. 33–36.
17. There are twenty lines of references in Merle Curti, *The Growth of American Thought* (New York, 1945), under index: "Jefferson, Thomas"; Dumas Malone, *Jefferson and the Rights of Man* (Boston, 1951), p. 287; Roland S. Morris, "Jefferson as a Lawyer," American Philosophical Society, *Proceedings*, LXXXVII (1944), 211–215—Attorney Jefferson had 227 cases in 1771.
18. Malone, *DAB*; Louis B. Wright, "Thomas Jefferson and the Classics," American Philosophical Society, *Proceedings*, LXXXVII (1944), 223–233; Gilbert Chinard, "Jefferson Among the Philosophers," *Ethics*, LIII (1942–43), 255–268; Van Wyck Brooks, "Thomas Jefferson, Man of Letters," American Academy of Arts and Letters, *Academy Papers*, II (1951), 174–182; E. Millicent Sowerby, *Catalogue of the Library of Thomas Jefferson* (5 vols., Washington, 1952–59); Sowerby, "Jefferson and His Library," pp. 213–214.
19. Fiske Kimball, "Jefferson and the Arts," American Philosophical Society, *Proceedings*, LXXXVII (1944), 238–245. Jefferson said he practiced the violin three hours daily for an eight-year stretch. In pre–Paganini days this expenditure of energy might have made virtuosity of even a meager talent.
20. H. M. Kallen, "The Arts and Thomas Jefferson," *Ethics*, LIII (1942–43), 269–283.
21. Charles A. Browne, "Thomas Jefferson and the Scientific Trends of His Time," *Chronica Botanica*, VIII (1944), 363–418; Daniel Joseph Boorstin, *The Lost World of Thomas Jefferson* (New York, 1948), pp. 8–26.
22. Dwight Bochm and Edward Schwartz, "Jefferson and the Theory of Degeneracy," *American Quarterly*, IX (1957), 448–453. While on the Board of Visitors of William and Mary College, Governor Jefferson helped to found the chairs of anatomy and medicine.
23. Harlow Shapley, "Notes on Thomas Jefferson as a Natural Philosopher," American Philosophical Society, *Proceedings*, LXXXVII (1944), 234–237.
24. Malone, *DAB*; George H. Knoles, "The Religious Ideas of Thomas Jefferson," *Mississippi Valley Historical Review*, XXX (1943), 187–204; Herbert W. Schneider, "The Enlightenment in Thomas Jefferson," *Ethics*, LIII (1942–43), 246–254; Henry Wilder Foote, *The Religion of Thomas Jefferson* (Boston, 1960).
25. Dr. Jefferson held the following honorary degrees: D.C.L., William and Mary, 1783; LL.D., Yale, 1786; LL.D., Harvard, 1788. Malone, *Jefferson the Virginian*, pp. 422, 422n. Any list of his "scientific" accomplishments will mainly comprise items of inventive genius rather than advances in pure science.

26. Joseph Charles, *The Origins of the American Party System, Three Essays* (Williamsburg, 1956), pp. 74–90. On Madison's political leadership in these years, see Irving Brant, *James Madison, Father of the Constitution* (Indianapolis, 1950).
27. Jefferson to Washington, Sept. 9, 1792, Gertrude Atherton (ed.), *A Few of Hamilton's Letters* (New York, 1903), pp. 162, 175; Broadus Mitchell, "The Secret of Alexander Hamilton," *Virginia Quarterly Review*, XXIX (1953), 595–609; Noble E. Cunningham, Jr., "John Beckley: An Early American Party Manager," *William and Mary Quarterly*, Third Series, XIII (1956), 41–45; Philip Marsh, "Jefferson and Journalism," *Huntington Library Quarterly*, IX (1946), 209–212.

James Madison and His Times

Irving Brant

Americans are prone to see history from Jefferson's presidency to that of Andrew Jackson as an obscure interlude in American political development, filled only by vague images of the continuing "Virginia Dynasty." Despite its indistinct flavor, however, the period produced its share of myths. Specifically, Irving Brant, biographer of James Madison and freelance historian, proposes that myths surround James Madison and his times. Positing a favorable interpretation of the "Father of the Constitution," Mr. Brant seeks to temper former preconceptions generated both by historians and what he sees as "the distorting shadows of political prejudice." Long overshadowed by the imposing figure of Thomas Jefferson, James Madison emerges as a significant governmental administrator in his own right. Rather than the "errand boy" of Jefferson, Madison was more often a positive force well-attuned to developing political realities.

In a recently published magazine article on the life portraits of James Madison, the following statement is quoted from the biographer of Charles Willson Peale: "Peale painted Jefferson in December, 1791. He tried to paint 'coming men' for his gallery, and in selecting them relied mostly on the advice of those whose judgment he trusted. It is a fairly safe supposition that Jefferson recommended Madison for this honor."[1]

Why should it be assumed that Jefferson was the one who recommended Madison? The Philadelphia painter had many contacts with Frenchmen. Might he not have heard that French Minister Luzerne, seven years earlier, had described Madison as the foremost member of the Continental Congress?[2] Could he not have heard, from almost anybody in public life, that Madison was at least the godfather of the new Constitution? As a Philadelphian, Peale might have heard the complaint of Senator Maclay of Pennsylvania in 1789 that Madison "already affects to govern" President Washington.[3] The recommendation might even have come from Madison's principal adversary in Congress, Fisher Ames, who wrote of him in that same year: "He is our first man."[4]

In rejecting the supposition that Madison needed sponsorship in 1791, I do not mean to disparage Mr. Sellers, the author of the very excellent life of Peale. The biographer of an artist, when he deals with statesmen, naturally

From "James Madison and His Times," by Irving Brant, in *American Historical Review* (July 1952). Reprinted by permission of the publisher and author.

relies on the verdicts of historians and political biographers. Why should he not suppose that Jefferson was responsible for Madison's inclusion in the portrait gallery, when everything else in his life—his education, his political and constitutional opinions, his career in public office; everything you can think of, except, perhaps, his birth—has been placed to Jefferson's credit? In making this comment, I should at once point out some conspicuous exceptions. There is nothing like this in Dumas Malone's life of Jefferson, nor in Miss Koch's studies of the philosophy and letters of Jefferson and Madison. I might add that according to some reports, Douglass Adair's doctoral thesis at Yale was so favorable to Madison that it almost paralyzed some of the examining professors.

Pick out at random a dozen histories of the double decade ending in 1800. In how many of them will you find a factual basis for the statements of Luzerne and Fisher Ames? In how many will you find that Madison laid the foundations of the Democratic party, by his opposition to Hamilton's funding system, while Jefferson was still on his way from the American legation in France to the cabinet of President Washington? In how many will you learn that, as late as 1795, Federalists in Congress were calling their opponents "the Madisonians"?[5]

For an example of the way history has been perverted to support a preconception, consider this extract from Beveridge's *Life of Marshall*, dealing with events of 1793: "Jefferson was keeping pace with the anti-Nationalist sentiment of the masses—drilling his followers into a sternly ordered political force. 'The discipline of the [Republican] party,' wrote Ames, 'is as severe as the Prussian.' "[6]

Compare that with what Ames actually wrote: ". . . the discipline of the party is as severe as the Prussian. Deserters are not spared. Madison is become a desperate party leader, and I am not sure of his stopping at any ordinary point of extremity."[7]

Beveridge, I am sure, did not intend to distort. He merely reshaped the material to fit the distortions of earlier writers. These he brought to a magnificent climax of his own, brilliantly epitomizing a hundred years of error, in the statement that Madison was the valley between the mountain peaks of Jefferson and Hamilton.[8]

To a great extent this impression reflects the interplay of hero and devil worship. Until the American people subscribe to Confucianism, there is no possibility that they will deify James Madison. As long as half of them look upon Jefferson as a god and Hamilton as a devil, while the other half sees them in opposite roles, there is little likelihood of building a really commodious American Pantheon. What has actually happened is that a fairly level Jefferson-Madison-Hamilton plateau has been converted into two mountains and a valley by the unremitting activities of cairn-builders and rock-throwers. Some political geologists are beginning to suspect that this plateau, instead of being depressed in the middle, may originally have had a few bulges upward there.

Disparagement of Madison as a supposed satellite did not begin with historians. It began as a defense mechanism of Federalist politicians. During the formation of the new government, Madison and Hamilton were linked in the public mind. They were the outstanding advocates of the Constitution, and a few close friends knew them as joint authors of the *Federalist.*

When the great political cleavage came, in 1790, it was a direct break between Madison and Hamilton. Madison delivered his opening speech against Hamilton's financial system on February 11, 1790. On that day, in that speech, the wheels of Hamiltonian federalism and Jeffersonian democracy started rolling down the political highway.

Jefferson did not even know this was going on. The debate was over, the vote was taken, the fundamental cleavage in American politics was indelibly recorded, four weeks before he arrived at the capital to enter Washington's cabinet. Now that implied no defect in Jefferson's principles or in his perception. It was no reflection on him that a letter telling him of Hamilton's report on public credit took nineteen days to reach Monticello.[9] But there were reasons, deep in human nature, why neither Federalists nor Jeffersonians could admit that Madison laid the cornerstone of the Democratic party and continued to be an independent, creative force in its development.

During the ensuing years, it became apparent that between Jefferson and Madison there existed perfect harmony of feeling and a close correspondence of political views. Each time the basic issue arose in some new form, Madison took the lead in Congress, Jefferson in the cabinet, both working to the same end. The Federalists, tied up with rich speculators, were under constant compulsion to deny the moral flaws in their own position. They must see themselves, they must be seen, as the representatives of morality, intelligence, and respectability. On that score, Madison's opposition was far more distressing than Jefferson's. It was easy to endow Jefferson with diabolical traits, especially after the six years he had spent in Paris, the devil's paradise. But Madison was beyond the reach of ordinary attack. The principal architect of the new Constitution could not be suspected of a malicious desire to tear it down or to ruin the national credit which he had been working for ten years to establish. How could it be explained to the public that a man of his acknowledged wisdom, stability, and integrity was on the wrong side? That proved quite easy. He had gone over to please Jefferson. A good man had been seduced by Satan.

So said Hamilton, though he knew it was not true. So said a hundred others, and believed it.[10] But that was just the beginning. Once this explanation was given, Madison's character had to be reshaped to make it credible. A little earlier, he had been accused of twisting George Washington around his fingers. Jefferson was still in transit when Madison's challenge of the money power inspired a Massachusetts newspaper writer to exclaim: "Happy there is a Madison who fearless of the bloodsuckers will step forward and boldly vindicate the rights of the widows and orphans, the original creditors and the war worn soldier."[11]

Bold? Fearless? That did not fit the new story. What sort of man would change his political convictions to please a friend? Only a soft-willed man, a weak and timid man. So Madison was pictured as the submissive errand boy of Thomas Jefferson, perverting his intellectual genius to political purposes alien to his mind. Federalists dared not admit that Madison had sacrificed his dominant position in Congress, sacrificed his influence over President Washington, for the sake of principle. So they made a double assault—an assault on Jefferson for political immorality and on Madison for weakness and timidity.

The technique of the big lie, the big smear, was not invented in our day. It was brought to perfection against Jefferson and Madison, but with differing results. Madison was admired, for his mental endowments, by friends and foes alike, and he made warm friendships. But he had no political glamour. Jefferson, a symbol as well as a leader of democracy, had personal qualities which made people either worship or hate him. His admirers threw back the slanders against him. Did they likewise reject the perverted picture of Madison? On the contrary they made it their own, and thereby placed Jefferson on a still higher pedestal. So there you had both Federalists and Democrats, for totally different reasons, agreeing on a characterization of Madison which was not only unsupported by the record but was refuted by it at every turn.

At this point historians and biographers took over from the politicians. The big lie became the lasting misconception. The historians had testimony from both sides that Madison drew his ideas from the master of Monticello and did what he was told to do. If everybody said it, it must be true.

Let us see how this operated in the fight over federal assumption of state war debts. The conventional story is that about June 20, 1790, Hamilton and Jefferson made a trade. Jefferson agreed to assumption in exchange for the national capital on the Potomac, and induced Madison, his henchman, to help it through Congress. Apply the chronological test to that story of events in 1790, and what do you get?

March, 1783—Madison, in the Continental Congress, proposed federal assumption of state debts.[12]

July, 1783—Madison proposed a national capital on the Potomac.[13]

February, 1790—Madison spoke against *unqualified* assumption.

March 2—Madison proposed a qualified assumption, which the Hamiltonians rejected.

March 20—Jefferson returned from his diplomatic exile.

June 17—Madison wrote to a friend that to save the whole funding bill from defeat and national credit from destruction, assumption probably would have to be admitted in some form, and the Potomac might show up in the business.

June 20—Hamilton and Madison, brought together by Jefferson on Hamilton's initiative, agreed to a compromise—the national capital on the Potomac, in exchange for qualified assumption, which Madison had offered three months before without a *quid pro quo*.[14]

In other words, both of the basic policies originated with Madison. Both features of the compromise came from him and so did the idea of linking them. All he got out of it was a reputation for weakness and timidity. The valley travailed and brought forth two mountains.

Next came the great conflict over the power to create a national bank. I quote from Beveridge: "Jefferson was already opposing, through the timid but resourceful Madison and the fearless and aggressive Giles, the Nationalist statesmanship of Hamilton. Thus it came about that when Washington asked his cabinet's opinion upon the bill to incorporate the Bank of the United States, Jefferson promptly expressed with all his power the constitutional theory of the Virginia legislature." To this Beveridge affixed a footnote: "and see Madison's argument against the constitutionality of the Bank Act in Annals, 1st Congress, February 2, 1791."[15]

What would have been the effect if Beveridge had omitted the Virginia legislature, which had no more to do with it than the parliament of Timbuktu, and had stated the simple, chronological truth? This was that Madison launched the attack against the national bank on February 2, and Jefferson, thirteen days later, paraphrased Madison's speech in a report to the President. That couldn't be told. It would have ruined a preconception.[16]

Madison was Secretary of State throughout the two Jefferson administrations. You can imagine how contemporary politicians and many historians have treated these eight years. The prevalent practice has been to credit Jefferson with every policy, every action, every document of any importance that came from the State Department. If Madison is mentioned at all, he is the errand boy, the amanuensis, obeying implicitly every order handed to him. One of our standard diplomatic histories does not even mention that Jefferson had a Secretary of State. Another mentions him only once.

Now it happens that a very different appraisal of Madison was recorded in 1806 by a Federalist senator, along with his own conventional one. Senator Plumer of New Hampshire, in his diary, quoted Senator Adair of Kentucky, a Democrat, as saying: "The President [Jefferson] wants nerve—he has not even confidence in himself. For more than a year he has been in the habit of trusting almost implicitly in Mr. Madison. Madison has acquired a complete ascendancy over him." To this the New Hampshire Federalist replied: "I observed that I considered Mr. Madison as an honest man—but that he was too cautious—too fearful and too timid to direct the affairs of the nation."[17]

Here, it would seem, was a sharp challenge to historians, especially to those equipped with the instruments of modern scholarship—in this instance, the writings of Jefferson and Madison and their associates and the diplomatic archives of the United States, Great Britain, France, and Spain. That brings us to Henry Adams, the first historian who tapped these rich sources of information. Adams wrote nine volumes whose effect is to sustain the negative side of both appraisals. His history sustains Senator Adair's conclusion that Jefferson lacked nerve and confidence in himself, and Plumer's opinion that Madison was fearful and timid. Henry Adams leaves it uncertain which of these two weaklings ruled the other, but, employing endless condemnation and an irony far more deadly, he created the impression that between them, in their successive presidencies, they reduced the United States to the depths of national degradation. And what shape was the country in at the end of this period of humiliation? Its area and population, Adams noted, had doubled, and it was on a tidal wave of prosperity and confidence. I quote from his ninth volume:

> These sixteen years set at rest the natural doubts that had attended the nation's birth. . . . Every serious difficulty which seemed alarming to the people of the Union in 1800 had been removed or had sunk from notice in 1816. . . . Not only had the people during these sixteen years escaped from dangers, they had also found the means of supplying their chief needs. . . . The continent lay before them, like an uncovered ore-bed.

That was the economic picture. And the national character? I quote once more from Adams:

> In 1815 for the first time Americans ceased to doubt the path they were to follow. Not only was the unity of the nation established, but its probable divergence from older societies was also well defined. . . . The public seemed obstinate only in believing that all was for the best, as far as the United States were concerned, in the affairs of mankind.[18]

This mighty material and spiritual advance had been brought about, if we may believe Adams, not with the aid of Jefferson and Madison but in spite of their blundering and cowardice. It was the communal product of Mother Nature and the Goddess of Luck, with a little timely assistance from Albert Gallatin, John Armstrong, and John Quincy Adams, Henry's grandfather.

One would suppose that the grotesque inconsistency between Adams' premises and his conclusions would raise suspicion in the minds of his more critical readers. But the magnitude of his research was enough in itself to discourage skeptical inquiry. His conclusions as to Jefferson and Madison were in line with contemporary Federalist verdicts, while the historian himself, though plainly a Federalist in his sympathies, drove away the thought of bias by damning the Essex Junto with a violence he never employed upon the chiefs of administration. So the Adams history has become the accepted classic, virtually unchallenged by historians, biographers, journalists, or statesmen, except in the emotional resentment of admirers of Jefferson. That emotional rebellion, plus the Louisiana Purchase, was enough to lift Jefferson into the lists of great Presidents. Madison was left buried under 750,000 disparaging words, marked with the same stamp of goodness, weakness, timidity, and blundering that was originally placed on him by Federalist politicians to fortify their own self-esteem.

The Adams history, as most people know, is a compendium of documents as well as an interpretation. The factual material has been selected with very little bias, and the interpretations are honest. But isolate the documents from the interpretation and strange results ensue. The documents will support, nay they are likely to demand, a drastically different set of conclusions.

As I read Henry Adams, he was neither partial nor impartial. He was just a solid mass of conditioned reflexes. His Federalist leanings conditioned him against Jefferson and Madison. His family descent conditioned him against every President not named Adams, and against every enemy of President John Adams—against Hamilton and Wolcott, against Pickering and the whole traitorous gang who sabotaged the War of 1812. His life in his father's American embassy during the Civil War conditioned him against British diplomats—against Canning, Castlereagh, and Wellesley. He needed no conditioning against Napoleon and Talleyrand. Among these objects of his dislike, Henry Adams played no favorites. He hit them all whenever their heads came up, and thus achieved the air of magnificent impartiality, with devastating effect upon the capacity of many later historians for independent judgment.

I shall come back to Henry Adams, but first let us pursue a more basic inquiry. Was Madison weak and timid? To what extent was he Jefferson's errand boy, and to what extent did he direct policy, during his eight years as Secretary of State?

The errand-boy assumption runs up against some curious facts. In the summer of 1801, British Chargé d'Affaires Thornton complained to Madison that a certain action by French seamen violated the Anglo-American treaty of 1794. Madison and Jefferson were at their homes in Virginia, and the policy adopted would be put into effect by Gallatin. Madison wrote to Jefferson that the circumstances admitted an easy reply "that the case is not considered as within the purview of the treaty." Jefferson replied that he thought the vessel "must fairly be considered as a prize made on Great Britain to which no shelter is to be given in our ports according to our treaty." But he wanted Madison to feel free to revise this opinion and act as he thought best. Madison wrote at once to Gallatin: "It was readily decided that the treaty of '94 is inapplicable to the case." The President, he said, "has thought, as I do," that the ship should be sent away under a different sanction. And when Madison communicated the decision to Thornton, the British diplomat replied that he found himself "entirely at a loss to comprehend the ground on which the

President is pleased to regard the case . . . as in no manner falling within the provisions of the treaty of 1794." Here you have not only an instantaneous reversal of Jefferson's judgment by Madison, but a total concealment from Gallatin and Thornton that there had been any difference of opinion.[19]

There was in fact no basic difference. Thornton was trying to give British prizes a preferred position over French prizes in American ports. Madison realized this. Jefferson did not, but Madison knew that the President would approve in retrospect. This was a minor incident, but consider what it means when applied to Madison's position, character and conduct. Was there weakness? Was there vacillation? Was there timidity? Was there subordination of intellect and will? Was there inferiority of judgment?

Turn now to the most important event and greatest achievement of the Jefferson administration—the Louisiana Purchase. Historians have tried for generations to decide how Louisiana was won. From Henry Adams we hear that Madison invited France to build an empire west of the Mississippi, and that Jefferson had no means of preventing it until the French military downfall in San Domingo made American hostility troublesome to France. "President Jefferson [I quote from Adams] had chiefly reckoned on this possibility as his hope of getting Louisiana; and slight as the chance seemed, he was right."[20] From various other commentators, we hear of the diplomatic skill and relentless pressure of Minister Robert Livingston or of the shrewd and forceful guidance of Jefferson. And we are told by Professor Channing that Napoleon "suddenly . . . threw the province" at the American government, with no credit to anybody else except for catching and holding it.[21] As to Madison, the only question raised would seem to be: Was he an absolute nonentity, or did he surrender to France, failing even to discern, as Jefferson did, that French defeat in San Domingo held the hope of American success?

There can be no doubt that the wiping out of General Leclerc's army, in the war with Toussaint Louverture, was the crucial factor in the cession of Louisiana. It destroyed the fulcrum of French power in the Western Hemisphere. Now let us trace the American attitude toward Leclerc. His army reached San Domingo in February, 1802. He carried instructions which included this sentence: "Jefferson has promised that the instant the French army arrives, all measures will be taken to starve Toussaint and to aid the army."[22]

That promise was made to the French chargé d'affaires, Pichon, in the summer of 1801. Reporting this joyously to his government, Pichon said it relieved him of fears derived from a prior talk with Madison. The Secretary of State, he said, had seemed ready to support Toussaint, and in the same talk had given warning that collision between the United States and France would be inevitable if the latter should take possession of Louisiana from Spain. That, please observe, was in July, 1801, seven months before the French opened their campaign to reconquer San Domingo and nearly two years before Napoleon offered Louisiana to the United States. One month later, Pichon wrote that Madison's San Domingo policy still seemed to be in effect. Six months later he reported that he had complained once more to Jefferson about it, and "I found him very reserved and cold, while he talked to me, though less explicitly, in the same sense as Mr. Madison."[23]

Here we have a repetition of the Thornton incident, this time at the highest level of national policy. Madison realized instantly what San Domingo meant. Jefferson did not, but swung over to Madison's policy when the realities were placed before him. The result? The United States allowed American ships to go on trading with the Negro rebels while guerrilla warfare and yellow fever wiped out the army of occupation. That was tough power politics—brutal politics. It did not come from a weak and vacillating errand boy.

Let us jump a year or two. On April 10, 1803, Easter Sunday, Napoleon sent for his finance minister, Marbois. Before Marbois left the palace Napoleon said to him: "I renounce Louisiana. It is not only New Orleans that I mean to cede, it is the whole colony without reserving any of it." It is well known that Napoleon made this decision two days after he read the resolutions of Senator Ross of Pennsylvania authorizing military occupation of New Orleans. But that was not the latest news he had from America. In the course of the talk with Marbois, Napoleon remarked: "The London cabinet is informed of the *resolutions taken* at Washington."[24] That means that Napoleon had received the London diplomatic pouch of April 7. He sent for Marbois after reading, in the London *Times* of that date, that the United States Senate had passed a bill to construct fifteen gunboats for use at the mouth of the Mississippi and that Congress was about to authorize the raising of 80,000 men for invasion purposes. Napoleon renounced Louisiana a few hours after he read the following London summary of American policy:

> Whether Spain continues in possession of Louisiana, or possession is taken by France, it is no longer doubtful that the deliberations of Congress are in unison with the feelings of the people. . . . The government and people seem to be aware that a decisive blow must be struck before the arrival of the expedition now waiting in the ports of Holland.

This was no thunderclap out of a clear sky. For two years the French legation in Washington had been describing the clouds that were rolling up, and here was evidence that there was lightning in them. It was not merely the danger of British seizure of Louisiana that Napoleon faced—he could have sidestepped that by leaving the country in the hands of Spain. The prospect that confronted him was both a danger and an opportunity—the certain prospect that some day the United States would take the country away from either Spain or France, and the reassuring certainty that they would never let it pass into the hands of Great Britain. These considerations were decisive, provided they were enforced by evidence of American strength and determination. Did Livingston provide that evidence? I quote from his letter of January 18, 1803, to Talleyrand, urging the cession of Florida and part of Louisiana to the United States:

> Under any other plan, sir . . . the whole of this establishment must pass into the hands of Great Britain. . . . France, by grasping at a desert and an insignificant town, and thereby throwing the weight of the United States into the scale of Britain, will render her [Great Britain] mistress of the new world.[25]

Madison had instructed Livingston to assure France that American self-interest forbade either a "voluntary or compulsive transfer" of these provinces from Spain to Great Britain.[26] Instead, the minister pictured the United States as supinely submitting to encirclement and domination through a compulsive transfer from France to Britain.

Was it from Jefferson that Napoleon heard of American strength and determination? The President wrote many forceful letters which did not go to the First Consul, and at times made threats which did, but observe what he said at the moment of highest crisis. I quote Pichon's report of what Jefferson said to him on January 12, 1803, explaining the decision made two days earlier to send Monroe to France:

> That Mr. Monroe was so well known to be a friend of the Western people that his mission would contribute more than anything else to tranquillize them and prevent unfortunate incidents; that he will be authorized jointly with Messrs. Pinckney and Livingston to treat with France or Spain, according to the state of things, in order to bring the affairs of the Mississippi to a definite conclusion. That the administration would try peaceful means to the last moment and they hoped that France would be disposed to concur in their views for the preservation of harmony.[27]

Livingston described the effect of this conciliatory attitude upon a promise just given him to confirm American treaty rights at New Orleans: "Unfortunately, dispatches arrived at that moment from Mr. Pichon, informing them that the appointment of Mr. Monroe had tranquillized everything . . . they determined to see whether the storm would not blow over."[28]

Six days later more dispatches arrived, giving Madison's far different account of the reasons for sending Monroe—reasons which "imperatively required that this mission should have a prompt conclusion." Instead of quoting from his veiled threats of war, I present Pichon's comments upon them:

> The implicit language of Mr. Madison . . . brings to light ideas too general to be neglected. . . . Louisiana in the first moment of war will answer for the behavior of our administration. . . . The crisis grows greater every day, and we cannot push it into the distant future. . . . I should fail in my duty if I did not tell you that these feelings of concern which Mr. Madison expressed to me are generally felt and that public opinion in the latest circumstances expresses itself at least as strongly and energetically as the government.[29]

That was the last diplomatic word from Washington before Napoleon read about the fifteen gunboats and 80,000 men. Who put the heat on Bonaparte?

Now let us come back to Henry Adams. I spoke of his charge that Madison invited France to build an empire west of the Mississippi. That amounted to nothing. Adams merely failed to recognize a threat of war in thirteen-letter words like "circumstances" and "eventualities."[30] But he was well aware that for two years Madison had been working incessantly against French occupation of the trans-Mississippi country. Ignoring all that, he relied on one cryptic passage in one letter to brand the Secretary of State as a blundering nincompoop.

That was the way Adams operated. Without a particle of mental dishonesty in his makeup, he always searched for the worst and never failed to find it. A British diplomat wrote: "Madison is now as obstinate as a mule."[31] A man cannot be obstinate as a mule without having that trait show up again and again. It does not show up in Adams' history, even though he quoted that particular statement. There you find that Madison was fretful, he was irritable, he had "a feminine faculty for pressing a sensitive point."[32] Always the adjectives imply weakness. There is nothing to account for the fact that, as one foreign diplomat after another took him on, those who were hostile went home in discomfiture. Consider, as the most extreme case, the man who described Madison's obstinacy. Francis James Jackson—"Copenhagen Jackson"—was the hatchet man of the British Foreign Office. On his arrival at Washington he wrote to Canning that his predecessor had told him "of the most violent things said to him" by President Madison. Erskine, he observed, had turned the other cheek, but "I shall give blow for blow."[33] Jackson delivered one blow and was ordered out of the country.

Let us examine the most damning characterization of Madison to be found in the Adams history—an account by French Minister Turreau of his protest to Madison against the filibustering expedition of General Miranda. General Turreau was a tough guy. He hammered his wife with a club while his secretary played on the French horn to drown her screams[34] and he aspired to be just as brutal in diplomacy. "I have never yet beheld a face so cruel and sanguinary as his," wrote a United States senator. On the occasion told of by Adams, he was acting as the agent of Spanish Minister Yrujo, with whom Madison had refused to have any more dealings. I quote from Adams' translation of Turreau's letter to the Spaniard: "I was this morning with Madison. . . . He was in a state of extraordinary prostration while I was demanding" etc., etc.[35]

It is a vivid picture—Madison collapsing with weakness and fright before the terrible Turreau. Let us look now at the French text. Turreau wrote: "*Il était dans un abattement extraordinaire.*" [36] I asked two Frenchmen on the Library of Congress staff to translate that. The first one said: "He was in very low spirits." The second: "He was very dejected." I showed the Adams translation to Ambassador Bonnet and he exclaimed: "How could anybody make a mistake like that?" It could be done, quite readily, by anybody who would also say that to hold a man in suspense means to hang him by the neck. For sixty years, this false picture of James Madison has blackened the canvas of history.

Adams' favorite technique against Madison was the left-hand, right-hand, left-hand punch—condemnation first, then quotation, then condemnation. In 1805, when England was at war with France and Spain, American Minister Armstrong in Paris sent home the "well-considered suggestion," as Henry Adams called it, that the United States take Texas away from Spain by force. Jefferson, Adams writes, "seized Armstrong's idea, and uniting it with his own, announced the result to Madison as the true solution." The United States should first obtain a promise from England not to make peace without American consent, then Congress should grant the President discretionary authority to make war on Spain. "Here at length," Adams commented, "was a plan—uncertain indeed because dependent on British help, but still a scheme of action." And then Madison knocked it on the head by observing that England was unlikely to bind herself positively not to make peace unless the United States bound itself positively to make war. Madison, Adams commented, "had nothing to propose except negotiation without end."

At this moment news reached America of William Pitt's second coalition against Napoleon. The whole continent of Europe was flaring into battle. International alignments were melting like wax. Madison's reaction opened the way for a one-two-three. Adams began with condemnation: "Upon Madison's mind this European convulsion acted as an additional reason for doing nothing."

Then quotation to prove it. Madison to Jefferson: "I think it very questionable whether a little delay may not be expedient," but meanwhile the United States should order Morales, Casa Calvo, and Yrujo out of the country.

Then final condemnation based on the quotation: "Madison's measures and conduct toward Europe showed the habit of avoiding the heart of every issue, in order to fret its extremities."[37]

All this because Madison thought a little delay would be expedient before jumping into the Napoleonic wars. Adams' specific complaint was that Madison "disregarded Armstrong's idea of seizing Texas." But when Madison, as President, seized West Florida on the same theory advanced by Armstrong for Texas, that it had been paid for in the Louisiana Purchase, Adams described it as "filching a petty sandheap," an action imbued with force and fraud, and he quoted at length the protesting preachment of a British diplomat against "wresting a province from a friendly power . . . at the time of her adversity." In brief, Madison was damned if he did and damned if he didn't.[38]

All through the controversy over West Florida, Adams supported Spain with a zeal which cannot be accounted for by his conviction that there was no merit in the American position. The glee with which he upheld the foreign side of international disputes was in exact proportion to the opportunities they gave him to pillory Madison and condemn Jefferson. Early in 1804, Congress authorized the President to make Mobile Bay part of a customs district. The Spanish minister, Adams writes, sent Madison "a note so severe as to require punishment, and so able as to admit of none. . . . Madison could neither maintain the law nor annul it; he could not even explain it away. . . . The President came to Madison's relief. By a proclamation," he limited the district to places lying within the United States. The proclamation—which Adams condemned as a perversion of a perverse law—was based entirely on the reply Madison already had written to Yrujo, that Section 11 (on Mobile) was subordinate to Section 4, which set up a more inclusive customs district but contained the limiting words, "lying within the United States." If anybody came to anybody's relief, Madison came to the President's, and in doing so, did just what Adams said he could not do—explained away what Yrujo had objected to.[39]

My final impression is that Henry Adams did not understand the policies of Jefferson and Madison at all. He saw weakness and national humiliation in their failure to go to war over this or that outrage—to war with England over impressment, or to avenge the attack on the *Chesapeake*; to war with France because of the Berlin and Milan decrees. Jefferson and Madison saw three choices—war, submission, or economic pressure and negotiation while the fast-growing nation gathered basic strength. They chose this third course, well knowing that war was the ultimate and probable alternative. Adams and a host of other writers have construed this course as submission, and have treated the War of 1812 as evidence of its failure.

Go back ten years. Go back to July 7, 1802, and read what Pichon wrote to Talleyrand on that day about the purposes of Jefferson and Madison: "They fear exceedingly to be forced to war, as they go on the principle that they ought not to try their strength within ten years, by which time they count on diminution of debt, growth of population and riches."

This was said in telling of an interview in which "Mr. Madison talked to me with much coolness, much method, and as if he had been prepared." The subject was Louisiana. It should be recognized, said Madison, "that France cannot long preserve Louisiana against the United States." As for other colonies of the European powers—in South America, the West Indies—the United States had no desire to possess them. But, said Madison, by joining England in the next war, they could throw all these distant territories into her hands, and "could without difficulty, in ten years, divide with her . . . all the export and import trade of these colonies."[40]

He was saying, in effect, that England and the United States could handle France at any time, and that in ten years the United States by itself would be strong enough to compel England to abandon its system of colonial monopoly.

For two reasons, and two only, the compulsive system which Madison threatened against both France and England was put into operation against England alone. France escaped it by ceding Louisiana. England brought it on by the blundering obstinacy of Canning, Wellesley, and Castlereagh. And the war started just three weeks short of the ten years Madison allowed for postponement of a showdown.

There is plenty to criticize in the presidencies of Jefferson and Madison. But their weaknesses were in general the weaknesses of the American people. Their major difficulty was one that we can appreciate today—that of living and working in a power-mad world dominated by lunatics. Study the work of Madison in that light, without the distorting shadows of political prejudice, and you will find the clear-cut lines of greatness in it.

I began writing the life of Madison without the slightest suspicion that the prevailing estimates of him were incorrect. Not in the remotest fashion did I suspect that in their political symbiosis, Jefferson might owe as much to Madison as Madison to Jefferson. My interest was in Madison the political philosopher, the architect of the Constitution, the author of the Bill of Rights —fields in which his primacy was universally acknowledged. Everything after 1789 was expected to be anticlimax. That has not proved true. The ultimate verdict upon Madison depends in part upon the future of the American people—upon their continued devotion to liberty, self-government, and personal honor. But, granted this fidelity, I have no doubt of the final verdict. Madison the diplomatist, Madison the President, will be found to measure up to the father of the Constitution. Washington, Jefferson, Jackson, Lincoln, Wilson, Roosevelt. Move over a little, gentlemen.

Notes

1. Quoted by Theodore Bolton in "The Life Portraits of James Madison," *William and Mary Quarterly*, VIII (January, 1951), 28–29.
2. Chevalier de la Luzerne, "Liste des Membres du Congrès depuis 1779 jusqu'en 1784," Archives des Affaires Etrangères, Mémoires et Documents, Etats-Unis, vol. 1, ff. 253–87.
3. *The Journal of William Maclay*, ed. Edgar S. Maclay (New York, 1890), July 1, 1789, p. 97.
4. Fisher Ames to George R. Minot, May 3, 1789, *Works of Fisher Ames*, ed. Seth Ames (Boston, 1854), I, 36.
5. Ames to Minot, January 20, 1795, *ibid.*, I, 165.
6. Albert J. Beveridge, *The Life of John Marshall* (Boston, 1916–19), II, 81.
7. Ames to Thomas Dwight, January, 1793, *Ames*, I, 127.
8. "He [Madison] was easily influenced by such lordly wills as Hamilton, easily seduced by such subtle minds as Jefferson. Thus his public service was a series of contradictions, compromises, doubts and fears. . . . Between those tremendous mountain peaks of power, Hamilton and Jefferson, standing over against each other, Madison was the valley." Albert J. Beveridge, quoted in the Madison volume of "Autographs of the Presidents," Morgan Library, New York.

9. Madison to Jefferson, January 24, 1790, *The Writings of James Madison,* ed. Gaillard Hunt (New York, 1900–10), V, 434; received February 12, Epistolary Record, Jefferson Papers, Library of Congress.
10. Alexander Hamilton to Edward Carrington, May 26, 1792, *The Works of Alexander Hamilton,* ed. Henry Cabot Lodge (New York, 1904), IX, 528–29.
11. *Columbian Centinel* (Boston), February 24, 1790.
12. Irving Brant, *James Madison,* II: *The Nationalist* (Indianapolis, 1948), 233; Papers of the Continental Congress, No. 26, pp. 438–40; Notes of Debates, March 7, 1783, *Writings of James Madison,* I, 399.
13. Brant, II, 300; Madison to Edmund Randolph, July 28, 1783, *Writings of James Madison,* II, 4.
14. Brant, *James Madison,* III: *Father of the Constitution* (Indianapolis, 1950), pp. 306–18. The June 20 date is approximate.
15. Beveridge, *John Marshall,* II, 71, n. 2.
16. February 2, 8, 1791, *Annals of Congress* (Washington, 1834), II, cols. 1944–52, 2008–12: "Opinion against the Constitutionality of a National Bank," February 15, 1791, *The Writings of Thomas Jefferson,* ed. A. A. Lipscomb and A. E. Bergh (Washington, 1903–1904), III, 145. Jefferson enlarged Madison's argument by contending that the "necessary and proper" clause of the Constitution restricted Congress "to those means without which the grant of power would be nugatory"—a test which would invalidate any action to which there was a possible alternative.
17. William Plumer, diary, April 8, 1806 (Library of Congress), quoted by Charles E. Hill in *The American Secretaries of State and Their Diplomacy,* ed. Samuel F. Bemis (New York, 1927–29), III, 7.
18. Henry Adams, *History of the United States,* IX, 173, 220, 240.
19. Madison to Jefferson, August 12 (received), 18, 27, 1801, Jefferson Papers, Library of Congress. Jefferson to Madison, August 22, 1801, Madison Papers, Library of Congress. Madison to Gallatin (private), August 29, 1801, Gallatin Papers, New York Historical Society. Edward Thornton to Madison, July 23, November 11, 1801, National Archives, General Records of the Department of State, Notes from the British Legation, II (1796–1803).
20. Adams, II, 54–55.
21. Edward Channing, *History of the United States,* IV, 319n.
22. *Lettres du Général Leclerc,* Appendix I, 269: Carl L. Lokke, "Jefferson and the Leclerc Expedition," *American Historical Review,* XXXIII (January, 1928), 324, 327–28.
23. L. A. Pichon to Talleyrand, July 22, August 11, 1801, February 24, 1802, Arch. Aff. Etr., correspondance politique, Etats-Unis, vol. 53, f. 179; vol. 54, f. 161.
24. François Barbé-Marbois, *Histoire de la Louisiane* (Paris, 1829), pp. 298, 301; R. R. Livingston to Madison, April 11, 1803, *American State Papers, Foreign Affairs,* II, 552 (hereafter cited as *State Papers*). The italics in the quotation are added.
25. Livingston to Talleyrand, January 18, 1803, *State Papers,* II, 531. This letter is dated January 10, 1803, in *State Papers* and "20 Nivose an XI (January 10, 1803)" in the State Department copy (National Archives, Diplomatic Dispatches, France, VIII, enclosure to Livingston dispatch of January 24, 1803) from which it was taken for publication. It is dated January 18 in Livingston's letterbook (New York Historical Society) and January 18 in a copy in Monroe Papers, VII, Library of Congress. At the end of the original letter (Arch. Aff. Etr., Etats-Unis, Supp., vol. 7, ff. 310–13) is the date 20 Frimaire an XI (December 11, 1802). This cannot be correct because the letter opens with a

reference to the closing of New Orleans to American commerce by Spain, news of which did not reach France until January. Arthur B. Darling (in *Our Rising Empire, 1763–1803* [London, 1940], p. 447), observing no signature to the letter, concluded that this was Livingston's December 11 memoir to Joseph Bonaparte, wrongly addressed to Talleyrand by somebody who transcribed it in the foreign ministry. The letter is actually in the handwriting of Livingston's usual copyist, and is signed "Robt. R. Livingston," but the faded ink of the signature is almost invisible in the photographic reproduction in the Library of Congress. News of the New Orleans closure reached Livingston on or just before January 7 (Livingston to Joseph Bonaparte, January 7, 1803, *State Papers*, II, 536). Talleyrand learned of it between January 10 and 14 (Talleyrand to General Bernadotte, January 10, 14, 1803, Arch. Aff. Etr., Etats-Unis, vol. 55, ff. 164, 170). The original letter is indorsed as received on 30 Nivose (January 20), which confirms the date of January 18 found on two manuscript copies of it. What happened, apparently, was that Livingston wrote a paragraph about New Orleans and directed his clerk to add the Bonaparte memoir of December 11 to it. The clerk copied it date and all, then noticed the error while preparing a copy for Madison and changed 20 Frimaire to 20 Nivose, both wrong. Minus the opening paragraph, it is, as Darling concluded, the only known text of the memoir to Joseph Bonaparte.

26. Madison to Livingston, September 28, 1801, National Archives, General Records of the Department of State, Instructions to Consular Representatives, I (1800–1806). In the published instructions (*State Papers*, II, 510), the words "from Spain to Great Britain" appear as "from Spain to France," making the whole sentence nonsensical.
27. Pichon to Talleyrand, January 21, 24, 1803, Arch. Aff. Etr., Etats-Unis, vol. 55, ff. 184v, 192.
28. Livingston to Madison, March 24, 1803, *State Papers*, II, 549; Talleyrand to Livingston, 1 Germinal an 11 (March 22, 1803, misdated March 21), *ibid.*, II, 550.
29. Pichon to Talleyrand, January 24, 1803, Arch. Aff. Etr., Etats-Unis, vol. 55, ff. 196–98v.
30. *Ibid.*; Adams, II, 54.
31. Francis James Jackson, October 26, 1809, quoted in Adams, V, 130.
32. Adams, II, 74; V, 187.
33. Francis J. Jackson to Canning, September 14, 1809, Foreign Office, 353, vol. 60.
34. Register, I, 181, William Plumer Papers, Library of Congress. Ordinarily, Turreau needed no provocation to beat his wife, but in this instance she had just hit him with a flatiron.
35. *Ibid.*, I, 105; Adams, III, 192–95.
36. General Turreau to the Marquis d'Yrujo, February 7, 1806, Archives Hist. Nac. Madrid, leg. 5544 pt. 1.
37. Adams, III, 69–74.
38. Adams, V, 309, 315. One's belief that Henry Adams did not distort intentionally is put to quite a strain at finding three distortions on one page (II, 69), all designed to prove that Minister Robert R. Livingston did not think that the portion of West Florida lying west of the Perdido River was included in the Louisiana Purchase until several weeks after the treaty negotiated by him and James Monroe had been signed. Adams wrote: (1) "In the preceding year one of the French ministers had applied to Livingston 'to know what we understand in America by Louisiana'; and Livingston's answer was on record in the State Department at Washington: 'Since the possession of the Floridas by Britain and the treaty of 1762, I think there can be no doubt as to the precise

meaning of the terms.' " This alleged answer was actually a comment by Livingston upon a letter from John Graham at Madrid, and concerned ancient French claims to the Ohio country as part of *Louisiane Orientale.* On the query of the French minister Livingston merely wrote: "You can readily conceive my answer." Where would Adams have been if he had quoted what Livingston wrote only two weeks later on the subject really at issue: "I find all the old French maps mark the river Perdido as the boundary between Florida and Louisiana." Livingston to Madison, July 30, August 16, 1802, *State Papers,* II, 519, 524. (2) "He had himself drafted an article which he tried to insert in Marbois' *projet,* pledging the First Consul to interpose his good offices with the King of Spain to obtain the country east of the Mississippi." The article actually covered all Spanish territory "on the continent of North America laying to the east of the river"–a description which did not make the Mississippi the boundary (Monroe Papers, VII, 1270v). Livingston and Monroe jointly asked aid in obtaining "so much of his [the king of Spain's] territories as lay *to the east of the ceded territory* . . ." Livingston and Monroe to Marbois, May 2, 1803, Arch. Aff. Etr., Etats-Unis, vol. 55, f. 416. (3) "As late as May 12, Livingston wrote to Madison: 'I am satisfied that . . . if they [the French] could have concluded with Spain, we should also have had West Florida.' " This did not refer to the negotiations of Livingston and Monroe, nor to the treaty they signed on May 2, 1803, but was a speculation about what the French might have been willing to do in the previous year, when Livingston made a bid for West Florida and the country above the Arkansas River.

39. Adams, II, 257–63; the marquis of Casa Yrujo to Madison, March 7, 1804, National Archives, General Records of the Department of State, Notes from the Spanish Legation, II; Madison to Yrujo, March 19, 1804, Monroe Papers; *Annals of Congress,* XIII, col. 1253 (the "Mobile Act"). Adams' methods of creating adverse impressions find an illustration (II, 262) in the way he quoted from Madison's letter to Livingston, March 31, 1804, about the belatedness of Yrujo's protest: "The Act had been for many weeks depending in Congress with these sections, word for word, in it; . . . it must in all probability have been known to the Marquis d'Yrujo in an early stage of its progress." The statement would have sounded less like an unsupported conjecture if Adams had not omitted part of it: "as two copies are by a usage of politeness always allotted for each foreign minister here it must in all probability" etc.

40. Pichon to Talleyrand, July 7, 1802, Arch. Aff. Etr., Etats-Unis, vol. 54, f. 410.

Myths Surrounding the Monroe Doctrine

Wayne S. Cole

In this article, Wayne S. Cole, a diplomatic historian at the University of Maryland, takes issue with the stock textbook interpretation of the Monroe Doctrine. He centers his attack on several myths, concluding that the doctrine "was not a treaty, not an executive agreement, not an act of Congress, not a multilateral inter-American policy, and not international law." He questions whether the principles of the doctrine originated with Monroe, as well as challenging the myth of immediate effective United States enforcement. Professor Cole does warn against overdepreciating the doctrine's place in history, reminding us that the idea of the Monroe Doctrine grew in influence and stature in the American mind following the Civil War. This development became particularly evident "as both the interests and the power of the United States grew in Latin America."

No policy statement in the history of American foreign affairs has captured such an enduring and revered hold on American thought as President James Monroe's statement in 1823. That Monroe Doctrine was not a treaty, not an executive agreement, not an act of Congress, not a multilateral inter-American policy, and not international law. Its principles were not original with Monroe. It was not effectively enforced by the United States for many years. And it was not even called the Monroe Doctrine until long after Monroe left the Presidency. It was simply a statement of policy included in the President's message to Congress on December 2, 1823.

In its original form it had three main premises. First, it warned the Quadruple Alliance against extending European political systems to the Western Hemisphere:

> The political system of the allied powers is essentially different . . . from that of America. . . . we should consider any attempt on their part to extend their system to any portion of this hemisphere as dangerous to our peace and safety. With the existing colonies or dependencies of any European power we have not interfered and shall not interfere. But with the Governments who have declared their independence and maintained it, and whose independence we have, on great consideration and on just principles, acknowledged, we could not view any interposition for the purpose of oppressing them, or controlling in any other manner their destiny, by any European power in any other light than as the manifestation of an unfriendly disposition toward the United States.

Reprinted with permission from Wayne Cole, *An Interpretive History of American Foreign Relations* (Homewood, Ill.: The Dorsey Press, 1968), No. 150, pp. 134–39.

Second, Monroe advanced the noncolonization principle:

> . . . the occasion has been judged proper for asserting, as a principle in which the rights and interests of the United States are involved, that the American continents, by the free and independent condition which they have assumed and maintain, are henceforth not to be considered as subjects for future colonization by any European powers.

And third, Monroe endorsed the American policy of nonintervention in Europe:

> In the wars of the European powers in matters relating to themselves we have never taken any part, nor does it comport with our policy so to do. . . . Our policy in regard to Europe . . . remains the same, which is, not to interfere in the internal concerns of any of its powers; to consider the government *de facto* as the legitimate government for us; to cultivate friendly relations with it, and to preserve those relations by a frank, firm, and manly policy, meeting in all instances the just claims of every power, submitting to injuries from none.

Monroe's statement was aimed against two apparent external threats to American interests in the Western Hemisphere and was triggered by a British proposal to the United States. First, the Monroe Doctrine was aimed against the danger that the Concert of Europe might use its power (as it had in Italy and Spain) to put down the Latin-American revolutions and reestablish monarchical governments there. Second, the Monroe Doctrine was aimed against Russian colonial expansion south into the Oregon Territory. In 1821, under Czar Alexander I, Russia issued a ukase that, in effect, extended the southern boundary of its Alaskan colony to the fifty-first parallel. The Ukase of 1821 gave Russians exclusive trading and navigation rights down to 51° north latitude. It also barred foreign ships from approaching within 115 miles of that coast on pain of seizure.

Like the United States, Great Britain preferred an independent Latin America and objected to efforts by the Quadruple Alliance (or one of its members) to reestablish European control there. In August, 1823, the British Foreign Secretary, George Canning, suggested to Richard Rush, the United States Minister in London, that Britain and the United States issue a joint declaration. That statement would have questioned Spain's ability to recover its colonies; it would have renounced any desire by the United States or Britain to seize Latin America; and it would have opposed the transfer of any part of Latin America to any other state. The idea appealed to Rush who promptly transmitted it to his government in Washington. President Monroe, too, was favorably disposed, as were the two former Presidents, Jefferson and Madison, that he consulted. Secretary of State John Quincy Adams, however, objected. He did not believe the European powers would intervene in Latin America and, in any event, he opposed a joint statement with Britain. He believed it would be more dignified for the United States to act unilaterally rather "than to come in as a cock-boat in the wake of the British man-of-war." Consequently, the United States rejected Canning's proposal, but his suggestion led directly to Monroe's statement in his message to Congress.

Not only did external challenges and a foreign proposal lead to the Monroe Doctrine, but circumstances and developments abroad also prevented the threats from materializing. Contrary to American mythology, neither the Quadruple Alliance nor Russia actually endangered the Western Hemisphere at the time Monroe issued his message. So far as the Concert of Europe was concerned, neither Austria nor Prussia had any interest in Latin America or any plans to intervene. Russia had not formulated its policies on the matter by December, 1823, and ironically Czar Alexander I did not even toy with the possibility of intervention until after Monroe's message. Even then it was just a passing consideration unaffected by United States opposition. France had considered the possibility of establishing independent Bourbon monarchies in Latin America but had not acted on the idea. In October, Canning discussed the matter with the French Ambassador to Britain, the Prince de Polignac. As a result, in the so-called Polignac Memorandum of October 12, 1823, France "disclaimed . . . any intention or desire . . . to appropriate to Herself any part of the Spanish Possessions in America. . . . She adjured, in any case, any design of acting against the Colonies by force of arms." Thus British diplomacy and power checked the slight possibility of French intervention nearly two months before the Monroe Doctrine.

So far as Russian colonial expansion in the Northwest was concerned, Secretary of State Adams had protested against the Ukase of 1821 through regular diplomatic channels long before Monroe's message. Alexander I had no colonial ambitions in America. He was not impressed by the United States, but he did view America as a potential adversary of Britain and did not want to antagonize America. The Czar decided to yield on the boundary matter as early as July, 1822, a year and a half before the Monroe Doctrine. In 1824, in the first treaty between Russia and the United States, Russia accepted 54°40′ north latitude as the southern boundary of Alaska and agreed to freedom of seas in the North Pacific. That favorable treaty, however, was not due to the Monroe Doctrine. As Dexter Perkins, the leading scholar on the Monroe Doctrine, phrased it: "From the standpoint of its immediate results, it was close to futility."

In addition to external influences, the Monroe Doctrine was consistent with the dominant domestic ideological, political, and economic patterns within the United States. Its antiforeign, antiEuropean, and antimonarchical tenor reflected American chauvinism in the Era of Good Feelings. The Doctrine's unilateralism and noninterventionism (the central ingredients of isolationism) expressed American nationalism.

Furthermore, like political patterns in the Era of Good Feelings, the Monroe Doctrine was consistent with the desires of both the urban shipping–commercial interests on the one hand and the farmer–agrarian interests on the other. That was symbolized in its authorship. President Monroe of planter Virginia was responsible for the statement aimed against intervention by the Quadruple Alliance in Latin America. He was also responsible for presenting the policy in his message to Congress. Secretary of State Adams from commercial Massachusetts was responsible for the noncolonization principle, for emphasizing nonintervention in Europe, and for making it a unilateral policy rather than a joint statement with Britain. That dual authorship symbolized the temporary political alliance of planter and merchant during the Era of Good Feelings.

The Monroe Doctrine appealed to both wings of that political alliance by keeping the door open for continued expansion by both commercial and agrarian interests. American merchants wanted to increase trade in Latin America. They feared that reestablishment of Spanish control, intervention by the Quadruple Alliance, or any European colonial expansion in Latin America, would conflict with their commercial ambitions there. The noncolonization principle did not apply to the United States (unlike Canning's original proposal). It opposed only European competitors of American territorial expansion. Thus the Monroe Doctrine was in tune with the expansionist ambitions of both agrarian and commercial groups within the United States.

The immediate impetus for the Monroe Doctrine came from external influences, but it was consistent with American emotions and sentiments in that nationalistic era. It was directed against European expansion, but it also left the door open for continued commercial and territorial expansion by the United States in the Western Hemisphere. It would have been difficult to formulate any foreign policy that appealed more neatly to the interests and ambitions of the two main economic groups in the United States than did the Monroe Doctrine.

It did not, however, get nearly so much attention in 1823 as it won subsequently. European and Latin-American leaders were not awed by it. Colombia in 1824 and Brazil in 1825 responded by seeking defensive alliances with the United States. The United States rebuffed their approaches, however, and for more than a century the Monroe Doctrine remained a unilateral United States policy, not a multilateral policy shared with other states in the Western Hemisphere.

Simon Bolivar organized a Pan-American Conference in Panama in 1826. He envisaged a confederation of Spanish-American states, but the United States was invited to the meeting. John Quincy Adams, then President, and his Secretary of State, Henry Clay, did not object to accepting the invitation. Many congressmen, however, feared entangling alliances and involvement in Latin-American affairs. The Senate finally approved the two delegates named by Adams, but one died on the way and the other arrived after the conference ended. Only Colombia, Mexico, Peru, and Central America were represented at Panama, though Britain and the Netherlands had observers on hand. The Conference approved a treaty of confederation, but only Colombia ratified it.

Not only did the Monroe Doctrine win little attention or respect but European states frequently violated it with impunity. Britain seized the Falkland Islands off Argentina in 1833. In 1838 France blockaded Mexico at Vera Cruz and invaded and blockaded Argentina. Britain extended the boundaries of British Honduras and seized one of the Bay Islands off Honduras in 1838. From 1845 to 1849 Britain and France jointly intervened in Argentina. The United States government either ignored each of those episodes or made only token protests. In no case did the United States compel the European state to withdraw.

The failure to invoke the Monroe Doctrine effectively before the Civil War was the result of America's limited interests and limited power. The agrarians who controlled the government most of the time before 1861 were interested in those parts of Latin America adjoining the United States, including Florida, Texas, New Mexico, and California. Some were even attracted by Cuba and Central America. But they had no interest in South America. New England traders might be affected by developments in Argentina, but generally they did not control American foreign policies. Even America's security interests in South America were not so great as they became later. Argentina was farther from the United States than Great Britain was. With the relatively limited mobility of nineteenth-century military forces, and with no isthmian canal to defend, European intervention in Argentina did not seem to represent so much of a threat to American security as it would have in the twentieth century. United States relations with Latin-American states generally were not very close before the Civil War. The United States did not even maintain diplomatic relations with Argentina from 1830 to 1844.

In addition to America's limited interests in South America, the United States also lacked the power necessary to enforce the Monroe Doctrine effectively. In those parts of Latin America that adjoined the United States, American power was adequate. In South America, however, and in much of the Caribbean and Central America, the United States was not strong enough to make its will prevail, even if its interests there had been much greater than they were. In the nineteenth century, Great Britain, not the United States, was the most powerful outside state in South America. And in international affairs, principles (even good ones) cannot prevail if they are not backed with sufficient power.

Nevertheless, as Dexter Perkins wrote of the Monroe Doctrine, ". . . we must not . . . err on the side of too complete a depreciation of its place in the history of American foreign policy. . . . it became in later years an American shibboleth, powerful in its appeal, and far-reaching in its influence." It obtained that greater importance as both the interests and the power of the United States grew in Latin America.

Suggested Further Reading for Chapter 3

Harry Ammon, "James Monroe and the Era of Good Feelings," *The Virginia Magazine of History and Biography,* 66 (1958).

Carl Becker, "What Is Still Living in the Political Philosophy of Thomas Jefferson?" *American Historical Review,* 48 (1943).

Marcus Cunliffe, *George Washington: Man and Monument* (Boston: Little, Brown, and Company, 1958).

David H. Fischer, "The Myth of the Essex Junto," *The William and Mary Quarterly,* 21 (1964).

Felix Gilbert, *The Beginnings of American Foreign Policy: To the Farewell Address* (New York: Harper & Row, Publishers, 1965).

Dumas Malone, "The Relevance of Mr. Jefferson," *Virginia Quarterly Review,* 37 (1961).

Bernard Mayo, *Myths and Men: Patrick Henry, George Washington, Thomas Jefferson* (Athens: University of Georgia Press, 1959).

Irby C. Nichols, Jr., "The Russian Ukase and the Monroe Doctrine: A Reevaluation," *Pacific Historical Review,* 36 (1967).

Armin Rappaport (ed.), *The Monroe Doctrine* (New York: Holt, Rinehart & Winston, Inc., 1966).

Clinton Rossiter, "Which Jefferson Do You Quote?" *The Reporter,* 13 (1955).

Mason Locke Weems, *Biography of George Washington,* edited with introduction by Marcus Cunliffe (Cambridge: The Belknap Press, 1962).

The object of this history is to follow the steps by which a favoring Providence, calling our institutions into being, has conducted the country to its present happiness and glory. God himself, working through the course of history, was behind the common man.

George Bancroft
The History of the United States of America from the Discovery of the Continent, 1879

4

MYTHS FROM THE "AGE OF THE COMMON MAN"

New Perspectives on Jacksonian Politics
Richard P. McCormick

Andrew Jackson and the Rise of Southwestern Democracy
Thomas P. Abernethy

The Mountain Man as Jacksonian Man
William H. Goetzmann

The Antislavery Myth
C. Vann Woodward

America as Peaceful Belligerent: Myth or Reality?
Glenn C. Price

George Caleb Bingham, "The Verdict of the People." Collection of the Boatman's National Bank of St. Louis.

The verdict of the people: democratic upheaval in the Age of the Common Man?

Henry Sargent, "The Dinner Party" (1821). Courtesy, Museum of Fine Arts, Boston.

The dinner party: persistent elitism in the Age of the Common Man?

Introduction

After Abraham Lincoln, Andrew Jackson ranks as perhaps the greatest of America's political-folk heroes. A substantial mythology, along with a certain symbolism and mystique, surrounds our historical understanding of both these men. In the case of Andrew Jackson, historical judgment suffers most from the fact that Jackson was allegedly America's first "popular" President. Jackson's popularity stemmed not so much from the degree to which his countrymen came to admire him (for certainly George Washington before him was thus admired), but rather from the degree to which he is said to have represented the "common man." Indicative of the degree to which Jackson was attuned to the political pulse of "the people," we are told, was the fact that he was the first "outsider" to become President. To many, Jackson personified the interests, the values, and the prejudices of newly-emergent Frontier America. But in addition to his identification with expansive "upland democracy," Jackson was also viewed as challenging precedent, in that Presidents before him had always risen from the ranks of cabinet service—a national apprenticeship that Jackson never served. Similarly, Andrew Jackson was the first President close enough to the people to be known by a nickname—"Old Hickory." So close an association between "Old Hickory" and the masses has been traditionally supposed, in fact, that the era of his presidency has long been affectionately labeled the "Age of the Common Man."

It is precisely the affinity between Andrew Jackson and the "common man" that recent historical scholarship has sought to reexamine. Legitimate questions have been raised as to the extent of democratization during Jackson's term as President, as to whether Jackson was a cause or consequence of his age, and as to whether Andrew Jackson himself was in fact a Jacksonian. "Jacksonian Democracy" eludes simple historical explanation, then, not only because of "Old Hickory's" personal and symbolic presence, but also because of the complex developments in American society that were contemporary with him, such as social and political reform, Manifest Destiny, and the Mexican War. As such, neither the myth nor the reality of either Jackson the man, or the times in which he lived, has as yet been finally determined.

New Perspectives on Jacksonian Politics

Richard P. McCormick

Questions as to the political character of Jacksonian Democracy have precipitated considerable intellectual debate among historians. The controversy has revolved around one central issue: What was the extent of voter participation in the American political process during the age of Andrew Jackson? Related to this issue is the question: Was Andrew Jackson a cause or a consequence of his times? Richard P. McCormick, Jackson scholar and Professor of History at Rutgers University, offers new insight into this continuing debate. Through his analysis of voter participation in presidential elections during the early-to-middle nineteenth century, McCormick demonstrates conclusively that the so-called "mighty democratic uprising" did not occur until 1840; in the process he destroys the myth that Jackson was swept to the presidency on a wave of popular voter sentiment.

The historical phenomenon that we have come to call Jacksonian democracy has long engaged the attention of American political historians, and never more insistently than in the past decade. From the time of Parton and Bancroft to the present day scholars have recognized that a profoundly significant change took place in the climate of politics simultaneously with the appearance of Andrew Jackson on the presidential scene. They have sensed that a full understanding of the nature of that change might enable them to dissolve some of the mysteries that envelop the operation of the American democratic process. With such a challenging goal before them, they have pursued their investigations with uncommon intensity and with a keen awareness of the contemporary relevance of their findings.

A cursory view of the vast body of historical writing on this subject suggests that scholars in the field have been largely preoccupied with attempts to define the content of Jacksonian democracy and identify the influences that shaped it. What did Jacksonian democracy represent, and what groups, classes, or sections gave it its distinctive character? The answers that have been given to these central questions have been—to put it succinctly—bewildering in their variety. The discriminating student, seeking the essential core of Jacksonianism, may make a choice among urban workingmen, southern planters, venturous conservatives, farm-bred *nouveaux riches*, western frontiersmen, frustrated entrepreneurs, or yeoman farmers. Various as are these

From "New Perspectives on Jacksonian Politics," by Richard P. McCormick, in *American Historical Review* (January 1960). Reprinted by permission of the author.

interpretations of the motivating elements that constituted the true Jacksonians, the characterizations of the programmatic features of Jacksonian democracy are correspondingly diverse. Probably the reasonable observer will content himself with the conclusion that many influences were at work and that latitudinarianism prevailed among the Jacksonian faithful.

In contrast with the controversy that persists over these aspects of Jacksonian democracy, there has been little dissent from the judgment that "the 1830's saw the triumph in American politics of that democracy which has remained pre-eminently the distinguishing feature of our society." The consensus would seem to be that with the emergence of Jackson, the political pulse of the nation quickened. The electorate, long dormant or excluded from the polls by suffrage barriers, now became fired with unprecedented political excitement. The result was a bursting forth of democratic energies, evidenced by a marked upward surge in voting. Beard in his colorful fashion gave expression to the common viewpoint when he asserted that "the roaring flood of the new democracy was... [by 1824] foaming perilously near the crest...." Schlesinger, with his allusion to the "immense popular vote" received by Jackson in 1824, creates a similar image. The Old Hero's victory in 1828 has been hailed as the consequence of a "mighty democratic uprising."

That a "new democracy, ignorant, impulsive, irrational" entered the arena of politics in the Jackson era has become one of the few unchallenged "facts" in an otherwise controversial field. Differences of opinion occur only when attempts are made to account for the remarkable increase in the size of the active electorate. The commonest explanations have emphasized the assertion by the common man of his newly won political privileges, the democratic influences that arose out of the western frontier, or the magnetic attractiveness of Jackson as a candidate capable of appealing with singular effectiveness to the backwoods hunter, the plain farmer, the urban workingman, and the southern planter.

Probably because the image of a "mighty democratic uprising" has been so universally agreed upon, there has been virtually no effort made to describe precisely the dimensions of the "uprising." Inquiry into this aspect of Jacksonian democracy has been discouraged by a common misconception regarding voter behavior before 1824. As the authors of one of our most recent and best textbooks put it: "In the years from the beginning of the government to 1824, a period for which we have no reliable election statistics, only small numbers of citizens seemed to have bothered to go to the polls." Actually, abundant data on pre-1824 elections is available, and it indicates a far higher rate of voting than has been realized. Only by taking this data into consideration can voting behavior after 1824 be placed in proper perspective.

The question of whether there was indeed a "mighty democratic uprising" during the Jackson era is certainly crucial in any analysis of the political character of Jacksonian democracy. More broadly, however, we need to know the degree to which potential voters participated in elections before, during, and after the period of Jackson's presidency as well as the conditions that apparently influenced the rate of voting. Only when such factors have been analyzed can we arrive at firm conclusions with respect to the dimensions of the political changes that we associate with Jacksonian democracy. Obviously in studying voter participation we are dealing with but one aspect of a large problem, and the limitations imposed by such a restrictive focus should be apparent.

In measuring the magnitude of the vote in the Jackson elections it is hardly significant to use the total popular vote cast throughout the nation. A comparison of the total vote cast in 1812, for example, when in eight of the seventeen states electors were chosen by the legislature, with the vote in 1832, when every state except South Carolina chose its electors by popular vote, has limited meaning. Neither is it revealing to compare the total vote in 1824 with that in 1832 without taking into consideration the population increase during the interval. The shift from the legislative choice of electors to their election by popular vote, together with the steady population growth, obviously swelled the presidential vote. But the problem to be investigated is whether the Jackson elections brought voters to the polls in such enlarged or unprecedented proportions as to indicate that a "new democracy" had burst upon the political scene.

The most practicable method for measuring the degree to which voters participated in elections over a period of time is to relate the number of votes cast to the number of potential voters. Although there is no way of calculating precisely how many eligible voters there were in any state at a given time, the evidence at hand demonstrates that with the exception of Rhode Island, Virginia, and Louisiana the potential electorate after 1824 was roughly equivalent to the adult white male population. A meaningful way of expressing the rate of voter participation, then, is to state it in terms of the percentage of the adult white males actually voting. This index can be employed to measure the variations that occurred in voter participation over a period of time and in both national and state elections. Consequently a basis is provided for comparing the rate of voting in the Jackson elections with other presidential elections before and after his regime as well as with state elections.

Using this approach it is possible, first of all, to ascertain whether or not voter participation rose markedly in the three presidential elections in which Jackson was a candidate. Did voter participation in these elections so far exceed the peak participation in the pre-1824 election as to suggest that a mighty democratic uprising was taking place? The accompanying data (Table I) provides an answer to this basic question.

In the 1824 election not a single one of the eighteen states in which the electors were chosen by popular vote attained the percentage of voter participation that had been reached before 1824. Prior to that critical election, fifteen

TABLE I. Percentages of Adult White Males Voting in Elections

State	Highest Known % AWM Voting before 1824 Year	% AWM	Presidential Elections 1824	1828	1832	1836	1840	1844
Maine	1812g	62.0	18.9	42.7	66.2*	37.4	82.2	67.5
New Hampshire	1814g	80.8	16.8	76.5	74.2	38.2	86.4*	65.6
Vermont	1812g	79.9	—	55.8	50.0	52.5	74.0	65.7
Massachusetts	1812g	67.4	29.1	25.7	39.3	45.1	66.4	59.3
Rhode Island	1812g	49.4	12.4	18.0	22.4	24.1	33.2	39.8
Connecticut	1819[1]	54.4	14.9	27.1	45.9	52.3	75.7*	76.1
New York	1810g	41.5	—	70.4*	72.1	60.2	77.7	73.6
New Jersey	1808p	71.8	31.1	70.9	69.0	69.3	80.4*	81.6
Pennsylvania	1808g	71.5	19.6	56.6	52.7	53.1	77.4*	75.5
Delaware	1804g	81.9	—	—	67.0	69.4	82.8*	85.0
Maryland	1820[1]	69.0	53.7	76.2*	55.6	67.5	84.6	80.3
Virginia	1800p	25.9	11.5	27.6*	30.8	35.1	54.6	54.5
North Carolina	1823c	70.0#	42.2	56.8	31.7	52.9	83.1*	79.1
Georgia	1812c	62.3	—	35.9	33.0	64.9*	88.9	94.0
Kentucky	1820g	74.4	25.3	70.7	73.9	61.1	74.3	80.3*
Tennessee	1817g	80.0	26.8	49.8	28.8	55.2	89.6*	89.6
Louisiana	1812g	34.2	—	36.3*	24.4	19.2	39.4	44.7
Alabama	1819g	96.7	52.1	53.6	33.3	65.0	89.8	82.7
Mississippi	1823g	79.8	41.6	56.6	32.8	62.8	88.2*	89.7
Ohio	1822g	46.5	34.8	75.8*	73.8	75.5	84.5	83.6
Indiana	1822g	52.4	37.5	68.3*	61.8	70.1	86.0	84.9
Illinois	1822g	55.8	24.2	51.9	45.6	43.7	85.9*	76.3
Missouri	1820g	71.9	20.1	54.3	40.8	35.6	74.0*	74.7
Arkansas		—	—	—	—	35.0	86.4	68.8
Michigan		—	—	—	—	35.7	84.9	79.3
National Average			26.5	56.3	54.9	55.2	78.0	74.9

* Exceeded pre-1824 high
g Gubernatorial election
p Presidential election
Estimate based on incomplete returns
c Congressional election
[1] Election of legislature

of those eighteen states had recorded votes in excess of 50 percent of their adult white male population, but in 1824 only two states—Maryland and Alabama—exceeded this modest mark. The average rate of voter participation in the election was 26.5 percent. This hardly fits the image of the "roaring flood of the new democracy . . . foaming perilously near the crest. . . ."

There would seem to be persuasive evidence that in 1828 the common man flocked to the polls in unprecedented numbers, for the proportion of adult white males voting soared to 56.3 percent, more than double the 1824 figure. But this outpouring shrinks in magnitude when we observe that in only six of the twenty-two states involved were new highs in voter participation established. In three of these—Maryland, Virginia, and Louisiana—the recorded gain was inconsiderable, and in a fourth—New York—the bulk of the increase might be attributed to changes that had been made in suffrage qualifications as recently as 1821 and 1826. Six states went over the 70 percent mark, whereas ten had bettered that performance before 1824. Instead of a "mighty democratic uprising" there was in 1828 a voter turnout that approached—but in only a few instances matched or exceeded—the maximum levels that had been attained before the Jackson era.

The advance that was registered in 1828 did not carry forward to 1832. Despite the fact that Jackson was probably at the peak of his personal popularity, that he was engaged in a campaign that was presumably to decide issues of great magnitude, and that in the opinion of some authorities a "well-developed two party system on a national scale" had been established, there was a slight decline in voter participation. The average for the twenty-three states participating in the presidential contest was 54.9 percent. In fifteen states a smaller percentage of the adult white males went to the polls in 1832 than in 1828. Only five states bettered their pre-1824 highs. Again the conclusion would be that it was essentially the pre-1824 electorate—diminished in most states and augmented in a few—that voted in 1832. Thus, after three Jackson elections, sixteen states had not achieved the proportions of voter participation that they had reached before 1824. The "new democracy" had not yet made its appearance.

A comparison of the Jackson elections with earlier presidential contests is of some interest. Such comparisons have little validity before 1808 because few states chose electors by popular vote, and for certain of those states the complete returns are not available. In 1816 and 1820 there was so little opposition to Monroe that the voter interest was negligible. The most relevant elections, therefore, are those of 1808 and 1812. The accompanying table (Table II) gives the percentages of adult white males voting in 1808 and 1812 in those states for which full returns could be found, together with the comparable percentages for the elections of 1824 and 1828. In 1824 only one

TABLE II.
PERCENTAGES OF ADULT WHITE MALES VOTING IN PRESIDENTIAL ELECTIONS

State	1808	1812	1824	1828
Maine	Legis.	50.0	18.9	42.7
New Hampshire	62.1	75.4	16.8	76.5
Massachusetts	Legis.	51.4	29.1	25.7
Rhode Island	37.4	37.7	12.4	18.0
New Hampshire	71.8	Legis.	31.1	70.9
Pennsylvania	34.7	45.5	19.6	56.6
Maryland	48.4	56.5	53.7	76.2
Virginia	17.7	17.8	11.5	27.6
Ohio	12.8	20.0	34.8	75.8

Note: No complete returns of the popular vote cast for electors in Kentucky or Tennessee in 1808 and 1812 and in North Carolina in 1808 could be located.

state—Ohio—surpassed the highs established in either 1808 or 1812. Four more joined this list in 1828—Virginia, Maryland, Pennsylvania, and New Hampshire—although the margin in the last case was so small as to be inconsequential. The most significant conclusion to be drawn from this admittedly limited and unrepresentative data is that in those states where there was a vigorous two-party contest in 1808 and 1812 the vote was relatively high. Conversely, where there was little or no contest in 1824 or 1828, the vote was low.

When an examination is made of voting in other than presidential elections prior to 1824, the inaccuracy of the impression that "only small numbers of citizens" went to the polls becomes apparent. Because of the almost automatic succession of the members of the "Virginia dynasty" and the early deterioration of the national two-party system that had seemed to be developing around 1800, presidential elections did not arouse voter interest as much as did those for governor, state legislators, or even members of Congress. In such elections at the state level the "common man" was stimulated by local factors to cast his vote, and he frequently responded in higher proportions than he did to the later stimulus provided by Jackson.

The average voter participation for all the states in 1828 was 56.3 percent. Before 1824 fifteen of the twenty-two states had surpassed that percentage. Among other things, this means that the 1828 election failed to bring to the polls the proportion of the electorate that had voted on occasion in previous elections. There was, in other words, a high potential vote that was frequently realized in state elections but which did not materialize in presidential elections. The unsupported assumption that the common man was either apathetic or debarred from voting by suffrage barriers before 1824 is untenable in the light of this evidence.

In state after state (see Table I) gubernatorial elections attracted 70 percent or more of the adult white males to the polls. Among the notable highs recorded were Delaware with 81.9 percent in 1804, New Hampshire with 80.8 percent in 1814, Tennessee with 80.0 percent in 1817, Vermont with 79.9 percent in 1812, Mississippi with 79.8 percent in 1823, and Alabama with a highly improbable 96.7 percent in its first gubernatorial contest in 1819. There is reason to believe that in some states, at least, the voter participation in the election of state legislators was even higher than in gubernatorial elections. Because of the virtual impossibility of securing county-by-county or district-by-district returns for such elections, this hypothesis is difficult to verify.

Down to this point the voter turnout in the Jackson elections has been compared with that in elections held prior to 1824. Now it becomes appropriate to inquire whether during the period 1824 through 1832 voters turned out in greater proportions for the three presidential contests than they did for the contemporary state elections. If, indeed, this "new democracy" bore some special relationship to Andrew Jackson or to his policies, it might be anticipated that interest in the elections in which he was the central figure would stimulate greater voter participation than gubernatorial contests, in which he was at most a remote factor.

Actually, the election returns show fairly conclusively that throughout the eight-year period the electorate continued to participate more extensively in state elections than in those involving the presidency. Between 1824 and 1832 there were fifty regular gubernatorial elections in the states that chose their electors by popular vote. In only sixteen of these fifty instances did the vote for President surpass the corresponding vote for governor. In Rhode Island, Delaware, Tennessee, Kentucky, Illinois, Mississippi, Missouri, and Georgia the vote for governor consistently exceeded that for President. Only in Connecticut was the reverse true. Viewed from this perspective, too, the remarkable feature of the vote in the Jackson elections is not its immensity but rather its smallness.

Finally, the Jackson elections may be compared with subsequent presidential elections. Once Jackson had retired to the Hermitage, and figures of less dramatic proportions took up the contest for the presidency, did voter participation rise or fall? This question can be answered by observing the percentage of adult white males who voted in each state in the presidential elections of 1836 through 1844 (Table I). Voter participation in the 1836 election remained near the level that had been established in 1828 and 1832, with 55.2 percent of the adult white males voting. Only five states registered percentages in excess of their pre-1824 highs. But in 1840 the "new democracy" made its appearance with explosive suddenness.

In a surge to the polls that has rarely, if ever, been exceeded in any presidential election, four out of five (78.0 percent) of the adult white males cast their votes for Harrison or Van Buren. This new electorate was greater than that of the Jackson period by more than 40 percent. In all but five states—Vermont, Massachusetts, Rhode Island, Kentucky, and Alabama—the peaks of voter participation reached before 1824 were passed. Fourteen of the twenty-five states involved set record highs for voting that were not to be broken throughout the remainder of the ante bellum period. Now, at last, the common man—or at least the man who previously had not been sufficiently aroused to vote in presidential elections—cast his weight into the political balance. This "Tippecanoe democracy," if such a label is permissible, was of a different order of magnitude from the Jacksonian democracy. The elections in which Jackson figured brought to the polls only those men who were accustomed to voting in state or national elections, except in a very few states. The Tippecanoe canvass witnessed an extraordinary expansion of the size of the presidential electorate far beyond previous dimensions. It was in 1840, then, that the "roaring flood of the new democracy" reached its crest. And it engulfed the Jacksonians.

The flood receded only slightly in 1844, when 74.9 percent of the estimated potential electorate went to the polls. Indeed, nine states attained their record highs for the period. In 1848 and 1852 there was a general downward trend in voter participation, followed by a modest upswing in 1856 and 1860. But the level of voter activity remained well above that of the Jackson elections. The conclusion to be drawn is that the "mighty democratic uprising" came after the period of Jackson's presidency.

Now that the quantitative dimensions of Jacksonian democracy as a political phenomenon have been delineated and brought into some appropriate perspective, certain questions still remain to be answered. Granted that the Jacksonian electorate—as revealed by the comparisons that have been set forth—was not really very large, how can we account for the fact that voter participation doubled between the elections of 1824 and 1828? It is true that the total vote soared from around 359,000 to 1,155,400 and that the percentage of voter participation more than doubled? Traditionally, students of the Jackson period have been impressed by this steep increase in voting and by way of explanation have identified the causal factors as the reduction of suffrage qualifications, the democratic influence of the West, or the personal magnetism of Jackson. The validity of each of these hypotheses needs to be reexamined.

In no one of the states in which electors were chosen by popular vote was any significant change made in suffrage qualifications between 1824 and 1828. Subsequently, severe restrictions were maintained in Rhode Island until 1842, when some liberalization was effected, and in Virginia down to 1850. In Louisiana, where the payment of a tax was a requirement, the character of the state tax system apparently operated to restrict the suffrage at least as late as 1845. Thus with the three exceptions noted, the elimination of suffrage barriers was hardly a factor in producing an enlarged electorate during the Jackson and post-Jackson periods. Furthermore, all but a few states had extended the privilege of voting either to all male taxpayers or to all adult male citizens by 1810. After Connecticut eliminated its property qualification in 1818, Massachusetts in 1821, and New York in 1821 and 1826, only Rhode Island, Virginia, and Louisiana were left on the list of "restrictionist" states. Neither Jackson's victory nor the increased vote in 1828 can be attributed to the presence at the polls of a newly enfranchised mass of voters.

Similarly, it does not appear that the western states led the way in voter participation. Prior to 1824, for example, Ohio, Indiana, and Illinois had never brought to the polls as much as 60 percent of their adult white males. Most of the eastern states had surpassed that level by considerable margins. In the election of 1828 six states registered votes in excess of 70 percent of their adult white male populations. They were in order of rank: New Hampshire, Maryland, Ohio, New Jersey, Kentucky, and New York. The six leaders in 1832 were: New Hampshire, Kentucky, Ohio, New York, New Jersey, and Delaware. It will be obvious that the West, however that region may be defined, was not leading the "mighty democratic uprising." Western influences, then, do not explain the increased vote in 1828.

There remains to be considered the factor of Jackson's personal popularity. Did Jackson, the popular hero, attract voters to the polls in unprecedented proportions? The comparisons that have already been made between the Jackson elections and other elections—state and national—before, during, and after his presidency would suggest a negative answer to the question. Granted that a majority of the voters in 1828 favored Jackson, it is not evident that his partisans stormed the polls any more enthusiastically than did the Adams men. Of the six highest states in voter participation in 1828, three favored Adams and three were for Jackson, which could be interpreted to mean that the convinced Adams supporters turned out no less zealously for their man than did the ardent Jacksonians. When Van Buren replaced Jackson in 1836, the voting average increased slightly over 1832. And, as has been demonstrated, the real manifestation of the "new democracy" came not in 1828 but in 1840.

The most satisfactory explanation for the increase in voter participation between 1824 and 1828 is a simple and obvious one. During the long reign of the Virginia dynasty, interest in presidential elections dwindled. In 1816 and 1820 there had been no contest. The somewhat fortuitous termination of the Virginia succession in 1824 and the failure of the congressional caucus to solve the problem of leadership succession threw the choice of a President upon the electorate. But popular interest was dampened by the confusion of choice presented by the multiplicity of candidates, by the disintegration of the old national parties, by the fact that in most states one or another of the candidates was so overwhelmingly popular as to forestall any semblance of a contest, and possibly by the realization that the election would ultimately be decided by the House of Representatives. By 1828 the situation had altered. There were but two candidates in the field, each of whom had substantial sectional backing. A clear-cut contest impended, and the voters became sufficiently aroused to go to the polls in moderate numbers.

One final question remains. Why was the vote in the Jackson elections relatively low when compared with previous and contemporary state elections and with presidential votes after 1840? The answer, in brief, is that in most states either Jackson or his opponent had such a one-sided advantage that the result was a foregone conclusion. Consequently there was little incentive for the voters to go to the polls.

This factor can be evaluated in fairly specific quantitative terms. If the percentage of the total vote secured by each candidate in each state in the election of 1828 is calculated, the difference between the percentages can be used as an index of the closeness, or one-sidedness, of the contest. In Illinois, for example, Jackson received 67 percent of the total vote and Adams, 33; the difference—thirty-four points—represents the margin between the candidates. The average difference between the candidates, taking all the states together, was thirty-six points. Expressed another way this would mean that in the average state the winning candidate received more than twice the vote of the loser. Actually, this was the case in thirteen of the twenty-two states (see Table III). Such a wide margin virtually placed these states in the "no contest" category.

A remarkably close correlation existed between the size of the voter turnout and the relative closeness of the contest. The six states previously listed as having the greatest voter participation in 1828 were among the seven states with the smallest margin of difference between the candidates. The exception was Louisiana, where restrictions on the suffrage curtailed the vote. Even in this instance, however, it is significant that voter participation in Louisiana reached a record high. In those states, then, where there was a close balance of political forces the vote was large, and conversely, where the contest was very one sided, the vote was low.

Most of the states in 1828 were so strongly partial to one or another of the candidates that they can best be characterized as one-party states. Adams encountered little opposition in New England, except in New Hampshire, and Jackson met with hardly any resistance in the South. It was chiefly in

TABLE III.
DIFFERENTIAL BETWEEN PERCENTAGES OF TOTAL VOTE OBTAINED BY MAJOR PRESIDENTIAL CANDIDATES, 1824–1844

State	1828	1832	1836	1840	1844
Maine	20	10	20	1	13
New Hampshire	7	13	50	11	19
Vermont	50	10	20	29	18
Massachusetts	66	30	9	16	12
Rhode Island	50	14	6	23	20
Connecticut	50	20	1	11	5
New York	2	4	9	4	1
New Jersey	4	1	1	4	1
Pennsylvania	33	16	4	1	2
Delaware	—	2	6	10	3
Maryland	2	1	7	8	5
Virginia	38	50	13	1	6
North Carolina	47	70	6	15	5
Georgia	94	100	4	12	4
Kentucky	1	9	6	29	8
Tennessee	90	90	16	11	1
Louisiana	6	38	3	19	3
Alabama	80	100	11	9	18
Mississippi	60	77	2	7	13
Ohio	3	3	4	9	2
Indiana	13	34	12	12	2
Illinois	34	37	10	2	12
Missouri	41	32	21	14	17
Arkansas	—	—	28	13	9
Michigan	—	—	9	4	26
Average Differential	36	36	11	11	6

the middle states and the older West that the real battle was waged. With the removal of Adams from the scene after 1828, New England became less of a one-party section, but the South remained extremely one sided. Consequently it is not surprising that voter participation in 1832 failed even to match that of 1828.

Here, certainly, is a factor of crucial importance in explaining the dimensions of the voter turnout in the Jackson elections. National parties were still in a rudimentary condition and were highly unbalanced from state to state. Indeed, a two-party system scarcely could be said to exist in more than half of the states until after 1832. Where opposing parties had been formed to contest the election, the vote was large, but where no parties, or only one, took the field, the vote was low. By 1840, fairly well-balanced parties had been organized in virtually every state. In only three states did the margin between Harrison and Van Buren exceed twenty points, and the average for all the states was only eleven points. The result was generally high voter participation.

When Jacksonian democracy is viewed from the perspectives employed in this analysis, its political dimensions in so far as they relate to the behavior of the electorate can be described with some precision. None of the Jackson elections involved a "mighty democratic uprising" in the sense that voters were drawn to the polls in unprecedented proportions. When compared with the peak participation recorded for each state before 1824, or with contemporaneous gubernatorial elections, or most particularly with the vast outpouring of the electorate in 1840, voter participation in the Jackson elections was unimpressive. The key to the relatively low presidential vote would seem to be the extreme political imbalance that existed in most states as between the Jacksonians and their opponents. Associated with this imbalance was the immature development of national political parties. Indeed, it can be highly misleading to think in terms of national parties in connection with the Jackson elections. As balanced, organized parties subsequently made their appearance from state to state, and voters were stimulated by the prospect of a genuine contest, a marked rise in voter participation occurred. Such conditions did not prevail generally across the nation until 1840, and then at last the "mighty democratic uprising" took place.

Andrew Jackson and the Rise of Southwestern Democracy

Thomas P. Abernethy

The association of Andrew Jackson with the emergent democracy of early nineteenth-century America is legend—or at least so says Thomas P. Abernethy, of the University of Virginia. According to Abernethy, Jackson's political career was schizophrenic. Jackson's political attitudes and behavior in the state of Tennessee bear little resemblance to the yet more famous Jackson of the national political arena. There is more to Jackson than his military exploits and his presence as a symbolic President. Abernethy concludes that "The truth of the matter is that Jackson had little to do with the development of the democracy of the West." Jackson was much more the product than the champion of the democratic awakening we so readily associate with his age.

The name of Andrew Jackson is inseparably linked with the rise of Western democracy, but the biographers of the general have confined their attention largely to his military exploits and to his contest for and occupancy of the presidency. It is not these phases of his life, however, which connect him most intimately with the struggle of the pioneer and early Western farmer for political power. Before he was a general or a presidential possibility, he was a Tennessee politician. In this capacity he was closely associated with those events which constituted an integral part of the democratic movement of the West. A study of this phase of his career, and of the setting in which he worked, should give a better idea of the man and of the cause for which his name has come to stand.

In 1796 Tennessee adopted her first constitution. Jackson was a member of the committee which drafted it. For its day it was a liberal document, but among its provisions were two which later attracted much unfavorable attention. One provided that the justices of the peace should be chosen by the general assembly for life terms, and that the justices should choose, with a few exceptions, the other county officials;[1] the second stipulated that all acreage should be taxed at the same rate, regardless of value.[2]

These provisions make it clear that the democracy of the West had not grown to full stature by 1796. The peculiarities of the early frontier go far toward explaining this fact. The familiar portraits of John Sevier show him

From "Andrew Jackson and the Rise of Southwestern Democracy," by Thomas P. Abernethy, in *American Historical Review* (October 1927). Reprinted by permission of the author and publisher.

in military costume of the Continental type, such as officers of the line wore during the Revolutionary War, but in his fighting days he wore a hunting shirt as did the men who followed him as he tracked the elusive Indian through the forest.[3] Distinctions existed on the border, but they were not patent to the eye and the simple backwoodsman was not alive to them. The voters who elected delegates to the constitutional convention of 1796 did not realize to what extent they were smoothing the way for the self-aggrandizement of their leaders, the colonels, the legislators, and the land-grabbers —classifications which greatly overlapped.

The years which elapsed between 1796 and 1812 were years of relative peace and considerable growth for the Southwest, but frontier conditions persisted throughout the period. The settlers, whether in town or country, continued, in the main, to live in log cabins and wear homespun. The acquisition of Louisiana and the final opening of the Mississippi River to the trade of the West was a boon to the country. Such towns as Nashville began to emerge from the primitive and to take on the appearance of civilization. Yet it was only with great difficulty that the rivers could be ascended by keel boats, and the majority of the roads were mere trails through the woods. Money was scarce, and the interchange of goods was difficult and hazardous. Barter was still commonly employed in conducting commercial transactions.[4]

The War of 1812 ushered in a change. Tennessee troops saw considerable service in the campaigns against the Indians and the British, and the supplies necessary for their maintenance were secured largely in the West. This brought ready money into regions which had previously known little of its use,[5] and money meant purchasing power, and luxuries, and trade. Moccasins gave place to shoes, and log cabins to brick and frame houses. The Indians caused less trouble after Jackson's conquest of the Creeks in 1813, and large tracts of land were wrested from the natives. The depression suffered by our infant industries as a result of the dumping of British goods on the American market at the end of the long European wars, and the depleted condition of the soils of the South Atlantic states were conditions tending to force population westward.[6] The Cotton Kingdom of the Gulf region was planted in these years.[7] The high price of the staple, which reached thirty-four cents a pound in 1817,[8] hastened this movement, and the steamboat came just in time to facilitate the commercial side of the development.[9]

Specie payments had been suspended by the banks south of New England in 1814, and cheap paper money had been one of the elements conducive to the rapid exploitation of the West which followed the war.[10] In 1817 the Second Bank of the United States went into operation, and it was hoped that it would, by bringing pressure to bear upon doubtful state banks, be able to restore the currency of the country to a sound basis.[11] This meant the retirement of much worthless paper money issued by the state banks, and a consequent restraint on speculative operations.

In order to offset this curtailment of currency and credit, Tennessee chartered a "litter" of state banks in 1817.[12] Kentucky did likewise during the next year.[13] At the same time, the legislature of Tennessee prevented the establishment of a branch of the Bank of the United States within her borders by levying a tax of $50,000 a year upon any such institution.[14] This prohibitive measure was sponsored by Hugh Lawson White,[15] while the opposition was led by Felix Grundy[16] and supported by William Carroll and Andrew Jackson.[17] Its passage seems to indicate the jealousy felt by local financial interests rather than the influence of constitutional scruples on the subject.

The period of speculation was followed by the panic of 1819. East Tennessee had largely escaped the financial excesses of the post-war boom,[18] for her valleys were not suited to the culture of cotton, and transportation was so difficult as to make commercial expansion almost impossible. In Middle Tennessee, however, the growing of cotton was far more widespread during these years than it is at the present time. It was, for instance, Jackson's principal crop at the Hermitage, whereas one now has to travel many miles south of Nashville before reaching cotton country. The very high price which the staple commanded from 1815 to 1819 was the primary cause of this expansion, and the result was that thousands of farmers in this section were ruined when the price fell and the panic came on in 1819. Between five and six hundred suits for debt were entered at one term of the court of Davidson County[19]—the county of which Nashville is the seat of justice.

The indications are that the panic of 1819 hit the small farmers of the Southwest harder than has any succeeding financial disaster. After settled conditions are established and farms are paid for, economic crises do their worst only among the trading and speculating classes, but in new country the farmers are the speculators. The result in this case was that the democracy, for the first time, rose up to demand legislative relief.

In Tennessee the agitation was led by Felix Grundy, who piloted through the assembly a bill providing for the establishment of a loan office.[20] The state was to furnish the capital, the legislature was to elect the directors, and the loans were to be apportioned among the counties according to the taxes paid in each. A "stay" law was also enacted which provided that any creditor who refused to receive the notes issued by the loan office, or state bank, as it was called, would be required to wait two years before he could enforce collection of his debt.[21] These measures were passed by the votes of Middle Tennessee, East Tennessee being opposed.[22] For the first and last time, the debtors of the state were clearly in the saddle.

Within a few months Kentucky established a loan office similar to that of Tennessee,[23] and in 1823 Alabama launched a state-owned bank.[24] Relief legislation was quite general throughout the states south of New England.[25]

The only prominent men in Middle Tennessee who were conspicuous for their opposition to these measures were Edward Ward and Andrew Jackson. They addressed a memorial of protest to the assembly which that body refused to accept on the ground that its language was disrespectful to the law-makers. The memorial did, in fact, charge the members who voted for the loan office act with perjury since they had taken an oath to support the Constitution of the United States, and now assented to a law which made something beside gold and silver a tender in payment of debts.[26]

In 1821 Tennessee experienced one of her most exciting gubernatorial elections. The candidates were Edward Ward and William Carroll. The former was he who had, together with Jackson, protested against the loan office; he was a native of Virginia, a man of education and wealth, and a neighbor to General Jackson.[27] The latter was a merchant from Pennsylvania who had opened the first nail store in Nashville. He was a young man of energy and address, and Jackson had befriended him in his early days. As major-general of Tennessee militia he had served with signal distinction at the battle of New Orleans, but a break, the causes of which are obscure, developed between him and Jackson in 1816.[28]

In the contest of 1821 Jackson used his influence in support of Ward, and looked upon Carroll and his friends as a group of demagogues.[29] The press of the state entered heartily into the campaign and Carroll was touted as a man of the people—an unpretentious merchant, without wealth and without social prestige—whereas Ward's wealth, his slaves, and his education were held against him. He was pictured in the press as a snobbish representative of the aristocracy of the planters.[30]

Both candidates were opposed to the loan office of 1820. Ward advocated a centralized state-banking system in place of it,[31] whereas Carroll simply stressed a policy of retrenchment.[32] The people appear to have discovered that the legislative relief was no panacea for their financial ills, and they were ready to accept Carroll's harsher doctrine of economy. They were beginning to understand that farmers, whose profits did not often run above five percent, could not afford to borrow from banks at six percent. Carroll carried every county in the state except two,[33] and the mere magnitude of the victory indicates that his success was due to his reputation for democracy rather than to his merchant-class economic ideas.

With the exception of a one-term intermission made necessary by the state constitution, William Carroll presided over the government of Tennessee continuously until 1835. He was the most constructive governor who ever held office in the state, for, curiously enough, it was he who, staunchly opposed by Jackson, established "Jacksonian democracy" within her borders. He believed in government of, for, and by the people, but he also believed in a financial policy of specie payments and legislative non-interference between debtor and creditor. Under his leadership, Tennessee disavowed the kind of democracy which had mounted into the saddle on the heels of the panic of 1819, and of which Felix Grundy had been the protagonist.

In his first message to the general assembly, the new chief magistrate outlined his policy. He stuck tenaciously to his program throughout his twelve years in office, and, though it was slow work, nearly every item of his platform was finally carried into effect. In 1821 he advocated the erection of a penitentiary and the abolition of the use of the whipping post, the pillory, and the branding iron. These changes were finally brought about in 1831.[34] Imprisonment for debt was abolished at the same time.[35] In 1821 the "stay" law of 1820 was held unconstitutional by the supreme court of the state.[36] In 1826 the law of 1817, which prevented the establishment of a branch of the Bank of the United States in Tennessee, was repealed with few dissenting votes in the lower house of the legislature,[37] and accordingly that institution established an office in Nashville during the following year. In 1831 the loan office of 1820 was abolished upon Carroll's recommendation,[38] and in 1832 and 1833 several important privately-owned banks of the usual commercial type were established.[39] The sales of the public lands belonging to the state, which had been put upon a credit basis in 1819, were put upon a cash basis in 1823,[40] and the prices were graduated according to the principle later advocated in Congress by Thomas H. Benton.[41] Finally, after several unsuccessful attempts had been made in the legislature to bring the question before the people, a referendum was held and a constitutional convention assembled in 1834.[42] The new instrument of government which was now drawn up and adopted provided for a revision of the judicial system which would facilitate the collection of debts, for popular election of county officials, and for the taxation of real estate according to its value. Thus democracy won its victory in Tennessee, and the guiding spirit was that of William Carroll.

Up to this time, the state had gone through three distinct political phases. The first, extending from 1796 until the panic of 1819, was a period during which the people gratefully and implicitly accepted the leadership of a group of outstanding citizens. The frontiersman was busy with his clearings and he gladly accepted the services of such energetic men as would organize governments and fight the Indians. The fact that these same men were usually land speculators did not disturb him even if he knew it. Land was cheap.

The second period was that of the panic of 1819 during which economic ills aroused the people to a consciousness of their political power. Felix Grundy was the first to see the possibilities of the situation and to organize the movement for his own advancement. He was the first, but by no means the last, demagogue of Tennessee. Carroll won the people away from him and inaugurated the third period, which was one of constructive social and conservative economic legislation. It is noteworthy that until 1829 both Carroll and the legislature favored federal as well as state banks, nor does anything in the history of the state indicate that there was any general feeling against such institutions before Jackson became President.

It was well for Tennessee that Carroll remained so long in office, for the demagogue was not dead. The people had been aroused and Grundy had taught a lesson to the politicians. Public office was eagerly sought by the young lawyers and others, and electioneering, unknown in the earlier days, grew rapidly in vogue during the period following 1819. Stump speaking came to be an art and cajolery a profession, while whiskey flowed freely at the hustings. The politicians could most easily attain their object by appealing to the prejudices of the masses. Colleges were said to exist for the rich, and the ignorant were asked to elect the ignorant because enlightenment and intelligence were not democratic.[43] America, to say nothing of Tennessee, has not outlived this brand of democracy.

It was during the years of Carroll's supremacy that the Jackson presidential boom took shape and ran its course. The relation between this movement and the rise of Western democracy is of considerable interest for the reason that the two have ordinarily been considered as amounting to practically the same thing. The truth of the matter is that Jackson had little to do with the development of the democracy of the West. The movement made him President, but he contributed to it not one idea previously to his election in 1828. He rode into office upon a military reputation and the appeal which a self-made man can make so effectively to self-made men.

It did not take as astute a politician as Aaron Burr to see the possibility of making the Hero of New Orleans President of the United States. Not only Burr, but Edward Livingston and others saw it shortly after January 8, 1815.[44] In fact, the general himself probably saw it, but did not admit it. He at least began taking a keen interest in national politics and set himself the agreeable task of helping Monroe keep Crawford out of the chief magistracy,[45] for the enmity between the general and the secretary dates from 1816. It arose as a result of an agreement which Crawford negotiated with the Cherokees during that year, according to the terms of which the Indians were allowed to retain three million acres of land which the Creeks had claimed and which had been ceded to the government by Jackson's treaty of 1813. The Cherokees were also allowed damages for depredations alleged to have been committed by Jackson's troops during the course of the Creek campaign.[46] The general considered this a slur on his military reputation, and the author of it was duly condemned. It was also good political material, for Crawford was made to appear an enemy of the Western heroes and an opponent of westward expansion. It was only after the election of 1820, however, that the friends of Jackson could tactfully avow their intention to make him President, and the movement did not actually take shape until after his retirement from the governorship of Florida in 1821.

At the time when Jackson resigned this commission and returned to the Hermitage to spend his declining years "surrounded by the pleasures of domestic felicity," a little group of friends in Nashville was forming to make plans of campaign for their distinguished fellow-townsman. The leaders of this group were William B. Lewis, John Overton, and John H. Eaton.

The first-named was a planter and Jackson's neighbor. He was a close personal friend and adviser of long standing, but he was not a man of large affairs. Parton has overestimated his importance because he obtained much of his information on the campaign from Lewis himself.[47] John Overton was a former member of the supreme court in Tennessee and one of the richest men in the state. At that time he and Jackson were partners in a large land deal: namely, the establishment of a trading-town on the Mississippi by the name of Memphis.[48] They were closely associated in Jackson's political venture, too, and Overton later burned the papers relating thereto so that the curious might not pry into its details.[49] In 1816 John H. Eaton, then comparatively unknown in Tennessee, undertook to complete a biography of Jackson.[50] In 1818 he was appointed to the United States Senate,[51] and in 1819 he defended the general when the Seminole campaign was before that body for investigation.[52] From his vantage-point in Washington he served as field agent for the little group of Nashville managers.

Both Overton and Eaton were accused of having entertained Federalist opinions in their early days.[53] There was certainly nothing in the background or the connections of the group to tie it up with the democratic movement which was in full tide about them. In 1823 a former judge who had sat with Overton in the supreme court of the state wrote to him: "True republicanism must supersede the Democracy of the present day before public employment will be suited to my taste. . . . There are too many who would prefer a directly contrary state of things."[54] At about this time Jackson himself was keenly interested in a legal scheme to throw open to question the titles to about half the occupied lands in Tennessee. This, of course, was in the interest of speculators like himself. The legislature however set itself against the plan and it failed miserably.[55]

The general had no personal dealings with either Grundy or Carroll during the early years of his candidacy, and though Grundy, with an eye to personal advancement, refused to break with him politically, and Carroll was later reconciled, it is significant that the latter is the only outstanding Tennessee Democrat who did not, sooner or later, receive federal recognition at the hands of Jackson's party.

Yet Jackson's political views were little known outside Tennessee at the time when he began to be looked upon as presidential timber. His strength lay in his military reputation, in his connection with the expansion of the West at the expense of the Spanish and Indians, and in the fact that he was not closely connected with the intrigue of Washington politics. A movement to turn out the "Virginia dynasty" and to forestall Crawford, the "heir apparent," was inevitable. The dissatisfied element in the Southern and Middle states instinctively turned to Jackson as the logical instrument for this purpose, and certainly no rôle could have been more congenial to the general than one which cast him in opposition to William H. Crawford.

The first statement that he was being definitely considered for the presidency came from Pennsylvania in 1821, where the leaders were said to have canvassed the situation and found that he was the logical man.[56] North Carolina followed the lead of Pennsylvania,[57] and word came from Virginia that the people were for Jackson, but that leadership was needed in order that the politicians be overthrown.[58]

The movement in Tennessee was brought to the surface in 1822 when it was proposed that the general assembly present the general's name to the nation as a suitable candidate for the presidency. The proposition was carried by that body without a dissenting vote.[59] This in the face of the fact that Jackson's candidate for the governorship had been defeated during the previous year by an overwhelming majority. This apparently conflicting vote merely shows that national and state politics were not closely related at that time. The general had been repudiated in no uncertain manner as a state politician, but as a national hero he was a success. Discredited because of his conservative stand in the state, he was chosen to lead the progressive movement in the nation.

A sidelight on the situation is afforded by an incident which occurred during the next year. Colonel John Williams, of Knoxville, had represented Tennessee in the United States Senate since 1815, and had attacked Jackson during the Seminole investigation of 1819.[60] His term expired in 1823, and he was up for re-election with excellent prospects of success. Jackson's friends decided that his presidential prospects would be blighted by the election of one of his bitterest enemies to the Senate from his own state, and when no other candidate could develop sufficient strength to defeat Williams, the general himself was, at the last minute, induced to run.[61] A number of the members of the legislature had already pledged their votes to Williams and could not change, but the ballot, when counted, stood twenty-five to thirty-five in favor of Jackson. The names of those voting were not recorded in the journal —a significant omission. Tennesseans would not permit Jackson to dictate to them, but his personal prestige was great, and there were few who dared stand against him face to face.

Jackson went to the Senate against his will. Back in 1798 he had resigned from that body after a year of uncongenial service. He was now returned to the national forum at the behest of friends who had previously devoted their best efforts to keeping him quiet. Yet it was not because he was afraid to speak his mind that he shrank from the Senate. Above all things, save perhaps a good fight, the general liked to speak his mind. That he gave in so often to his advisers shows that he was not devoid of political discretion. His real objection to Washington, as he so often stated, was its partisan intrigue. There was too much competition in the capital.

There was no doubt but that, before the presidential election, Jackson's hand would be revealed in regard to the important questions which were agitating the country. It was a brave stand for a general in politics to take, but he took it unequivocally. He voted consistently for internal improvements and for the tariff of 1824.[62]

Jackson posed as a Jeffersonian, as did nearly all the Southern Republicans of his day, and in 1822 he had written to Monroe congratulating him upon the veto of the Cumberland Road bill.[63] Yet Tennessee needed internal improvements and ardently desired them. As late as 1825 James K. Polk advocated federal aid for such purposes.[64] In voting as he did in 1824, Jackson represented the interests of his constituents, but during the same year he expressed the opinion that the consent of the state should be secured before the national government should give assistance.[65] During 1827 his supporters in the Tennessee legislature were said to have opposed a federal aid project because of the effect that the agitation of such a question by them might have upon the presidential election in Pennsylvania and Virginia.[66] Finally, when the general became President, he vetoed the Maysville Road bill on the ground that the thoroughfare in question was one of only local importance. The fact was, however, that it was the main highway—an extension of the old Cumberland Road—along which the eastern mail was, at the very time, being carried to Nashville and the Southwest.[67]

In his stand on the tariff question in 1824, Jackson stressed the military importance of domestic manufactures, and also argued for the development of a home market for agricultural products.[68] In this matter he doubtless voiced his personal convictions. The home-market argument had an appeal for the grain farmers of the West, and there were more grain farmers in Tennessee than there were cotton planters, yet Jackson himself belonged to the latter group and protection was not popular with them as a class. Furthermore, despite the rise of democracy, the wealthy cotton planters still had a large share in the creation of public opinion, and there were, in Tennessee, few active advocates of a high tariff before 1840.[69]

In regard to the Bank of the United States, Jackson's views were not developed until after the period of his senatorial services. He certainly did not take a stand against that institution before 1826. In 1827 he began making unfavorable comments on it, but public opposition did not develop until after his election to the presidency.[70] This was clearly not a question of long-standing prejudice with him, and the evidence seems to point to Van Buren as the source of his opinions on the subject.[71] In addition to this, Jackson knew that most of the branches of the bank were in the hands of his opponents and had good reason to believe that their influence was used against him during the election of 1828.[72] It was entirely Jacksonian for him to form his opinion upon such grounds.

Jackson had once been a merchant and he was still a man of business affairs. He had long been a believer in a sound currency and the rights of the creditor. His early economic ideas were in accord with those of William Carroll, and there was nothing here to bring him into conflict with the Bank of the United States. The motives of his opposition were political, not economic.

No historian has ever accused Jackson, the great Democrat, of having had a political philosophy. It is hard to see that he even had any political principles. He was a man of action, and the man of action is likely to be an opportunist. Politically speaking, Jackson was certainly an opportunist. If he gave any real help or encouragement before 1828 to any of the movements which, under men like Carroll, aimed at the amelioration of the condition of the masses, the fact has not been recorded. He belonged to the moneyed aristocracy of Nashville, yet he was a self-made man and devoid of snobbishness. He thought he was sincere when he spoke to the people, yet he never really championed their cause. He merely encouraged them to champion his.

It seems clear that Jackson's political habits were formed in the period of the early settlement of the Southwest when a few leaders were able to shape the public mind and use their official positions as an aid to their exploitation of the land. He never failed, for instance, to use the patronage of office for the promotion of the interests of his friends. The democratic awakening which took such hold upon the people of Tennessee after the panic of 1819 failed to enlist his sympathy. He was called upon to lead the national phase of this movement, but played no part in the formulation or promotion of its constructive program. He did, however, in 1824, represent the needs of the West for improved commercial facilities, and he was a nationalist from early conviction. After 1824 he came under political influence—that of Van Buren, it seems, being paramount[73]—which caused him to change his earlier opinions in several respects. This accounts for the fact that his presidential policy favored the seaboard staple growers rather than the grain producers of the West. Yet he failed, in the main, to capture the support of the cotton planters of the South, for many of them either sympathized with nullification or desired a United States bank and internal improvements. He was a political hybrid—too strong a nationalist for some, too strong a state-rights man for others. On the other hand, he held to the end the loyalty of the small farmers, for the Jacksonian tradition was deeply rooted in them, and Jackson's bank policy looked to them like democracy. Banks often worked to their disadvantage, and they could manage without commercial facilities. They constituted the rank and file of the Democratic party in the South until the Whig organization went to pieces and the planters were thereby forced to accept, at a late date, the bait which Jackson had proffered them in vain.

Notes

1. Article V., section 12; article VI., section 1.
2. Article I., section 26.
3. J. G. M. Ramsey, *Annals of Tennessee* (Kingsport, Tenn., 1926), p. 711.
4. Account book of H. Tatum, merchant, Nashville, 1793–1798, Tennessee Historical Society MSS., Box T–1, no. 5; *Correspondence of Andrew Jackson*, ed. J. S. Bassett (Washington, 1926), I. 89–90, 99–101.
5. Nashville *Gazette*, Oct. 29, 1820.
6. A. O. Craven, *Soil Exhaustion as a Factor in the Agricultural History of Virginia and Maryland* (Urbana, Ill., 1926), pp. 118–121.
7. T. P. Abernethy, *Formative Period in Alabama* (Montgomery, Ala., 1922), pp. 50–56.
8. U. S. Department of Agriculture, Office of Farm Management, *Atlas of American Agriculture* (Washington, 1918), part V., section A, 20.
9. Moore and Foster, *Tennessee, the Volunteer State* (Chicago, 1923), II. 85–86; Nashville *Banner*, Apr. 14, 1827.
10. D. R. Dewey, *Financial History of the United States* (New York, 1920), pp. 144–145.
11. *Ibid.*, pp. 145–151.
12. Tennessee, *Public Acts*, 1817, pp. 163–180.
13. McMaster, *History of the People of the United States* (New York, 1895), IV. 508.
14. Tennessee, *Public Acts*, 1817, pp. 138–139.
15. John Catron to Polk, June 17, 1837, Papers of James K. Polk in Library of Congress; *A Memoir of Hugh Lawson White*, ed. Nancy N. Scott (Philadelphia, 1856), pp. 19–23.
16. St. George L. Sioussat, "Some Phases of Tennessee Politics in the Jackson Period," in *American Historical Review*, XIV. 60; Nashville *Whig*, Feb. 7, 1818.
17. James Phelan, *History of Tennessee* (Boston, 1888), pp. 394–395; R. C. H. Catterall, *Second Bank of the United States*, p. 183.
18. Thos. Emmerson to John Overton, Oct. 24, 1820, John Overton Papers in Tennessee Historical Society library; P. M. Miller to Jackson, Aug. 9, 1820, Jackson Papers in Library of Congress; Nashville *Gazette*, June 20, 1820; Knoxville *Register*, June 20, 1820.
19. Jackson to Capt. James Gadsden, Aug. 1, 1819, *Correspondence of Andrew Jackson*, ed. J. S. Bassett, II. 421; Nashville *Clarion*, July 13, 1819.
20. Knoxville *Register*, July 18, 1820.
21. Tennessee, *Public Acts*, 1820, p. 13.
22. Tennessee Assembly, *Journal of the House*, 1820, p. 129.
23. Nashville *Gazette*, Dec. 9, 1820.
24. T. P. Abernethy, *Formative Period in Alabama*, p. 99.
25. Thos. H. Benton, *Thirty Years' View* (New York, 1854), I. 5.
26. Nashville *Clarion*, July 25, 1820; Knoxville *Register*, Aug. 15, 1820.
27. Hale and Merritt, *A History of Tennessee and Tennesseans* (Chicago, 1913), II. 267.
28. Jackson to Coffee, Feb. 2, 1816, Papers of John Coffee in Tennessee Historical Society library.
29. Jackson to Coffee, July 26, 1821, *ibid.*; Jackson to Capt. John Donelson, Sept. 2, 1821, Jackson Papers.
30. Knoxville *Register*, July 17, 1821; Nashville *Clarion*, July 18, 1821.

31. Nashville *Gazette*, June 2, 1821; Nashville *Clarion*, June 13, 1821; Knoxville *Register*, June 16, 1821.
32. Nashville *Clarion*, June 27, 1821.
33. *Ibid.*, Aug. 15, 1821.
34. See messages of 1821 and 1823, Tennessee Assembly, *Journal of the Senate*, 1821, pp. 86–99, and *Journal of the House*, 1823, pp. 9–15.
35. Tennessee, *Public Acts*, 1831, p. 56.
36. Townsend *v.* Townsend *et al.*, *Tennessee Reports* (Peck), pp. 1–21.
37. Tennessee, *Public Acts*, 1826, p. 18; Tennessee Assembly, *Journal of the House*, 1826, pp. 173–174.
38. Tennessee Assembly, *Journal of the Senate*, 1831, pp. 6–9, *Journal of the House*, 1831, pp. 41 *et seq.*
39. Tennessee, *Public Acts*, 1832, pp. 2–13, and 1833, pp. 30–42; Phelan, *History of Tennessee*, pp. 267–268.
40. Whitney, *Land Laws of Tennessee* (Chattanooga, 1891), pp. 387–394.
41. *Ibid.*, pp. 398–400; see also Sioussat, "Tennessee Politics in the Jackson Period," *loc. cit.*, pp. 54–58.
42. The question of calling a convention was voted on by the assembly and defeated in 1821, 1823, and 1826. It was finally carried by the assembly and ratified by popular vote in 1833.
43. For suggestions on this topic, see J. W. M. Breazeale, "Satirical Burlesque upon the Practice of Electioneering," in *Life as It Is* (Knoxville, 1842), pp. 158–226; and "An Address to Farmers and Mechanics," in *Works of Philip Lindsley* (Philadelphia, 1866), III. 265–316.
44. J. S. Bassett, *Life of Andrew Jackson* (New York, 1925), p. 279; William Carroll to Jackson, Oct. 4, 1815, *id.*, *Correspondence of Andrew Jackson*, II. 217–218; James Parton, *Life of Andrew Jackson* (Boston, 1887), II. 350.
45. A. P. Hayne to Jackson, Jan. 21, 1819, Jackson Papers; *id.* to *id.*, Mar. 6, 1819, Jackson to Governor Clark of Georgia, Apr. 20, 1819, *Correspondence of Andrew Jackson*, ed. J. S. Bassett, II. 412, 416; Address of Enoch Parsons, Mar. 25, 1819, Jackson Papers; Jackson to Coffee, Apr. 3, 1819, Coffee Papers.
46. Parton, *Jackson*, II. 355–356; Bassett, *Jackson*, p. 281; Nashville *Whig*, July 31, 1819; Jackson to Monroe, Oct. 10, 1823, Jackson Papers; Jackson to Crawford, June 10, 13 ?, and 16, 1816, *Correspondence of Andrew Jackson*, ed. J. S. Bassett, II. 243–250.
47. Parton, *Jackson*, III. 17.
48. Phelan, *History of Tennessee*, p. 317.
49. W. W. Clayton, *History of Davidson County, Tennessee* (Philadelphia, 1880), p. 99.
50. Nashville *Whig*, June 4, 1816.
51. C. A. Miller, *Official and Political Manual of the State of Tennessee* (Nashville, 1890), p. 173.
52. Jackson to William Williams, Sept. 25, 1819, Bassett, *Correspondence of Andrew Jackson*, II. 430.
53. Nashville *Clarion*, Jan. 5, 1819; Phelan, *History of Tennessee*, p. 241.
54. Thos. Emmerson to John Overton, May 25, 1823; see also *id.* to *id.*, Dec. 26, 1823, and June 3, 1824, Overton Papers.
55. This had to do with a decision of the state supreme court which overruled former decisions and declared that titles to land, in order to be valid, must be connected by an unbroken chain with the original grant, and that occupiers might be ejected even though they held under color of title. The legislature added another justice to the court, and John Catron, afterward justice of the United States Supreme Court, was appointed to fill the place in order that this

decision might be annulled. Jackson had a personal interest in the matter and denounced the action of the legislature. See Jackson to Coffee, April 15, and May 24, 1823, Coffee Papers. For the legal phase of the question, see Barton's Lessee *v.* Shall, *Tennessee Reports* (Peck), p. 172.

56. S. R. Overton to Jackson, Aug. 1, 1821, Jackson Papers.
57. A. D. Murphy to John H. Eaton, Jan. 16, 1824, Overton Papers.
58. Thos. G. Watkins to Jackson, Mar. 13, 1822, Jackson Papers.
59. Jackson to Dr. J. C. Bronaugh, Aug. 1, 1822, S. R. Overton to Jackson, Sept. 10, 1822, Jackson Papers; Nashville *Whig*, July 31, 1822. See also Grundy to Jackson, June 27, 1822, Jackson Papers.
60. Jackson to William Williams, Sept. 25, 1819, Bassett, *Correspondence of Andrew Jackson*, II. 430.
61. Thos. L. Williams to Overton, Sept. 10, 1823, Overton Papers; Wm. Brady and Thos. Williamson to Jackson, Sept. 20, 1823, Jackson to Brady and Williamson, Sept. 27, 1823, Jackson Papers; Jackson to Coffee, Oct. 5, 1823, Coffee Papers; Knoxville *Register*, Oct. 10, 1823.
62. Bassett, *Jackson*, pp. 344–345.
63. Jackson to Monroe, July 26, 1822, Jackson Papers.
64. Phelan, *History of Tennessee*, p. 396.
65. Jackson to James W. Lanier, May (?), 1824, Jackson Papers; Jackson to Polk, Dec. 4, 1826, Polk Papers.
66. Knoxville *Enquirer*, Jan. 9, 1828.
67. J. P. Bretz, "Early Land Communication with the Lower Mississippi Valley," in *Mississippi Valley Historical Review*, XIII. 27–29.
68. Jackson to Coffee, May 7, 1824, Jackson to John Overton, June 18, 1824, Coffee Papers; Parton, *Jackson*, III. 35–36.
69. Phelan, *History of Tennessee*, p. 425.
70. Catterall, *Second Bank of the United States*, pp. 183–184.
71. R. L. Colt to Biddle, Jan. 7, 1829, June 10, 1830, Henry Clay to Biddle, June 14, 1830, *The Correspondence of Nicholas Biddle*, ed. R. C. McGrane, pp. 66–67, 104, 105.
72. Wm. B. Lewis to Biddle, Oct. 16, 1829, pp. 79–80, Biddle to Geo. Hoffman, Nov. 22, 1829, *ibid.*, pp. 87–88.
73. Bassett, *Jackson*, pp. 484–489; *David Crockett's Circular*, pamphlet in Library of Congress (Washington, 1831), pp. 2–5.

The Mountain Man as Jacksonian Man*

William H. Goetzmann

William H. Goetzmann, history professor at the University of Texas, offers new data as to the social and economic behavior of the Mountain Men during the Jacksonian period. Faced with the fact that "the Mountain Man exists as a figure of American mythology rather than history," Goetzmann offers a vigorous and effective statement concerning this elusive hero of American folklore. The Mountain Man has most often been considered the exemplar of a free and unrestrained existence; like all lasting myths, those that surrounded him had enough validity to gain acceptance. Yet in analyzing those who lived close to nature as they worked the Rocky Mountain fur trade, Goetzmann concludes that few were willing to remain "free agents of nature" if given the chance at other occupations. Most shared a distinct desire to return to civilized comforts. Most sought, and many attained, the respectability and success so valued by the society they had left behind. In the end, the Mountain Man rather fit the pattern of most "Jacksonian Men"—he was a "venturous conservative."

*The term "Jacksonian Man" is used throughout this essay in a general rather than a particular sense. It is intended to describe a fictional composite, the average man of the period under consideration regardless of whether or not he was a follower of Andrew Jackson and his party. Those qualities which I take to be general enough to characterize the average man are defined in my quotations from Richard Hofstadter, Marvin Meyers and Alexis de Tocqueville. It should not be inferred from this that I seek to portray the Mountain Men as members of Andrew Jackson's political party nor that I mean to suggest that the particular objectives of the Democratic Party were necessarily those described by Hofstadter, Meyers and Tocqueville. Rather their terms seem to characterize to some extent men of all political persuasions in this period. Lee Benson, in his recent book, *The Concept of Jacksonian Democracy,* has shown that in New York State, at least, the Jackson party had no particular monopoly on such terms as "egalitarianism" and "democracy," and that indeed most parties in the state, including the Whigs, actually preceded the Jackson men in their advocacy of these views. He thus demonstrates that there were certain values and goals common to all men of the day. Benson then concludes that instead of calling the period "The Age of Jackson," it should properly be called "The Age of Egalitarianism." His evidence indicates to me, however, that a still more precise term for the period might well be "The Age of Expectant Capitalism," and following Hofstadter and Meyers, and before them Frederick Jackson Turner, I have seen this as the most generally applicable descriptive concept for the period. Thus it forms the basis for my definition of "Jacksonian Man," or *Genus Homo Americanus* during the years of the presidency of Andrew Jackson and his successor Martin Van Buren.

From "The Mountain Man as Jacksonian Man," by William H. Goetzmann, in *American Quarterly,* XV, No. 3 (Fall 1963), 402–415.

One of the most often studied and least understood figures in American history has been the Mountain Man. Remote, so it would seem, as Neanderthal, and according to some almost as inarticulate, the Mountain Man exists as a figure of American mythology rather than history. As such he has presented at least two vivid stereotypes to the public imagination. From the first he has been the very symbol for the romantic banditti of the forest, freed of the artificial restrictions of civilization—a picturesque wanderer in the wilderness whose very life is a constant and direct association with Nature.

> There is perhaps, no class of men on the face of the earth," said Captain Bonneville [and through him Washington Irving], "who lead a life of more continued exertion, peril, and excitement, and who are more enamoured of their occupations, than the free trappers of the west. No toil, no danger, no privation can turn the trapper from his pursuit. His passionate excitement at times resembles a mania. In vain may the most vigilant and cruel savages beset his path; in vain may rocks, and precipices, and wintry torrents oppose his progress; let but a single track of a beaver meet his eye, and he forgets all dangers and defies all difficulties. At times, he may be seen with his traps on his shoulder, buffeting his way across rapid streams amidst floating blocks of ice: at other times, he is to be found with his traps on his back clambering the most rugged mountains, scaling or descending the most frightening precipices, searching by routes inaccessible to the horse, and never before trodden by white man, for springs and lakes unknown to his comrades, and where he may meet with his favorite game. Such is the mountaineer, the hardy trapper of the west; and such as we have slightly sketched it, is the wild, Robin Hood kind of life, with all its strange and motley populace, now existing in full vigor among the Rocky mountains."[1]

To Irving in the nineteenth century the Mountain Man was Robin Hood, a European literary convention. By the twentieth century the image was still literary and romantic but somewhat less precise. According to Bernard De Voto, "For a few years Odysseus Jed Smith and Siegfried Carson and the wing-shod Fitzpatrick actually drew breath in this province of fable," and Jim Beckwourth "went among the Rockies as Theseus dared the wine-dark seas. Skirting the rise of a hill, he saw the willows stirring; he charged down upon them, while despairing Blackfeet sang the death-song—and lo, to the clear music of a horn, Roland had met the pagan hordes. . . ."[2]

On the other hand, to perhaps more discerning eyes in his own day and down through the years, the Mountain Man presented another image—one that was far less exalted. Set off from the ordinary man by his costume of greasy buckskins, coonskin cap and Indian finery, not to mention the distinctive odor that went with bear grease and the habitual failure to bathe between one yearly rendezvous and the next, the Mountain Man seemed a forlorn and pathetic primitive out of the past. "They are stared at as though they were bears," wrote Rudolph F. Kurz, a Swiss artist who traveled the Upper Missouri.[3]

The Mountain Man, so it was said, was out of touch with conventional civilization and hence not quite acceptable.[4] Instead in his own time and even more today he has been viewed as a purely hedonistic character who lived for the year's end rendezvous where he got gloriously drunk on diluted rot-gut company alcohol, gave his beaver away for wildly inflated company trade goods and crawled off into the underbrush for a delirious orgy with some unenthusiastic Indian squaw. In this view the romantic rendezvous was nothing more than a modern company picnic, the object of which was to keep the employees docile, happy and ready for the coming year's task.

Pacified, satisfied, cheated, impoverished, and probably mortified the next day, the Mountain Man, be he free trapper or not, went back to his dangerous work when the rendezvous was over. He was thus to many shrewd observers not a hero at all but a docile and obedient slave of the company. By a stretch of the imagination he might have seemed heroic, but because of the contrast between his daring deeds and his degraded status he seemed one of the saddest heroes in all history. Out of date before his time was up, he was a wild free spirit who after all was not free. He was instead an adventurer who was bringing about his own destruction even as he succeeded in his quest to search out the beaver in all of the secret places of the mountain West. A dependent of the London dandy and his foppish taste in hats, the Mountain Man was Caliban. He was a member of a picturesque lower class fast vanishing from the face of America. Like the Mohican Indian and quaint old Leatherstocking he was a vanishing breed, forlorn and permanently class-bound in spite of all his heroics.[5]

Both of these stereotypes embody, as do most effective stereotypes, more than a measure of reality. The Mountain Man traveled far out ahead of the march of conventional civilization, and the job he did required him to be as tough, primitive and close to nature as an Indian. Moreover, it was an out-of-doors life of the hunt and the chase that he often grew to like. By the same token because he spent much of his time in primitive isolation in the mountains, he very often proved to be a poor businessman ignorant of current prices and sharp company practices. Even if aware of his disadvantageous position he could do nothing to free himself until he had made his stake.

The fact is, however, that many Mountain Men lived for the chance to exchange their dangerous mountain careers for an advantageous start in civilized life. If one examines their lives and their stated aspirations one discovers that the Mountain Men, for all their apparent eccentricities, were astonishingly similar to the common men of their time—plain republican citizens of the Jacksonian era.

Jacksonian Man, according to Richard Hofstadter, "was an expectant capitalist, a hardworking ambitious person for whom enterprise was a kind of religion."[6] He was "the master mechanic who aspired to open his own shop, the planter, or farmer who speculated in land, the lawyer who hoped to be a judge, the local politician who wanted to go to Congress, the grocer who would be a merchant. . . ."[7] To this list one might well add, the trapper who hoped some day, if he hit it lucky and avoided the scalping knife, to be one or all of these, or perhaps better still, a landed gentleman of wealth and prestige.

"Everywhere," writes Hofstadter, the Jacksonian expectant capitalist "found conditions that encouraged him to extend himself."[8] And there were many like William Ashley or Thomas James who out of encouragement or desperation looked away to the Rocky Mountains, teeming with beaver and other hidden resources, and saw a path to economic success and rapid upward mobility. In short, when he went out West and became a Mountain Man the Jacksonian Man did so as a prospector. He too was an expectant capitalist.

Marvin Meyers has added a further characterization of Jacksonian Man. He was, according to Meyers, the "venturous conservative,"[9] the man who desired relative freedom from restraint so that he might risk his life and his fortune, if not his sacred honor, on what appeared to be a long-term, continent-wide boom. Yet at the same time he wished to pyramid his fortune within the limits of the familiar American social and economic system, and likewise to derive his status therefrom. Wherever he went, and especially on the frontier, Jacksonian Man did not wish to change the system. He merely wished to throw it open as much as possible to opportunity, with the hope that by so doing he could place himself at the top instead of at the bottom of the conventional social and economic ladder. "They love change," wrote Tocqueville, "but they dread revolutions."[10] Instead of a new world the Jacksonian Man wished to restore the old where the greatest man was the independent man—yeoman or mechanic, trader or ranchero—the man who basked in comfort and sturdy security under his own "vine and fig tree."

The structure of the Rocky Mountain fur trade itself, the life stories of the trappers and on rare occasions their stated or implied aspirations all make it clear that if he was not precisely the Meyers-Hofstadter Jacksonian Man, the Mountain Man was most certainly his cousin once removed, and a clearly recognizable member of the family.

It is a truism, of course, to state that the Rocky Mountain fur trade was a business, though writers in the Mountain Man's day and since have sometimes made it seem more like a sporting event. The Mountain Man himself often put such an ambiguous face on what he was doing.

> "Westward! Ho!" wrote Warren Ferris, an American Fur Company trapper. "It is the sixteenth of the second month A.D. 1830, and I have joined a trapping, trading, hunting expedition to the Rocky Mountains. Why, I scarcely know, for the motives that induced me to this step were of a mixed complexion,—something like the pepper and salt population of this city of St. Louis. Curiosity, a love of wild adventure, and perhaps also a hope of profit,—for times *are* hard, and my best coat has a sort of sheepish hang-dog hesitation to encounter fashionable folk—combined to make me look upon the project with an eye of favor. The party consists of some thirty men, mostly Canadian; but

a few there are, like myself, from various parts of the Union. Each has some plausible excuse for joining, and the aggregate of disinterestedness would delight the most ghostly saint in the Roman calendar. Engage for money! no, not they;—health, and the strong desire of seeing strange lands, of beholding nature in the savage grandeur of her primeval state,—these are the only arguments that *could* have persuaded such independent and high-minded young fellows to adventure with the American Fur Company in a trip to the mountain wilds of the great west."[11]

Ambiguous though the Mountain Man 's approach to it may have been, it is abundantly clear that the Rocky Mountain fur trade was indeed a *business,* and not an invariably individualistic enterprise at that. The unit of operation was the company, usually a partnership for the sake of capital, risk and year-round efficiency. Examples of the company are The Missouri Fur Company, Gantt and Blackwell, Stone and Bostwick, Bean and Sinclair, and most famous of all, the Rocky Mountain Fur Company and its successors, Smith, Jackson, and Sublette, Sublette & Campbell, and Sublette, Fitzpatrick, Bridger, Gervais and Fraeb. These were the average company units in the Rocky Mountain trade and much of the story of their existence is analogous to Jackson's war on the "Monster Bank" for they were all forced to contend against John Jacob Astor's "Monster Monopoly," the American Fur Co., which was controlled and financed by eastern capitalists.

Perhaps the most interesting aspect of the independent fur companies was their fluid structure of leadership. There was indeed, "a baton in every knapsack" or more accurately, perhaps, in every "possibles" bag. William Ashley, owner of a gun powder factory and Andrew Henry, a former Lisa lieutenant, and lead miner, founded the Rocky Mountain Fur Company.[12] After a few years of overwhelming success, first Henry, and then Ashley, retired, and they were succeeded by their lieutenants, Jedediah Smith, David Jackson and William Sublette, three of the "enterprising young men" who had answered Ashley's advertisement in the St. Louis *Gazette and Public Advertiser* in 1823. When Smith and Jackson moved on to more attractive endeavors, first William Sublette and Robert Campbell, then Tom "Broken Hand" Fitzpatrick, James "Old Gabe" Bridger, Henry Fraeb, Milton "Thunderbolt" Sublette and Jean Baptiste Gervais moved up to fill their entrepreneurial role.

In another example Etienne Provost was successively an employee of Auguste Chouteau, partner with LeClair and leader of his own Green River brigade, and servant of American Fur.[13] Sylvestre Pattie became a Santa Fe trader, then an independent trapper, then manager of the Santa Rita (New Mexico) Copper Mines and ultimately leader of an independent trapping venture into the Gila River country of the far Southwest—a venture that ended in disaster when he was thrown into a Mexican prison in California and there left to die.[14] Most significant is the fact that few of the trappers declined the responsibility of entrepreneurial leadership when it was offered them. On the contrary, the usual practice was to indenture oneself to an established company for a period of time, during which it was possible to acquire the limited capital in the way of traps, rifles, trade goods, etc., that was needed to become independent and a potential brigade leader. Referring to his arrangement with the old Missouri Fur Company in 1809, Thomas James wrote,

> We Americans were all private adventurers, each on his own hook, and were led into the enterprise by the promises of the Company, who agreed to subsist us to the trapping grounds, we helping to navigate the boats, and on our arrival there they were to furnish us each with a rifle and sufficient ammunition, six good beaver traps and also four men of their hired French, to be under our individual commands for a period of three years.
>
> By the terms of the contract each of us was to divide one-fourth of the profits of our joint labor with the four men thus to be appointed to us.[15]

James himself retired when he could from the upper Missouri trade and eventually became an unsuccessful storekeeper in Harrisonville, Illinois.[16]

In addition to the fact of rapid entrepreneurial succession within the structure of the independent fur companies, a study of 446 Mountain Men (perhaps 45 percent of the total engaged in this pursuit between 1805 and 1845) indicates that their life-patterns could be extremely varied. One hundred seventeen Mountain Men definitely turned to occupations other than trapping subsequent to their entering the mountain trade. Of this number 39 followed more than one pursuit. As such they often worked at as many as four or five different callings.[17]

Moreover beyond the 117 definite cases of alternative callings, 32 others were found to have indeterminate occupations that were almost certainly not connected with the fur trade,[18] making a total of 149 out of 154 men for whom some occupational data exists who had turned away from the trapping fraternity before 1845. Of the remaining men in the study, 110 men yielded nothing to investigation beyond the fact that they had once been trappers, 182 can be listed as killed in the line of duty and only five men out of the total stayed with the great out-of-doors life of the free trapper that according to the myth they were all supposed to love.

TABLE 1

Total Number of Cases	446
Persons whose other occupations are known	117
Persons whose other occupations are probable	32
Persons with more than one other occupation	39
Persons who stayed on as trappers	5
Persons whose status is unknown	110
Persons killed in the fur trade	182

The list of alternative callings pursued by the trappers is also revealing. Twenty-one became ranchers, fifteen farmers, seventeen traders (at stationary trading posts), eight miners, seven politicians, six distillers, five each storekeepers and army scouts, four United States Indian agents, three carpenters, two each bankers, drovers and hatters and at least one pursued each of the following occupations: sheepherder, postman, miller, medium, ice dealer, vintner, fancy fruit grower, baker, saloon keeper, clockmaker, cattle buyer, real estate speculator, newspaper editor, lawyer, lumberman, superintendent of schools, tailor, blacksmith, and supercargo of a trading schooner. Moreover many of these same individuals pursued secondary occupations such as that of hotel keeper, gambler, soldier, health resort proprietor, coal mine owner, tanner, sea captain, horse thief and opera house impresario.

TABLE 2. LIST OF OCCUPATIONS

Occupation	No.	Occupation	No.
A. *Primary*			
1. Farmer	15	17. Blacksmith	1
2. Rancher	21	18. Tailor	1
3. Politician	7	19. Supercargo	1
4. Sheepherder	1	20. Superintendent of Schools	1
5. Scout [For Govt.]	5	21. Lumberman	2
6. Trader	17	22. Newspaper Editor	1
7. Miner	8	23. Carpenter	3
8. Postman	1	24. Cattle Buyer	1
9. Distiller	6	25. Clockmaker	1
10. Miller	1	26. Saloon Keeper	1
11. Storekeeper	5	27. Baker	1
12. Medium	1	28. Fruit Grower	1
13. Banker	2	29. Vintner	1
14. Drover	2	30. Ice Dealer	1
15. Hatter	2	31. Real Estate Speculator	1
16. Indian Agent	4	32. Lawyer	1
B. *Secondary*			
1. Trader	4	12. Lumberman	2
2. Transportation	2	13. Gambler	3
3. Scout	5	14. Blacksmith	1
4. Hotel Keeper	1	15. Soldier	1
5. Miner	2	16. Spa Keeper	1
6. Farmer	5	17. Coal Mine Operator	1
7. Politician	3	18. Tanner	1
8. Rancher	5	19. Opera House Impresario	1
9. Storekeeper	4	20. Sea Captain	1
10. Miller	3	21. Carpenter	1
11. Real Estate	3	22. Horse Thief	1

From this it seems clear that, statistically at least, the Mountain Man was hardly the simple-minded primitive that mythology has made him out to be. Indeed it appears that whenever he had the chance, he exchanged the joys of the rendezvous and the wilderness life for the more civilized excitement of "getting ahead." In many cases he achieved this aim, and on a frontier where able men were scarce he very often became a pillar of the community, and even of the nation. From the beginning, as Ashley's famous advertisement implied, the Mountain Men were men of "enterprise" who risked their lives for something more than pure romance and a misanthropic desire to evade civilization. The picturesqueness and the quaintness were largely the creation of what was the literary mentality of an age of artistic romanticism. For every "Cannibal Phil" or Robert Meldrum or "Peg-Leg" Smith there was a Sarchel Wolfskill (vintner), a George Yount (rancher) and a William Sublette (banker-politician).

Two further facts emerge in part from this data. First, it is clear that though the Jeffersonian agrarian dream of "Arcadia" bulked large in the Mountain Man's choice of occupations, it by no means obscured the whole range of "mechanical" or mercantile pursuits that offered the chance for success on the frontier. Indeed, if it suggests anything a statistical view of the Mountain Man's "other life" suggests that almost from the beginning the Far Western frontier took on the decided aspect of an urban or semi-urban "industrial" civilization. Secondly, though it is not immediately apparent from the above statistics, a closer look indicates that a surprising number of the Mountain Men succeeded at their "other" tasks to the extent that they became regionally and even nationally prominent.

William H. Ashley became Congressman from Missouri and a spokesman for the West, Charles Bent an ill-fated though famed governor of New Mexico. "Doc" Newell was a prominent figure in the organization of Oregon Territory. Elbridge Gerry, William McGaa and John Simpson Smith were the founders and incorporators of Denver. Lucien Maxwell held the largest land grant in the whole history of the United States.

Joshua Pilcher was a famous superintendent of Indian Affairs. William Sublette, pursuing a hard money policy, saved the Bank of Missouri in the panic of 1837 and went on to be a Democratic elector for "young hickory" James K. Polk in 1844. Benjamin Wilson was elected first mayor of Los Angeles. James Clyman and his Napa Valley estate were famous in California as were the ranches of George Yount and J. J. Warner, while Sarchel Wolfskill was a co-founder of the modern California wine industry. James Waters built the first opera house in Southern California, and Kit Carson, in his later years a silver miner, received the supreme tribute of finding a dime novel dedicated to his exploits in plunder captured from marauding Apache Indians who had recently attacked and massacred a wagon train.[19]

Many of the Mountain Men achieved fame and national status through works that they published themselves, or, as in the case of Carson, through works that immortalized correctly, or as was more usual, incorrectly, their exploits. Here one need only mention Kit Carson's *Autobiography* and his favorable treatment at the hands of Jessie Benton Frémont, T. D. Bonner's

Life and Adventures of James Beckwourth, Francis Fuller Victor's *River of the West* (about Joe Meek), James Ohio Pattie's *Personal Narrative,* Thomas James' *Three Years Among the Indians and Mexicans,* H. L. Conard's *Uncle Dick Wooton,* David Coyner's *The Lost Trappers* (about Ezekial Williams), Irving's portrait of Joseph Reddeford Walker in *The Adventures of Captain Bonneville,* Zenas Leonard's *Narrative,* Peg-Leg Smith's "as told to" exploits in *Hutchings' California Magazine,* Stephen Meek's *Autobiography,* Warren Ferris' letters to the Buffalo, New York, *Western Literary Messenger,* John Hatcher's yarns in Lewis H. Garrard's *Wah To Yah and The Taos Trail* and perhaps most interesting of all, trapper John Brown's pseudo-scientific *Mediumistic Experiences,* to realize the extent and range of the Mountain Man's communication with the outside world in his own day. Not only was he a typical man of his time, he was often a conspicuous success and not bashful about communicating the fact in somewhat exaggerated terms to his fellow countrymen.

Direct evidence of the Mountain Men's motives is scarce, but it is clear their intentions were complex.

"Tell them that I have no heirs and that I hope to make a fortune," wrote Louis Vasquez ("Old Vaskiss" to Bernard De Voto) in 1834 from "Fort Convenience" somewhere in the Rockies.[20] Later as he set out on one last expedition in 1842 he added somewhat melodramatically, "I leave to make money or die."[21] And finally Colonel A. G. Brackett, who visited Fort Bridger (jointly owned by Bridger and Vasquez), described him as "a Mexican, who put on a great deal of style, and used to ride about the country in a coach and four."[22]

"It is, that I may be able to help those who stand in need, that I face every danger," wrote Jedediah Smith from the Wind River Mountains in 1829, "most of all, it is for this, that I deprive myself of the privilege of Society and the satisfaction of the Converse of My Friends! but I shall count all this pleasure, if I am allowed by the Alwise Ruler the privilege of Joining my Friends. . . ." And he added "let it be the greatest pleasure that we can enjoy, the height of our ambition, now, when our Parents are in the decline of Life, to smooth the Pillow of their age, and as much as in us lies, take from them all cause of Trouble."[23] So spoke Jedediah Smith of his hopes and ambitions upon pursuing the fur trade. No sooner had he left the mountains, however, than he was killed by Plains Indians before he could settle down in business with his brothers as he had intended.[24] Noble and ignoble were the motives of the Mountain Men. Colonel John Shaw, starting across the southern plains and into the Rockies in search of gold; Thomas James, desperate to recoup his failing fortunes; the Little Rock *Gazette* of 1829 "confidently" believing "that this enterprise affords a prospect of great profit to all who may engage in it"; the St. Louis *Enquirer* in 1822 labeling the Rocky Mountains "the Shining Mountains," and innocently declaring, "A hunter pursuing his game found the silver mines of Potosi, and many others have been discovered by the like accidents, and there is no reason to suppose that other valuable discoveries may not be made";[25] Ashley calling clearly and unmistakably for men of "enterprise," all added up to the fact that the Mountain Man when he went West was a complex character. But in his complexity was a clearly discernible pattern—the pattern of Jacksonian Man in search of respectability and success in terms recognized by the society he had left behind. His goal was, of course, the pursuit of happiness. But happiness, contrary to Rousseauistic expectations, was not found in the wilderness; it was an integral product of society and civilization.

If the Mountain Man was indeed Jacksonian Man, then there are at least three senses in which this concept has importance. First, more clearly than anything else a statistical and occupational view of the various callings of the Mountain Man tentatively indicates the incredible rate and the surprising *nature* of social and economic change in the West. In little more than two decades most of the surviving enterprising men had left the fur trade for more lucrative and presumably more useful occupations. And by their choice of occupations it is clear that in the Far West a whole step in the settlement process had been virtually skipped. They may have dreamed of "Arcadia," but when they turned to the task of settling the West as fast as possible, the former Mountain Men and perhaps others like them brought with them all the aspects of an "industrial," mercantile and quasi-urban society. The opera house went up almost simultaneously with the ranch, and the Bank of Missouri was secured before the land was properly put into hay.

Secondly, as explorers—men who searched out the hidden places in the western wilderness—the Mountain Men as Jacksonian Men looked with a flexible eye upon the new land. Unlike the Hudson's Bay explorer who looked only for beaver and immediate profit, the Mountain Man looked to the future and the development of the West, not as a vast game preserve, but as a land like the one he had known back home.

> "Much of this vast waste of territory belongs to the Republic of the United States," wrote Zenas Leonard from San Francisco Bay in 1833. "What a theme to contemplate its settlement and civilization. Will the jurisdiction of the federal government ever succeed in civilizing the thousands of savages now roaming over these plains, and her hardy freeborn population here plant their homes, build their towns and cities, and say here shall the arts and sciences of civilization take root and flourish? Yes, here, even in this remote part of the Great West before many years will these hills and valleys be greeted with the enlivening sound of the workman's hammer, and the merry whistle of the ploughboy . . . we have good reason to suppose that the territory *west* of the mountains will some day be equally as important to the nation as that on the east."[26]

In 1830 in a famous letter to John H. Eaton, the Secretary of War, Jedediah S. Smith, David E. Jackson and William L. Sublette aired their views on the possibilities of the West. Smith made clear that a wagon road route suitable for settlers existed all the way to Oregon, and Sublette dramatized the point when he brought ten wagons and two dearborns and even a milch cow over the mountains as far as the Wind River rendezvous. Their report made abundantly clear that in their opinion the future of the West lay with settlers rather than trappers. Indeed they were worried that the English at Fort Vancouver might grasp this fact before the American government.[27] In short, as explorers and trappers theirs was a broad-ranging, flexible, settler-oriented, public view of the Far West.

Tied in with this and of the greatest significance is a third and final point. Not only did they *see* a settler's future in the West, but at least some of the Mountain Men were most eager to see to it that such a future was *guaranteed* by the institutions of the United States Government which must be brought West and extended over all the wild new land to protect the settler in the enjoyment of his own "vine and fig tree." The Mexican Government, unstable, and blown by whim or caprice, could not secure the future, and the British Government, at least in North America, was under the heel of monopoly. France was frivolous and decadent. Russia was a sinister and backward despotism. Only the free institutions of Jacksonian America would make the West safe for enterprise. So strongly did he feel about this that in 1841 the Mountain Man Moses "Black" Harris sent a letter to one Thornton Grimsley offering him the command of 700 men, of which he was one, who were eager to "join the standard of their country, and make a clean sweep of what is called the Origon [*sic*] Territory; that is clear it of British and Indians." Outraged not only at British encroachments, he was also prepared to "march through to California" as well.[28] It may well have been this spirit that settled the Oregon question and brought on the Mexican War.[29]

Settlement, security, stability, enterprise, free enterprise, a government of laws which, in the words of Jackson himself, confines "itself to equal *protection*, and as Heaven does its rains, showers its favors alike on the high and the low, the rich and the poor,"[30] all of these shaped the Mountain Man's vision of the West and his role in its development. It was called Manifest Destiny. But long before John L. O'Sullivan nicely turned the phrase in the *Democratic Review*,[31] the Mountain Man as Jacksonian Man—a "venturous conservative"—was out in the West doing his utmost to lend the Almighty a helping hand. James Clyman perhaps put it most simply:

> Here lies the bones of old Black Harris
> who often traveled beyond the far west
> and for the freedom of Equal rights
> He crossed the snowy mountain Hights
> was free and easy kind of soul
> Especially with a Belly full.[32]

Notes

1. Washington Irving, *The Rocky Mountains: or, Scenes, Incidents, and Adventures in the Far West* (2 vols.; Philadelphia, 1837), I, 27.
2. Bernard De Voto, "Introduction," *The Life and Adventures of James P. Beckwourth*, ed. T. D. Bonner (New York, 1931), p. xxvii.
3. Quoted in Dorothey O. Johansen, "Introduction," *Robert Newell's Memoranda* (Portland, Ore., 1959), p. 2.
4. *Ibid.*, pp. 2–3; see also Ray A. Billington, *The Far Western Frontier* (New York, 1956), p. 44.
5. Billington, pp. 46–47; Robert Glass Cleland, *This Reckless Breed of Men* (New York, 1952), pp. 24–25; Bernard De Voto, *Across the Wide Missouri* (Boston, 1947), pp. 96–104. See also Henry Nash Smith, *Virgin Land* (Boston, 1950), pp. 59–70, 81–89. My portrait is a composite derived, but not quoted from the above sources.
6. Richard Hofstadter, *The American Political Tradition* (New York, 1955), p. 57.
7. *Ibid.*, p. 59.
8. *Ibid.*, p. 57.
9. Marvin Meyers, *The Jacksonian Persuasion* (New York, 1960), pp. 33–56.
10. Quoted in *ibid.*, p. 43.
11. W. A. Ferris, *Life in the Rocky Mountains*, ed. Paul C. Phillips (Denver, Colo., 1940), p. 1.
12. Harrison C. Dale, *The Ashley-Smith Explorations and the Discovery of a Central Route to the Pacific, 1822–1829*, rev. ed. (Glendale, Calif., 1941), pp. 57–61.
13. Dale L. Morgan, *Jedediah Smith* (Indianapolis and New York, 1953), pp. 145–48; Ferris, pp. 150, 156, 158.
14. James Ohio Pattie, *Personal Narrative*, ed. Timothey Flint (Cincinnati, 1831), *passim.*
15. Thomas James, *Three Years Among the Indians and Mexicans*, ed. Milo M. Quaife (Chicago, 1953), pp. 9–10.
16. *Ibid.*, p. 100. When his store failed, Thomas James set out in May 1821 on a trading venture to Santa Fe. By July of 1822 he had returned to his home in Illinois.
17. This study is based upon the lives of the Mountain Men whose entrance into the Rocky Mountain fur trade during the period 1805–45 can be proven, and who fit the criteria listed below. As anyone who has worked in the field will undoubtedly understand, the estimated one-thousand-man total given for those who would possibly qualify for consideration under these criteria represents merely an informed guess, since it is impossible with present-day evidence to determine with accuracy *all* of the Mountain Men who entered the West during this period. The data upon which this study is based is the sum total of men and careers that the extensive investigation described below has yielded. The author believes this to be the most extensive such investigation undertaken to date and also the largest number of such Mountain Men and careers located as of this time. However, in presenting this statistical analysis, the author wishes to stress the tentativeness of the conclusions herein reached. Further study of those whose "other occupations were indeterminable," and those "whose other occupations are probable" quite obviously might alter the present statistical results to a significant degree, and though the attempt was made to determine the occupations of as many men as possible, the author wishes specifically to acknowledge this possibility.

The basic sources for this sample study were: 1) General histories of the western states. In this respect the pioneer register in H. H. Bancroft's *History of California* proved to be particularly useful. 2) Original and modern editions of the relevant fur trade classics listed in Henry Raup Wagner and Charles Camp, *Plains and Rockies.* 3) The many available monographs and biographies relating to the fur trade such as those by Hiram M. Chittenden, Paul C. Phillips, Dale L. Morgan and John E. Sunder. 4) The files of historical journals containing materials on the fur trade of the Far West. 5) Reports submitted to the United States Government and published in the House and Senate document series. 6) Newspapers and periodicals for the fur trade period. In this latter category the author's research was by no means complete, nor was it possible to carry out the research project to the extent of consulting the multitude of local and county histories that almost certainly would have yielded further information. Enough research was conducted in these latter two categories of materials, however, to indicate the probable extent of their utility, which the author deemed insufficient for the present purposes.

The criteria for selecting the men to be included in the study are relatively simple. 1) They must have been associated with the fur trapping enterprise during the period 1805–45. 2) They must have pursued their trapping activities in the Rocky Mountains, northern or southern; hence the term Mountain Man. 3) They could not be employees of the American Fur Company, nor engagées at any of the Missouri River trading posts. The American Fur Company men are excluded from this study for two reasons: first, because the majority of them were river traders, not Mountain Men and they have never been classified under the old stereotyped images; secondly, of those few American Fur men who did go into the mountains in this period a large percentage were killed. Further study of the survivors, however, indicates that they too changed occupations much as did the Mountain Men. (See for example the career of Warren A. Ferris.)

18. This conclusion is deduced by the author primarily upon the basis of their residence during this period in places far removed from fur trapping or trading activities.
19. Kit Carson, *Autobiography,* ed. Milo M. Quaife (Chicago, 1935), p. 135.
20. Quoted in Leroy Hafen, "Louis Vasquez," *The Colorado Magazine,* X (1933), 17. De Voto's nickname for Vasquez appears in *Across the Wide Missouri,* p. xxvi.
21. *Ibid.,* p. 19.
22. *Ibid.,* p. 20.
23. Jedediah Smith to Ralph Smith, Wind River, East Side of the Rocky Mountains, December 24, 1829. MS. Kansas State Historical Society. Also reproduced in Morgan, *Jedediah Smith,* pp. 351–54.
24. Jedediah S. Smith to Ralph Smith, Blue River, fork of Kansas, 30 miles from the Ponnee Villages, September 10, 1830. MS. Kansas State Historical Society. Also reproduced in Morgan, *Jedediah Smith,* pp. 355–56.
25. St. Louis *Enquirer* quoted in Donald McKay Frost, *Notes on General Ashley* (Barre, Mass., 1960), p. 67. Little Rock *Gazette* quoted in Leroy R. Hafen, "The Bean-Sinclair Party of Rocky Mountain Trappers, 1830–32," *The Colorado Magazine,* XXXI (1954), 163.
26. Zenas Leonard, *Narrative of the Adventures of Zenas Leonard,* ed. John C. Ewers (Norman, Okla., 1959), pp. 94–95.
27. Reproduced in Morgan, *Jedediah Smith,* pp. 343–48.
28. Quoted in Charles L. Camp, ed. *James Clyman Frontiersman* (Portland, Ore., 1960), pp. 61–62.

29. Ray Allen Billington, *The Far Western Frontier*, pp. 154–73. See also Frederick Merk, *Manifest Destiny and Mission in American History* (New York, 1963).
30. James D. Richardson, ed. *A Compilation of the Messages and Papers of the Presidents 1789–1897* (1900), II, 590–91. Italics mine.
31. John L. O'Sullivan, "Annexation," unsigned article, *United States Magazine and Democratic Review*, XVII (July-August 1845), 797–98. See also his more popular statement in the New York *Morning News*, December 27, 1845.
32. Camp, *James Clyman Frontiersman*, p. 64.

The Antislavery Myth

C. Vann Woodward

Layers of fantasy and romance have come to cloud the historical reality of the Northern position on the slavery issue before the Civil War. Marshalling his facts with sophistication and skill, C. Vann Woodward, former President of the American Historical Association and Sterling Professor of History at Yale, reviews the status of historical study on the antislavery question. Noting that the antislavery myth gained its greatest measure of vitality only after the Civil War was ended, Woodward takes direct aim at the mythological trappings that still adhere to the Underground Railroad; and, more importantly, the revered notion that racial inhumanity was a condition only to be found in the pre-war South. Woodward's thesis suggests that the Antislavery Myth was a Northern exercise in atonement for social guilt. The Mason-Dixon Line did not successfully divide slavery from freedom in antebellum America.

Slavery and the Civil War were prolific breeders of myth, and their fertility would seem to wax rather than wane with the passage of time. Neither the proslavery myths of the South nor the antislavery myths of the North ceased to grow after the abolition of the Peculiar Institution. In fact they took on new life, struck new roots and flourished more luxuriantly than ever. Both myths continually found new sources of nourishment in the changing psychological needs and regional policies of North and South. The South used the proslavery myth to salve its wounds, lighten its burden of guilt and, most of all, to rationalize and defend the system of caste and segregation that was developed in place of the old order. The North, as we shall see, had deeply felt needs of its own to be served by an antislavery myth, needs that were sufficient at all times to keep the legend vital and growing to meet altered demands.

In late years the proslavery myth and the plantation legend have been subjected to heavy critical erosion from historians, sociologists and psychologists. So damaging has this attack been that little more is heard of the famous school for civilizing savages, peopled with happy slaves and benevolent masters. Shreds and pieces of the myth are still invoked as props to the crumbling defenses of segregation, but conviction has drained out of it, and it has been all but relegated to the limbo of dead or obsolescent myths.

From "The Antislavery Myth," by C. Vann Woodward. Reprinted from *The American Scholar*, XXXI (Spring 1962), 312–328.

Nothing like this can be said of the antislavery myth. Its potency is attested by a steady flow of historical works by journalists and reputable scholars. It is obvious that the myth can still dim the eye and quicken the pulse as well as warp the critical judgment. Apart from the fact that it is a creation of the victor rather than the vanquished, there are other reasons for the undiminished vitality of the antislavery myth. One is that it has not been subjected to as much critical study as has the proslavery myth.

Before turning to certain recent evidence of the exuberant vitality of the antislavery myth, however, it is interesting to note two penetrating critical studies of some of its components. Larry Gara, in *The Liberty Line: The Legend of the Underground Railroad,* addresses himself to a limited but substantial element of the myth. No aspect of the myth has so deeply engaged the American imagination and entrenched itself in the national heritage as the underground railroad, and no aspect so well reflects what we fondly believe to be the more generous impulses of national character. It is a relief to report that Mr. Gara is a temperate scholar and has avoided handling his subject with unnecessary rudeness. By the time he finishes patiently peeling away the layers of fantasy and romance, however, the factual substance is painfully reduced and the legend is revealed as melodrama. Following the assumptions that the better critics of the proslavery legend make about the slave, he assumes that "abolitionists, after all, were human," and that the "actual men and women of the abolition movement, like the slaves themselves, are far too complex to fit into a melodrama."

One very human thing the authors of the melodrama did was to seize the spotlight. They elected themselves the heroes. It was not that the abolitionists attempted to stage *Othello* without the princely Moor, but they did relegate the Moor to a subordinate role. The role assigned him was largely passive—that of the trembling, helpless fugitive completely dependent on his noble benefactors. The abolitionist was clearly the hero, and as Gerrit Smith, one of them, put it, the thing was brought off by the "Abolitionists and the Abolitionists only." As Mr. Gara points out, however, it took a brave, resourceful and rebellious slave to make good an escape, not one temperamentally adapted to subordinate roles—no Uncle Tom, as abolitionists often discovered. Moreover, by the time he reached the helping hands of the underground railroad conductors—if he ever did in fact—he had already completed the most perilous part of his journey, the southern part.

Another important actor in the drama of rescue who was crowded offstage by the abolitionists was the free Negro. According to the antislavery leader James G. Birney, the assistance of the fugitives was "almost uniformly managed by the colored people. I know nothing of them generally till they are past." The fugitive slaves had good reason to mistrust any white man, and in the opinion of Mr. Gara the majority of those who completed their flight to freedom did so without a ride on the legendary U.G.R.R.

Still another human failing of the legendmakers was exaggeration, and in this the abolitionists were ably assisted by their adversaries, the slaveholders, who no more understated their pecuniary losses than the abolitionists underestimated their heroic exploits. Under analysis the "flood" of fugitives diminishes to a trickle. As few as were the manumissions, they were double the number of fugitives in 1860 according to the author, and by far the greater number of fugitives never got out of the slave states. Another and even more fascinating distortion is the legend of conspiracy and secrecy associated with the U.G.R.R. The obvious fact was that the rescue of fugitive slaves was the best possible propaganda for the antislavery cause. We are mildly admonished that the U.G.R.R was "not the well-organized and mysterious institution of the legend." "Far from being secret," we are told, "it was copiously and persistently publicized, and there is little valid evidence for the existence of a widespread underground conspiracy."

But there remains the haunting appeal and enchantment of the secret stations, the disguised "conductors," and the whole "underground" and conspiratorial aspect of the legend that is so hard to give up. "Stories are still repeated," patiently explains Mr. Gara, "about underground tunnels, mysterious signal lights in colored windows, peculiarly placed rows of colored bricks in houses or chimneys to identify the station, and secret rooms for hiding fugitives." These stories he finds to be without basis in fact. While we must continue to bear with our Midwestern friends and their family traditions, we are advised that, "Hearsay, rumor, and persistent stories handed down orally from generation to generation are not proof of anything."

The most valuable contribution this study makes is the revelation of how the legend grew. It was largely a postwar creation, and it sprang from a laudable impulse to be identified with noble deeds. Family pride, local pride and regional pride were fed by abolitionist reminiscences and floods of memoirs and stories. "Every barn that ever housed a fugitive, and some that hadn't," remarks Mr. Gara, "were listed as underground railroad depots." There were thousands of contributors to the legend, but the greatest was Professor Wilbur H. Siebert, whose first book, *The Underground Railroad from Slavery to Freedom,* appeared in 1898. In the nineties he painstakingly questioned hundreds of surviving antislavery workers, whose letters and responses to questionnaires Mr. Gara has reexamined. Mr. Siebert accepted their statements at face value "on the ground that the memories of the aged were more accurate than those of young people." The picture that emerged in his big book was that of "a vast network of secret routes," connecting hundreds of underground stations, operated by 3,200 "conductors"—the very minimum figure, he insisted. This work fathered many subsequent ones, which borrowed generously from it. There has been no lag in legend-building since. "The greater the distance," observes Mr. Gara, "the more enchantment seems to adhere to all aspects of the underground railroad, the legend that grew up around it, and its role in America's heritage."

A second and more elaborate aspect of the antislavery myth is the legend that the Mason and Dixon Line not only divided slavery from freedom in antebellum America, but that it also set apart racial inhumanity in the South from benevolence, liberality and tolerance in the North. Like the Underground Railroad Legend, the North Star Legend (for lack of another name) was a postwar creation. Looking back through a haze of passing years that obscured historical realities, the myth-makers credited the North with the realization in its own society of all the war aims for which it fought (or eventually proclaimed): not only Union and Freedom, but Equality as well. True, the North did not win the third war aim (or if it did, quickly forfeited it), but it nevertheless practiced what it preached, even if it failed to get the South to practice it, and had been practicing it in exemplary fashion for some time.

For a searching examination of the North Star Legend we are indebted to Leon F. Litwack, *North of Slavery: The Negro in the Free States, 1790–1860*. He starts with the assumption that, "The inherent cruelty and violence of southern slavery requires no further demonstration, but this does not prove northern humanity." On racial attitudes of the two regions he quotes with approval the observation of Tocqueville in 1831: "The prejudice of race appears to be stronger in the states that have abolished slavery than in those where it still exists." White supremacy was a national, not a regional credo, and politicians of the Democratic, the Whig and the Republican parties openly and repeatedly expressed their allegiance to the doctrine. To do otherwise was to risk political suicide. "We, the Republican party, are the white man's party," declared Senator Lyman Trumbull of Illinois. And, as Mr. Litwack observes, "Abraham Lincoln, in his vigorous support of both white supremacy and denial of equal rights for Negroes, simply gave expression to almost universal American convictions." These convictions were to be found among Free Soil adherents and were not unknown among antislavery and abolitionist people themselves.

One reason for the unrestrained expression of racial prejudice from politicians was that the Negro was almost entirely disfranchised in the North and was therefore politically helpless. Far from sharing the expansion of political democracy, the Negro often suffered disfranchisement as a consequence of white manhood suffrage. By 1840 about 93 percent of the free Negroes in the North were living in states that excluded them from the polls. By 1860 only 6 percent of the Northern Negro population lived in the five states that provided legally for their suffrage. In only three states were they allowed complete parity with whites in voting. Even in those New England states doubts lingered concerning the practical exercise of equal political rights. As late as 1869, the year before the ratification of the 15th Amendment, New York State voted against equal suffrage rights for Negroes. Four Western states legally excluded free Negroes from entry.

In Northern courtrooms as at Northern polls racial discrimination prevailed. Five states prohibited Negro testimony when a white man was a party to a case, and Oregon prohibited Negroes from holding real estate, making contracts or maintaining lawsuits. Only in Massachusetts were Negroes admitted as jurors, and that not until the eve of the Civil War. The absence of Negro judges, jurors, witnesses and lawyers helps to explain the heavily disproportionate number of Negroes in Northern prisons.

Custom, extralegal codes and sometimes mob law served to relegate the Negro to a position of social inferiority and impose a harsh rule of segregation in Northern states. According to Mr. Litwack:

> In virtually every phase of existence, Negroes found themselves systematically separated from whites. They were either excluded from railway cars, omnibuses, stagecoaches, and steamboats or assigned to special "Jim Crow" sections; they sat, when permitted, in secluded and remote corners of theaters and lecture halls; they could not enter most hotels, restaurants, and resorts, except as servants; they prayed in "Negro pews" in white churches, and if partaking of the sacrament of the Lord's Supper, they waited until the whites had been served the bread and wine. Moreover, they were often educated in segregated schools, punished in segregated prisons, nursed in segregated hospitals, and buried in segregated cemeteries.

Housing and job opportunities were severely limited. A Boston Negro wrote in 1860 that "it is five times as hard to get a house in a good location in Boston as it is in Philadelphia; and it is ten times as difficult for a colored mechanic to get work here as it is in Charleston." The earlier verdict of Tocqueville continued to ring true. "Thus the Negro is free," he wrote, "but he can share neither the rights, nor the pleasures, nor the labor, nor the afflictions, nor the tomb of him whose equal he has been declared to be; and he cannot meet him upon fair terms in life or in death."

In Northern cities with large Negro populations, violent mob action occurred with appalling frequency. Between 1832 and 1849 mobs touched off five major anti-Negro riots in Philadelphia. Mobs destroyed homes, churches and meeting halls, and forced hundreds to flee the city. An English Quaker visiting Philadelphia in 1849 remarked that there was probably no city "where dislike, amounting to hatred of the coloured population, prevails more than in the city of brotherly love!"

The Southern historian will be struck with the remarkable degree to which the South recapitulated a generation later the tragic history of race relations in the North. Once slavery was destroyed as a means of social control and subordination of the Negro, and Reconstruction was overthrown, the South resorted to many of the devices originally developed in the North to keep the Negro in his "place." There was more delay in the resort to segregation than generally supposed, but once it came toward the end of the century it was harsh and thorough. One important difference was that in the antebellum North the Negro was sometimes free to organize, protest and join white sympathizers to advance his cause and improve his position.

His success in these efforts was unimpressive, however, for by 1860, as Mr. Litwack says, "despite some notable advances, the Northern Negro remained largely disfranchised, segregated, and economically oppressed." The haven to which the North Star of the legend guided the fugitive from slavery was a Jim Crow haven.

While these two studies of the antislavery myth are valuable and significant, they are slight in scope and modest in aim when compared with the far more ambitious—and traditional—book of Dwight Lowell Dumond, *Antislavery: The Crusade for Freedom in America.* Elaborately documented, profusely illustrated and ornately bound, this massive volume is easily twice the bulk of an average-sized book. It covers the entire scope of the organized antislavery movement in this country, as well as preorganizational beginnings, and is the most extensive work on the subject in print. Represented as the result of "more than thirty years" of research by the Michigan historian, it is the outcome of a lifetime absorption in antislavery literature. It is doubtful that any other scholar has lavished such devoted study upon this vast corpus of writings.

The author's total absorption with his source materials is, indeed, the key to the theory of historiography upon which this remarkable work would appear to be based. That theory is that the purest history is to be derived from strict and undivided attention to source materials—in this case chiefly the writings, tracts and propaganda, running to millions upon millions of words, of the antislavery people themselves. If the author is aware of any of the scholarly studies of slavery and antislavery that have appeared in the last generation or more, he does not betray awareness by reference to the questions they have raised, by use of methods they have developed, or by incorporation of findings they have published. Neither the problems of slavery and antislavery that have been pressed upon the historian by new learning in psychology, anthropology, sociology and economics, nor the questions that have been raised by fresh encounters with Africa and Afro-Americans and by new experience with reformers and revolutionists and their motivation, receive any attention from the author. It is difficult to comment intelligently upon a work that so persistently and successfully avoids engagement with the contemporary mind, its assumptions, its preoccupations, its urgent questions, its whole frame of reference.

Mr. Dumond's treatment of slavery and the abolitionists admits of no complexities or ambiguities beyond the fixed categories of right and wrong. All of his abolitionists are engaged in a single-minded crusade wholly motivated by a humanitarian impulse to destroy an evil institution and succor its victims. They are moral giants among the pygmies who cross their will or fail to share their views. The single exception is William Lloyd Garrison, for whom he shares the strong distaste of his onetime collaborator Gilbert H. Barnes, the Midwestern historian. "In fact," writes Dumond (the italics are his), *"he was a man of distinctly narrow limitations among the giants of the antislavery movement."* Why Garrison falls so far short of the stature of the giants is not quite clear, but we are assured that he was "insufferably arrogant," given to "cheap cynicism" and withal "a timid soul except when safely behind the editorial desk."

Apart from Garrison, the antislavery leaders command Mr. Dumond's unqualified admiration, and his praise of them is unbounded. "What a combination of intellect, courage, and Christian faith!" he exclaims in describing the founders of the American Antislavery Society. The abolitionists are indeed due a redress of grievances at the hands of the historians, for they have had something less than justice from the craft. They are remembered more as pictured by caricatures such as Henry James drew in *The Bostonians* than for their good works and genuine merits. The wild eccentricities, the fierce come-outerism, the doctrinaire extravagancies and the armchair bloodlusts of some of the abolitionists have been stressed and repeated to the neglect of the dedicated and fearless work they did in the face of ridicule, mob violence and all the pressures that wealth and established order can bring to bear upon dissenters. Their cause was just, and among their numbers were men and women of courage, intelligence and moral force. They deserve their due and need a sympathetic defender.

The trouble with Mr. Dumond as historian of the antislavery movement is his total involvement. This involvement extends beyond hatred of slavery and approval of abolition. It commits him as well to the style and tone and temper, the immediacy of indignation, the very idiom and rhetoric of a movement of thought that took its shape from intellectual influences and social conditions existing nearly a century and a half ago. The effect is startling. The rhythm and color of his prose is in perfect keeping with the style and tone of the scores of lithographs and prints from old abolitionist tracts that serve appropriately to illustrate the book. The author paints just what he sees, but he sees everything through the eyes of the 1830's. The result is more than an anachronism. It gives the effect of a modern primitive, a Henri Rousseau of historiography.

Any treatment of the antislavery movement necessarily involves some treatment of the institution it opposed. Mr. Dumond's conception of slavery would seem to have taken shape in considerable degree from the antislavery literature he has so thoroughly mastered. At any rate, he quotes liberally from this literature in characterizing slavery. Among other things, he quotes a poem by Timothy Dwight, published in 1794, the year before he became president of Yale. The last stanza of it reads as follows:

> Why shrinks yon slave, with horror, from his meat? / Heavens! 'tis his flesh, the wretch is whipped to eat. / Why streams the life-blood from that female's throat? / She sprinkled gravy on a guest's new coat!

"Poetic license?" asks the historian. "Exaggeration? Fantasy? *Only half the truth, if a thousand witnesses are to be believed.*" And they, he assures us, are to be believed.

Mr. Dumond selects Theodore Dwight Weld's *American Slavery As It Is,* published in 1839, as "the greatest of the antislavery pamphlets," and still the best historical authority on slavery. "It is an encyclopedia of knowledge. It is a book of horrors," he writes. Weld himself correctly described it as "a work of incalculable value" to the abolitionist cause. "Facts and testimonies are troops, weapons and victory, all in one," he wrote. The principles governing its composition are suggested by a letter to Weld from two editorial advisors, Sereno and Mary Streeter: "Under the head of personal cruelty [you] will be obliged to reject much testimony; and this is not because the facts are not well authenticated but because those which are merely *horrid* must give place to those which are absolutely diabolical." Absolutely diabolical or not, in the opinion of Professor Dumond, "It is as close as history can come to the facts." According to his theory of historical evidence, "Diaries and plantation records are largely worthless because slaveholders never kept a record of their own evil ways."

The strong sexual theme that pervades antislavery literature often took a prurient turn, but in Mr. Dumond's hands the pruriency is transmuted by bold treatment. The presence of miscegenation is attested by the Census of 1860 and the proportion of the colored population of the South that was of mixed blood. But to Mr. Dumond, sexual exploitation becomes very nearly the basis of the institution of slavery. "Its prevalence leads to the inescapable conclusion," he writes, "that it was the basis—unspoken to be sure—of much of the defense of the institution." Ulrich B. Phillips, the Southern historian of slavery, doubtless betrayed a certain blindness when he reported that in all the records he studied he could find only one instance of deliberate "breeding" of slaves, and that an unsuccessful one in colonial Massachusetts. To Mr. Dumond, however, it is plain as day that the "breeding" was practiced by *all* slaveholders: "That is exactly what slave owners did with the slaves, and there were no exceptions." To the Georgia historian there were no instances, to the Michigan historian no exceptions! What is one to tell the children?

Mr. Dumond's main subject, of course, is not slavery but antislavery. In his treatment of this great theme the myth is slightly muted, but it nevertheless pulses powerfully through the whole narrative. The Underground Railroad is described as "a highly romantic enterprise" that became "well organized." In these pages it operates with all the enchanting conspiracy and secrecy of the legend, with fugitive slaves "secreted in livery stables, in attics, in storerooms, under featherbeds, in secret passages, in all sorts of out of the way places." There was one hayloft in Detroit that "was always full of Negroes."

In Professor Dumond's history the North Star Legend is given very nearly full credence. In striking contrast with the account rendered in detail by Mr. Litwack, we are informed that Negroes "continued to vote without interruption in New Hampshire, Vermont, Rhode Island, and in the two slave states of New York and New Jersey," and that there were never "any distinctions whatever in criminal law, judicial procedure, and punishments" in any New England states. "Negroes were citizens in all of these [free?] states," he writes (leaving it unclear how many). "They were citizens by enjoyment of full political equality, by lack of any statements to the contrary in any constitution or law, by complete absence of legal distinctions based on color, and by specific legal and constitutional declaration, and any statements to the contrary by courts, federal or state, were contrary to historical fact and are worthless as historical evidence." There is no hint of the thoroughgoing system of Northern segregation described by Mr. Litwack. It is admitted that one might "find a less liberal attitude toward free Negroes" in the Midwestern states, but that is easily accounted for: "There was a preponderance of Southern immigrants in the populations." In spite of this, we learn that in Jackson's time, "the Northern people, freeing themselves of the last vestiges of slavery, moved forward in a vast liberal reform movement."

The theory Mr. Dumond applies to the antislavery movement colors and coerces his reading of the whole of American history from the Revolution through the Civil War. This reading amounts to a revival of the long discredited theory of the Slave Power Conspiracy, a dominant hypothesis two or three generations ago. Slavery, we are told, "gave clay feet to Patrick Henry . . . and I suspect to Washington and Jefferson as well." Of the Revolutionary leaders he writes: "Those men were perfectly willing to spread carnage over the face of the earth to establish their own claim to freedom, but lacked the courage to live by their assertion of the natural rights of men." Of the Presidential contest of 1800 we are told: "This election enabled Jefferson to lay solidly the foundations of the party of agrarianism, slavery, and decentralization." Any mention of Jefferson is accompanied by a reminder that he owned slaves. The achievement of a group is discredited with the phrase, "slaveholders all." The Virginia Dynasty, its heirs and successors of the next three decades, and most of their acts and works including the Constitution, fare pretty harshly under this restricted historical criterion.

The whole sectional conflict that eventually erupted in the Civil War is construed, of course, in terms of right versus wrong, North against South. Civil War historians will be interested to learn that "there was complete coordination by the Congress, the President, and the field commanders of the Army" in their mutual determination to abolish slavery at the earliest possible moment. This revelation will require a good deal of revision in accepted views, which take into account a great lack of coordination among those distracted branches of the wartime government.

It is possible that Professor Dumond's interpretations of American history might be traced directly to an unfortunate theory of historical method. Neither this nor the extended criticism of his work already undertaken would be worth the effort, however, were it not for what the book reveals about the present vitality and amazing persistence of the antislavery myth. His book is the latest and fullest embodiment of the myth. Yet it comes with endorsements of unqualified praise from leading authorities in the field. The wide flaps of the dust jacket bear such recommendations from the three foremost present-day historians of the American Civil War, followed by the equally enthusiastic praise of prominent historians from four of our most respected universities. These are not men who share Mr. Dumond's restrictive concepts of historiography, nor are they given to bestowing praise lightly. They undoubtedly mean what they say. What two of them say is that this book is "definitive," and all agree that from their point of view it is wholly satisfying.

One would like to know more about their reasoning. Several of them refer directly or obliquely to present-day social problems that are a heritage of slavery, meaning segregation and the movement for Negro rights. But surely one can establish his position upon such clear-cut contemporary moral problems as these without compromising the standards of historical criticism. And by this time, one hopes, it is possible to register a stand on the slavery issue without feigning the apocalyptic rages of a John Brown. No, these are not adequate or convincing explanations, at least for the reactions of these particular historians.

In all probability the real reason why this ponderous, fierce and humorless book is handled with such piety and solemnity is the very fact that it does embody one of the great American myths. We have never faced up to the relationship between myth and history. Without tackling the semantic difficulties involved, we know that *myth* has more than pejorative usages and that it can be used to denote more than what one deems false about the other man's beliefs. In the non-pejorative sense myths are images, or collections of them, charged with values, aspirations, ideals and meanings. In the words of Mark Schorer, they are "the instruments by which we continually struggle to make our experience intelligible to ourselves." Myths *can* be, in short, "a good thing." No man in his right mind, and surely not a responsible historian, will knowingly and wantonly destroy a precious thing. And no doubt some would hesitate to lay hands on a book that, improperly though it may be, got itself identified as a repository of cherished values.

Serious history is the critique of myths, however, not the embodiment of them. Neither is it the destruction of myths. One of the great national myths is the equality of man, embodied in the Declaration of Independence. Tocqueville's study of equality in America is a valid critique of the myth, with neither the intention nor the effect of destroying it or doing it injury. Henry Nash Smith's *Virgin Land* provides a valid critique of the West's Myth of the Garden and symbols of the frontier without succumbing to impulses of iconoclasm. There is no comparable critique of the more elaborate myth—one might say mythology—of the South. What has been done in this respect has been mainly the work of imaginative writers rather than historians of the South. Historians have made a beginning, however, and a recent contribution by William R. Taylor, *Cavalier and Yankee,* which illuminates the legend of aristocratic grandeur, is an excellent illustration of what is needed.

As a result of such studies, intelligent, contemporary Americans can speak of the myth of equality without self-consciousness or cynicism, and embrace it without striking the pose of a defiant Jacksonian of the 1830's. Contemporary westerners are able to cherish and preserve frontier values without assuming the role of a Davy Crockett. And southerners can even salvage some of the aristocratic heritage without wallowing in the Plantation Legend.

As yet, however, the Yankee remains to be fully emancipated from his own legends of emancipation. Confront him with a given set of symbols and he will set his sense of humor aside, snap to attention and come to a full salute. In the ensuing rigidities of that situation, conversation tends to lag. The pertinent interjections by Mr. Gara on the U.G.R.R. and by Mr. Litwack on the North Star Legend, already noticed, may help to break the ice, but the thawing will probably be slow. The provocative suggestions of Stanley M. Elkins, in *Slavery: A Problem in American Institutional and Intellectual Life,* have been gravely rebuked for impropriety, if not impiety. The orthodox text is obviously still the gospel according to Mr. Dumond.

The big assignment on the Antislavery Myth still awaits a taker. The eventual taker, like any historian who would make myth the proper subject of his study, should be involved without running the risks of total involvement. It would help a great deal if he could contrive to bring detachment as well as sympathy to his task. It is also to be hoped that he might make legitimate use of irony as well as compassion. And, finally, no aspirant with inappropriate regional identifications need apply.

America as Peaceful Belligerent: Myth or Reality?

Glenn C. Price

Mission, destiny, and purpose have been bywords of the American past. They have often served as rationale for American expansionism, both internal and external. America's self-image as "redeemer nation," however, fits rather badly with what Glenn C. Price of Sonoma State College in California calls the "rhetoric of peace." The Mexican War clearly documents this inherent contradiction between professed values and overt actions. Testifying that as regards our basic national myths, "little difference is to be found between the intellectual community and the mass culture," Professor Price concludes that James K. Polk's justifications as to our conflict with Mexico "are classic formulations of the American illusion." This illusion of America as "peaceful belligerent" still enjoys a distinct measure of currency today.

The history of the United States since the founding of the nation by a war against Great Britain has certainly been no more pacific than that of other countries. There was the aggression against the Spanish in the Floridas; the unsuccessful invasion of Canada during the War of 1812; the War with Mexico in 1846–1848 and the filibustering expeditions of Americans into Mexico and Central America and the Caribbean during the 1850's; the war against Spain and the brutal war against the Filipinos for several years thereafter; and in this century the use of American military power in small Latin American countries as well as American participation in two world wars. This is not a record which indicates a disinclination to resort to mass violence. Perhaps some nations of Western Christendom have been more aggressive, some less so; but it is quite impossible to make out the American experience as uniquely restrained in the use of force, or as resorting to force for defensive purposes only.

The United States, however, has produced a rhetoric of peace which is unmatched by any other nation, and this continues to the present day. A typical current example of this prevailing American self-image is in a statement of McGeorge Bundy in July of 1965, when he was President Lyndon B. Johnson's special assistant for national security affairs. In an article defending American foreign policy he asserted that "a commitment to peace" is one of the "great strands" in "the operations of the United States in its relationships to the world." Bundy comes out of an American elite subculture,

From *Origins of the War with Mexico: the Polk-Stockton Intrigue,* by Glenn C. Price, The University of Texas Press (1967). Reprinted by permission of the publisher.

but the language he used demonstrates that on our basic national myths little difference is to be found between the intellectual community and the mass culture. He used the phrases in which generations of Americans have expressed such self-appraisals: "It is right to understand this country as a country of peace. It is a country built by people who came from struggle and strife in other countries." We have, Bundy granted, an "American tradition of battle" to be sure, but this has quite obviously been in the pursuit of peace, for "the inspiration of the nation, the purpose of its people, and therefore, by extension, the purpose of those who are elected by its people must be of peace."[1]

These assertions can be assessed meaningfully only as judgments of the United States in comparison with other nations; and when that assessment is made one must state flatly that Bundy's generalizations on the American record are simply wrong, that his statements are untrue. But it is appropriate that these expressions of self-esteem, these distortions of the American war record, should issue from the office of the President in 1965; they are in the authentic tradition of the American rhetoric of peace. It demonstrates, if demonstration were needed, the continuing necessity for a candid historical analysis of our wars—and of our explanations of our wars.

We have no more instructive experience in our past on this subject than the War against Mexico. It provides an extensive documentation of the unreconciled internal contradiction between professed values and patterns of action. The character of that war, in contrast to the American explanation of the War, is a classic form of the dilemma; this is at least partly because it occurred in a period when the faith in American virtue was wholly undiluted by sobering experience, when the belief in American uniqueness was still untouched by any felt ambiguities.

The two men who played the chief roles in the war intrigue of 1845 were representative men. President James K. Polk and Commodore Robert F. Stockton expressed their faith in American righteousness in their actions, and they expressed the myth of American innocence in their writings and addresses. A display of the contents of their minds about the United States as a nation among nations is the appropriate beginning for an analysis of the historical record on their actions.

In his Inaugural Address President Polk referred to the government of which he was assuming the executive leadership simply as "this most admirable and wisest system of well-organized self-government among men ever devised by human minds." This was not rodomontade for a ceremonial occasion; Polk was expressing the faith that was in him. Near the end of his term of office he wrote in his Diary that he had "filled the highest station on earth."[2]

The American mission, in Polk's mind, was literally a divine mission; he would have missed the sarcasm in the jibe that Americans thought of their nation as God's last, supreme effort to make a new start in the history of mankind. Polk's addresses are punctuated with references to God and God's country. In his Third Annual Message to Congress he said: "No country has been so much favored, or should acknowledge with deeper reverence the manifestations of the divine protection. An all-wise Creator directed and guarded us in our infant struggle for freedom and has constantly watched over our surprising progress until we have become one of the great nations of the earth."[3]

The United States, he said on another occasion, has achieved eminence painlessly. While "other nations have achieved glory at the price of suffering, distress, and impoverishment of their people," the people of the United States have won theirs "in the midst of an uninterrupted prosperity and of an increasing individual comfort and happiness."[4]

Polk's explanations of American foreign relations are classic formulations of the American illusion. In his Inaugural Address he complained that the United States was misunderstood by other nations: "Foreign powers do not seem to appreciate the true character of our government. Our Union is a confederation of independent States, whose policy is peace with each other and all the world. To enlarge its limits is to extend the dominions of peace over additional territories and increasing millions."[5]

During the War with Mexico the President informed Congress that it was "a source of high satisfaction to know that the relations of the United States with all other nations, with a single exception, are of the most amicable character." He followed this expression of gratification that the United States was engaged in only one war at the time with a statement of the American "spirit" on war and peace: "Sincerely attached to the policy of peace early adopted and steadily pursued by this government, I have anxiously desired to cultivate and cherish friendship and commerce with every foreign power. The Spirit and habits of the American people are favorable to the maintenance of such international harmony."[6]

The conviction of righteousness, the assurance of perfect virtue while waging war against Mexico, is nowhere better displayed than in a message which Polk sent to Congress, prepared by his Secretary of the Treasury, Robert J. Walker. In this document the Administration recommended the imposition of "burdensome" and "onerous" duties upon imports in Mexico through ports held by the armed forces of the United States; Polk thought this imposition would induce the Mexican people to seek relief from their suffering by forcing their rulers to accept the peace terms of the United States. The financial burden should be placed "upon our enemies, the people of Mexico, and not upon ourselves," the President explained, and then he communicated this remarkable formulation of American self-righteousness: "In the meantime it is not just that Mexico, by her obstinate persistence in this contest, should compel us to overthrow our own financial policy and arrest this great nation in her high and prosperous career."[7]

The President constantly spoke of the American devotion to peace. During the last months of the War against Mexico he said: "It has ever been our cherished policy to cultivate peace and good will with all nations, and this policy has been steadily pursued by me."[8] At the close of his term, when the United States had acquired half the area of Mexico as the fruit of the War, Polk began his address to Congress with high praise for American virtue. The representatives of the people had again gathered "under the benignant providence of Almighty God," he said, to "deliberate for the public good." He continued:

> The gratitude of the nation to the Sovereign Arbiter of All Human Events should be commensurate with the boundless blessings which we enjoy.
>
> Peace, plenty, and contentment reign throughout our borders, and our beloved country presents a sublime moral spectacle to the world.[9]

Polk was not a popular President. He was the first "dark horse" in the history of the office, and the experiment did not seem to be a success, either to his contemporaries or to historians for a half century and more following. During the last few decades, however, the President who acquired California by means of war against Mexico and thereupon announced that the United States presented a "sublime moral spectacle to the world" has been sharply upgraded by American historians. That curious revisionism has not been the consequence of new information; it is rather the product of a sufficiently self-advertised, tough-minded sophistication among historians in the United States in recent years. The current strength of the revisionist appraisal of Polk constitutes another reason for a more thorough analysis of the 1845 war intrigue in Texas.

Commodore Robert F. Stockton, Polk's agent in Texas in 1845, is not a major figure in American history and his career and his ideas are not well known. Here it will be helpful to look at some of Stockton's views on the role of the United States in the world in the middle of the nineteenth century.

A few years following the War with Mexico, Stockton was a United States senator from New Jersey. He spoke in the Senate in 1852 on the issue of "interventionism" by one nation in the affairs of other nations, an issue which had been raised by the unsuccessful effort of the Hungarians to establish their independence in 1848. That effort had been crushed by the intervention of the Russian army, and the "friends of freedom" in the United States welcomed Louis Kossuth, the Hungarian leader who had gone into exile. Most public men in America who spoke for the Hungarian cause attacked the Russian government for its intervention and asserted that it must be established as a principle of international law that no nation had the right to intervene in such a revolution under any conditions. Stockton did not agree. He said it would be a mistake for the United States to take that position "as long as there is a single despotic government existing whose people rise to demand the blessings of liberty." He described the situation in the world in the seventy-sixth year of the existence of the United States of America:

> Sir, when we cast our eyes over the world, everywhere, with the exception of America, we see the surface of the whole earth appropriated by absolute monarchs. The only country which enjoys Republican Government, and whose people adequately appreciate free institutions, is the United States. Those free institutions comprehend all that survives of free principles and political liberty. In them is concentrated all that is valuable of what man has ever achieved in qualifying himself for self-government. . . .
>
> We are, in truth, the residuary legatees of all that the blood and treasure of mankind, expended for four thousand years, have accomplished in the cause of human freedom. In our hands alone is the precious deposit. Before God and the world, we are responsible for the legacy. Not for our own benefit only, but the benefit of the whole family of man.

A man with that kind of vision of the unique value of his own society is not apt to hold himself to conventional rules and technicalities in the relations of men or of nations as he endeavors to preserve and enlarge a precious heritage. That "precious deposit" of liberty, Stockton said, should be developed and extended by war only under "peculiar circumstances," but it is apparent that he thought such circumstances would arise not infrequently. Since the "whole world, wherever you look," except for the United States was under monarchical governments, he desired to know "how the oppressed and fettered nations of the earth are to break their chains, and maintain themselves against the armies of despotism" if there should be a law of nations against intervention in their behalf.

Stockton concluded that the United States had "an indisputable and perfect right to interfere [in another nation] whenever, by such interference, she can promote her own interests and advance the cause of liberty."[10]

During the Presidency of James K. Polk the United States did intervene in a neighboring country; it promoted its own interests, in Stockton's words, and in the language of President Polk, it "extended the dominions of peace over additional territories." An understanding of the origins of that intervention is not to be found on the eve of the action. An examination of Mexican-American relations for the score of years before the War is necessary to comprehend the forces operating in the Polk-Stockton intrigue.

Notes

1. McGeorge Bundy, "The Uses of Responsibility: A Reply to Archibald MacLeish," *Saturday Review*, XLVIII (July 3, 1965), 13.
2. Inaugural Address, given on March 4, 1845, Richardson (ed.), *A Compilation of Messages and Papers*, IV, 375. The Diary entry was on Thursday, November 2, 1848, Milo Milton Quaife (ed.), *The Diary of James K. Polk*, IV, 177.

3. Third Annual Message, December 7, 1847, Richardson (ed.), *A Compilation of Messages and Papers*, IV, 533.
4. Fourth Annual Message, December 5, 1848, *ibid.*, p. 629.
5. Inaugural Address, given on March 4, 1845, *ibid.*, p. 375.
6. Second Annual Message, December 8, 1846, *ibid.*, p. 472.
7. Message given on March 30, 1847, *ibid.*, pp. 525–529.
8. Message given on December 7, 1847, *ibid.*, p. 533.
9. Message given on December 5, 1848, *ibid.*, p. 629.
10. [Samuel John Bayard], *A Sketch of the Life of Commodore Robert F. Stockton*, Appendix E, pp. 94–98.

Suggested Further Reading for Chapter 4

Lee Benson, *The Concept of Jacksonian Democracy: New York as a Test Case* (Princeton: Princeton University Press, 1961).

James L. Bugg (ed.), *Jacksonian Democracy: Myth or Reality?* (New York: Holt, Rinehart & Winston, Inc., 1962).

Larry Gara, "Propaganda Uses of the Underground Railroad," *Mid-America*, 34 (1952).

Marvin Meyers, *The Jacksonian Persuasion: Politics and Belief* (New York: Vintage Books, 1957).

Samuel Eliot Morison, Frederick Merk and Frank Freidel, *Dissent in Three American Wars* (Cambridge: Harvard University Press, 1970).

Edward Pessen, "The Egalitarian Myth and the American Social Reality: Wealth, Mobility and Equality in the 'Era of the Common Man,'" *American Historical Review*, 72 (1971).

Henry Nash Smith, *Virgin Land: The American West as Symbol and Myth* (New York: Vintage Books, 1962).

John William Ward, *Andrew Jackson: Symbol for an Age* (New York: Oxford University Press, 1955).

Barbara Welter, "The Cult of True Womanhood, 1820–1860," *American Quarterly*, 18 (1966).

"Those are the Confederate dead," said Sally Carrol simply.

They walked along and read the inscriptions, always only a name and a date, sometimes quite indecipherable.

"The last row is the saddest—see, 'way over there. Every cross has just a date on it, and the word 'Unknown.' "

She looked at him and her eyes brimmed with tears.

"I can't tell you how real it is to me, darling—if you don't know."

"How you feel about it is beautiful to me."

"No, no, it's not me, it's them—that old time that I've tried to have live in me. These were just men, unimportant evidently or they wouldn't have been 'unknown'; but they died for the most beautiful thing in the world—the dead South. You see," she continued, her voice still husky, her eyes glistening with tears, "people have these dreams they fasten onto things, and I've always grown up with that dream. It was so easy because it was all dead and there weren't any disillusions comin' to me. I've tried in a way to live up to those past standards of noblesse oblige—there's just the last remnants of it, you know, like the roses of an old garden dying all round us—streaks of strange courtliness and chivalry in some of these boys an' stories I used to hear from a Confederate soldier who lived next door, and a few old darkies. Oh, Harry, there was something, there was something! I couldn't ever make you understand, but it was there."

F. Scott Fitzgerald
The Ice Palace

5

THE MYTHOLOGY OF THE SOUTH

George Cochran Lambden, "The Consecration, 1861" (1865). Courtesy, Indianapolis Museum of Art, James E. Roberts Fund.

The Consecration: Southern romance.

English wood engraving, 1861. The Granger Collection.

The Desecration: Southern tragedy.

Introduction

The South is more than a geographical expression; it is at once a way of life and a way of mind. It remains a region struck by a sense of its uniqueness and proud of its traditions, its past, and its ceremonial style. Burdened with a history of frustration, poverty, defeat, and prejudice, in the view of the noted southern historian C. Vann Woodward, the southern imagination has sought compensation through mythical images. The vision of a hospitable and mannered society populated by contented Blacks, aristocratic cavaliers, and virtuous belles has come to supplant the South's true historical experience. In short, the South's collective consciousness has sought escape and isolation behind a boundary of sentiment. One of those to recognize the pervasiveness of the myth was the "progressive" historian Vernon Louis Parrington, who observed:

> A golden light still lingers upon the old plantation. Memories are still too dear to the Virginian to suffer any lessening of the reputed splendors of ante bellum days. The tragedy of a lost cause has woven itself into the older romance and endowed the tradition with an added sanction. It has long since spread beyond the confines of Virginia and become a national possession. North as well as South is so firmly convinced of its authenticity that realism has never had the temerity to meddle with it.

Thus has the South's search for a usable past and a sectional image signaled a retreat from reality and the enforcement of rigid opinions concerning her history.

The prevailing mood of the South—its distinct regional identification and mystique—balanced against the complexity of its historical past, then, has often proved an enigma to the historian. Forced to combat longstanding impressions, they have found doubly difficult the task of piecing together the dislocated and fragmentary evidence with which all history must deal. It is only of late that the interrelationships between the mythical and the historical South are becoming clear, as historians seek to reconsider southern history within the context of mythology.

Out of the process of reviewing hardening southern stereotypes—the collective products of southerners and northerners, at times abetted by historians themselves—has emerged yet another South. This new view suggests a region of complex social structure, populated not only by a southern gentry but also by frontiersmen, small farmers, and Unionists. The mythological approach to understanding the southern past has yielded significant new historical insight; and as the native southern historian George B. Tindall suggests in the article that leads this chapter, mythology can indeed become the "new frontier in Southern history." The way thus seems open to pursuing the theme of southern mythology more forcefully; in the interest of exploring this "new frontier" in some detail a separate chapter has been set aside to deal with it exclusively.

Mythology: A New Frontier in Southern History

George B. Tindall

Any discussion of the "reality" of history must take into account both that which actually happened (a difficult enough determination, to be sure) and that which has been perceived. This point finds particular emphasis in the essay which follows. George B. Tindall, Professor of History at the University of North Carolina, suggests that a proper rendering of southern historical reality must take particular account of the varied and elusive ways in which the American South has come to view herself and has been viewed by the nation at large.

The idea of the South—or more appropriately, the ideas of the South—belong in large part to the order of social myth. There are few areas of the modern world that have bred a regional mythology so potent, so profuse and diverse, even so paradoxical, as the American South. But the various mythical images of the South that have so significantly affected American history have yet to be subjected to the kind of broad and imaginative historical analysis that has been applied to the idea of the American West, particularly in Henry Nash Smith's *Virgin Land: The American West as Symbol and Myth.* The idea of the South has yet to be fully examined in the context of mythology, as essentially a problem of intellectual history.

To place the ideas of the South in the context of mythology, of course, is not necessarily to pass judgment upon them as illusions. The game of debunking myths, Harry Levin has warned us, starts "in the denunciation of myth as falsehood from the vantage-point of a rival myth." Mythology has other meanings, not all of them pejorative, and myths have a life of their own which to some degree renders irrelevant the question of their correlation to empirical fact. Setting aside for the moment the multiple connotations of the term, we may say that social myths in general, including those of the South, are simply mental pictures that portray the pattern of what a people think they are (or ought to be) or what somebody else thinks they are. They tend to develop abstract ideas in more or less concrete and dramatic terms. In the words of Henry Nash Smith, they fuse "concept and emotion into an image."

They may serve a variety of functions. "A myth," Mark Schorer has observed, "is a large, controlling image that gives philosophical meaning to

From "Mythology: A New Frontier in Southern History," by George Tindall, in Frank E. Vandiver (ed.), *The Idea of the South: Pursuit of a Central Theme,* pp. 1–15. Reprinted by permission of the author and the University of Chicago Press.

Published 1964. Composed and printed by the University of Chicago Press, Chicago, Illinois, U.S.A.

the facts of ordinary life; that is, which has organizing value for experience." It may offer useful generalizations by which data may be tested. But being also "charged with values, aspirations, ideals and meanings," myths may become the ground for belief, for either loyalty and defense on the one hand and hostility and opposition on the other. In such circumstances a myth itself becomes one of the realities of history, significantly influencing the course of human action, for good or ill. There is, of course, always a danger of illusion, a danger that in ordering one's vision of reality, the myth may predetermine the categories of perception, rendering one blind to things that do not fit into the mental image.

Since the Southern mind is reputed to be peculiarly resistant to pure abstraction and more receptive to the concrete and dramatic image, it may be unusually susceptible to mythology. Perhaps for the same reason our subject can best be approached through reference to the contrasting experiences of two Southerners—one recent, the other about forty-five years ago.

The first is the experience of a contemporary Louisiana writer, John T. Westbrook.

> During the thirties and early forties [Westbrook has written] when I was an English instructor at the University of Missouri, I was often mildly irritated by the average northerner's Jeeter-Lester-and-potlikker idea of the South. Even today the northern visitor inertia-headedly maintains his misconception: he hankers to see eroded hills and rednecks, scrub cotton and sharecropper shacks.
>
> It little profits me to drive him through Baton Rouge, show him the oil-ethyl-rubber-aluminum-chemical miles of industry along the Mississippi River, and say, "This . . . is the fastest-growing city of over 100,000 in America. We can amply substantiate our claim that we are atomic target number one, that in the next war the Russians will obliterate us first. . . ."
>
> Our northerner is suspicious of all this crass evidence presented to his senses. It bewilders and befuddles him. He is too deeply steeped in William Faulkner and Robert Penn Warren. The fumes of progress are in his nose and the bright steel of industry towers before his eyes, but his heart is away in Yoknapatawpha County with razorback hogs and night riders. On this trip to the South he wants, above all else, to sniff the effluvium of backwoods-and-sand-hill sub-humanity and to see at least one barn burn at midnight. So he looks at me with crafty misgiving, as if to say, "Well, you *do* drive a Cadillac, talk rather glibly about Kierkegaard and Sartre . . . but, after all, you *are* only fooling, aren't you? You do, don't you, sometimes, go out secretly by owl-light to drink swamp water and feed on sowbelly and collard greens?"

The other story was the experience of a Southern historian, Frank L. Owsley, who traveled during World War I from Chicago via Cincinnati to Montgomery with a group of young ladies on the way to visit their menfolk at an army camp. He wrote later that, "despite everything which had ever been said to the contrary," the young ladies had a romantic conception of the "Sunny South" and looked forward to the journey with considerable excitement. "They expected to enter a pleasant land of white columned mansions, green pastures, expansive cotton and tobacco fields where Negroes sang spirituals all the day through." Except in the bluegrass basins of central Kentucky and Tennessee, what they actually found "were gutted hill-sides; scrub oak and pine; bramble and blackberry thickets, bottom lands once fertile now senile and exhausted, with spindling tobacco, corn, or cotton stalks . . . ; unpainted houses which were hardly more than shacks or here and there the crumbling ruins of old mansions covered with briars, the homes of snakes and lizards." The disappointment of Dr. Owsley's ladies was, no doubt, even greater than that of Mr. Westbrook's friend in Baton Rouge.

There is a striking contrast between these two episodes, both in the picture of Southern reality and in the differing popular images that they present. The fact that they are four decades apart helps to account for the discrepancies, but what is not apparent at first is the common ancestry of the two images. They are not very distant cousins, collateral descendants from the standard image of the Old South, the plantation myth. The version of Owsley's lady friends is closer to the original primogenitor, which despite its advancing age and debility, still lives amid a flourishing progeny of legendary Southern gentility. According to Francis Pendleton Gaines, author of *The Southern Plantation,* the pattern appeared full-blown at least as early as 1832 in John Pendleton Kennedy's romance, *Swallow Barn.* It has had a long career in story and novel and song, in the drama and motion picture. The corrosions of age seem to have ended its Hollywood career, although the old films still turn up on the late late. It may still be found in the tourist bait of shapely beauties in hoop skirts posed against the backdrop of white columns at Natchez, Orton, or a hundred other places.

These pictures are enough to trigger in the mind the whole euphoric pattern of kindly old marster with his mint julep; happy darkies singing in fields perpetually white to the harvest or, as the case may be, sadly recalling the long lost days of old; coquettish belles wooed by slender gallants in gray underneath the moonlight and magnolias. It is a pattern that yields all too easily to caricature and ridicule, for in its more sophisticated versions the figure of the planter carries a heavy freight of the aristocratic virtues: courtliness, grace, hospitality, honor, *noblesse oblige,* as well as many no less charming aristocratic vices: a lordly indifference to the balance sheet, hot temper, profanity, overindulgence, a certain stubborn obstinacy. The old-time Negro, when not a figure of comedy, is the very embodiment of loyalty. And the Southern belle: "Beautiful, graceful, accomplished in social charm, bewitching in coquetry, yet strangely steadfast in soul," Gaines has written, "she is perhaps the most winsome figure in the whole field of our fancy." "The plantation romance," Gaines says, "remains our chief social idyl of the past; of an Arcadian scheme of existence, less material, less hurried, less prosaically equalitarian, less futile, richer in picturesqueness, festivity, in realized pleasure that recked not of hope or fear or unrejoicing labor."

But there is still more to the traditional pattern. Somewhere off in the piney woods and erosion-gutted clay hills, away from the white columns and gentility, there existed Po' White Trash: the crackers; hillbillies; sand-hillers; rag, tag, and bobtail; squatters; "po' buckra" to the Negroes; the Ransy Sniffle of A. B. Longstreet's *Georgia Scenes* and his literary descendants like Jeeter Lester and Ab Snopes, abandoned to poverty and degeneracy—the victims, it was later discovered, of hookworm, malaria, and pellagra. Somewhere in the pattern the respectable small farmer was lost from sight. He seemed to be neither romantic nor outrageous enough to fit in. His neglect provides the classic example in Southern history of the blind spots engendered by the power of mythology. It was not until the 1930's that Frank L. Owsley and his students at Vanderbilt rediscovered the Southern yeoman farmer as the characteristic, or at least the most numerous, ante bellum white Southerner. More about the yeoman presently; neglected in the plantation myth, he was in the foreground of another.

In contrast to the legitimate heirs of the plantation myth, the image of John T. Westbrook's Yankee visitor in Baton Rouge seems to be descended from what might be called the illegitimate line of the plantation myth, out of abolition. It is one of the ironies of our history that, as Gaines put it, "two opposing sides of the fiercest controversy that ever shook national thought agreed concerning certain picturesque elements of plantation life and joined hands to set the conception unforgettably in public consciousness." The abolitionists found it difficult, or even undesirable, to escape the standard image. It was pretty fully developed even in *Uncle Tom's Cabin*. Harriet Beecher Stowe made her villain a Yankee overseer, and has been accused by at least one latter-day abolitionist of implanting deeply in the American mind the stereotype of the faithful darkey. For others the plantation myth simply appeared in reverse, as a pattern of corrupt opulence resting upon human exploitation. Gentle old marster became the arrogant, haughty, imperious potentate, the very embodiment of sin, the central target of the antislavery attack. He maintained a seraglio in the slave quarters; he bred Negroes like cattle and sold them down the river to certain death in the sugar mills, separating families if that served his purpose, while Southern women suffered in silence the guilty knowledge of their men's infidelity. The happy darkies in this picture became white men in black skins, an oppressed people longing for freedom, the victims of countless atrocities so ghastly as to be unbelievable except for undeniable evidence, forever seeking an opportunity to follow the North Star to freedom. The masses of the white folks were simply poor whites, relegated to ignorance and degeneracy by the slavocracy.

Both lines of the plantation myth have been remarkably prolific, but the more adaptable one has been that of the abolitionists. It has repeatedly readjusted to new conditions while the more legitimate line has courted extinction, running out finally into the decadence perpetrated by Tennessee Williams. Meanwhile, the abolitionist image of brutality persisted through and beyond

Reconstruction in the Republican outrage mills and bloody shirt political campaigns. For several decades it was more than overbalanced by the Southern image of Reconstruction horrors, disarmed by prophets of a New South created in the image of the North, and almost completely submerged under the popularity of plantation romances in the generation before Owsley's trainload of ladies ventured into their "Sunny South" of the teens. At about that time, however, the undercurrents began to emerge once again into the mainstream of American thought. In the clever decade of the twenties a kind of neo-abolitionist myth of the Savage South was compounded. It seemed that the benighted South, after a period of relative neglect, suddenly became an object of concern to every publicist in the country. One Southern abomination after another was ground through their mills: child labor, peonage, lynching, hookworm, pellagra, the Scopes trial, the Fundamentalist crusade against Al Smith. The guiding genius was Henry L. Mencken, the hatchet man from Baltimore who developed the game of South-baiting into a national pastime, a fine art at which he had no peer. In 1917, when he started constructing his image of "Baptist and Methodist barbarism" below the Potomac, he began with the sterility of Southern literature and went on from there. With characteristic glee he anointed one J. Gordon Coogler of South Carolina "the last bard of Dixie" and quoted his immortal couplet:

> Alas, for the South! Her books have grown fewer—
> She never was much given to literature.

"Down there," Mencken wrote, "a poet is now almost as rare as an oboe-player, a dry-point etcher or a metaphysician." As for "critics, musical composers, painters, sculptors, architects . . . there is not even a bad one between the Potomac mud-flats and the Gulf. Nor an historian. Nor a sociologist. Nor a philosopher. Nor a theologian. Nor a scientist. In all these fields the south is an awe-inspiring blank. . . ." It was as complete a vacuity as the interstellar spaces, the "Sahara of the Bozart," "The Bible Belt." He summed it all up in one basic catalogue of Southern grotesqueries: "Fundamentalism, Ku Kluxry, revivals, lynchings, hog wallow politics—these are the things that always occur to a northerner when he thinks of the south." The South, in short, had fallen prey to its poor whites, who would soon achieve apotheosis in the Snopes family.

It did not end with the twenties. The image was reinforced by a variety of episodes: the Scottsboro trials, chain gang exposés, Bilbo and Rankin, Senate filibusters, labor wars; much later by Central High and Orval Faubus, Emmett Till and Autherine Lucy and James Meredith, bus boycotts and Freedom Riders; and not least of all by the lush growth of literature that covered Mencken's Sahara, with Caldwell's *Tobacco Road* and Faulkner's *Sanctuary* and various other products of what Ellen Glasgow labeled the Southern Gothic and a less elegant Mississippi editor called the "privy school" of literature. In the words of Faulkner's character, Gavin Stevens, the North suffered from a curious "gullibility: a volitionless, almost helpless capacity and eagerness to believe anything about the South not even provided it be derogatory but merely bizarre enough and strange enough." And Faulkner, to be sure, did not altogether neglect that market. Not surprisingly, he was taken in some quarters for a realist, and the image of Southern savagery long obscured the critics' recognition of his manifold merits.

The family line of the plantation myth can be traced only so far in the legendary gentility and savagery of the South. Other family lines seem to be entirely independent—if sometimes on friendly terms. In an excellent study, "The New South Creed, 1865–1900," soon to be published, Paul M. Gaston has traced the evolution of the creed into a genuine myth. In the aftermath of the Civil War, apostles of a "New South," led by Henry W. Grady, preached with almost evangelical fervor the gospel of industry. Their dream, Gaston writes, "was essentially a promise of American life for the South. It proffered all the glitter and glory and freedom from guilt that inhered in the American ideal." From advocacy, from this vision of the future, the prophets soon advanced to the belief that "their promised land [was] at hand, no longer merely a gleaming goal." "By the twentieth century . . . there was established for many in the South a pattern of belief within which they could see themselves and their section as rich, success-oriented, and just . . . opulence and power were at hand . . . the Negro lived in the best of all possible worlds."

As the twentieth century advanced, and wealth did in fact increase, the creed of the New South took on an additional burden of crusades for good roads and education, blending them into what Francis B. Simkins has called the "trinity of Southern progress": industrial growth, good roads, and schools. When the American Historical Association went to Durham in 1929 for its annual meeting, Robert D. W. Connor of the University of North Carolina presented the picture of a rehabilitated South that had "shaken itself free from its heritage of war and Reconstruction. Its self-confidence restored, its political stability assured, its prosperity regained, its social problems on the way to solution. . . ." Two months before Connor spoke, the New York Stock Exchange had broken badly, and in the aftermath the image he described was seriously blurred, but before the end of the thirties it was being brought back into focus by renewed industrial expansion that received increased momentum from World War II and postwar prosperity.

Two new and disparate images emerged in the depression years, both with the altogether novel feature of academic trappings and affiliations. One was the burgeoning school of sociological regionalism led by Howard W. Odum and Rupert B. Vance at the University of North Carolina. It was neither altogether the image of the Savage South nor that of industrial progress, although both entered into the compound. It was rather a concept of the "Problem South," which Franklin D. Roosevelt labeled "the Nation's Economic Problem No. 1," a region with indisputable shortcomings but with potentialities that needed constructive attention and the application of rational social planning. Through the disciples of Odum as well as the agencies of the New Deal, the vision issued in a flood of social science monographs and programs for reform and development. To one undergraduate in Chapel Hill at the time, it seemed in retrospect that "we had more of an attitude of service to the South as the South than was true later. . . ."

The regionalists were challenged by the Vanderbilt Agrarians, who developed a myth of the traditional South. Their manifesto, *I'll Take My Stand,* by Twelve Southerners, appeared by fortuitous circumstance in 1930 when industrial capitalism seemed on the verge of collapse. In reaction against both the progressive New South and Mencken's image of savagery they championed, in Donald Davidson's words, a "traditional society . . . that is stable, religious, more rural than urban, and politically conservative," in which human needs were supplied by "Family, bloodkinship, clanship, folkways, custom, community. . . ." The ideal of the traditional virtues took on the texture of myth in their image of the agrarian South. Of course, in the end, their agrarianism proved less important as a social-economic force than as a context for creative literature. The central figures in the movement were the Fugitive poets John Crowe Ransom, Donald Davidson, Allen Tate, and Robert Penn Warren. But, as Professor Louis Rubin has emphasized, "Through their vision of an agrarian community, the authors of *I'll Take My Stand* presented a critique of the modern world. In contrast to the hurried, nervous life of cities, the image of the agrarian South was of a life in which human beings existed serenely and harmoniously." Their critique of the modern frenzy "has since been echoed by commentator after commentator."

While it never became altogether clear whether the Agrarians were celebrating the aristocratic graces or following the old Jeffersonian dictum that "Those who labor in the earth are the chosen people of God . . . ," most of them seemed to come down eventually on the side of the farmer rather than the planter. Frank L. Owsley, who rediscovered the ante bellum yeoman farmer, was one of them. Insofar as they extolled the yeoman farmer, the Agrarians laid hold upon an image older than any of the others—the Jeffersonian South. David M. Potter, a Southerner in exile at Stanford University, has remarked how difficult it is for many people to realize that the benighted South "was, until recently, regarded by many liberals as the birthplace and the natural bulwark of the Jeffersonian ideal. . . ." The theme has long had an appeal for historians as well as others. Frederick Jackson Turner developed it for the West and William E. Dodd for the South. According to Dodd the democratic, equalitarian South of the Jeffersonian image was the norm; the plantation slavocracy was the great aberration. Dodd's theme has been reflected in the writing of other historians, largely in terms of a region subjected to economic colonialism by an imperial Northeast: Charles A. Beard, for example, who saw the sectional conflict as a struggle between agrarianism and industrialism; Howard K. Beale, who interpreted Reconstruction in similar terms; C. Vann Woodward, defender of Populism; Arthur S. Link, who first rediscovered the Southern progressives; and Walter Prescott Webb, who found the nation divided between an exploited South and West on the one hand, and a predatory Northeast on the other. Jefferson, like the South, it sometimes seems, can mean all things to all men, and the Jefferson image of agrarian democracy has been a favorite recourse of Southern liberals, just as his state-rights doctrines have nourished conservatism.

In stark contrast to radical agrarianism there stands the concept of monolithic conservatism in Southern politics. It seems to be a proposition generally taken for granted now that the South is, by definition, conservative—and always has been. Yet the South in the late nineteenth century produced some of the most radical Populists and in the twentieth was a bulwark of Wilsonian progressivism and Roosevelt's New Deal, at least up to a point. A good case has been made out by Arthur S. Link that Southern agrarian radicals pushed Wilson further into progressivism than he intended to go. During the twenties Southern minority leadership in Congress kept up such a running battle against the conservative tax policies of Andrew Mellon that, believe it or not, there was real fear among some Northern businessmen during the 1932 campaign that Franklin D. Roosevelt might be succeeded by that radical Southern income-taxer, John Nance Garner! The conservative image of course has considerable validity, but it obscures understanding of such phenomena as Albert Gore, Russell Long, Lister Hill, John Sparkman, Olin D. Johnston, William Fulbright, the Yarboroughs of Texas, or the late Estes Kefauver. In the 1960 campaign the conservative image seriously victimized Lyndon B. Johnson, who started in politics as a vigorous New Dealer and later maneuvered through the Senate the first civil rights legislation since Reconstruction.

The infinite variety of Southern mythology could be catalogued and analyzed endlessly. A suggestive list would include the Proslavery South; the Confederate South; the Demagogic South; the State Rights South; the Fighting South; the Lazy South; the Folklore South; the South of jazz and the blues; the Booster South; the Rapacious South running away with Northern industries; the Liberal South of the interracial movement; the White Supremacy South of racial segregation, which seems to be for some the all-encompassing "Southern way of life"; the Anglo-Saxon (or was it the Scotch-Irish?) South, the most American of all regions because of its native population; or the Internationalist South, a mainstay of the Wilson, Roosevelt, and Truman foreign policies.

The South, then, has been the seedbed for a proliferation of paradoxical myths, all of which have some basis in empirical fact and all of which doubtlessly have, or have had, their true believers. The result has been, in David Potter's words, that the South has become an enigma, "a kind of Sphinx on the American land." What is really the answer to the riddle, what is at bottom the foundation of Southern distinctiveness has never been established with finality, but the quest for a central theme of Southern history has repeatedly engaged the region's historians. Like Frederick Jackson Turner, who extracted the essential West in his frontier thesis, Southern historians have sought to distill the quintessence of the South into some kind of central theme.

In a recent survey of these efforts David L. Smiley of Wake Forest College has concluded that they turn upon two basic lines of thought: "the causal effects of environment, and the development of certain acquired characteristics of the people called Southern." The distinctive climate and weather of the South, it has been argued, slowed the pace of life, tempered the speech of the South, dictated the system of staple crops and Negro slavery—in short, predetermined the plantation economy. The more persuasive suggestions have resulted from concentration upon human factors and causation. The best known is that set forth by U. B. Phillips. The quintessence of Southernism, he wrote in 1928, was "a common resolve indomitably maintained" that the South "shall be and remain a white man's country." Whether "expressed with the frenzy of a demagogue or maintained with a patrician's quietude," this was "the cardinal test of a Southerner and the central theme of Southern history." Other historians have pointed to the rural nature of Southern society as the basic conditioning factor, to the prevalence of the country gentleman ideal imported from England, to the experience of the South as a conscious minority unified by criticism and attack from outside, to the fundamental piety of the Bible Belt, and to various other factors. It has even been suggested by one writer that a chart of the mule population would determine the boundaries of the South.

More recently, two historians have attempted new explanations. In his search for a Southern identity, C. Vann Woodward advances several crucial factors: the experience of poverty in a land of plenty; failure and defeat in a land that glorifies success; sin and guilt amid the legend of American innocence; and a sense of place and belonging among a people given to abstraction. David M. Potter, probing the enigma of the South, has found the key to the riddle in the prevalence of a folk society. "This folk culture, we know, was far from being ideal or utopian," he writes, "and was in fact full of inequality and wrong, but if the nostalgia persists was it because even the inequality and wrong were parts of a life that still had a relatedness and meaning which our more bountiful life in the mass culture seems to lack?"

It is significant that both explanations are expressed largely in the past tense, Potter's explicitly in terms of nostalgia. They recognize, by implication at least, still another image—that of the Dynamic or the Changing South. The image may be rather nebulous and the ultimate ends unclear, but the fact of change is written inescapably across the Southern scene. The consciousness of change has been present so long as to become in itself one of the abiding facts of Southern life. . . . As far back as the twenties it was the consciousness of change that quickened the imaginations of a cultivated and sensitive minority, giving us the Southern renaissance in literature. The peculiar historical consciousness of the Southern writer, Allen Tate has suggested, "made possible the curious burst of intelligence that we get at a crossing of the ways, not unlike, on an infinitesimal scale, the outburst of poetic genius at the end of the sixteenth century when commercial England had already begun to crush feudal England." Trace it through modern Southern writing, and at the center—in Ellen Glasgow, in Faulkner, Wolfe, Caldwell, the Fugitive-Agrarian poets, and all the others–there is the consciousness of change, of suspension between two worlds, a double focus looking both backward and forward.

The Southerner of the present generation has seen the old landmarks crumble with great rapidity: the one-crop agriculture and the very predominance of agriculture itself, the one-party system, the white primary, the poll tax, racial segregation, the poor white (at least in his classic connotations), the provincial isolation—virtually all the foundations of the established order. Yet, sometimes, the old traditions endure in surprising new forms. Southern folkways have been carried even into the factory, and the Bible Belt has revealed resources undreamed of in Mencken's philosophy—but who, in the twenties, could have anticipated Martin Luther King?

One wonders what new images, what new myths, might be nurtured by the emerging South. Some, like Harry Ashmore, have merely written *An Epitaph for Dixie.* It is the conclusion of two Southern sociologists, John M. Maclachlan and Joe S. Floyd, Jr., that present trends "might well hasten the day when the South, once perhaps the most distinctively 'different' American region, will have become . . . virtually indistinguishable from the other urban-industrial areas of the nation." U. B. Phillips long ago suggested that the disappearance of race as a major issue would end Southern distinctiveness. One may wonder if Southern distinctiveness might even be preserved in new conditions entirely antithetic to his image. Charles L. Black, Jr., another *émigré* Southerner (at Yale Law School) has confessed to a fantastic dream that Southern white and Negroes, bound in a special bond of common tragedy, may come to recognize their kinship. There is not the slightest warrant for it, he admits, in history, sociology, or common sense. But if it should come to pass, he suggests, "The South, which has always felt itself reserved for a high destiny, would have found it, and would have come to flower at last. And the fragrance of it would spread, beyond calculation, over the world."

Despite the consciousness of change, perhaps even more because of it, Southerners still feel a persistent pull toward identification with their native region as a ground for belief and loyalty. Is there not yet something more than nostalgia to the idea of the South? Is there not some living heritage with which the modern Southerner can identify? Is there not, in short, a viable myth of the South? The quest for myth has been a powerful factor in recent Southern literature, and the suspicion is strong that it will irresistibly affect any historian's quest for the central theme of Southern history. It has all too clearly happened before—in the climatic theory, for example, which operated through its geographical determinism to justify the social order of the plantation, or the Phillips thesis of white supremacy, which has become almost a touchstone of the historian's attitude toward the whole contemporary issue of race. "To elaborate a central theme," David L. Smiley has asserted, is "but to reduce a multi-faceted story to a single aspect, and its result . . . but to find new footnotes to confirm revealed truths and prescribed views." The trouble is that the quest for the central theme, like Turner's frontier thesis, becomes absorbed willy-nilly into the process of myth making.

To pursue the Turner analogy a little further, the conviction grows that the frontier thesis, with all its elaborations and critiques, has been exhausted (and in part exploded) as a source of new historical insight. It is no derogation of insights already gained to suggest that the same thing has happened to the quest for the central theme, and that the historian, *as historian,* may be better able to illuminate our understanding of the South now by turning to a new focus upon the regional mythology.

To undertake the analysis of mythology will no longer require him to venture into uncharted wilderness. A substantial conceptual framework of mythology has already been developed by anthropologists, philosophers, psychologists, theologians, and literary critics. The historian, while his field has always been closely related to mythology, has come only lately to the critique of it. But there now exists a considerable body of historical literature on the American national mythology and the related subject of the national character, and Smith's stimulating *Virgin Land* suggests the trails that may be followed into the idea of the South.

Several trails, in fact, have already been blazed. Nearly forty years ago, Francis Pendleton Gaines successfully traced the rise and progress of the plantation myth, and two recent authors have belatedly taken to the same trail. Howard R. Floan has considerably increased our knowledge of the abolitionist version in his study of Northern writers, *The South in Northern Eyes,* while William R. Taylor has approached the subject from an entirely new perspective in his *Cavalier and Yankee.* Shields McIlwaine has traced the literary image of the poor white, while Stanley Elkins' *Slavery* has broken sharply from established concepts on both sides of that controversial question. One foray into the New South has been made in Paul Gaston's "The New South Creed, 1865–1900." Yet many important areas—the Confederate and Reconstruction myths, for example—still remain almost untouched.

Some of the basic questions that need to be answered have been attacked in these studies; some have not. It is significant that students of literature have led the way and have pointed up the value of even third-rate creative literature in the critique of myth. The historian, however, should be able to contribute other perspectives. With his peculiar time perspective he can seek to unravel the tangled genealogy of myth that runs back from the modern Changing South to Jefferson's yeoman and Kennedy's plantation. Along the way he should investigate the possibility that some obscure dialectic may be at work in the pairing of obverse images: the two versions of the plantation, New South and Old, Cavalier and Yankee, genteel and savage, regionalist and agrarian, nativist and internationalist.

What, the historian may ask, have been the historical origins and functions of the myths? The plantation myth, according to Gaines and Floan, was born in the controversy and emotion of the struggle over slavery. It had polemical uses for both sides. Taylor, on the other hand, finds its origin in the psychological need, both North and South, to find a corrective for the grasping, materialistic, rootless society symbolized by the image of the Yankee. Vann Woodward and Gaston have noted its later psychological uses in bolstering the morale of the New South. The image of the Savage South has obvious polemical uses, but has it not others? Has it not served the function of national catharsis? Has it not created for many Americans a convenient scapegoat upon which the sins of all may be symbolically laid and thereby expiated—a most convenient escape from problem solving? To what extent, indeed, has the mythology of the South in general welled up from the subconscious depths? Taylor, especially, has emphasized this question, but the skeptical historian will also be concerned with the degree to which it has been the product or the device of deliberate manipulation by propagandists and vested interests seeking identification with the "real" South.

Certainly any effort to delineate the unique character of a people must take into account its mythology. "Poets," James G. Randall suggested, "have done better in expressing this oneness of the South than historians in explaining it." Can it be that the historians have been looking in the wrong places, that they have failed to seek the key to the enigma where the poets have so readily found it—in the mythology that has had so much to do with shaping character, unifying society, developing a sense of community, of common ideals and shared goals, making the region conscious of its distinctiveness? Perhaps by turning to different and untrodden paths we shall encounter the central theme of Southern history at last on the new frontier of mythology.

There Was Another South

Carl N. Degler

As a student of both individual and social behavior, the historian must constantly seek to establish the tenuous line between the truth of the particular and that of the general. In that the profiles of history have generally been drawn either in terms of its "great men" or in terms of its general "movements," the difficulty seems to lie in striking a balance, as to emphasis, between the two. The historian's problem is to find true generalizations that neither distort nor violate truth. Such a balance is offered by Carl Degler of Stanford University, as he treats the subjects of slavery and secession in the antebellum South. As Degler suggests, contrary to popular generalizations, the South before the Civil War did not represent a monolithic point of view on these issues. In the prewar South there was a scarcity neither of abolitionists nor of unionists.

The stereotype of the South is as tenacious as it is familiar: a traditionally rebellious region which has made a dogma of states' rights and a religious order of the Democratic party. Here indeed is a monotonous and unchanging tapestry, with a pattern of magnolia blossoms, Spanish moss, and the inevitable old plantations running ceaselessly from border to border. To this depiction of almost willful backwardness, add the dark motif of the Negro problem, a few threads of poor white, and the picture is complete.

Such is the mythical image, and a highly inaccurate one it is, for the South is a region of immense variety. Its sprawling landscape ranges from the startlingly red soil of Virginia and North Carolina to the black, sticky clay of the Delta; from the wild and primitive mountain forests of eastern Kentucky to the lush, junglelike swamps of southern Louisiana; from the high, dry, wind-swept plains of the Texas Panhandle to the humid tidelands of the South Carolina coast. An environment so diverse can be expected to produce social and political differences to match, and in fact, it always has.

Today, with the South in ferment, we have come to recognize increasingly the wide variety of attitudes that exist in the region. But this denial of the southern stereotype is a relatively new development, even among historians. For too long the history of the region has been regarded as a kind of unbroken plain of uniform opinion. This is especially true of what has been written about the years before the Civil War; a belief in states' rights, the legality of secession, and the rightfulness of slavery has been accepted almost without question as typical of southern thought. In a sense, such catch phrases do represent what many southerners have believed; but at the same time there were many others who both denied the legality of secession and denounced slavery. It is time this "other South" was better known.

Let us begin with the story of those southerners who so cherished the Union that they refused to accept the doctrine of nullification and secession. They included not only humble farmers and remote mountain men, but some of the greatest names in the history of the South; their devotion to the Union was tested in several bitter clashes with states' righters during the antebellum decades. The first of these contests came over the question of the high protective tariffs which many southerners felt would hurt the cotton trade; the arguments advanced at the beginning set forth the basic lines of debate that were followed thereafter. South Carolina's *Exposition and Protest* of 1828, which John C. Calhoun wrote secretly in opposition to the tariff passed that year, embodied the classic defense of state sovereignty. In the *Exposition,* Calhoun contended that nullification of federal legislation by a state and even secession were constitutional—a doctrine rejected by many prominent southerners in 1828 and after.

Foremost among them was former President James Madison, the reputed "father of the Constitution." As a Jeffersonian in politics and a Virginian by birth and heritage, Madison was no friend of the protective tariff, and certainly not of the monstrous one of 1828, which had been promulgated by the Jacksonian faction in Congress in an effort to discredit the Adams administration. But he could not accept even that politically inspired tariff as sufficient reason for nullification. Indeed, he could not accept the constitutional doctrine of nullification on any grounds. It is worthwhile to consider briefly Madison's views on nullification, because virtually all subsequent southern defenses of the Union followed his line of thought; at the time, no man in the South carried more authority on the meaning and interpretation of the Constitution that the venerable Virginian, who celebrated his eightieth birthday in 1830, and was the last surviving signer of that document.

Many political leaders sought his views all through the tariff crisis of 1828–33, and to all of them Madison reiterated the same conclusions. The United States was a "mixed government" in which the states were supreme in some areas and the federal government in others. In the event of conflict between them, the Supreme Court was the intended arbiter under the Constitution; the Court, Madison wrote, was "so constituted as to be impartial as it could be made by the mode of appointment and responsibility of the judges."

If confidence were lacking in the objectivity of the judges, Madison continued, then there were further remedies: the impeachment of offending officials, election of a new government, or amendments to the Constitution.

But neither nullification nor secession was legal, he tirelessly pointed out. Of course, if tyrannized sufficiently, a state could invoke its natural right to overthrow its oppressor; but that was a right of revolution, and not a constitutional right as Calhoun and his followers maintained.

As a southern Unionist, Madison did not stand alone, either at the time of the nullification crisis or later. In Calhoun's own state, in fact, the Unionists were a powerful and eloquent minority. Hugh S. Legare (pronounced Legree, curiously enough), Charleston aristocrat, intellectual, and one-time editor of the *Southern Review*, distinguished himself in defense of the Union, vigorously opposing Calhoun during the heated debates in Charleston in 1832. (Eleven years later, as United States Attorney General, Legare again differed with the majority of southerners when he offered the official opinion that free Negroes in the United States enjoyed the same civil rights as white men.)

James Petigru and Joel Poinsett (who, as minister to Mexico, gave his name to the Poinsettia) were two other prominent Charlestonians who would not accept the doctrine that a state could constitutionally withdraw from the Union. Unlike Legare and Poinsett, Petigru lived long enough to fight nullification and secession in South Carolina until that state left the Union. (When asked by a stranger in December, 1860, where the insane asylum was, he contemptuously pointed to the building where the secession convention was meeting.)

Andrew Jackson is often ignored by those who conceive of the South as a monolith of states' rights and secession. A Carolinian by birth and a Tennessean by choice, Jackson acted as an outspoken advocate of the Union when he threatened South Carolina with overwhelming force in the crisis of 1832–33. Jackson's fervently nationalistic proclamation to the people of the dissident state was at once a closely reasoned restatement of the Madisonian view that the United States was a "mixed government," and a highly emotional panegyric to the Union. Though there can be no question of Jackson's wholehearted acceptance of every patriotic syllable in that proclamation, it comes as no surprise to those acquainted with the limited literary abilities of Old Hickory that its composition was the work of an adviser. That adviser, it is worth noting, was a southerner, Secretary of State Edward Livingston of Louisiana.

There were few things on which Henry Clay of Kentucky and Andrew Jackson could agree, but the indissolubility of the Union was one of them. Clay never concurred with those southern leaders who accepted Calhoun's position that a state could nullify national legislation or secede from the Union. As a matter of fact, Henry Clay's Whig party was probably the most important stronghold of pro-Union sentiment in the antebellum South. Unlike the Democratic party, the Whigs never succumbed, in defending slavery, to the all-encompassing states' rights doctrine. Instead, they identified themselves with the national bank, internal improvements, the tariff, and opposition to the "tyranny" of Andrew Jackson. Despite the "unsouthern" sound of these principles to modern ears, the Whig party was both powerful and popular, capable of winning elections in any southern state. In the heyday of the Whigs, a solidly Democratic South was still unimaginable.

In 1846, the attempt of antislavery forces to prohibit slavery in the vast areas about to be acquired as a result of the Mexican War precipitated another bitter sectional struggle. But as much as they might support the "peculiar institution," the southern Whigs stood firm against Calhoun's efforts to commit the whole South to a states' rights position that once more threatened the existence of the Union. When, in 1849, Calhoun invited southern Congressmen to join his Southern Rights movement in order to strengthen resistance against northern demands, forty of the eighty-eight he approached refused to sign the call. Almost all of them were Whigs.

Throughout the Deep South in the state elections of 1851, Unionist Democrats and Whigs combined to stop the incipient secessionist movement in its tracks. In Georgia, Howell Cobb, the Unionist candidate for governor, received 56,261 votes to 37,472 for his opponent, a prominent Southern Rights man; in the legislature the Unionists captured 101 of the 127 seats. After the same election the congressional delegation of Alabama consisted of two secessionists and five Union supporters. In the Calhoun stronghold of Mississippi, where Jefferson Davis was the best-known spokesman for the Southern Rights movement, Davis was defeated for the governorship, 28,738 to 27,729, by his Unionist opponent, Henry S. Foote. Even in fire-eating South Carolina itself, the anti-Calhoun forces won overwhelmingly, 25,045 to 17,710.

By the time of the Kansas-Nebraska Act of 1854, the Whig party had all but disappeared, the victim of a widening sectional schism. Bereft of its traditional political organization, southern Unionism was, for the time, almost voiceless, but it was not dead. In the election of 1860, it reappeared in the shape of the Constitutional Union party. Its candidate was John Bell of Tennessee, an old-line Whig and staunch Unionist who, in order to prevent disruption of the nation, made his platform the Union itself. That year, in a four-party race, the Constitutional Unionists were the effective second party to the southern Democrats; for Stephen A. Douglas, the candidate of the northern Democrats, received few votes outside the border states, and Lincoln was not even on a ballot in ten of the fifteen slave states.

The Constitutional Unionists gave the dominant Democratic party a hot fight in every southern state. Of the upper southern states, Virginia, Kentucky, and Tennessee went to Bell outright, while Maryland gave him forty-five per cent and North Carolina forty-seven per cent of their votes.

Bell's showing in the Deep South was not as strong as in the upper South, but it nonetheless demonstrated that those southerners still willing to be counted for the Union were a large minority in almost all of the states.

From the whole South, Bell received forty percent of the popular vote to southern Democrat Breckinridge's forty-five.

A clear indication of the continuity of Unionism from the days of the Whigs to the election of 1860 is that Bell's support in the Deep South centered in the same general areas where the Whigs had been most powerful in the 1840's. Many of the delta counties along the Mississippi River—in Arkansas, Mississippi, and Louisiana—which were always strongholds of Whiggery, went for Bell. Whig votes had always been conspicuous in the black belt counties of central Alabama and Georgia, and so were Bell's in 1860.

Surprisingly enough, the wealthy, slaveholding counties of the South were more often Whig than Democratic in the years before the war. Ever since the days of Jackson, the Democracy had been predominantly the party of the small planter and non-slaveholder. Regardless of the serious threat to slavery posed by the Republican party in 1860, many slaveholders could still not bring themselves to violate their traditional political allegiances and vote for a Democratic candidate identified with states' rights.

A further test of southern Unionism was provided in the election of delegates to the state secession conventions in the winter of 1860–61. Unfortunately, the voting figures do not tell us as much as we would like to know. To most southerners at the time, the issue was not simply the Union versus the right of a state to secede; more often it was whether secession was expedient, with little thought about its constitutionality. Therefore, those delegates who favored a course other than immediate secession did not necessarily support the Union under all and every circumstance.

Nevertheless, these voting returns make clear that even on the verge of secession, tens of thousands in all the states of the Deep South were still opposed to a break with the Union. In Alabama, for example, 28,200 voted against immediate secession to 35,700 for; furthermore, one third of the delegates to the convention refused to sign the secession ordinance because it would not be submitted to the people. In Georgia, 37,123 were against secession to 50,243 in favor; in Louisiana the Unionists were an even larger minority: 17,296 against secession, 20,448 for. In Texas, despite much intimidation of Unionists, twenty-two percent of the voters still opposed secession.

Before Sumter was fired upon and Lincoln called for volunteers, the states of the upper South refused to join the seceding states. Early in 1861, the people of Tennessee voted against having a secession convention, 68,282 to 59,449; the vote of the people of Arkansas against secession in February, 1861, was 22,000 to 17,000. North Carolina, in a popular vote, also turned down a call for a secession convention. As late as April 4, the Virginia convention voted down a proposal to draw up an ordinance of secession by an almost two-to-one majority. Even after Sumter, when the upper South states did secede, it is clear that loyalty to the Union was still a powerful sentiment.

Throughout the war southern Unionists were active in opposition to the Confederacy. Areas of strong Unionist feeling, like eastern Tennessee, western Virginia, northern Alabama, and the mountain counties of Arkansas, quickly come to mind. In eastern Tennessee, for example, Unionist sentiment was so widespread and deep-felt that for a large part of the war, the courts of the Confederacy in that area could not function without military support and not always even then. After the war broke out, Charles Galloway, a staunch Unionist who had opposed secession in Arkansas, led two companies of his fellow southerners to Springfield, Missouri, where they were mustered into the Union Army. Galloway then led his men back to Arkansas to fight the Confederates. Some 48,000 white southern Unionists, it has been estimated, served voluntarily in the Army of the United States. In northern Alabama and Georgia in 1863 and after, peace societies, replete with secret grips, passwords and elaborate security precautions, worked to encourage desertion from the Confederate Army.

A recent study of the Southern Claims Commission provides the most explicit and detailed evidence of the character of southern Unionism during the war. The commission was set up by the United States government at the end of hostilities in order to reimburse those southerners who had sustained certain kinds of property losses because of their loyalty to the Union. (Only actual material losses incurred by loyal southerners in behalf of the Union armies were to be honored; acts of charity or mercy, or losses occasioned by Confederate action, for example, were not included.) Since all claimants first had to offer ironclad proof of loyalty before their losses could even be considered, those who did file claims may well be taken as the hard core of southern Unionism. There must have been thousands more who, because they lacked the opportunity or the substance to help the Union armies, went uncounted. Still others may not have been able to meet the high standards set for proof of loyalty, though their devotion to the Union was unquestioned. Under these circumstances, 22,298 claimants is an impressive number.

One of the striking facts that emerges from a study of the records of the commission is the great number of southern Unionists who were people of substance. The total amount of the claims was $22.5 million, and 701 claims were for losses of $10,000 or more—a very substantial sum in the 1860's. The wealthy claimants were mainly planters, owners of great plantations and large numbers of slaves. Despite their wealth, or perhaps because of it, they stood with the Union when the storm of secession broke upon them—though to do so often meant obloquy and harassment at the very least, and not infrequently confiscation of property and personal danger.

Southern Unionism also played its part in the complicated history of Reconstruction. Tennessee, for example, probably escaped radical congressional Reconstruction because of the large number of Unionists in the state. William "Parson" Brownlow, an old Whig and Unionist turned Republican, was able to gain control of the state after the war, and under his leadership Tennessee managed to avoid the military occupation that was the retribution visited upon its more recalcitrant neighbors.

In Louisiana, the first Republican governor, Michael Hahn, was also a lifelong Unionist, though originally a Democrat; he had opposed secession and during the war had refused to take a pledge of loyalty to the Confederacy. About a third of the members of the Mississippi legislature during Reconstruction were so-called scalawags; but far from being the disreputable persons usually associated with that label, most of them were actually respectable former Whig Unionists turned Republican.

This shift in allegiance from Whig to Republican—by no means a rarity in the Reconstruction South—is not so strange when it is recalled that Lincoln, the first Republican President, was once a confirmed Whig. Indeed, to many former southern Whigs it must have seemed that the Republican party—the party of business, national authority, sound money, and internal improvements—was a most fortunate reincarnation of Henry Clay's old organization. And now that slavery was no more, it seemed that southerners could once again divide politically as their interests dictated.

The opportunity, however, proved to be short-lived, for to resist effectively the excesses of the Radicals during Reconstruction, all southerners of consequence became Democrats as a matter of necessity. But though they may have been Democrats in name, in principles they were Whigs, and as such worked quite easily with northern Republicans to end Reconstruction and to bring new railroads and industry to the South in the 1880's.

Most Americans assume that between 1830 and 1860 all southerners favored slavery. This is not so. In the earlier years of the Republic, the great Virginians had not defended the institution but only excused it as an undeniable evil that was exceptionally difficult to eradicate. It was not until the 1830's that it began to be widely upheld as something to be proud of, a positive good. Here too, as in the nullification controversy, Calhoun's thought dominated the southern mind. He had been among the first prominent southerners to shake off the sense of guilt over slavery and to proclaim it a "great moral revolution." At the same time, however, many men and women in the South continued to doubt the utility, the wisdom, and the justice of slavery. These, too, constituted another South.

Although there were some southerners who opposed slavery for reasons of Christian ethics, many more decried it for economic and political reasons. Cassius Marcellus Clay of Kentucky, a cousin of the more famous Henry, was prominent among those who abominated slavery because it retarded the economic growth of the South. The son of a wealthy slaveholder, Clay was educated at Yale, where his future is supposed to have been decided by hearing William Lloyd Garrison present an abolitionist lecture. Regardless of the cause for Clay's subsequent antislavery views, he emancipated his slaves in 1833, soon after his graduation, and devoted himself to ridding his state of slavery. Despite his proclaimed hostile sentiments on the subject, Clay gained a large following in state and national politics.

The nature of Clay's objections to slavery were made clear in a speech he delivered before the Kentucky legislature in 1841:

> Gentlemen would import slaves "to clear up the forests of the Green River country." Take one day's ride from this capital and then go and tell them what you have seen. Tell them that you have looked upon the once most lovely and fertile lands that nature ever formed; and have seen it in fifty years worn to the rock . . . tell them of the depopulation of the country and the consequent ruin of the towns and villages; tell them that the white Kentuckian has been driven out by slaves, by the unequal competition of unpaid labor; tell them that the mass of our people are uneducated; tell them that you have heard the children of white Kentuckians crying for bread, whilst the children of the African was [*sic*] clothed, and fed, and laughed! And then ask them if they will have blacks to fell their forests.

The troublesome race question effectively prevented some antislavery southerners from taking any concrete steps to end slavery; others saw a threat in the possibility of a large free Negro population. To many, the return of former slaves to Africa seemed the necessary first step in any movement toward emancipation. Cassius Clay was both more radical and more realistic. He recognized that colonization was as illusory a solution to the evils of slavery and the Negro problem as it actually proved to be; many more Negroes were born each year than could possibly be sent to Liberia in a generation. Instead, Clay boldly advocated gradual emancipation, with the owners of the slaves being compensated by the state.

Hinton Rowan Helper is better known today as an antislavery southerner than Clay, though the latter was certainly the more prominent at the time. Helper was the son of a poor North Carolina farmer; with the publication of his book, *The Impending Crisis of the South*, in 1857, he became a nationally known figure. In an effort to demonstrate the material and cultural backwardness of the slave states, Helper brought together statistics from the Census of 1850—compiled by that most indefatigable southern publicist, J. D. B. De Bow, and therefore unimpeachable in southern eyes—to show that in number of libraries, newspapers, and schools, as well as in wealth, manufactures, population, and commerce, the North far outdistanced the South. Helper pointed out that even in agriculture, the vaunted specialty of Dixie, northern production exceeded southern. Almost contemptuously, he observed that the value of the Cotton Kingdom's chief staple was surpassed by that of the North's lowly hay crop. The cause for all these discrepancies, Helper contended, was slavery.

Helper's indictment of slavery was sufficiently telling to arouse violent southern attacks. He also serves to illustrate the variety of motives underlying the southern antislavery movement. He was more disturbed about what slavery did to the poor white man than about what it did to the Negro. Many antislavery men felt the same, but Helper went further; his concern for the white man was coupled with an almost pathological hatred of the black.

Not its economic disadvantages, but its essential incompatibility with the genius of America, was the more compelling argument against slavery for some southerners. The great Virginians of the eighteenth century—men like Washington, Marshall, Patrick Henry, Madison, Jefferson, and Monroe—all felt that it somehow contradicted their ideal of a new republic of freemen. Echoes of this view were heard by Frederick Law Olmsted when he traveled through the back country of the South in the 1850's. One mountain dweller told Olmsted that he "was afraid that there was many a man who had gone to the bad world, who wouldn't have gone if he hadn't had any slaves."

Though less moralistic in his conclusions, Henry Clay was of much the same opinion. "I am no friend to slavery," he wrote to an Alabaman in 1838. "I think it is an evil; but I believe it better that slaves should remain slaves than to be set loose as free men among us. . . ." For Clay, as for many antislavery southerners, it was difficult to believe that emancipated Negroes and whites could live together peacefully in the same country. This deep-seated belief in the incompatibility of the two races constituted the great dilemma in the minds of antislavery southerners; often it paralyzed all action.

The effects of this dilemma were certainly evident in the course of the remarkable debate on slavery in the Virginia legislature in 1832.

The event which precipitated it was a brief but violent uprising of slaves in Southampton County on August 21, 1831. Led by Nat Turner, a slave preacher given to visions and prophecies, the insurrectionists deliberately killed some sixty white people, mainly women and children. But even the rapidity and efficiency with which the might of the white man had been mobilized against the runaway slaves did not assuage the fear that surged through the minds of southerners everywhere. And so it was that on January 11, 1832, there began one of the most searching debates on slavery ever held by the elected representatives of a slaveholding people. For two weeks the venerable institution was subjected to the frankest kind of criticism.

Three quarters of the members of the House of Delegates held slaves, yet more than half of that body spoke out against the institution in one fashion or another. In analyzing the statements and the notes of the members, one historian concluded that 60 of the 134 delegates were consistently antislavery, working for legislation that would eventually terminate Negro bondage in Virginia. Twelve more, whom he calls the compromisers, were antislavery in belief, but were not prepared to vote for any measure which would, at that time, commit the state to emancipation. It was this latter group, in league with the sixty or so defenders of the *status quo,* who defeated the efforts to initiate gradual emancipation in 1832.

Though individual opponents of slavery remained in the South right up to the Civil War, it is impossible to ascertain their numbers. However, a glimpse into the mind of one such southerner has been afforded by the publication of the diary of Mary Minor Blackford. Mrs. Blackford lived in Fredericksburg, Virginia, across the street from a slave trader's house, a location which permitted her to see slavery at its worst. And it was slavery as a moral evil rather than as an economic fallacy which troubled her: how could people otherwise good and humane, kind and Christian, hold fellow human beings in bondage? For unlike some northern abolitionists, she knew slave owners too well to think them innately evil. Her answer was not surprising: material self-interest morally blinded them.

The tragedy of the South's history was woven into the fabric of Mary Minor Blackford's life. Despite her long opposition to slavery, she proudly saw five of her sons serve in the Confederate Army. Yet with its defeat, she could still write early in 1866: "A New Era has dawned since I last wrote in this book. Slavery has been abolished!!!"

Other individual opponents of slavery in the South could be cited, but perhaps it would be best to close by mentioning an antislavery organization. The American Colonization Society, founded in 1817 by southern and northern antislavery men, always included prominent southerners among its leaders. In the course of its half century of operations, the society managed to send more than six thousand Negroes to its African colony in Liberia.

The society was strongest in the South; indeed, it was anathema to the New England and middle western abolitionists. Though it is true that antislavery was never a popular cause in the South, it was never a dead one, either, so long as thousands of southerners refused to view slavery as anything but an evil for their region.

As we have seen, the South was even less united on nullification and secession than it was on the question of slavery. In fact, it is now clear that if a majority of southerners ever did support secession—and there is real doubt on this—it was never a big majority, and it was not achieved until the very eve of the Civil War. In short, the South, rather than being a monolith of undivided opinion, was not even of one mind on the two most vital issues of the thirty years that led up to the war.

The Myth of "Cavalier" Confederate Leadership

Wilbur Cash

Central to the southern myth is its legendary sociology—the belief in the ascendancy of a southern aristocracy in the antebellum period. Thus, the mythical structure of the prewar South comprised three classes: Aristocrat, "Cracker," and Black. True, the South had come to cultivate a taste for form, formality, and the ornamental quality of life. But, as the native southern journalist Wilbur Cash imaginatively observes here, neither *time* nor the essential *frontier* character of the early South was conducive to the development of a Cavalier society. Some had become *nouveaux riches*, but yeoman farmers—not planter aristocrats—and log cabins—not white-columned mansions—were the measure of life as the South then knew it.

How account for the ruling class, then? Manifestly, for the great part, by the strong, the pushing, the ambitious, among the old coon-hunting population of the backcountry. The frontier was their predestined inheritance. They possessed precisely the qualities necessary to the taming of the land and the building of the cotton kingdom. The process of their rise to power was simplicity itself. Take a concrete case.

A stout young Irishman brought his bride into the Carolina up-country about 1800. He cleared a bit of land, built a log cabin of two rooms, and sat down to the pioneer life. One winter, with several of his neighbors, he loaded a boat with whisky and the coarse woolen cloth woven by the women, and drifted down to Charleston to trade. There, remembering the fondness of his woman for a bit of beauty, he bought a handful of cotton seed, which she planted about the cabin with the wild rose and the honeysuckle—as a flower. Afterward she learned, under the tutelage of a new neighbor, to pick the seed from the fiber with her fingers and to spin it into yarn. Another winter the man drifted down the river, this time to find the half-way station of Columbia in a strange ferment. There was a new wonder in the world—the cotton gin—and the forest which had lined the banks of the stream for a thousand centuries was beginning to go down. Fires flared red and portentous in the night—to set off an answering fire in the breast of the Irishman.

Land in his neighborhood was to be had for fifty cents an acre. With twenty dollars, the savings of his lifetime, he bought forty acres and set himself to clear it. Rising long before day, he toiled deep into the night, with his wife holding a pine torch for him to see by. Aided by his neighbors, he piled the trunks of the trees into great heaps and burned them, grubbed up the stumps, hacked away the tangle of underbrush and vine, stamped out the poison ivy and the snakes. A wandering trader sold him a horse, bony and half-starved, for a knife, a dollar, and a gallon of whisky. Every day now—Sundays not excepted—when the heavens allowed, and every night that the moon came, he drove the plow into the earth, with uptorn roots bruising his shanks at every step. Behind him came his wife with a hoe. In a few years the land was beginning to yield cotton—richly, for the soil was fecund with the accumulated mold of centuries. Another trip down the river, and he brought home a mangy black slave—an old and lazy fellow reckoned of no account in the ricelands, but with plenty of life in him still if you knew how to get it out. Next year the Irishman bought fifty acres more, and the year after another black. Five years more and he had two hundred acres and ten Negroes. Cotton prices swung up and down sharply, but always, whatever the return, it was almost pure velvet. For the fertility of the soil seemed inexhaustible.

When he was forty-five, he quit work, abandoned the log house, which had grown to six rooms, and built himself a wide-spreading frame cottage. When he was fifty, he became a magistrate, acquired a carriage, and built a cotton gin and a third house—a "big house" this time. It was not, to be truthful, a very grand house really. Built of lumber sawn on the place, it was a little crude and had not cost above a thousand dollars, even when the marble mantel was counted in. Essentially, it was just a box, with four rooms, bisected by a hallway, set on four more rooms bisected by another hallway, and a detached kitchen at the back. Wind-swept in winter, it was difficult to keep clean of vermin in summer. But it was huge, it had great columns in front, and it was eventually painted white, and so, in this land of wide fields and pinewoods it seemed very imposing.

Meantime the country around had been growing up. Other "big houses" had been built. There was a county seat now, a cluster of frame houses, stores, and "doggeries" about a red brick courthouse. A Presbyterian parson had drifted in and started an academy, as Presbyterian parsons had a habit of doing everywhere in the South—and Pompeys and Caesars and Ciceros and Platos were multiplying both among the pickaninnies in the slave quarters and among the white children of the "big houses." The Irishman had a piano in his house, on which his daughters, taught by a vagabond German, played as well as young ladies could be expected to. One of the Irishman's sons went to the College of South Carolina, came back to grow into the chief lawyer in the county, got to be a judge, and would have been Governor if he had not died at the head of his regiment at Chancellorsville.

As a crown on his career, the old man went to the Legislature, where he was accepted by the Charleston gentlemen tolerantly and with genuine liking.

He grew extremely mellow in age and liked to pass his time in company, arguing about predestination and infant damnation, proving conclusively that cotton was king and that the damyankee didn't dare do anything about it, and developing a notable taste in the local liquors. Tall and well-made, he grew whiskers after the Galway fashion—the well-kept whiteness of which contrasted very agreeably with the brick red of his complexion—donned the long-tailed coat, stove-pipe hat, and string tie of the statesmen of his period, waxed innocently pompous, and, in short, became a really striking figure of a man.

Once, going down to Columbia for the inauguration of a new Governor, he took his youngest daughter along. There she met a Charleston gentleman who was pestering her father for a loan. Her manner, formed by the Presbyterian parson, was plain but not bad, and she was very pretty. Moreover, the Charleston gentleman was decidedly in hard lines. So he married her.

When the old man finally died in 1854, he left two thousand acres, a hundred and fourteen slaves, and four cotton gins. The little newspaper which had recently set up in the county seat spoke of him as "a gentleman of the old school" and "a noble specimen of the chivalry at its best"; the Charleston papers each gave him a column; and a lordly Legaré introduced resolutions of respect into the Legislature. His wife outlived him by ten years—by her portrait a beautifully fragile old woman, and, as I have heard it said, with lovely hands, knotted and twisted just enough to give them character, and a finely transparent skin through which the blue veins showed most aristocratically.

The Confederate Myth

Frank E. Vandiver

Looking backward with fondness and nostalgia, the American South has succeeded in manufacturing an elaborate "Confederate Myth." It is the product of every man's appetite for historical romance. The "Confederate Myth" has been fed by a social psychology receptive to such patterns of thought, both North and South; it is here challenged by Frank E. Vandiver, Provost of Rice University. Vandiver, a student of the southern mind and its mystique, systematically tries to destroy, each in turn, the major pillars of the Confederate mythical edifice. Wedded in the antebellum period, nurtured during the war between the states, and fashioned in "marble images" during the postwar era, the myth of the Confederacy, Vandiver claims, has withstood the test of time but has burdened the South with a "pseudo-past."

In the states of the old Confederacy the Centennial celebration of the Civil War is to be largely a refurbishing of the Confederate myth. The Confederate myth is a vital part of life in the South. According to this legend, sanctified southern ancestors fought valiantly against virtually hopeless odds to sustain a "way of life" peculiar to the section of long, hot summers, and Negro field hands. This "way of life" never seemed to be wholly understood, but it found description in various paeans of nostalgia and in the self-image of all southerners. Key elements in the southern mode of living were tradition, dedication to the protocols of lineage, land, cotton, sun, and vast hordes of blacks. Tending southern life were a special breed represented by the planters. Not everybody by any means was a planter, but the myth holds that everybody wanted to be and that all had the same chance to rise to that pinnacle of grace—all save the noncitizens with dark skin. The planters came to hoard their status with a certain grim zeal. Under increasing pressure throughout the 1830's, 40's, and 50's, they turned to all types of protection—censorship, intimidation, propaganda, open hostility to fellow-Americans.

But their tactics were glossed by myth into a creditable struggle for self-determination against a tide of urban nationalism which threatened extinction of the "way of life" so happy and so alien to the time.

The crusade of the planters spread to a campaign for Southern Rights, and hence the small farmer, the town merchant, the southern clergy found

From "The Confederate Myth," by Frank E. Vandiver. Reprinted with permission of the publisher and author from *Southwest Review*, XLVI (Summer 1961), 199–204.

themselves sharing the planter's war. What was good for the planter was good for the South.

War, according to the myth, may not have been the only way to save the social and economic order, but it showed how deeply dedicated were the southerners to their inarticulated "rights." Against forces most formidable the southerner pitted himself, his small fortune, his Lilliputian industry, his life, and his girded honor. He lost, but lost magnificently. He lost wholly, utterly, but out of the ashes of his homes, his cities, his broken generation, he salvaged his sacred honor. And with this scrap of victory he could build the myth that has sustained him, has shackled him to a false image, and has convinced him of a lasting difference between himself and the rest of the United States.

Marshall Fishwick, in a brave and controversial essay, "Robert E. Lee: The Guardian Angel Myth" (*Saturday Review*, March 4, 1961), points out that Lee's noble virtues, peerless leadership, and heroic acceptance of defeat fixed in the southern mind the meaning of the Lost Cause. That cause represented the true acme of southern achievement; for it died the flower of the South, and those who yielded up their blood were such southerners as all those who came since would like to be. They were the shining model, the marble image, the men above men who lived a brief moment as destiny's chosen. They were the South.

They still are the South, for they stand above, around, and beyond what the South now is, and loom as silent prophets to lesser men in troubled times. And so they are God and curse, inspiration and death. Their stone faces look from countless shafts to the past, and their sons, grandsons, and great-grandsons look with them. They are different from the present; they were alien to their time. So, too, the modern southerner who points to difference, to his ageless "white man's burden" and his genteel poverty. His ancestors lurking from musty picture frames stood against the leviathan state and its leveling tendencies. He, too, stands with his own perception of past obligations and future duties. If the rest of the nation has lost its agrarian innocence, the southerner remembers. He, at least, is faithful to a dim Jeffersonian image and to a Greek democracy ideal which came, was fleetingly touched by life and sustained by blood, and faded to the pantheon of lost glories. But the brief blood bath lent a strange endurance and gave hope to generations held tight in inertia, fear, poverty, and the horror of a lost dream and a shattered mirror. The broken image had to be conjured again, and when it came it was twisted into a grotesque sort of plaster beauty which satisfied its designers and doomed the past it seemed to limn to a hundred years of distortion.

Distorting Civil War southerners was not easy. They lived larger than most, fought, raged, cowed, bled, spoke, and died with the nobility of desperation. They were, like their northern brethren, touched with timeless animation. They were unique and so should have been immune to the myth-makers and falsifiers of history. But myth-makers are determined and their works often approved by necessity. So the Confederate changed from a human, striving, erring being to something much different. All Confederates automatically became virtuous, all were defenders of the rights of states and individuals, all were segregationists, all steadfast, all patriotic.

Like all lasting myths, this one had enough validity to sound good. The Lost Cause came on to the present as the last American resistance against the Organization State, against racial indistinction, against mass and motor.

And while post-Civil War southerners were pushing as fast as they could into the New South, were grasping Yankee dollars with enthusiasm, they purified their motives in the well of Lost Causism. Politicians found it a bottomless source of bombast and ballots, preachers found it balm and solace to somewhat reluctant middle-class morals, writers found it a noble and salable theme. What the South had been could be the touchstone for the future, could be the fundament of a section going into the industrial age with part of its heart and holding firm to the past with the other.

Lost Causism came to fulfill a role similar to that of the pro-slavery argument in antebellum times. It offered justification for resistance to the leveling tendencies continued by harsh Reconstruction measures. It cloaked the lawless Klansman and lent license to the segregating Christian. It was, finally, the cornerstone of the New South.

The tragedy is that the Confederate myth is so wrong. That the Confederacy could come to represent in the present things it never represented in its lifetime is an irony of the present southern dilemma.

What, then, are some of the axioms of the Confederate myth?

First: The Confederate States represented the unified nationalistic yearning of all the states' rights advocates in the South.

Wrong. States' righters were not unified and there is considerable doubt that they were in the majority when the Confederacy took form in February, 1861. Certain it is that they failed to gain control of the government under Jefferson Davis, and although they did much to impede the Confederate war effort, they did not dominate the high councils.

Second: The Confederacy was defended to the last by gaunt gray heroes who went with Lee and Johnston and others to the bitterest end.

Wrong again. There was probably more per capita desertion from Confederate ranks than from the ranks of the Union. Far more Rebel troops were absent from roll call at the end of the war than were with the colors. Much bravery, even shining, incredible heroism the southern men did display, but that they were all blind patriots is demonstrably untrue.

Third: Any Confederate could lick ten Yankees.

Possibly, but in the end the Rebels were "overwhelmed."

Fourth: Everyone behind the Confederate lines showed the same dauntless dedication to oblivion as the soldiery. Men, women, and children all served the cause to the last shred of cloth, the last window weight, the last crust of bread.

Not so. While there were many magnificent examples of fate-defying loyalty by southern civilians, there were also many examples of petty speculation, wanton brigandage, Unionism, criminal selfishness, and treason. Defection behind the lines, open resistance to Confederate laws, became a matter of national scandal before the conflict ended.

Fifth: All Confederate leaders were unswervingly dedicated to the cause and would have preferred to perish rather than survive under a despised and crushing victor.

Still wrong. Many Confederate leaders, including Davis, Stephens, Lee, and Stonewall Jackson, looked on secession with a jaundiced eye. Legal they thought it to be, but they doubted its practicality. And when the war ended only a few of the leaders who survived buried themselves in the past. Davis did, and so did lasting disservice to the section he strove to defend. Lee, on the other hand, put the war behind him and worked unsparingly for a prosperous New South sharing fully the destiny of a re-United States. His example set the tone for most veterans. Numbers of former generals, to be sure, used their combat records to gain some personal advantage, but most wanted that advantage to further a career in business or politics and hence partook of the new industrial age.

Sixth: The Confederacy fought not only for states' rights, but also and especially to preserve racial integrity. The government and the people of the embattled southern states were solidly against letting down racial barriers and understood that a northern victory would mean abolition. The Negro was kept in his place in the Confederacy, was used only for agricultural and menial tasks, and what was good enough for the Confederates is good enough for us.

False, and this is false on two levels. During the war the South did attempt for a time to shore up the bonds of servitude, but when the pressure of defeat grew grim, various southern leaders, including Lee and Davis, came to advocate the use of slaves in the army; some even suggested freedom in return for service. And after the war, on the level of special pleading, the South engaged in a long paper conflict with northern historians about the causes of the fighting. A point which the southerners strove staunchly to sustain was that the war had not been fought to preserve slavery, but to preserve the "Southern Way of Life," of which slavery was only an aspect. Finally some argued that the war had been fought solely to gain independence, and cited the offer to England in March, 1865, of total freedom in exchange for recognition as proof.

Seventh: The Confederate government was a supreme, unsullied example of a states' rights organization that remained loyal to the principles of Calhoun, even in face of defeat.

This is the wrongest of all assumptions. Davis and his administration tried for a while to do what seemed constitutional under the narrow southern view of law, but war and a curiously unnoticed strain of mind in the South changed the course of governmental conduct.

Union sentiment, long-standing in many parts of the South, united with conservative Democratic sentiment and with latent Whiggery to introduce a new element in southern politics. Men who looked on violent change with repugnance banded together to prevent the secessionists from carrying the Confederacy to revolutionary excesses. These men, including Davis himself, kept the Montgomery Convention in hand, saw to it that the trend toward vast, ruinous upheaval was halted by moderate counsel. The result of moderate control at Montgomery was a Confederate constitution much like that of the Union, a government based on established and familiar federal principles, and a president who had not camped with the fire-eaters. Many with these cautious views were elected to the various Confederate congresses and so held some authority through the war.

Caution and the natural conservatism of some Democrats and Whigs did not mean that these members of the Confederate Congress were unwilling to fight a hard war. Most of these southern moderates were men dedicated to strong central government as the main bulwark of law and order. They hated disturbance and resisted disruption of the Union. But when it came, they "went with their state," they stayed with family and land. They stayed, too, with principles of steady government, strong law, and established order. Consequently they stood for power in the hands of the executive, power in the federal government and a stern war effort.

It was these Whiggish moderates who came to represent the Confederate "left" and to urge big government to fight a big war. They knew something of the corporate state, saw that it had virtues for organization, and urged Davis and his cabinet to centralize and command. These neo-organization men supported the growth of a large army, strict taxation (in keeping with sound Whig monetary views), conscription, impressment of private property, and finally the use of Negro slaves in the ranks—even to the point of manumission in return for service. When the war ended, these same "leftists" of the Confederacy moved into the New South.

Many became leaders in new southern industries, some went into politics and supported the coming of northern capital, most stood for sound finances, restoration of order, and the onward march of business. These moderates, these quiet men who abhorred revolution but used it when they had to, were the ones who brought about the greatest revolution of the South. They changed the Confederacy right under the eyes of the rabid secessionists from a localistic community into a small industrial power run along centralized lines. They aroused resistance from the Confederate "right"—states' righers and fire-eaters—but kept control and forced their opponents to adopt modern centralist measures to resist them. When their attempt to remake the wartime South ended in defeat, they continued their efforts with the aid of Radical Republicans and ultimately achieved their goal. The Old South disappeared in the smoke of Chattanooga's and Birmingham's iron furnaces, in the dust of Alabama's coal pits, in the busy marts of Atlanta, Houston, Memphis, and New Orleans. These quiet, soft action men were the ones who set the base for the rise of a new industrial giant south of Mason and Dixon's Line, a giant whose future, according to Professor Walter Prescott Webb, is limitless because of its natural resources.

But in one salient respect these Whiggish gentlemen failed to remold their native section: this boundless potential painted by Webb and many chambers of commerce is sharply restricted by the Confederate myth. Although the moderate businessmen of the Confederate and New South were willing and partially able to set the black man free, and did break the bonds of southern agriculture, they could not unshackle the mind of the South—the Negro became a symbol of all troubles, and the Confederacy lingered as the herald of the South's greatness. The myth holds that the South was so great when it fought with piteous ardor for a twisted past and for principles aged and vestigial, that there was no future left for it. Its future lay buried with its gray dead.

This stultifying acceptance of decline is the wages of the Confederate myth. What was, was pure and better than what is, and in what was lies a sort of self-realization. While the South was transformed by Confederates into a moderately modern, progressive nation, the myth twists the achievement of the rebellious generation and dooms descendants to cheating themselves. Acceptance of the illusion of rabid Confederate racism, for instance, leads the modern Confederate to waste a vast source of manpower—a source which could be of inestimable value if the South is to move into the rosy future that some have predicted for it.

The Centennial years could best be devoted to revising the Confederate myth and bringing it up to date. Instead of standing for a pseudo-past, for false traditions and sham virtues, it should be repaired by the reality of perspective into what it has always been. Lee, Davis, members of the Confederate Congress, many soldiers who fell gallantly on scores of fields, were alert, forward-looking southerners. They were willing, for the sake of their cause, to abandon old shibboleths, to change the very nature of their body politic and body social. Instead of looking back and making war with weapons withered by age, they looked at the new ones their enemies used and copied, improved, progressed. The Confederate States of America did not have America in the name for nothing. Confederates were Americans, too, and so had no fear of challenge. The Rebels accepted challenge and almost met it. Most of them surely would regard with scorn their descendants who look backward in frustration.

Robert E. Lee: The Guardian Angel Myth

Marshall Fishwick

It was the English historian and social critic Thomas Carlyle who most fully endorsed the notion of the "Great Man Theory" of history, contending that historical change is the product of great men inspired by pure ideas. The South's foremost "historical hero" has undoubtedly been Robert E. Lee. Demonstrating that at times myth is indeed at one with the reality of history, Marshall Fishwick, Director of the American Studies Institute at Lincoln University in Pennsylvania, here confronts the problem of the continuing impact of Robert E. Lee on southern social psychology. Since leading the "crusade of the planters" to the doors of Appomattox, Lee has come to serve as symbol of the "lost cause" and "guardian angel" to succeeding generations of southerners.

Robert E. Lee was the most remarkable man the American South has produced. Others were more versatile, intelligent, learned, and articulate, but Lee has been the most influential. Unsuccessful as a soldier, he was turned into a saint. Now even those whose Union he almost destroyed reverence him. The man who could not save the Confederacy as a general now hovers over it like a guardian angel.

As the Civil War Centennial begins I write not to exalt Lee the general (that has been done deservedly and repeatedly) but to exorcise Lee the guardian angel.

His life completely reversed the American success pattern. He did not begin life in a log cabin but in a Georgian manor house. He was definitely not one of the boys. Thomas Lee, an ancestor, had been the only native Virginian to serve as royal governor. When Stratford Hall, the Lee mansion, burned, the English Queen gave money from the privy purse to help rebuild it. In a family-centered region, his was *the* family. But with Robert E. Lee the family luck seemed to run out. After a military career with very infrequent promotions (he was a captain for twenty-one years) he decided to serve the Confederacy, even though he opposed secession. That he fought exceedingly well no one can seriously question. But he lost, and he died a prisoner on parole.

His last five years were spent at an obscure little college. During that time he refused to speak in his own defense (he alone of all the generals on either side wrote no memoirs) or to have others speak for him. Lord Acton wrote

From "Robert E. Lee: The Guardian Angel Myth," by Marshall Fishwick. *Saturday Review* (March 4, 1961).

him with word of a new publication, and pledged that "the new review shall follow the course which you prescribe and that any communication with which you may honour me shall be kept in strictest confidence." Lee offered no prescription.

Indifferent to political theory and practice, he seems to have had no interest whatever in the Confederacy as a government, or in industrialization, Darwinism, and the other major issues of his time. He simply did not have a conceptualizing mind. His religion was fundamental and his conduct was gentlemanly. All his life he was a creature of method and routine. "Robert was always good," his father wrote in 1817. And so men have said ever since.

It is this unspectacular and unsuccessful life that has thrown a long shadow over the whole South for a century. "He had been dead for years and yet his spirit seemed so close to us that I was afraid," James Street wrote of his own North Carolina boyhood. "He was always watching me and when I did bad things, like write dirty words on a fence or chunk at birds, he shook his head and disapproved. God, my grandmother, and Robert E. Lee were always watching me. He was the archangel Michael, away off yonder beyond my reach—pure white, godly, and cold."

"To this day," Cleveland Amory writes in "Who Killed Society?", "so great is the deference to Lee's name that Southerners control any and all matters of manners, morals, and mores by the mildest mention of him. 'Whenever we did something bad,' a lady from Lynchburg says of her school days, 'the head mistress would quietly turn Lee's picture to the wall—and that was enough.' "

The old revere him no less than the young. I have stood at the deathbed of an elderly lady and heard her say, "I'm not afraid to die. I'm going to heaven. Then I'll see the three I've always loved—my husband, Jesus, and Robert E. Lee."

What is behind such an attitude? And what effect has it had on the region and the nation to which, willy-nilly, the South is organically welded?

The switch from Lee the general to Lee the guardian angel seems to have been instantaneous. The Lee Memorial Society was organized on October 12, 1870—the day the general died. The charter read that "no duty is more sacred than that of making manifest the love of his countrymen for the character and genius of Robert E. Lee."

Soon Richmond ladies had formed the Ladies' Lee Monument Association and were collecting funds, in a desolate and bankrupt South, for a sixty-foot statue featuring Lee bedecked in sash and cavalry sword. Executed by the French sculptor Jean Mercié, it reached Richmond in three boxes. Each was dragged to the site by willing human helpers: the first by ex-Confederates, the second by townsmen, the third by women and girls. Here was one heavy chore for which delicate ladies vied; and sections of the ropes used are still prized as relics.

As impressive as the monument was, Thomas Nelson Page was quite right when he said: "His monument is the adoration of the South; his shrine is in every Southern heart."

The law of compensation was at work. The North had the victory, but the South had Robert E. Lee. He became, instantaneously, the symbol of all that the South *had been,* and the North *could never be,* no matter how many smokestacks it erected. When men are not attracted by the present or future, they turn inevitably to an idolization of the past. The glories (real and imagined) of the Good Old Days become an impregnable castle from which flies the invincible banner of "the Lost Cause." So it was south of the Potomac.

Some Southerners, at least, have admitted it. Writes Clarence Cason: "Eating the cornbread and sorghum of 1870, the impoverished and discouraged Southerners bravely drew mental pictures of tables laden with pheasant and Burgundy. The psychological reaction constituted a typical flight from reality." Leading this fleeing army was not Lee the general, but Lee the guardian angel. And the result was much more disastrous than Gettysburg.

To the consequences we give the name Reconstruction, although it also bore many signs of Retrogression. In place of *noblesse oblige* came white supremacy; in place of curiosity, bigotry; in place of democracy, demagoguery. No one in his right mind could blame the decline on Robert E. Lee; but his name was invoked in many of the acts, and his guardian angel was said to flutter close by and to bless them. More and more he came to be remembered not in military but in religious terms. From hundreds of examples, I choose two typical ones. At an 1883 memorial service, John W. Daniel used this analogy:

> Since the Son of Man stood upon the Mount, and saw "all the kingdoms of the world and the glory of them" stretched before him, and turned away to the agony and bloody sweat of Gethsemane, and to the Cross of Calvary beyond, no follower of the meek and lowly Savior had undergone more trying ordeals than Lee.

A second quotation, from a speech Henry T. Wickham made in the Virginia Senate during World War II, shows how little the rhetoric had altered in some sixty years:

> Some devout clergymen have, with the utmost reverence, likened Lee's last words, "Strike the tent," to the last words of the Savior on the cross of Calvary, "It is finished." I believe when Lee uttered those words that a vision of glory appeared before his closing eyes; a vision of the progress of a pilgrim.

While orators were busy linking Jesus and the guardian angel in heaven, things were going badly for many Southerners on earth. Dixie became a colonial outpost for Yankee money. In 1880 the per capita wealth in the South was a startling 57 percent below the national average, and the deficiency stood at 56.3 percent in 1900. A region-wide capitulation to racism developed; Jim Crow segregation laws took on the guise of a "permanent solution." In the 1890s, 1,111 Negroes were lynched in the United States. "Almost any offense was likely to be considered sufficiently sinister to lead to lynching," Francis Simkins writes, "such as slapping children, using offensive or boastful language, and seeking political or other employment deemed improper for members of an inferior caste."

When the Great Depression struck, Dixie's situation moved from pitiful to unbearable. Planters abandoned their lands and left tenants to starve. Hordes of people wandered into overcrowded city slums, looking for jobs that didn't exist. The South became, in the words of President Roosevelt's National Emergency Council, "the nation's number one economic problem."

Yet not even this social catastrophe, nor the war that followed on its heels, could turn a mesmerized South from the Civil War and the peerless knight who had led the heroes in gray. As Arnold Toynbee notes in "A Study of History":

> In the Southern states the memory of that catastrophe is as green in our generation as if the blow had fallen only yesterday; and "the war" still means the Civil War, though two fearful wars have since supervened.

Professor Toynbee points to the worst of all Southern diseases: myopia. Cultural nearsightedness has been more devastating than the boll weevil, hookworm, carpetbaggers, and the NAACP combined. It has deprived men of the outlook and resilience that would put other problems in perspective. Since World War II militant sectionalism has cropped up in the social, cultural, and political life of the South.

What is needed, desperately and quickly, is a change of strategy. Rather than re-enacting Confederate battles, the South should enact laws that would stop potential battles from taking place in our own time. Rather than arguing about what did happen at Gettysburg, Southerners should ask what is happening in Leopoldville and New Delhi—in the world South of which ours is a small but pivotal portion.

General Lee would have seen the need for a new strategy instantly; guardian angel Lee never will. "If the Great Man were here today" can form the basis for a cheap kind of game in which the author proves his point by making himself speak for the dead. I do not intend to do that with General Lee. But I do think it fair to quote from a scrap of paper found with his papers after his death, and to comment on its implications. There were the words he had written:

> The forbearing use of power does not only form a touchstone, but the manner in which an individual enjoys certain advantages over others is a test of a true gentleman. . . . The gentleman cannot only forgive, he can forget; and he strives for that nobleness of self and mildness of character which impart sufficient strength to *let the past be but the past.*

Has the South been willing to forgive, let alone forget, the defeat and miseries to which she was subjected a century ago? Have her leaders and policymakers been willing to "let the past be but the past"? Obviously not. Yet the very men who have flagrantly disregarded the words of the living Lee have called upon the dead Lee for succor.

They do not know their man. Instead of fighting change and growth, Lee encouraged and commended it. Look at his achievements after 1865, when he served as president of Washington College. Enrollment jumped from a handful to over 410, who came from twenty-six states. In 1866 he founded a "School of Law and Equity," and in 1867 a Students' Business School. The man who is taken as a symbol of agrarian aristocracy wrote to his Board of Trustees on January 8, 1869: "In recommending a Commercial School, it is proposed, not merely to give instruction in bookkeeping and the forms and details of business, but to teach the principles of Commercial Economy, Trade, and Mercantile Law."

That same year saw the College offer practical and theoretical courses in journalism (the first such offerings in any American college), and lay plans for courses in agriculture.

During these years Lee sought and won financial support not only from many Southern sympathizers, but also from such unlikely donors as Thomas A. Scott (Lincoln's assistant secretary of war) and Henry Ward Beecher.

All this suggests that a man who had such vision in the 1860s would see that in the 1960s the intellectual battlefield includes not only the Potomac, but the Congo, Nile, and Yellow rivers. With the launching of satellites, the basic premise of the human condition, man's bondage to the earth, was modified. We deal now with characteristics, not properties, with purpose, not causality; with process, not product. Notions of energy, matter, and time are in flux. Some fields are advancing so fast that they are almost unteachable. We are confronted by novelty without precedent, power without measurement. Scholars estimate that we are now doubling the knowledge in our intellectual storehouse every ten years. Little wonder: 90 percent of all scientists who ever lived are alive today.

The American South, perplexed by matters at home and abroad, confronts a paradox. To understand her own problems, she must study other men's. To preserve her basic distinctions, she must acknowledge human similarities.

And she must preserve her own flavor and history, no matter how terrifying the problems. To abandon these would be spiritual suicide. "If Southerners deny their inner beings," warns Cleanth Brooks, "the South can be only an exporter of raw materials and man power, and a consumer of imported cultural products. It will cease to export them. In the creative sense it will be numb and sterile."

So we come back to where we began, and ask with James Street: who wants a general for a guardian angel? No one, if when he is enshrined in cold, spotless marble all the heart and the fire that belonged to the man disappear forever. Let us enshrine instead the living Lee. In this Lee was a daring bugle sound; a swift-leaping reckless fire that cannot be put into marble or angel wings.

I cannot believe that Robert E. Lee wanted to become a guardian angel.

Instead I prefer to think that in our day, as in his, he would think not in terms of defense but offense. If our South would be as bold as was his, and as willing to risk everything for decent and honorable principles, she might become a challenge rather than an enigma to the free world.

The Enigma of the South

David M. Potter

Arguing from the conviction that the South has genuine and important features of distinctiveness, David Potter, late of Stanford University, questions whether the term *agrarianism* best describes southern uniqueness. Does agrarianism, Potter asks, convey the essence and nature of southernism? Despite the counter opinions of some historians and those of the southern literary tradition, Potter attests that the equation of southernism and agrarianism is a myth. The agrarian formula fits the South badly—it does not represent that which lies at the heart of Dixie. As Potter suggests: ". . . the whole idea of the South as an agrarian society now seems more and more an illusion, nourished by a wish."

Among the many flourishing branches of American historical study during the last half-century, one of the most robust has been the history of the South. Fifty years ago, there was already one large body of literature on the Southern Confederacy, especially in its military aspects, and another on the local history of various Southern states, but the history of the South as a region—of the whole vast area below the Potomac, viewed as a single entity for the whole time from the settlement of Jamestown to the present—is largely a product of the last five decades. Today, a multi-volume history, a number of college textbooks, a quarterly journal, and a substantial library of monographic studies all serve as measures of the extent of the development in this field.

Anyone who seeks an explanation for this interest in Southern history must take account of several factors. To begin with, the study of American regions is a general phenomenon, embracing not only the South but also New England, the Middle West, and the great physiographic provinces beyond the Mississippi. In a nation as vast and as diverse as ours, there is really no level higher than the regional level at which one can come to grips with the concrete realities of the land. But apart from this regional aspect, the Southern theme has held an unusual appeal for the people of the South because of their peculiarly strong and sentimental loyalty to Dixie as their native land, and for Americans outside the South because of the exotic quality of the place and because it bears the aura of a Lost Cause. Union generals, for some reason, have never held the romantic interest that attached to Stonewall Jackson, Jeb Stuart, George Pickett, Bedford Forrest, and, of course,

Robert E. Lee. Today, the predilection of Yankee children for caps, flags, and toys displaying the Rebel insignia bears further witness to the enduring truth that lost causes have a fascination even for those who did not lose them.

But it seems unlikely that either the South as an American region, or the South as Dixieland, or the South as a Lost Cause could hold so much scholarly and popular attention in focus if the South were not also an enigma. To writers for more than half a century the South has been a kind of sphinx on the American land.

To some who viewed it, this sphinx has seemed a great insensate monolith, a vast artifact of the past with no meaning behind its inscrutable expression. Its domain has been just what H. L. Mencken said it was—a cultural desert, a Sahara of the Bozart. But to others this sphinx has seemed to hold a secret, an answer to the riddle of American life.

To many people today, who think of the South in terms of Freedom Riders and lunch-counter sit-ins, of Tobacco Road and Central High School in Little Rock, of robed Klansmen and burning crosses, and perhaps of a Monkey Trial at Dayton, Tennessee, it may seem hard to believe that not long ago the South was regarded by many thoughtful and liberal-minded people as a kind of sanctuary of the American democratic tradition. What is now deplored as the "benighted South," or the "sick South," was, until recently, regarded by many liberals as the birthplace and the natural bulwark of the Jeffersonian ideal—a region where agrarian democracy still struggled to survive, fighting a gallant rearguard action against the commercialism and the industrial capitalism of the Northeast.

It would be a major undertaking to trace the evolution of this concept. The general idea that American democracy is essentially frontier democracy—which closely resembles agrarian democracy—is forever linked with Frederick Jackson Turner, but Turner gave it a Western rather than a Southern orientation. Certainly one of the earliest writers to apply it to the South was William E. Dodd. In 1911, when Dodd had been but recently appointed to the University of Chicago, and twenty-two years before Franklin Roosevelt sent him as our unswervingly democratic ambassador to Hitler's Berlin, he wrote a sketchy little book, now largely forgotten, entitled *Statesmen of the Old South,* with the significant subtitle, *From Radicalism to Conservative Revolt.* The statesmen whom he treated were Jefferson, Calhoun, and Jefferson Davis, and the theme which he developed was that the democratic or radical South of Thomas Jefferson—an equalitarian South of small subsistence farmers—had been subverted by the increasingly aristocratic and hierarchical South of the great slaveholders whose property interests found embodiment in Calhoun and Davis.

In three brief and seemingly artless chapters, Dodd achieved two very subtle effects. First, he defined to suit himself what may be called a normative South—the South of Thomas Jefferson—and thus established an arbitrary basis for indentifying all future developments of a Jeffersonian tenor as truly or intrinsically Southern, and for rejecting all conservative or hierarchical developments as aberrations of Southernism. Using this device, he then proceeded to dispose of the whole conservative, slaveholding South of antebellum fame as a kind of deviation or detour in the true course of Southern history. Thus he finessed the basic question whether the true and realistic image of the South might not be a dualism, with as much of Calhoun as of Jefferson in it, or even whether the true South, historically, is not hierarchical and conservative rather than radical and equalitarian.

In justice to Dodd, one must recognize that his version of Southernism was by no means without foundations. Jeffersonianism, as well as Jefferson, did have distinctively Southern origins, and at almost every decisive turning point in the advancement of American democracy—whether at the time of Jackson, or Bryan, or Wilson, or Franklin Roosevelt—the South has thrown crucial weight on the democratic side. Still, there was something of a tour de force about the way in which Dodd reconciled his love for his native South and his commitment to democracy, and, with very little disclosure of the wishful thinking which was involved, identified the land he loved with the values he cherished.

Whether later writers were directly influenced by Dodd or not, the theme of agrarianism has persisted ever since in the literature of the South, sometimes with the most startling implications. Thus when Charles and Mary Beard came to write about the Civil War in their *The Rise of American Civilization* (1927), they pictured it as a conflict between Southern agrarianism and Northern industrialism; in this way, the defenders of slavery were transmuted into democrats, more or less, since agrarianism was, in the Beards' lexicon, by definition democratic, and industrialism was anti-democratic. Again, at the hands of the Beards and of the late Howard K. Beale, in his *The Critical Year*, published in 1930, Reconstruction was not primarily a contest over the rights of Negro freedmen, but rather a series of coups by industrial capitalism to consolidate its ascendancy and to retain its wartime gains, consisting of tariffs, subsidies, and a monetary system favorable to creditors. The Fourteenth Amendment was not a Magna Carta of freedmen's rights, but rather a bulwark for property interests, disguised as a Negro rights measure in order to catch votes. Again, the implications were ironic: for instance, under this formula Andrew Johnson, a onetime slaveowner and an obdurate foe of Negro rights, appeared as a champion of democracy against the predatory capitalists. Thus Johnson received ecstatic praise in a biography (1929) by that archliberal attorney Lloyd Paul Stryker, who later became a crusading spokesman for Negro rights.

Through all of these treatments there runs a persistent implied affirmation of Dodd's cleverly articulated premise: that which is agrarian in the South is truly Southern; anything not in the agrarian tradition is somehow extraneous—a cowbird's egg in the Southern nest. Almost automatically, this formula reduced the factor of biracialism and caste to secondary importance, or even kept it out of sight altogether. Again, some interesting results follow in the literature. For instance, when Howard W. Odum and his associates at Chapel Hill prepared their great compendium *Southern Regions of the United States* (1936), they deployed no less than six hundred maps and charts to show that the agricultural South, despite its rich natural resources, was worse off in almost every measurable respect than the rest of the country. That is, they mapped, measured, and charted the plight of the agricultural South. But not one graph, map, or chart showed the relatively worse plight of the Negroes within the South. In other words, the most careful reader of this encyclopedic survey of Southern economic and social conditions could almost have overlooked the fact that a biracial system prevailed in the South and that under this system the Negroes experienced adverse differentials in almost every respect. No doubt Odum and his associates chose this presentation deliberately, and certainly not because of any blind agrarianism, for they advocated economic diversification for the South. Their purpose may even have been to avoid dulling the concern of white Southerners about differentials by admitting that these differentials fell more heavily upon the Negro than upon the white component in the Southern population. Or, they may have wished to treat Negroes and whites indiscriminately alike as being handicapped by regional differentials. But in any case, their survey of Southern problems left out the greatest problem of all. Like the doctrinal agrarians with whom they disagreed, they presented an image of the South which emphasized the plight of farmers rather than the plight of Negroes.

In quite a different way, the agrarian premise shows itself also in many of the writings of C. Vann Woodward, the foremost historian of the modern South. In Woodward's biography of Tom Watson (1938), for instance, the protagonist of the drama is Watson the agrarian, and the antagonists are the Bourbon Democrats who have betrayed the interests of the South to the forces of industrial capitalism. Or alternatively, one could say, the protagonist is the earlier Watson, who championed Populism and defended Negro rights, while the antagonist is the later Watson, a reactionary racist who betrayed the ideals of his youth. Though Woodward's treatment is deeply subtle and sensitive to complexities, while Dodd's was superficial and grossly oversimplified, both are alike in regarding the agrarian South as, almost *a priori*, the true South, and any force within the South which runs counter to it as an aberration. This is, of course, quite a different thing from merely favoring the agrarian cause.

Although a whole generation of writers has made this tempting equation between Southernism and agrarianism, it requires only a limited analysis to see that in many respects the Southern economy and the Southern society have not been agrarian at all—in fact, have embodied almost the antithesis of agrarianism. Agrarianism implies an escape from the commercialism of the money economy, but Southern cotton and tobacco and sugar cultivators have consistently been agricultural businessmen producing for market and for cash income. Agrarianism implies production for use rather than production for sale, and therefore diversification rather than specialization, but the Southern agriculturist stuck to his one-crop system in the past as tenaciously as he clings to segregation at the present. It implies the independence of a husbandman who looks to no one else either for his access to the land or for the necessities of his living, but the Southern cultivator has been historically either a slave or a sharecropper, without land and often without opportunity even to grow his own turnip greens in a garden patch. Meanwhile the Southern landowner, whether an absentee planter or a mortgage-holding bank, frequently failed to follow the ennobling agrarian practice of laboring in the earth. To one who is impressed by these aspects, it may seem realistic to regard Calhoun rather than Jefferson as the typical leader of the South; the plantation producing raw materials for the textile industry, rather than the subsistence farm producing for use, as the typical economic unit; hierarchy rather than equality as the typical social condition; and conservatism rather than radicalism as the typical mode of thought.

One man who was long the leading historian of the South saw the region to some extent in these terms. This was Ulrich B. Phillips, who began his career around the turn of the century with studies of Southern political history and the history of Southern transportation. But wherever his investigations began, they always led him, as he himself said, back to one feature of life in the South which was constant both before emancipation and after, namely the presence of Negroes and whites whose destinies were inextricably intertwined but whose paths in life were separated by a biracial system. Accordingly, Phillips gave only slight attention to the agrarian theme. Instead he concentrated on the staple-crop economy with its plantation units and its slave labor. With supreme thoroughness in research, he made what remains the basic study of slavery as a system of labor (*American Negro Slavery*, 1918). Later he developed an artistry in writing which matched his soundness in research, and he achieved a felicitous conjunction of both talents in a study of the society and economy of the antebellum period (*Life and Labor in the Old South*, 1929).

When Phillips looked at the Southern economy, the image which seemed visible to him was not an independent husbandman laboring in the soil, but a Negro field hand picking cotton. The persistence of this figure, either as a slave or as a sharecropper, and the persistence of the system which kept him in his subordinate role led Phillips, five years before his death in 1934, to write an essay, "The Central Theme of Southern History," in which he stated what he had found at the core of distinctive Southernism. This was not some agrarian ideal, but rather a fixed purpose on the part of the Southern whites to preserve biracialism, or, as he said, in unvarnished terms, to assure that the South "shall be and remain a white man's country."

Although Phillips' stature is still recognized even by his critics, liberal historians have been reluctant to accept his views. Kenneth Stampp has written a new account of slavery (*The Peculiar Institution*, 1956) which emphasizes, as Phillips never did, the harsh and exploitative aspects of the system; Richard Hofstadter has criticized Phillips for giving too much attention to the plantation, and not enough to the slaves held in small holdings; and at least two writers have questioned the "Central Theme."

It is in some ways ironical for liberals, concerned as they are with the "sick South," to reject a formula which explains so cogently the chronic nature of the illness. But what they found fault with was not in fact the accuracy of Phillips' conclusion; it was rather the lack of moral indignation in his statement of it. By asserting that the policy of biracialism is and will continue to be a central aspect of Southernism, without personally repudiating this policy, he made it difficult for liberals to identify with him. When Harry Ashmore, more recently, said in *An Epitaph for Dixie* (1958) that the South will cease to be the South when it ceases to be segregated, the statement was almost identical with that of Phillips, but liberals could accept Ashmore's because he expects the South, in the old sense, to vanish (hence "an epitaph"), whereas they could not accept Phillips', because he seemingly expected the South to survive, with the implied corollary that efforts at integration must fail. Moreover, in the case of liberals who want to love the South, as some do, but who find it psychologically impossible to love an embodiment of biracialism, the only recourse is a resort to Dodd's original formula: dispose of the factor which is troublesome (in this case the biracialism) by treating it as a great aberration. Here even so excellent a book as Vann Woodward's *Strange Career of Jim Crow* (1955) is a case in point, for though it was intended to emphasize a thoroughly valid observation—namely, that the patterns of biracialism have varied and are not immutable—it lends itself to being read as a statement that caste does not have very deep roots in the South. The preface to the paperback edition (1957) showed that Woodward was himself concerned that his work had been taken too much in this way.

When one considers the degree of hardheadedness and realism which went into Phillips' view that biracialism lay at the core of Southernism, and the vulnerability of the doctrine that agrarianism was the heart of the matter, it seems strange that writers have been so abstinent in accepting the former and so addicted to the latter. Clearly, the agrarian interpretation has drawn its strength from something other than the sheer weight of evidence, and it is worth pondering what the real basis of its acceptance is. In the purely historical literature, this basis is hard to detect, for the historian purports merely to be describing the agrarianism which he finds in the past—not to be advocating it. But in 1930 agrarianism enjoyed open advocacy at the hands of a group of writers, all centered at Vanderbilt University, in the famous manifesto entitled *I'll Take My Stand*. The twelve Southerners who joined in this profession of faith categorically rejected the industrial way of life, which they regarded as the prevailing or American way, and with equal conviction they subscribed to an agrarian way, which they identified as a Southern way. They hoped to carry this Southern way to the nation through "a national agrarian movement."

In the extensive and often heated discussion which followed, attention was focused very heavily upon the operative practicability of their proposals. They were accused of medievalism, and of quixotically renouncing all the benefits of modern science and technology. They were also accused, with somewhat more justice, of being in disagreement among themselves as to whether agrarianism was designed to provide a livelihood for dirt farmers or to restore cultural amenities for the landed gentry. Whether they advocated populism or elitism no one could quite make out. While controversy raged between them and their assailants, not much attention was given to the ideological implications of agrarianism, nor to the question why this particular line of thought had appeared at this particular time. Indeed, the historical significance of agrarian thought has still never been adequately analyzed.

But it is clearly evident that agrarianism appealed to many liberals, both before and after the Nashville group, partly because they were looking for an alternative to the prevailing American way of life. Some writers, like Charles A. Beard, used agrarianism so enthusiastically as a stick with which to beat capitalism that it had some of the appearance of a disguised Marxism. But its real significance lay in the fact that it offered an alternative to Marxism. Here, in fact, was a way in which a man could renounce industrial capitalism and all its works without becoming a Marxist. This is perhaps why the agrarian ideal held so much attraction for such a large number of social thinkers. It gave them a chance to express their dissent from the prevailing system without going outside the American tradition in order to do so.

Another significant feature in making agrarianism attractive was its affirmation that the South had something of value in its tradition to offer to the nation. The Nashville group really felt convinced that the Southern sphinx did have an answer to the riddle, if not of the universe, at least of American life. Their affirmation came at a time when it was being asserted by critics like Mencken that the Southern tradition amounted to little more than a sterile, backward-looking form of ancestor worship. Now suddenly men were saying in a fresh and arresting way that the Southern tradition was not merely a pressed flower in the nation's scrapbook of memories, but rather an urgent message which Americans, deafened by the roar of progress, had failed to hear. To Southerners who yearned to believe that there was some element of vitality in the history of their region, this idea seemed immensely appealing.

The continued acceleration of industrial growth and the failure of the Nashville group to rally a popular following soon showed that agrarianism had no future, but it was still widely believed to have a past, and historians continued to apply it to the interpretation of American history. Henry Bamford Parkes made brilliant use of it in his *The American Experience* (1947), and as recently as 1949, Frank L. Owsley, in his *Plain Folk of the Old South,* delineated the structure of antebellum society in terms in which large slaveholders and plain farmers were practically indistinguishable. In these and many other writings, a number of time-honored propositions continued to find acceptance: that American democracy has been nourished primarily from agrarian roots; that agrarian attitudes are inherently democratic; and that the South peculiarly embodies the agrarian tradition.

But of late the first two of these propositions have come under criticism, and the agrarian view has been attacked, for the first time, at its foundations. As long ago as 1945, Arthur Schlesinger, Jr., in his *The Age of Jackson,* offered the then heretical view that Jacksonian democracy owed more to the East and to class-conscious urban workingmen than to the frontier and its coonskin equality. More recently, Richard Hofstadter, in his *Age of Reform* (1955), has gone even further by arguing that Populism had little affinity with liberal democracy, and was in fact a seedbed for such illiberal manifestations as prohibition, nativism, immigration restriction, Red-baiting, and the like. Thus, according to Schlesinger, democracy was not agrarian, and according to Hofstadter, agrarianism was not democratic.

In literal form, the agrarian formula fitted the South remarkably badly. It envisioned a subsistence economy, agricultural diversification, a wide distribution of small landholdings, a large class of independent husbandmen, and an unstratified society. The cold fact is that none of these features has ever been dominant in the South. In the light of these flaws, as well as of recent criticisms, the whole idea of the South as an agrarian society now seems more and more an illusion, nourished by a wish. But once it is discarded, the question reverts to the enigma of the South. All theory aside, is the South, at a purely descriptive level, distinguishable? And if it is, does the distinction lie in anything more than the fact that biracialism takes a form in the South differing from the form it takes elsewhere?

This is a question which the literature of the future will perhaps explore further. Vann Woodward, in *The Burden of Southern History* (1960), has already moved in this direction with incisive and fertile arguments that certain distinctive experiences of the South have put their mark upon the Southern people: the experience of defeat and frustration, in an America of monotonous, taken-for-granted success; the experience of guilt because of the Negro, in an America with a cult of Adamic innocence; the experience of poverty, in an America with abundance which has caused people to confuse life with a standard of living. But though Woodward discusses these factors as experiences impinging upon the Southern culture, we still need a dissection of the culture itself upon which they impinge.

On the face of it, it seems a matter of observation and not of theory to say that the culture of the folk survived in the South long after it succumbed to the onslaught of urban-industrial culture elsewhere. It was an aspect of this culture that the relation between the land and the people remained more direct and more primal in the South than in other parts of the country. (This may be more true for the Negroes than for the whites, but then there is also a question whether the Negroes may not have embodied the distinctive qualities of the Southern character even more than the whites.) Even in the most exploitative economic situations, this culture retained a personalism in the relations of man to man which the industrial culture lacks. Even for those whose lives were narrowest, it offered a relationship of man to nature in which there was a certain fulfillment of personality. Every culture is, among other things, a system of relationships among an aggregate of people, and as cultures differ, the systems of relationship vary. In the folk culture of the South, it may be that the relation of people to one another imparted a distinctive texture as well as a distinctive tempo to their lives.

An explanation of the South in terms of a folk culture would not have the ideological implications which have made the explanation in terms of agrarianism so tempting and at the same time so treacherous. But on the other hand, it would not be inconsistent with some of the realities of Southern society, such as biracialism and hierarchy, whereas agrarianism is inconsistent with these realities. The enigma remains, and the historian must still ask what distinctive quality it was in the life of the South for which Southerners have felt such a persistent, haunting nostalgia and to which even the Yankee has responded with a poignant impulse. We must now doubt that this nostalgia was the yearning of men for an ideal agrarian utopia which never existed in reality. But if it was not that, was it perhaps the yearning of men in a mass culture for the life of a folk culture which did really exist? This folk culture, we know, was far from being ideal or utopian, and was in fact full of inequality and wrong, but if the nostalgia persists was it because even the inequality and wrong were parts of a life that still had a relatedness and meaning which our more bountiful life in the mass culture seems to lack?

Suggested Further Reading for Chapter 5

Wilbur Cash, *The Mind of the South* (New York: Vintage Books, 1951).

E. Garvin Davenport, *The Myth of Southern History* (Nashville: Vanderbilt University Press, 1971).

Eugene Genovese, *The Political Economy of Slavery: Studies in the Economy and Society of the Slave South* (New York: Pantheon Books, Inc., 1965).

Thomas P. Govan, "Was the Old South Different?" *Journal of Southern History*, 21 (1955).

Dewey W. Grantham, Jr. (ed.), *The South and the Sectional Image: The Sectional Theme Since Reconstruction* (New York: Harper & Row, Publishers, 1967).

Fletcher M. Green, "Democracy in the Old South," *Journal of Southern History*, 12 (1946).

Richard Hofstadter, "Ulrich B. Phillips and the Plantation Legend," *Journal of Negro History*, 29 (1944).
William K. Scarborough, *The Overseer: Plantation Management in the Old South* (Baton Rouge: Louisiana University Press, 1966).
Charles Grier Setters, Jr., "Who Were the Southern Whigs?" *American Historical Review*, 59 (1954).
William R. Taylor, *Cavalier and Yankee: The Old South and American National Character* (New York: Anchor Books, 1963).
C. Vann Woodward, *The Burden of Southern History* (Baton Rouge: Louisiana State University Press, 1960).
C. Vann Woodward, "Southern Mythology," *Commentary*, 42 (1965).
Howard Zinn, *The Southern Mystique* (New York: Alfred A. Knopf, Inc., 1964).

A great literature will yet arise out of the era of those four [Civil War] years, those scenes—era compressing centuries of native passion, first-class pictures, tempests of life and death—an inexhaustible mine for the histories, drama, romance, and even philosophy, of peoples to come—indeed the verteber of poetry and art (of personal character too) for all future America—far more grand, in my opinion, to the hands capable of it, than Homer's siege of Troy, or the French wars to Shakespeare.

Walt Whitman, 1879

MYTHS OF THE CIVIL WAR AND RECONSTRUCTION

Harper's Weekly. Courtesy, Virginia State Library.

The Glorious: John A. Logan in action.

The Terrible: Union dead after Gettysburg.

Introduction

Today the Civil War remains central to America's national historical experience. For many Americans the War between the States represents the greatest single event in their history. From the epic struggle emerges a gallery of heroic figures and memorable episodes—Lincoln and Lee, Shiloh and Gettysburg. *The War* enjoys the status of an American *Iliad*. As novelist and poet Robert Penn Warren suggested, the Civil War marked America's "Homeric Age." To Warren, the War between the States quickly became the great synthesis of the American experience and the inexhaustible reservoir of American symbol and myth:

> From the first, Americans had a strong tendency to think of their land as the Galahad among nations, and the Civil War, with its happy marriage of victory and virtue, has converted this tendency into an article of faith nearly as sacrosanct as the Declaration of Independence.

As Warren implies, ideas concerning the past often combine with emotion. Because of this, time, which is supposed to bring detachment and objectivity to one's historical understanding, very often has the opposite effect. The American Civil War proves an interesting case in point. Images of either the heroic (as with the war itself) or the tragic (as with the period of reconstruction that followed) have supplanted a proportioned view. Civil War and reconstruction history has been an exceptionally fertile breeding ground for distortion and myth.

The importance of recognizing what people think happened as against what did—the discrepancies between history as perceived and history as actuality—holds particular significance, then, to our historical judgments concerning the war and its aftermath. A proper view of our "Homeric Age" requires that the American penchant for overemphasizing both the heroic and tragic elements of history be challenged. A proper understanding of the era of the Civil War must yield much more than the pageantry and legend of the martyred Lincoln and the Christlike Lee. It must supply more than the tragic legend of the war's aftermath. One can begin to appreciate the entire era in its proper historical perspective only by noting the war's multiple causes, the complexity of Lincoln as politician, the conflict in both its glorious and terrible aspects, the war's importance as a stage in the development of modern nationalism and its significance to American industrial development, and reconstruction's subsequent importance to the course of American race relations. In the end, the Civil War and its heritage can indeed remain central to our national historical experience, but for reasons other than those which we might previously have imagined.

The Causes of the Civil War

David M. Potter

In what he describes as a "historiographical foray," David Potter, late Coe Professor of History at Stanford University, describes the dimensions of historical research as to the causes of the Civil War. Clearly reflecting the span of his academic experience, Potter speaks to both the causes of the Civil War *per se*, and those topics that bear directly upon the growing sectionalism between North and South. Through a discussion of the "revisionists" and the counter-attack that has been directed against their views, Potter concludes by redefining the question in terms of the problem of race—indeed the fulcrum upon which the delicate balance of the sections rested.

The last three decades have witnessed considerable advances in the historical understanding of many of the developments which preceded the Civil War, but it can hardly be said that they have brought us visibly closer to the point at which a jury of historians seems likely to arrive at a verdict which will settle the controversy as to causes. Indeed some of the most fundamental issues in the controversy, namely those turning upon the significance of the slavery question, have been reactivated and seem now to have given new dimensions to the whole dispute.

By 1940, the literature on the Civil War had already been accumulating for eighty years. During these eight decades, interpretation of the war had passed through three major phases. First, during the immediate postwar era, there had been a literature by participants and partisans, designed to justify their own course of conduct and therefore striving either to vindicate or indict. Both sides had appealed to absolute values: if they were partisans of the Union, they had explained the war in terms of slavery and disunion, appealing to the moral absolutes of human freedom and national unity; if they were partisans of the South, they had explained it in terms of the secession issue, appealing to the legal absolute inherent in the theory of state sovereignty and to the moral absolute of the right of self-government.

Second, in the period after the wounds of war began to heal, there had been a nationalistic interpretation, well exemplified in the seven-volume history by James Ford Rhodes (1893–1906), which avoided the attribution of blame and emphasized the sincerity and high motive of both the Blue and the Gray. Rhodes himself argued unequivocally that slavery was the cause of the war, but he held the nation rather than the South responsible for slavery, and if he blamed the South for secession, he blamed the North for

From *The South and the Sectional Conflict*, by David M. Potter (Baton Rouge, 1968). Reprinted by permission of Louisiana State University Press.

Reconstruction. In such an interpretation the concept of an inevitable or "irrepressible" conflict fitted well, for if the war could not possibly have been prevented, then no one could be blamed for failing to prevent it, and thus no one was guilty. Charles Francis Adams pushed this view to its logical limit in 1902 by declaring that "Everybody, in short, was right; no one wrong."

Third, in the 1920's, after ideas of economic determinism began to prevail widely in American intellectual circles, Charles and Mary Beard had published an immensely influential interpretation of the war in their *The Rise of American Civilization* (1927). Seeing the great contests of history as struggles for power, rather than for principle, and regarding moral and legal arguments as mere rationalizations, the Beards had denied that the South really cared about states' rights or the North about slavery. The South had simply used states' rights as a tactical device in defending a minority position. The Republicans had simply used the slavery issue to turn public opinion against the South, but in fact the Republicans had not been abolitionists and had done nothing to help the slaves, but had sought only to "contain" the power of the slaveholders by excluding them from the new territories. The war, therefore, had not been a contest over principles but a struggle for power—a clash of economic sections in which freedom did not necessarily combat slavery but industrialism most assuredly combated the planter interests.

These three were, in brief, the major interpretations which had held sway up to 1940. Since 1940, the major tendencies have been: (1) the development of a so-called "revisionist" interpretation which minimized the importance of slavery or any other fundamental factor as a cause of the war and also argued that the war could have been and should have been averted; (2) a counterattack upon the revisionists by writers who reassert the causative importance of the slavery question; and (3) a shifting of the question away from a sharp focus upon the "causes" of the hostilities as such, together with a more generalized concern with the relation between the war and the pattern of race relations in the United States.

Although sometimes mentioned as if they were a "school," the so-called revisionists have in fact been a number of distinctively independent scholars, working separately, disagreeing on occasion, and united only by their skepticism about the role of slavery as the heart of the sectional issue and by their doubt that the conflict was irrepressible.

These doubts are as old as the war itself, but modern revisionism possibly begins with Albert J. Beveridge, Republican Senator from Indiana and biographer of John Marshall. About 1920, Beveridge set out to write a biography of Lincoln. He approached this undertaking with the traditional Republican reverence for an almost superhuman being—the inevitable protagonist of the antislavery drama in which there had to be an antagonist or villain, and in which Stephen A. Douglas was inevitably stereotyped for the latter role. But when Beveridge began his research, he found the facts far more complex than the tradition, and when he came to the Lincoln-Douglas debates, he concluded that Douglas had acted with integrity and had represented a very respectable point of view—namely that the question of slavery in the territories was a fictitious issue, not worth a crisis which would endanger the nation. Because the abolitionists had "agitated" this issue in such a way as to precipitate the crisis, Beveridge formed an unfavorable opinion of them and began to think that, without them, there might have been no war—indeed that slavery might in time have disappeared peaceably under the pressure of economic forces.

In 1927, Beveridge died. His life of Lincoln, published in the following year, had been completed only to the year 1858, and we can never know what broad, overall interpretation he would have advanced. But certain of the ideas which he had foreshadowed continued to develop in the decade of the thirties. In 1933, Gilbert H. Barnes published an account of the early abolitionist movement (*The Anti-Slavery Impulse, 1830–1844*) in which he emphasized the neglected figure of Theodore Dwight Weld, and de-emphasized the importance of William Lloyd Garrison, at the same time condemning the fanaticism of the abolitionists in general. During the same year, Gerald W. Johnson of the Baltimore *Sun* published a small interpretive volume on *The Secession of the Southern States,* which stated brilliantly the argument that dogmatic, rigid adherence to "principle" on the part of both antislavery zealots like Charles Sumner of Massachusetts and doctrinaire legalists like John C. Calhoun of South Carolina had caused an unnecessary war in which "everybody was wrong and no one was right." Johnson's little book has been neglected, perhaps because he was not a professional historian, but it remains to this day one of the most vigorous and effective statements of a major thesis of revisionism. In 1934, George Fort Milton, editor of the Chattanooga *News,* brought out a full-scale biography of Douglas, based on extensive new manuscripts and bearing the significant title *The Eve of Conflict: Stephen A. Douglas and the Needless War.* Like Beveridge, Milton considered Douglas statesmanlike in his effort to play down the territorial issue, and believed that unwise political leadership was responsible for the war.

After these preliminaries, the full tide of the revisionist reaction struck in the late thirties and early forties, primarily as the result of the work of two men—James G. Randall and Avery O. Craven—advancing independently along somewhat parallel lines.

Craven first enunciated his views clearly in an article, "Coming of the War Between the States: An Interpretation," in 1936. He followed this with a brief interpretive volume, *The Repressible Conflict,* in 1939, and with a full-scale history of the years from 1830 to 1861 in *The Coming of the Civil War* in 1942. Since then he has continued to develop and to modify his ideas in a number of writings, including notably a volume in the History of the

South series, *The Growth of Southern Nationalism, 1848–1861* (1953), a set of interpretive lectures, *Civil War in the Making, 1815–1860* (1959), and a volume of essays, *An Historian and the Civil War* (1964).

Perhaps the crucial feature of Craven's interpretation is his belief that the basic and essential differences between North and South were not great enough to make war necessary. The dissimilarities between the agrarian society of the South and the industrial society of the Northeast were, to be sure, a fertile seedbed for friction and for misunderstandings, but these misunderstandings were not, on the whole, realistic. The great difference traditionally emphasized is that of slavery, but Craven argued that the economic condition of the Negro as an unskilled laborer engaged in the cotton culture was much more important in controlling the conditions of his life than his legal status as a chattel. Because of these economic factors the condition of the Negro after emancipation changed very little until the cotton economy itself changed in the 1930's. Craven also emphasized the fact that three-quarters of the Southern whites were not slaveholders and were not directly involved in the slavery complex. North and South did not, in fact, present polar extremes.

But if sectional antagonisms did not arise out of fundamental differences, what did they arise from? Craven believed that they resulted from the creation of false images of each section by the other, and from the charging of these images with a high, unreasoning emotional content. He believed that these stereotypes were to some extent manufactured by irresponsible political agitators, both North and South—that is by the "fire-eating" secessionists and by the abolitionists. In other words, the explanation lies more in psychological attitudes than in objective conditions. From this conclusion, it follows that we should beware of any arbitrary assumption that the conflict was irrepressible (though Craven later concluded that the opposite assumption should also be avoided, since the question really cannot be determined). It follows, too, that slavery should be played down: Craven suggested "the possibility that behind the determination to put slavery on the road to ultimate extinction there may have lain drives that had little to do with Negro slavery or the American South, as well as others that were the direct product of slavery itself and of the so-called 'Slave Power.' " Since, in his opinion, "the great body of Americans were moderate and conservative in their attitudes [and] . . . came to the brink of Civil War reluctantly," a heavy burden of what may really be called war guilt rests with the political leaders ("extremists") like Charles Sumner and Barnwell Rhett who played upon public emotions until they brought about a conflict which the circumstances did not require and which neither the Northern nor the Southern majority wanted.

While Craven was developing these themes at the University of Chicago, James G. Randall at the University of Illinois was concurrently working out an interpretation to which he himself applied the term "revisionist." His first clear-cut statement of this interpretation appeared, but was not heavily emphasized, in his *The Civil War and Reconstruction* in 1937. It was more fully elaborated in three important articles, "The Blundering Generation," "The Civil War Restudied," and "When War Came in 1861," all published in 1940. Finally, in *Lincoln, the President: Springfield to Gettysburg* (1945), he set forth his views in their fully matured form.

Critics sometimes discuss Craven and Randall as if their views were identical. It is easy to see why this happens, for both men held a number of major ideas in common: that sectional differences were not great enough to necessitate a war; that the crisis resulted more from the whipping-up of emotions than from the impact of realistic issues; that extremists on both sides were responsible for this emotional jag, but that the responsibility of the extremists of the North (i.e., the abolitionists), which had been disregarded by many historians, needed to be emphasized rather more than the responsibility of the extremists of the South (i.e., the fire-eating secessionists), whom historians had blamed excessively; and above all, that the war was both avoidable and unnecessary and that it occurred as the result of a failure of leadership. But within this broad framework of agreement, Craven and Randall each developed distinctive points of emphasis. Where Craven argued that the Civil War in particular ought not to have occurred, Randall showed greater concern with the problem of war as such, and writing at a time when the world was rapidly losing the international peace which World War I and the League of Nations were supposed to have won, he argued that war as such should be prevented, that it is a "fallacy" to believe that "fundamental motives produce war." Indeed, he contended that analysis of the causes of war must fail unless it takes into consideration psychopathic factors.

Because of his greater concern with the general problem of the causation of war, Randall was also more concerned than was Craven to refute the idea of economic determinism, in the Beardian sense, as an explanation of war. In some of his best analysis, Randall pointed out that economic determinists have a kind of "heads, I win—tails, you lose" formula. If a people who lack economic diversity make war, their belligerence can be explained in terms of the need for economic self-sufficiency. But if a people with diversity have an internal war, their conflict can be explained in terms of the clash of diverse interests. In either case, the explanation for war stands ready-made. As Randall argued, features of diversity may lead to mutual interdependence rather than to war, and the existence of economic differences creates no presumption that antagonism need follow. Where antagonism exists, it must be explained on specific grounds.

A second respect in which Randall's emphasis differed from Craven's is that where Craven discounted the significance of slavery as an institution, Randall minimized its significance as an issue. One of his most effective arguments was his contention that, while the broad issue of freedom versus slavery may be worth a war, the issue as defined by the opposing forces in 1861 was not that broad, and was not worth a war in the form in which they defined it. For the Republicans in 1861 did not propose to emancipate the slaves; they even agreed in 1861 to guarantee slavery in the existing slave states and to return fugitives to slavery. The one point on which they stuck was that they would not sanction slavery in any of the new territories. But since the climate and the economy of these new regions made them inhospitable to slavery anyway, the territorial question could be viewed as an abstraction—a contest over "an imaginary Negro in an impossible place," and a very inadequate cause for a war. The idea that the territorial issue was a fictitious one was not new—it had been vigorously expressed by James K. Polk—but Randall gave it a new application in his treatment of the causes of the war.

A third major expression of revisionism appeared in 1948, when Roy F. Nichols of the University of Pennsylvania published his *The Disruption of American Democracy*. Unlike Craven and Randall, Nichols did not undertake a general interpretation of the sectional crisis as a whole. Instead he set himself to the more specialized study of the impact of sectional antagonisms in shattering a national political party—the Democratic Party. His work, which won the Pulitzer Prize, was, therefore, an institutional study of the impact of sectional pressures upon American political machinery. But the findings fitted well with the revisionist thesis, for Nichols showed how the defects of the political system (excessive localism, the need for agitation in order to stimulate voters in the frequent elections, etc.) contributed to the breakdown of a national political organization under the weight of sectional pressures. Moreover, Nichols asserted in clear-cut terms his belief that the "hyperemotionalism" of the times made it possible for "irresponsible and blind operators of local political machinery" to exploit the inflammable issues which led to war.

Toward the end of the forties, revisionism had very largely swept the field of Civil War literature. With the partial exception of Allan Nevins' *Ordeal of the Union* (1947), all the major works on the Civil War for a decade had reflected a revisionist view. Revisionism had made its way into the textbooks and had been taken up by popular writers. It is perhaps symptomatic that, in 1951, William E. Woodward's posthumous history of the war, tentatively entitled *The Civil War: A National Blunder*, was finally issued under the title *Years of Madness*.

About nine years after Craven and Randall had sounded the first trumpets of a broad revisionism, Arthur Schlesinger, Jr., in his *The Age of Jackson* (1945) entered a dissenting opinion. In a brief discussion, made in passing, Schlesinger affirmed his belief that "the emotion which moved the North finally to battlefield and bloodshed was moral disgust with slavery." He also denied the Beardian thesis that slavery was resisted because it constituted an obstacle to industrial capitalism; on the contrary, he said, "the aspirations which were first felt to be menaced by the slave power were in actuality democratic aspirations." Four years later, in an article on Randall's contention, he returned to the subject for a more extended treatment. Attacking the revisionists for using the claim of objectivity and the concept of automatic progress as devices for avoiding consideration of the moral issue of slavery, Schlesinger argued that the focus of the slavery contest had fallen on the territories, not because industrialists on-the-make were covetous of power in new regions and indifferent to slave hardships in old ones, but because Americans found their moral scruples about slavery in conflict with their civic scruples to obey the Constitution, which protected slavery in the slave states. Therefore, their powerful impulse against human bondage was deflected from its natural target, slavery in the states, and was sublimated, as it were, into an attack on the peripheral question of slavery in the territories. But despite this displacement of the objective, Schlesinger felt no doubt that the moral question of slavery was basic in precipitating conflict between the sections.

During the same year when Schlesinger published this latter article, Pieter Geyl, an eminent Dutch historian of major stature, also published, in Dutch, a critique of Randall's idea that the war could have been avoided. (A part of this was published in English translation in 1951.) Geyl focused his attention especially on Randall's contention that because the majority did not want conflict, war should have been avoidable. He argued that the historical process is not as rational as Randall assumed, and that the issues of sectional disagreement could not be neatly separated from the emotions which they generated, and which ultimately got out of control. His criticism must rank with Schlesinger's as one of the two major rebuttals to the revisionist argument, but other voices have been raised as well. Bernard De Voto assailed the revisionists in two influential articles in *Harper's* which were notable for their early date (1946) as well as for their vigorous, hard-hitting tone. In 1950, Oscar Handlin, in a review of Nevins, deplored the practice of equating the abolitionists and the secessionists because both groups were fanatics: "There is surely a difference," he said, "between being a fanatic for freedom and being a fanatic for slavery."

Harry V. Jaffa has provided an important full-scale criticism of much of the revisionist position. Jaffa denied that slavery had reached the geographical limits of its expansion and that the political restriction was redundant. He denied also that Douglas' popular sovereignty and Lincoln's restrictionism would both have come to the same thing, that is, freedom in the territories, and that the two men's views did not conflict in any basic way. Instead he argued, Douglas was willing to sacrifice the principles of freedom and equality to the principle of majority rule, while Lincoln, though not a doctrinaire equalitarian, wanted "the highest degree of equality for which general [majority] consent could be obtained." Emphasizing this distinction as he did, he dismissed the idea that emotions of the crisis period were "whipped up" or unrealistic.

By the time Jaffa published his refutation, revisionism had reached the end of its active phase. James G. Randall's voice had been stilled by death in 1953, and Avery Craven had greatly modified his earlier arguments as to the irrepressibility of the conflict. In certain respects, revisionism, like many other historical correctives, had served its purpose—not by winning adoption of its own doctrinal views, but by forcing a correction of previous stereotypes and oversimplifications. Never again could well-trained historians explain the Civil War purely in terms of economic determinism or as a moral crusade against slavery. Nor could they dismiss questions of responsibility and the failure of leadership with an unsupported assertion that the conflict was irrepressible.

But much of the revisionist position remained under attack. One of the most protracted and intensive controversies that had ever occurred among American historians had not terminated in agreement. This was true despite the fact that revisionism was woven into such major historical studies as those of Randall, Craven, and Nichols, while most of the critics of revisionism had been essayists making their forays from other fields: Jaffa from political science, Geyl from Dutch history, and Schlesinger from the New Deals of Andrew Jackson and Franklin Roosevelt. Perhaps the dispute remained unresolved because, although it purported to be disagreement of an analytical sort about the nature of historical forces, it was also, in cryptic and indirect form, a disagreement of a philosophical sort about the relative importance of three moral objectives: the avoidance of war, the abolition of slavery, and the preservation of the American union. In each case there was an issue not only as to the relative moral priority of the objective (e.g., Was it more important to avoid war than to free slaves?), but also as to whether there were acceptable alternative ways of attaining the objectives (e.g., Could the slaves have been freed without waging a war? Could the Union have been preserved without sacrificing the objectives of ultimate emancipation? Could war have been averted without destroying the Union or leaving the blacks permanently enslaved?). The shifting emphases on first one moral objective and then another, without a corresponding shift in attitudes toward the contingent alternatives, had resulted in constant alterations of the questions which historians were trying to answer. For instance, Randall was so deeply preoccupied with the evil of war that he concentrated primarily on why it was not avoided, without giving full consideration to the evil of slavery, even as a secondary thought. Schlesinger and Kenneth Stampp have given primacy to the evil of slavery and have at least implied that while war is, in most situations, worse than the alternatives, there are cases such as that of Hitlerite Germany where war is preferable, and that the confrontation with slavery was such a case. In the historical writing of today, the Union is usually taken for granted, and historians no longer ask to what extent union has enough intrinsic worth to justify either a resort to the evil of war or a compromise with the evil of slavery. But in the 1860's, this was the crucial question for many. Paul C. Nagel's *One Nation Indivisible: The Union in American Thought, 1776–1861* furnishes striking evidence of the intensity with which the union was regarded, in the mid-nineteenth century, as an absolute value.

In short, while the revisionists and their critics systematically conducted their discourse in the terminology of causation, they were usually bent upon defending the moral priority of one objective over another. Insofar as this was true, they were engaged more in justification than in explanation. Disputes on points of moral justification cannot be settled by objective means. That is one reason why the results of the great revisionist controversy remained inconclusive despite the vast barrage of factual data that was thrown into the campaign by both the revisionists and their critics.

While much of the literature of revisionism and of the counterattack upon it was almost ostentatiously focused upon what purported to be systematic analysis, the shifting fortunes of the revisionist view were illuminated in an especially revealing way in a major work which scarcely attempted such analytical interpretation at all, but which undertook instead to provide the first modern, full-scale narrative of the period from 1850 to 1861. This was the work of Allan Nevins. Many years ago, Nevins began a study of the vast array of source materials that had accumulated in repositories throughout the country, and he set himself to write such a comprehensive and at the same time detailed history as no one had even attempted since James Ford Rhodes. The triumphant results of this enterprise began to appear in 1947 when Nevins published two volumes, *Ordeal of the Union,* covering the period 1850–57. Two more in 1950, *The Emergence of Lincoln,* carried the narrative to 1860, and a fifth and sixth, *The War for the Union,* in 1959 and 1960, have covered the outbreak of war and major aspects of the war itself.

The primary importance of Nevins' work, as I have tried to emphasize, is that it stands today as the only great overall narrative based upon modern research. But for the examination of historiographical trends, it is pertinent here to concentrate upon the rather brief and infrequent passages in which Nevins offers observations on the causative aspects of his theme. At times, especially in the earlier volumes, he seemed to some extent to share the ideas of the revisionists. He spoke of "the unrealities of passion" and of "the failure of American leadership" and he even stated a conviction that "the war should have been avoidable." It is worth noting, however, that this is by no means the same thing as saying that it could have been avoided. But in *The Emergence of Lincoln,* he struck at the chief weakness of revisionism by observing that "while hysteria was important, we have always to ask what basic reasons made possible the propaganda which aroused it." Also in 1950, he rejected the older simplistic idea that slavery in the strict sense of the chattel servitude of Negroes, was the crux of the controversy, and he offered instead the hypothesis that "the main root of the conflict (and there were minor roots) was the problem of slavery *with its complementary problem of race-adjustment*. . . . It was a war over slavery *and* the future position of the Negro race in North America."

Nevins' striking observation is valid or not, according to the level of meaning at which one reads it. If it is read to mean that the men who fought each other did so because they held opposing views about the future position of the Negro race in America, it is not tenable, for the evidence is abundant that North and South, in 1860, both regarded the subordination of the Negro as axiomatic. In this sense, it may be argued that although the war perhaps ought to have been about the future position of the Negro, in fact that is not what it was about, since American whites did not recognize that question as an issue. Just as Randall sought to refute the assertion that slavery was the cause of the war by showing that the Republicans, during the slavery controversy, disavowed any purpose to tamper with slavery, and declared their intention only to monopolize the territories for white settlers, so a critic of Nevins might even more persuasively refute the assertion that the future position of the Negro race was the main root of the conflict by showing that hardly anyone at that time contemplated raising the Negro from his position of inferiority, much less fighting a war for such a purpose. From this view, the tragedy of the war is that Americans sacrificed so much without tackling or even perceiving the ultimate question—without even recognizing what was really at stake.

But it is by no means certain historically that the participants in a war necessarily understand why they fight, nor that the conscious objectives of belligerents are an adequate measure of the historical meaning of a war. If Nevins' statement is read to mean that in the crisis leading to the Civil War the blind forces of history were working toward a long-protracted and agonizing readjustment of the future position of the Negro, it is entirely tenable, and may also be regarded as having a broad significance which previous explanations had lacked. In fact, coming as it did, four years before *Brown vs. the Board of Education*, and five years before Martin Luther King's Montgomery Improvement Association, Nevins' statement was historiographically prophetic in foreseeing the viewpoints of historians for at least the next two decades.

Even if historians between 1950 and 1968 had not been plying their trade in a society whose foremost development was the Negro Revolution, probably they would have corrected some of the excesses of the revisionist position simply because the revisionists had carried some of their claims to an extreme. For instance, from the time of Albert J. Beveridge through that of J. G. Randall, the prevailing treatment of Lincoln had insisted that his only greatness appeared after he became President, that there was little to choose between him and Stephen A. Douglas (except that Douglas was more straightforward), and that morally, Lincoln was an opportunist who skillfully contrived to win the votes of both antislavery men and Negrophobes.

The first serious refutation of this view in almost a generation appeared in Don E. Fehrenbacher's *Prelude to Greatness: Lincoln in the 1850's* (1962). Fehrenbacher shunned all the legendary melodrama which pictured Lincoln as a foreordained Emancipator, but he showed very accurately and specifically that Lincoln's position was fundamentally incompatible with that of Douglas, and that he was eager to emphasize the divergence. Fehrenbacher's Lincoln was politically ambitious, but not opportunistic, and his ambition "was leavened by moral conviction."

This emphasis upon Lincoln's moral stature and responsibility was a reaffirmation, at a more subtle and more scholarly level, of a view that had prevailed widely before the revisionist onslaught. But when the focus shifted from Lincoln to the abolitionists, there was very little in the way of accepted legend to build upon. Ever since the Civil War, every historian who sympathized with the South or gave a priority to peace or to Union over emancipation held the abolitionists answerable for driving the South into secession, and thus responsible for both disunion and war. Partly in consequence of these reactions and also perhaps because they did manifest more than the average amount of self-righteousness and moral absolutism, the abolitionists were customarily portrayed as "fanatics" or "extremists." But by 1960, a widespread sense of guilt about American racial attitudes had reached such a degree of intensity that many people, both inside and outside of the historical profession, had lost all interest in the complexities of the relationship between the slavery issue and the war, and had come to regard emancipation and equality for the Negro as the only meaningful aspects of the conflict. In short, the problem of justification had replaced the closely related problem of explanation. As it did so, there was a compulsion to understand the war once more not as a clash of interests but as a crusade against slavery. The shift is well indicated by the titles of the two principal books in the last thirty years which have covered the whole period from the Mexican War through the Civil War. The first of these, by Roy F. Nichols, published in 1961, was entitled *The Stakes of Power, 1845–1877*; the second, by Elbert B. Smith, published in 1967, was *The Death of Slavery, 1837–1865*.

To validate the crusade against slavery, it was, of course necessary to legitimize the crusaders (just as it had been necessary, in discrediting the crusade, to disparage the crusaders). David Donald discovered this historical correlation in 1960 when he published the first volume of his biography of the foremost political adversary of slavery, *Charles Sumner and the Coming of the Civil War*. Donald had researched his subject superbly, and in many respects it seems that he appreciated Sumner's qualities of conviction and devotion to all worthy causes. But he portrayed quite explicitly Sumner's rigid self-righteousness, his arrogance and tendency to quarrel even with his close friends, and his humorless egoism. Although he won a Pulitzer prize for his work, Donald was assailed in at least three articles or lengthy reviews for dealing so harshly with an antislavery leader. He had unwittingly violated an axiom which has served many writers, not all of them outside the historical profession: a man's character is to be inferred from the cause with which he is or was identified and not from the evidence of his personal behavior. Although the slavery question was certainly an ethical one, it does not follow that the vice or virtue of any given individual is a direct coefficient of his position on that question. But nonetheless, true believers will never doubt that if Sumner was sound on slavery, he was one of the good guys, and therefore must, by definition, have had a sense of humor.

This comment should not be read as a covert attack on the abolitionists. They may well have been maligned more indiscriminately in the past than they were lauded indiscriminately in the 1960's. But it is unfortunate that one school, which admires "moderation," tends to denounce the abolitionists as unmitigated bigots, while another school, which admires morality, cannot admit that moral absolutism leads to excessive self-righteousness. All parties tend to avoid facing the fact that every value has its cost. The cost of deep commitment is a certain measure, more or less, of intolerance, and the cost of tolerance is a certain measure, more or less, of moral apathy.

In a larger sense, the vital question concerning the abolitionists is not whether they were "fanatics," but first whether they were humanitarians in a broad sense—that is whether the dynamic of their antislavery was an outgoing concern for the welfare of others or a neurotic impulse to find outlets for psychological problems of their own—and second, whether they really perceived the problem of race adjustment in America, to which Nevins alludes, and which was the essence of the problem of slavery.

The literature of antislavery began to treat its theme somewhat more broadly beginning about 1930. Perhaps the first scholarly modern treatment appeared in 1933 when Gilbert H. Barnes published *The Anti-Slavery Impulse, 1830–1844*. This work broke the monopolistic focus upon William Lloyd Garrison as the one standard symbol of abolitionism by showing the great importance of Theodore Dwight Weld and others. At the same time, it shifted attention from New England to the Middle West. It also began to link antislavery with other forces by demonstrating the integral relationship of abolitionism with the fervent evangelical religion of which Weld was apostle. With the Garrisonian mold thus broken, other writers did much more to explore the social and intellectual origins and relationships of the antislavery movement. Illustrative of this tendency are: Alice Felt Tyler, *Freedom's Ferment* (1944), which deals comprehensively with the many-faceted movement of humanitarian reform, within the context of which the antislavery movement developed; Thomas E. Drake, *Quakers and Slavery in America* (1950), which focused attention again on some of the less sensational, less militant aspects of the resistance to slavery; Samuel Flagg Bemis, *John Quincy Adams and the Union* (1956), which told the story of Adams' career as an antislavery leader in Congress, and thus showed how broad the antislavery movement was in comparison with the abolitionists' campaign for immediate emancipation; and Philip S. Foner, *The Life and Writings of Frederick Douglass* (1950–55), which emphasized the role of free Negroes in the abolition movement.

Identification of the antislavery movement with the humanitarian movement usually implies a measure of approbation for the abolitionists. But, while this approval has certainly been prominent in part of the literature, there also remained a marked tendency to question the basic motivation of abolitionists, sometimes in modern psychological terms. The abolitionists have, of course, always been condemned by writers who attribute the disruption of the Union to the fanaticism of the antislavery crusade. But some of the recent criticism, coming from quite an opposite direction, reflects a belief that the abolitionists were motivated less by a concern for Negro welfare than by other objectives and even by a drive to fulfill certain peculiar psychological needs of their own.

This theme was implied in 1949, in Russel B. Nye's *Fettered Freedom* which argued that the slave system, both in itself and in its zealous defensiveness, constituted a threat to civil liberties and thus provoked the opposition of men who opposed the slave power without necessarily caring about the slave. At almost the same time, Richard Hofstadter, in his *The American Political Tradition,* described Lincoln as one who owed his success to his skill in finding a way "to win the support of both Negrophobes and antislavery men." Hofstadter did not picture the antislavery men as being Negrophobes themselves, but Joseph C. Furnas has actually carried the argument to this position in *Goodbye to Uncle Tom* (1956). Furnas castigates the abolitionists for paving the way to the later system of segregation by their acceptance of the idea of the inferiority of the Negro, and he shows very clearly that many abolitionists, although rejecting slavery, nevertheless did "type" the Negro as an inferior. Since his book appeared, Robert F. Durden's *James Shepherd Pike* (1957) has shown how the strands of antislavery and Negrophobia were strikingly united in the person of one of the editors of the New York *Tribune,* the most important journalistic organ of the antislavery cause.

More recently, biographies of Cassius M. Clay by David Smiley (1962), of George W. Julian by Patrick Riddleberger (1966), and of Hinton R. Helper by Hugh C. Bailey (1965) have illustrated other striking cases of men who hated slavery but had no love for the Negro.

Meanwhile, David Donald has advanced some generalizations about the abolitionists, based upon a study of the backgrounds of 106 prominent antislavery men. He found them, in general, conservative, indifferent to the exploitation of industrial labor, and hostile to Jacksonian democracy. He also suggested that many of them were descendants of New England clerical families who found their leadership challenged by the new industrialism and who turned to reform as a medium through which "their own class" could reassert "its former social dominance . . . an attack upon slavery was their best, if quite unconscious, attack upon the new industrial system."

In short, Donald applied to the abolitionists the same concept of status anxiety and status politics which Richard Hofstadter and the authors of *The New American Right* (1955) were applying, at about the same time, to the Progressives and to the McCarthy Era—and with the same disparaging results.

The treatment of individual abolitionists was usually more favorable than in the generalized accounts. This is true, for instance, of biographies of Gerrit Smith, by Ralph V. Harlow (1939), Harriet Beecher Stowe, by Forrest Wilson (1941), William Lloyd Garrison and Wendell Phillips, by Ralph Korngold (1950), Theodore Weld by Benjamin P. Thomas (1950), William Lloyd Garrison, by Russel B. Nye (1955), James G. Birney by Betty Fladeland (1955), and Wendell Phillips, by Oscar Sherwin (1958).

But the real watershed in antislavery histories came with the publication of Louis Filler's *The Crusade Against Slavery, 1830–1860* and Clifford S. Griffin's *Their Brothers' Keepers, Moral Stewardship in the United States, 1800–1865*, both in 1960, and Dwight L. Dumond's *Antislavery*, in 1961. Filler provided the first modern, general, scholarly account of the antislavery movement and one sympathetic to the cause whose history it recorded. Griffin identified antislavery with a reform tradition that was somewhat self-righteous, paternalistic, and given to the use of compulsory methods, but which was nevertheless high-minded, public-spirited, and civicly responsible. Dumond, who approached his subject with immense erudition (only partly reflected in his editing of the Weld and Grimke papers [2 vols., 1934] and the Birney Papers [2 vols., 1938]), launched the most learned, most extensive, and most uncritical history of antislavery since Pillsbury Parker had published *The Acts of the Antislavery Apostles* in 1883. This work, a kind of fifth gospel according to Dumond, asserted that the antislavery movement was "the greatest concentration of moral and intellectual power ever assembled in support of any cause before or since."

Dumond's hyperbole was such as to make his book, with all its learning, something of a curiosity, but any reader who compared his panegyric with previous acerbic treatments of the abolitionists could easily tell that "the times they are a-changing." Four years later, Martin Duberman, as editor of a collection of essays by various hands, *The Antislavery Vanguard*, made the same point with vastly more restraint and with strong effect. Duberman specifically rejected the stereotype of the abolitionist as a crank and a fanatic, and claimed for the antislavery movement an immense constructive value. No longer were abolitionists the irresponsible and bigoted men who brought disunion and civil war upon the country. Rather they were the defenders of freedom when none else would defend it.

This account of the literature of antislavery might be extended to include a discussion of biographies of Wendell Phillips by Irving H. Bartlett (1961—the best treatment), of Elijah P. Lovejoy by Merton L. Dillon (1961), of Thomas Wentworth Higginson by Mary Ann Wells (1963), of Lydia Maria Child by Helene G. Baer (1964—with some shortcomings), of John P. Hale by Richard H. Sewell (1965), of James Russell Lowell by Martin Duberman (1966), of Benjamin Lundy by Merton L. Dillon (1966), of Owen Lovejoy by Edward Magdol (1967), of Sarah and Angelina Grimke by Gerda Lerner (1967), and two 1963 biographies of William Lloyd Garrison, one by John L. Thomas, the other by Walter M. Merrill. Larry Gara's history of the fact and legend of the Underground Railroad, *The Liberty Line* (1961), should also be mentioned. Finally, it is important to note James M. MacPherson's *The Struggle for Equality* (1964), for MacPherson followed the careers of the antislavery men into the era of Reconstruction and argued with considerable force that many of the leading abolitionists were not racists, did not hold the unrealistic view that all the slaves needed was to be set legally free, did not abandon the freedman to his fate, and were motivated by concern for the welfare of the blacks and not by neurotic anxiety concerning their own status.

Since MacPherson's book deals with Reconstruction, it may seem completely misguided of me to include it in a discussion of the literature concerning the background of the Civil War. But it is pertinent because MacPherson is one of the first writers who applied Nevins' idea that the main root of the conflict—whether the participants knew it or not—was the problem of "slavery *and* of the future position of the Negro race in North America." For almost a century, the histories of slavery had treated it as something unique, and either did not consider its relation to the broader practice of the subordination of the blacks, or even treated the subordination as one result of the stigma of slavery. So long as slavery was conceived to be central, the two main questions were: what did slavery have to do with causing the Civil War and how necessary was the war to the ending of slavery? But by the 1960's, it was beginning to be recognized that slavery was only a special form of racial subordination, and not everyone would even agree that it was the severest of all forms, though it was certainly one of the most complete. But if racial subordination was the essence, and slavery was only an overt form, then the question had to be restated: what did racial subordination have to do with causing the Civil War and how did the war impinge on racial subordination? Unless the war played a vital part in these connections, perhaps it was really not as important as people had imagined, and not worth all the controversy that had raged for a century.

To express this in another way, the war was certainly vital in the history of slavery, but it was not necessarily significant in the history of racism, except insofar as the end of slavery transformed the real social position of the blacks, which clearly it did not do. Perhaps as a result, the focus on the war began to be diffused. In a somewhat anomalous way, a more pervasive influence was attributed to slavery as social subordination, while at the same time it was recognized that, as chattel bondage, it constituted only one dimension of the more enduring problem of racial caste.

Thus, Thomas Jefferson came under fire. Jefferson had always been the South's symbol of its own intrinsic liberalism, and in the eyes of Southern liberals, Calhoun had only been an unfortunate aberration. But Leonard Levy in 1963, in a study of *Jefferson and Civil Liberties: The Darker Side,* pictured the great Democrat as repressive and illiberal in many important respects. A year later, Robert McColley, in *Slavery in Jeffersonian Virginia,* made the most sustained assault ever launched upon the long-standing legend that Jefferson and Virginia would have abolished slavery if they had only gotten around to it. Similarly, for a century, the nullification crisis was believed to have turned upon the tariff issue, but in 1966, William W. Freehling approached the question in a new way. In *Prelude to Civil War: The Nullification Controversy in South Carolina, 1816–1936* he advanced the theory that slavery underlay nullification.

Slavery is now being emphasized more than ever before, to the exclusion of economic and other sectional factors which once received major stress. However, it is not slavery as chattel servitude, but slavery as racial subordination. Leon Litwack's *North of Slavery: The Negro in the Free States, 1790–1860* (1964) showed conclusively that complete segregation, formalized discrimination, and belief in Negro inferiority prevailed throughout the states that fought for the Union in the Civil War. How could the Union victory mean a defeat for racism, when both of the antagonists were racists? William Stanton, *The Leopard's Spots: Scientific Attitudes Toward Race in America,* shows how ideas of Negro biological inferiority were supported by a widely accepted doctrine that the races of men were actually distinct species. Philip J. Stadenraus, *The African Colonization Movement, 1816–1865* (1961), showed to what a great extent the idea of sending freed slaves to Liberia meant in fact deporting Negroes to Africa. Eugene F. Berwanger's *The Frontier Against Slavery: Western Anti-Negro Prejudice and the Slavery Extension Controversy* (1967) documented the antipathy toward Negroes which made so many Northern whites eager to keep them out of the territories. Finally, and perhaps most significant of all, David Brion Davis' groundbreaking *The Problem of Slavery in Western Culture* (1967) has shown the depth of the roots of ideological belief in slavery, and Winthrop Jordan's massive study, *White over Black: American Attitudes Toward the Negro, 1550–1812* (1968), has noted the protracted duration and the pervasiveness of the rejection of the Negro by American whites. On this long road, the Civil War scarcely seemed more than a jog.

Increasingly in recent years, the period preceding the Civil War has been discussed in terms of racism and the subordination of the Negro, rather than in terms of slavery alone, or of the territorial issue. Ironically, this emphasis leaves the explanation of the war even more remote than ever before. The work of men like Litwack, Stanton, Stadenraus, Berwanger, and Jordan shows that the dominant forces in both sections spurned and oppressed the Negro. Since this was true, it is difficult to understand why the particular form which this oppression took in the South should have caused acute tension, as it did, between the sections. Was it because Northerners hated and envied the aristocratic pretensions of the slaveholders, but at the same time stood aloof from the slaves? Was the South needlessly frightened into breaking up the Union, and was the issue of union really much more vital than we are now psychologically prepared to believe?

The overwhelming preoccupation with racial questions during the 1960's has to some extent diverted attention from analytical explanations of the war. Despite this general shift in focus away from what was for a time *the* central question in American historiography, a few genuinely analytical approaches are still being taken. Two especially may be mentioned here. First, Barrington Moore's chapter "The American Civil War: the Last Capitalist Revolution" in his *Social Origins of Dictatorship and Democracy* (1966), has been written with remarkable cogency and decisiveness. Moore argues that "the strictly economic issues were very probably negotiable"; he also accepts the view that the Northern public did not care enough about slavery to fight for its overthrow. As to conflict of interests, he regards the "tugging and hauling and quarreling and grabbing" by diverse interest groups as chronic in any society, and therefore useless for diagnostic purposes in explaining a civil war. Generally, slavery was a form of capitalism, not inherently incompatible with industrial capitalism: "There is no abstract general reason why the North and South had to fight. Special historical circumstances, in other words, had to be present." The special historical circumstance which brought on a war, as Moore sees it, was the fact that the slave system was an obstacle "to a *particular kind* of capitalism at a specific historical stage." The South wanted a capitalism with fixed hierarchical status; the North wanted "a competitive democratic capitalism" and "was still committed to notions of equal opportunity," deriving from "the Puritan, American, and French Revolutions." It was impossible "to establish political and social institutions that would satisfy both" North and South. The Civil War was the last of several major nineteenth-century conflicts waged by the bourgeois against the landed classes.

In Moore, old ideas are echoed in a new, somewhat Marxian context. A second important interpretation, also Marxist, but not at all literal-minded in its Marxism, has appeared in Eugene D. Genovese, "Marxian Interpretations of the Slave South," in *Towards a New Past: Dissenting Essays in American History* (Barton J. Bernstein, editor, 1968). The heart of Genovese's argument is to be found in his critique of Moore. The fallacy in Moore, he contends, is the view that since both slavery and industry were forms of capitalism, there was therefore no necessary ground for conflict between them, in general terms, and that specific circumstances had to be invoked. But, says Genovese, while slavery may have partaken of the nature of capital, it "simultaneously extruded a ruling class with strong pre-bourgeois qualities and economic interests." In short, if industrialists and slaveholders were both capitalists, the resemblance was purely semantic and at an abstract level. Concretely, they clashed partly because one group was bourgeois while the other, although not feudal (the distinction is brilliantly made), was pre-bourgeois.

Today, historians seem to have agreed on a good many points: that the North did not hate slavery enough to go to war about it; that slavery was too close to capitalism to justify the old antithesis of industrialism versus agrarianism; that the conflict of economic interests was negotiable and the conflict of civilizations was, to some extent, trumped up; that the power of the planters was real; that slavery was not a dying institution; and that the South was not a land primarily of Jeffersonian yeomen. Thus the "causes of the Civil War" remain moot.

Nevertheless, in every aspect, slavery was important. Economically, it was an immensely powerful property interest, somewhat inimical to the interests of free farming, because the independent farmer could not compete with the slave. Socially, it was the keystone of a static society of social hierarchy which challenged the dynamic, mobile, and equalitarian modes of life and labor that prevailed in the free states. Ideologically, it was a negation of the basic American principles of freedom and equality. It is futile to draw analytical distinctions between the slavery issue and (a) economic conflict of interest, (b) cultural incompatibilities, and (c) ideals as a social force. For the slavery issue was not, for explanatory purposes, an alternative to any of the others. It was part of the essence of all of them.

Abraham Lincoln and the Self-Made Myth

Richard Hofstadter

Rather than attempt to destroy the immense body of myth that surrounds Abraham Lincoln, Richard Hofstadter, late DeWitt Clinton Professor of American History at Columbia University, looks to the myth's origin, development, and final effect on its subject. Accepting the fact that elements of the myth are true, Professor Hofstadter finds that it was Lincoln himself who was the "first author of the Lincoln legend" and then continued to be its chief exponent. The "self-made myth" was propelled by Lincoln's political ambition for the presidency. The effects of the myth's fulfillment on the sensitive Lincoln were tragic; instead of glory, "he had found only ashes and blood."

> I happen, temporarily, to occupy this White House. I am a living witness that any one of your children may look to come here as my father's child has.
>
> Abraham Lincoln to the 166th Ohio Regiment

> His ambition was a little engine that knew no rest.
>
> William H. Herndon

The Lincoln legend has come to have a hold on the American imagination that defies comparison with anything else in political mythology. Here is a drama in which a great man shoulders the torment and moral burdens of a blundering and sinful people, suffers for them, and redeems them with hallowed Christian virtues—"malice toward none and charity for all"—and is destroyed at the pitch of his success. The worldly-wise John Hay, who knew him about as well as he permitted himself to be known, called him "the greatest character since Christ," a comparison one cannot imagine being made of any other political figure of modern times.

If the Lincoln legend gathers strength from its similarity to the Christian theme of vicarious atonement and redemption, there is still another strain in American experience that it represents equally well. Although his métier was politics and not business, Lincoln was a pre-eminent example of that self-help which Americans have always so admired. He was not, of course, the first eminent American politician who could claim humble origins, nor the first to exploit them. But few have been able to point to such a sudden ascent from relative obscurity to high eminence; none has maintained so completely while scaling the heights the aspect of extreme simplicity; and none has combined with the attainment of success and power such an intense awareness of humanity and moral responsibility. It was precisely in his attainments as a common man that Lincoln felt himself to be remarkable, and in this light that he interpreted to the world the significance of his career. Keenly aware of his role as the exemplar of the self-made man, he played the part with an intense and poignant consistency that gives his performance the quality of a high art. The first author of the Lincoln legend and the greatest of the Lincoln dramatists was Lincoln himself.

Lincoln's simplicity was very real. He called his wife "mother," received distinguished guests in shirtsleeves, and once during his presidency hailed a soldier out of the ranks with the cry: "Bub! Bub!" But he was also a complex man, easily complex enough to know the value of his own simplicity. With his morbid compulsion for honesty he was too modest to pose coarsely and blatantly as a Henry Clay or James G. Blaine might pose. (When an 1860 campaign document announced that he was a reader of Plutarch, he sat down at once to validate the claim by reading the *Lives*.) But he did develop a political personality by intensifying qualities he actually possessed.

Even during his early days in politics, when his speeches were full of conventional platform bombast, Lincoln seldom failed to strike the humble manner that was peculiarly his. "I was born and have ever remained," he said in his first extended campaign speech, "in the most humble walks of life. I have no popular relations or friends to recommend me." Thereafter he always sounded the theme. "I presume you all know who I am—I am humble Abraham Lincoln. . . . If elected I shall be thankful; if not it will be all the same." Opponents at times grew impatient with his self-derogation ("my poor, lean, lank face") and a Democratic journal once called him a Uriah Heep. But self-conscious as the device was, and coupled even as it was with a secret confidence that Hay called "intellectual arrogance," there was still no imposture in it. It corresponded to Lincoln's own image of himself, which placed him with the poor, the aged, and the forgotten. In a letter to Herndon that was certainly not meant to impress any constituency, Lincoln, near his thirty-ninth birthday, referred to "my old, withered, dry eyes."

There was always this pathos in his plainness, his lack of external grace. "He is," said one of Mrs. Lincoln's friends, "the *ungodliest* man you ever saw." His colleagues, however, recognized in this a possible political asset and transmuted it into one of the most successful of all political symbols—the hard-fisted rail-splitter. At a Republican meeting in 1860 John Hanks and another old pioneer appeared carrying fence rails labeled: "Two rails from a lot made by Abraham Lincoln and John Hanks in the Sangamon Bottom in the year 1830." And Lincoln, with his usual candor, confessed that he had no idea whether these were the same rails, but he was sure he had actually split rails every bit as good. The time was to come when little Tad could say: "Everybody in this world knows Pa used to split rails."

Humility belongs with mercy among the cardinal Christian virtues. "Blessed are the meek, for they shall inherit the earth." But the demands of Christianity and the success myth are incompatible. The competitive society out of which the success myth and the self-made man have grown may accept the Christian virtues in principle but can hardly observe them in practice. The motivating force in the mythology of success is ambition, which is closely akin to the cardinal Christian sin of pride. In a world that works through ambition and self-help, while inculcating an ethic that looks upon their results with disdain, how can an earnest man, a public figure living in a time of crisis, gratify his aspirations and yet remain morally whole? If he is, like Lincoln, a man of private religious intensity, the stage is set for high tragedy.

The clue to much that is vital in Lincoln's thought and character lies in the fact that he was thoroughly and completely the politician, by preference and by training. It is difficult to think of any man of comparable stature whose life was so fully absorbed into his political being. Lincoln plunged into politics almost at the beginning of his adult life and was never occupied in any other career except for a brief period when an unfavorable turn in the political situation forced him back to his law practice. His life was one of caucuses and conventions, party circulars and speeches, requests, recommendations, stratagems, schemes, and ambitions. "It was in the world of politics that he lived," wrote Herndon after his death. "Politics were his life, newspapers his food, and his great ambition his motive power."

Like his father, Lincoln was physically lazy even as a youth, but unlike him had an active forensic mind. When only fifteen he was often on stumps and fences making political speeches, from which his father had to haul him back to his chores. He was fond of listening to lawyers' arguments and occupying his mind with them. Herndon testifies that "He read specially for a special object and thought things useless unless they could be of utility, use, practice, etc."[1] When Lincoln read he preferred to read aloud. Once when Herndon asked him about it he answered: "I catch the idea by two senses, for when I read aloud I *hear* what is read and I see it . . . and I remember it better, if I do not understand it better." These are the reading habits of a man who is preparing for the platform.

For a youth with such mental habits—and one who had no business talents in the narrower sense—the greatest opportunities on the Illinois prairies were in the ministry, law, or politics. Lincoln, who had read Paine and Volney, was too unorthodox in theology for the ministry, and law and politics it proved to be. But politics was first: at twenty-three, only seven months after coming to the little Illinois community of New Salem, he was running for office. Previously he had worked only at odd jobs as ferryman, surveyor, postmaster, storekeeper, rail-splitter, farm hand, and the like; and now, without any other preparation, he was looking for election to the state legislature.

He was not chosen, but two years later, in 1834, Sangamon County sent him to the lower house. Not until his first term had almost ended was he sufficiently qualified as a lawyer to be admitted to the state bar.

From this time to the end of his life—except for the years between 1849 and 1854, when his political prospects were discouraging—Lincoln was busy either as officeholder or officeseeker. In the summer of 1860, for a friend who wanted to prepare a campaign biography, he wrote in the third person a short sketch of his political life up to that time: 1832—defeated in an attempt to be elected to the legislature; 1834—elected to the legislature "by the highest vote cast for any candidate"; 1836, 1838, 1840—re-elected; 1838 and 1840—chosen by his party as its candidate for Speaker of the Illinois House of Representatives, but not elected; 1840 and 1844—placed on Harrison and Clay electoral tickets "and spent much time and labor in both those canvasses"; 1846—elected to Congress; 1848—campaign worker for Zachary Taylor, speaking in Maryland and Massachusetts, and "canvassing quite fully his own district in Illinois, which was followed by a majority in the district of over 1500 for General Taylor"; 1852—placed on Winfield Scott's electoral ticket, "but owing to the hopelessness of the cause in Illinois he did less than in previous presidential canvasses"; 1854—". . . his profession had almost superseded the thought of politics in his mind, when the repeal of the Missouri Compromise aroused him as he had never been before"; 1856—"made over fifty speeches" in the campaign for Frémont; prominently mentioned in the Republican national convention for the vice-presidential nomination. . . .

The rest of the story is familiar enough. . . .

As an economic thinker, Lincoln had a passion for the great average. Thoroughly middle-class in his ideas, he spoke for those millions of Americans who had begun their lives as hired workers—as farm hands, clerks, teachers, mechanics, flatboat men, and rail-splitters—and had passed into the ranks of landed farmers, prosperous grocers, lawyers, merchants, physicians, and politicians. Theirs were the traditional ideals of the Protestant ethic: hard work, frugality, temperance, and a touch of ability applied long and hard enough would lift a man into the propertied or professional class and give him independence and respect if not wealth and prestige. Failure to rise in the economic scale was generally viewed as a fault in the individual, not in society. It was the outward sign of an inward lack of grace—of idleness, indulgence, waste, or incapacity.

This conception of the competitive world was by no means so inaccurate in Lincoln's day as it has long since become; neither was it so conservative as time has made it. It was the legitimate inheritance of Jacksonian democracy. It was the belief not only of those who had arrived but also of those who were pushing their way to the top. If it was intensely and at times inhumanly individualistic, it also defied aristocracy and class distinction. Lincoln's life was a dramatization of it in the sphere of politics as, say, Carnegie's was in business. His own rather conventional version of the self-help ideology[2] is expressed with some charm in a letter written to his feckless stepbrother, John D. Johnston, in 1851:

> Your request for eighty dollars I do not think it best to comply with now. At the various times when I have helped you a little you have said to me, "We can get along very well now"; but in a very short time I find you in the same difficulty again. Now, this can only happen by some defect in your conduct. What that defect is, I think I know. You are not lazy, and still you are an idler. I doubt whether, since I saw you, you have done a good whole day's work in any one day. You do not very much dislike to work, and still you do not work much, merely because it does not seem to you that you could get much for it. This habit of uselessly wasting time is the whole difficulty.

Lincoln advised Johnston to leave his farm in charge of his family and go to work for wages.

> I now promise you, that for every dollar you will, between this and the first of May, get for your own labor . . . I will then give you one other dollar. . . . Now if you will do this, you will soon be out of debt, and, what is better, you will have a habit that will keep you from getting in debt again. . . . You have always been kind to me, and I do not mean to be unkind to you. On the contrary, if you will but follow my advice, you will find it worth more than eighty times eighty dollars to you.

Given the chance for the frugal, the industrious, and the able—for the Abraham Lincolns if not the John D. Johnstons—to assert themselves, society would never be divided along fixed lines. There would be no eternal mud-sill class. "There is no permanent class of hired laborers among us," Lincoln declared in a public address. "Twenty-five years ago I was a hired laborer. The hired laborer of yesterday labors on his own account today, and will hire others to labor for him tomorrow. Advancement—improvement in condition—is the order of things in a society of equals." For Lincoln the vital test of a democracy was economic—its ability to provide opportunities for social ascent to those born in its lower ranks. This belief in opportunity for the self-made man is the key to his entire career; it explains his public appeal; it is the core of his criticism of slavery.

There is a strong pro-labor strain in all of Lincoln's utterances from the beginning to the end of his career. Perhaps the most sweeping of his words, and certainly the least equivocal, were penned in 1847. "Inasmuch as most good things are produced by labor," be began,

> it follows that all such things of right belong to those whose labor has produced them. But it has so happened, in all ages of the world, that some have labored, and others have without labor enjoyed a large proportion of the fruits. This is wrong and should not continue. To secure to each laborer the whole product of his labor, or as nearly as possible, is a worthy object of any good government.

This reads like a passage from a socialist argument. But its context is significant; the statement was neither a preface to an attack upon private property nor an argument for redistributing the world's goods—it was part of a firm defense of the protective tariff!

In Lincoln's day, especially in the more primitive communities of his formative years, the laborer had not yet been fully separated from his tools. The rights of labor still were closely associated in the fashion of Locke and Jefferson with the right of the laborer to retain his own product; when men talked about the sacredness of labor, they were often talking in veiled terms about the right to own. These ideas, which belonged to the age of craftsmanship rather than industrialism, Lincoln carried into the modern industrial scene. The result is a quaint equivocation, worth observing carefully because it pictures the state of mind of a man living half in one economy and half in another and wishing to do justice to every interest. In 1860, when Lincoln was stumping about the country before the Republican convention, he turned up at New Haven, where shoemakers were on strike. The Democrats had charged Republican agitators with responsibility for the strike, and Lincoln met them head-on:

> . . . I am glad to see that a system of labor prevails in New England under which laborers can strike when they want to, where they are not obliged to work under all circumstances, and are not tied down and obliged to labor whether you pay them or not! I like the system which lets a man quit when he wants to, and wish it might prevail everywhere. One of the reasons why I am opposed to slavery is just here. What is the true condition of the laborer? I take it that it is best for all to leave each man free to acquire property as fast as he can. Some will get wealthy. I don't believe in a law to prevent a man from getting rich; it would do more harm than good. So while we do not propose any war upon capital, we do wish to allow the humblest man an equal chance to get rich with everybody else. When one starts poor, as most do in the race of life, free society is such that he knows he can better his condition; he knows that there is no fixed condition of labor for his whole life. . . . That is the true system.

If there was a flaw in all this, it was one that Lincoln was never forced to meet. Had he lived to seventy, he would have seen the generation brought up on self-help come into its own, build oppressive business corporations, and begin to close off those treasured opportunities for the little man. Further, he would have seen his own party become the jackal of the vested interests, placing the dollar far, far ahead of the man. He himself presided over the social revolution that destroyed the simple equalitarian order of the 1840's, corrupted what remained of its values, and caricatured its ideals. Booth's bullet, indeed, saved him from something worse than embroilment with the radicals over Reconstruction. It confined his life to the happier age that Lincoln understood—which unwittingly he helped to destroy—the age that gave sanction to the honest compromises of his thought.

A story about Abraham Lincoln's second trip to New Orleans when he was twenty-one holds an important place in the Lincoln legend. According to John Hanks, when Lincoln went with his companions to a slave market they saw a handsome mulatto girl being sold on the block, and "the iron entered his soul"; he swore that if he ever got a chance he would hit slavery "and hit it hard." The implication is clear: Lincoln was half abolitionist and the Emancipation Proclamation was a fulfillment of that young promise. But the authenticity of the tale is suspect among Lincoln scholars. John Hanks recalled it thirty-five years afterward as a personal witness, whereas, according to Lincoln, Hanks had not gone beyond St. Louis on the journey. Beveridge observes that Lincoln himself apparently never spoke of the alleged incident publicly or privately,[3] and that for twenty years afterward he showed little concern over slavery. We know that he refused to denounce the Fugitive Slave Law, viciously unfair though it was, even to free Negroes charged as runaways. ("I confess I hate to see the poor creatures hunted down," he wrote to Speed, ". . . but I bite my lips and keep quiet.")

His later career as an opponent of slavery extension must be interpreted in the light of his earlier public indifference to the question. Always moderately hostile to the South's "peculiar institution," he quieted himself with the comfortable thought that it was destined very gradually to disappear. Only after the Kansas-Nebraska Act breathed political life into the slavery issue did he seize upon it as a subject for agitation; only then did he attack it openly. His attitude was based on justice tempered by expediency—or perhaps more accurately, expediency tempered by justice.

Lincoln was by birth a Southerner, a Kentuckian; both his parents were Virginians. His father had served on the slave patrol of Hardin County. The Lincoln family was one of thousands that in the early decades of the nineteenth century had moved from the Southern states, particularly Virginia, Kentucky, and Tennessee, into the Valley of Democracy, and peopled the southern parts of Ohio, Indiana, and Illinois.

During his boyhood days in Indiana and Illinois Lincoln lived in communities where slaves were rare or unknown, and the problem was not thrust upon him. The prevailing attitude toward Negroes in Illinois was intensely hostile. Severe laws against free Negroes and runaway slaves were in force when Lincoln went to the Springfield legislature, and there is no evidence of any popular movement to liberalize them. Lincoln's experiences with slavery on his journeys to New Orleans in 1828 and 1831 do not seem to have made an impression vivid enough to change his conduct. Always privately compassionate, in his public career and his legal practice he never made himself the advocate of unpopular reform movements.

While Lincoln was serving his second term in the Illinois legislature the slavery question was discussed throughout the country. Garrison had begun his agitation, and petitions to abolish slavery in the District of Columbia had begun to pour in upon Congress. State legislatures began to express themselves upon the matter. The Illinois legislature turned the subject over to a joint committee, of which Lincoln and his Sangamon County colleague, Dan Stone, were members. At twenty-eight Lincoln thus had occasion to review the whole slavery question on both sides. The committee reported proslavery resolutions, presently adopted, which praised the beneficent effects of white civilization upon African natives, cited the wretchedness of emancipated Negroes as proof of the folly of freedom, and denounced abolitionists.

Lincoln voted against these resolutions. Six weeks later—the delay resulted from a desire to alienate no one from the cause that then stood closest to his heart, the removal of the state capital from Vandalia to Springfield—he and Stone embodied their own opinions in a resolution that was entered in the Journal of the House and promptly forgotten. It read in part: "They [Lincoln and Stone] believe that the institution of slavery is founded on injustice and bad policy, but that the promulgation of abolition doctrines tends to increase rather than abate its evils." (Which means, the later Lincoln might have said, that slavery is wrong but that proposing to do away with it is also wrong because it makes slavery worse.) They went on to say that while the Constitution does not permit Congress to abolish slavery in the states, Congress can do so in the District of Columbia—*but* this power should not be exercised unless at "the request of the people of the District." This statement breathes the fire of an uncompromising insistence upon moderation. Let it be noted, however, that it did represent a point of view faintly to the left of prevailing opinion. Lincoln had gone on record as saying not merely that slavery was "bad policy" but even that it was unjust; but he had done so without jeopardizing his all-important project to transfer the state capital to Springfield.

In 1845, not long before he entered Congress, Lincoln again had occasion to express himself on slavery, this time in a carefully phrased private letter to a political supporter who happened to be an abolitionist.

> I hold it a paramount duty of us in the free States, due to the Union of the States, and perhaps to liberty itself (paradox though it may seem), to let the slavery of the other states alone; while, on the other hand, I hold it to be equally clear that we should never knowingly lend ourselves, directly or indirectly, to prevent that slavery from dying a natural death—to find new places for it to live in, when it can not longer exist in the old.

Throughout his political career he consistently held to this position.

After he had become a lame-duck Congressman, Lincoln introduced into Congress in January 1849 a resolution to instruct the Committee on the District of Columbia to report a bill abolishing slavery in the District. The bill provided that children born of slave mothers after January 1, 1850 should be freed and supported by their mothers' owners until of a certain age. District slaveholders who wanted to emancipate their slaves were to be compensated from the federal Treasury. Lincoln himself added a section requiring the municipal authorities of Washington and Georgetown to provide "active and efficient means" of arresting and restoring to their owners all fugitive slaves escaping into the District. (This was six years before he confessed that he hated "to see the poor creatures hunted down.") Years later, recalling this fugitive-slave provision, Wendell Phillips referred to Lincoln somewhat unfairly as "that slavehound from Illinois." The bill itself, although not passed, gave rise to a spirited debate on the morality of slavery, in which Lincoln took no part.

When Lincoln returned to active politics the slavery issue had come to occupy the central position on the American scene. Stephen Douglas and some of his colleagues in Congress had secured the passage of the Kansas-Nebraska Act, which, by opening some new territory, formally at least, to slavery, repealed the part of the thirty-four-year-old Missouri Compromise that barred slavery from territory north of 36° 30′. The measure provoked a howl of opposition in the North and split Douglas's party. The Republican Party, built on opposition to the extension of slavery, began to emerge in small communities in the Northwest. Lincoln's ambitions and interests were aroused, and he proceeded to rehabilitate his political fortunes.

His strategy was simple and forceful. He carefully avoided issues like the tariff, internal improvements, the Know-Nothing mania, or prohibitionism, each of which would alienate important groups of voters. He took pains in all his speeches to stress that he was not an abolitionist and at the same time to stand on the sole program of opposing the extension of slavery. On October 4, 1854, at the age of forty-five, Lincoln *for the first time in his life* denounced slavery in public. In his speech delivered in the Hall of Representatives at Springfield (and later repeated at Peoria) he declared that he hated the current zeal for the spread of slavery: "I hate it because of the monstrous injustice of slavery itself." He went on to say that he had no prejudice against the people of the South. He appreciated their argument that it would be difficult to get rid of the institution "in any satisfactory way." "I surely will not blame them for not doing what I should not know how to do myself. If all earthly power were given me, I should not know what to do as to the existing institution. My first impulse would be to free all the slaves and send them to Liberia, to their own native land." But immediate colonization, he added, is manifestly impossible. The slaves might be freed and kept "among us as underlings." Would this really better their condition?

> What next? Free them, and make them politically and socially our equals. *My own feelings will not admit of this,* and if mine would, we well know that those of the great mass of whites will not. Whether this feeling accords with justice and sound judgment is not the sole question, if indeed it is any part of it. A universal feeling, whether well or ill founded, cannot be safely disregarded.[4]

And yet nothing could justify an attempt to carry slavery into territories now free, Lincoln emphasized. For slavery is unquestionably wrong. "The great mass of mankind," he said at Peoria, "consider slavery a great moral wrong. [This feeling] lies at the very foundation of their sense of justice, and it cannot be trifled with. . . . No statesman can safely disregard it." The last sentence was the key to Lincoln's growing radicalism. As a practical politician he was naturally very much concerned about those public sentiments which no statesman can safely disregard. It was impossible, he had learned, safely to disregard either the feeling that slavery is a moral wrong or the feeling—held by an even larger portion of the public—that Negroes must not be given political and social equality.

He had now struck the core of the Republican problem in the Northwest: how to find a formula to reconcile the two opposing points of view held by great numbers of white people in the North. Lincoln's success in 1860 was due in no small part to his ability to bridge the gap, a performance that entitles him to a place among the world's great political propagandists.

To comprehend Lincoln's strategy we must keep one salient fact in mind: the abolitionists and their humanitarian sympathizers in the nation at large and particularly in the Northwest, the seat of Lincoln's strength, although numerous enough to hold the balance of power, were far too few to make a successful political party. Most of the white people of the Northwest, moreover, were in fact not only not abolitionists, but actually—and here is the core of the matter—Negrophobes. They feared and detested the very thought of living side by side with large numbers of Negroes in their own states, to say nothing of competing with their labor. Hence the severe laws against free Negroes, for example in Lincoln's Illinois.[5] Amid all the agitation in Kansas over making the territory a free state, the conduct of the majority of Republicans there was colored far more by self-interest than by moral principle. In their so-called Topeka Constitution the Kansas Republicans *forbade free Negroes even to come into the state*, and gave only to whites and Indians the right to vote. It was not bondage that troubled them—it was the Negro, free or slave. Again and again the Republican press of the Northwest referred to the Republican Party as the "White Man's Party." The motto of the leading Republican paper of Missouri, Frank Blair's *Daily Missouri Democrat*, was "White Men for Missouri and Missouri for White Men." Nothing could be more devastating to the contention that the early Republican Party in the Northwest was built upon moral principle. At the party convention of 1860 a plank endorsing the Declaration of Independence was almost hissed down and was saved only by the threat of a bolt by the antislavery element.

If the Republicans were to succeed in the strategic Northwest, how were they to win the support of both Negrophobes and antislavery men? Merely to insist that slavery was an evil would sound like abolitionism and offend the Negrophobes. Yet pitching their opposition to slavery extension on too low a moral level might lose the valued support of the humanitarians. Lincoln, perhaps borrowing from the old free-soil ideology, had the right formula and exploited it. He first hinted at it in the Peoria speech:

> The whole nation is interested that the best use shall be made of these Territories. *We want them for homes of free white people. This they cannot be, to any considerable extent, if slavery shall be planted within them.* Slave States are places for poor white people to remove from, not to remove to. New free States are the places for poor people to go to, and better their condition. For this use the nation needs these Territories.

The full possibilities of this line first became clear in Lincoln's "lost" Bloomington speech, delivered at a Republican state convention in May 1856. There, according to the report of one of his colleagues at the Illinois bar, Lincoln warned that Douglas and his followers would frighten men away from the very idea of freedom with their incessant mouthing of the red-herring epithet: "Abolitionist!" "If that trick should succeed," he is reported to have said,[6] "if free negroes should be made *things*, how long, think you, before they will begin to make *things* out of poor white men?"

Here was the answer to the Republican problem. Negrophobes and abolitionists alike could understand this threat; if freedom should be broken down they might themselves have to compete with the labor of slaves in the then free states—or might even be reduced to bondage along with the blacks! Here was an argument that could strike a responsive chord in the nervous system of every Northern man, farmer or worker, abolitionist or racist: *if a stop was not put somewhere upon the spread of slavery, the institution would become nation-wide.*[7] Here, too, is the practical significance of the repeated statements Lincoln made in favor of labor at this time. Lincoln took the slavery question out of the realm of moral and legal dispute and, by dramatizing it in terms of free labor's self-interest, gave it a universal appeal. To please the abolitionists he kept saying that slavery was an evil thing; but for the material benefit of all Northern white men he opposed its further extension.

The importance of this argument becomes increasingly clear when it is realized that Lincoln used it in every one of his recorded speeches from 1854 until he became the President-elect. He once declared in Kansas that preventing slavery from becoming a nation-wide institution "is *the purpose* of this organization [the Republican Party]." The argument had a great allure too for the immigrants who were moving in such great numbers into the Northwest. Speaking at Alton, in the heart of a county where more than fifty per-cent of the population was foreign-born, Lincoln went out of his way to make it clear that he favored keeping the territories open not only for native Americans, "but as an outlet for *free white people* everywhere, the world over—in which Hans, and Baptiste, and Patrick, and all other men from all the world, may find new homes and better their condition in life."

During the debates with Douglas, Lincoln dwelt on the theme again and again, and added the charge that Douglas himself was involved in a Democratic "conspiracy . . . for the sole purpose of nationalizing slavery."[8] Douglas and the Supreme Court (which a year before had handed down the Dred Scott decision) would soon have the American people "working in the traces that tend to make this one universal slave nation." Chief Justice Taney had declared that Congress did not have the constitutional power to exclude slavery from the territories. The next step, said Lincoln, would be

> another Supreme Court decision, declaring that the Constitution of the United States does not permit a *State* to exclude slavery from its limits. . . . We shall lie down pleasantly, dreaming that the people of Missouri are on the verge of making their State free; and we shall awake to the reality instead, that the Supreme Court has made Illinois a slave State.

So also the theme of the "House Divided" speech:

> I do not expect the Union to be dissolved—I do not expect the House to fall—but I do expect it to cease to be divided. It will become all one thing or all the other. Either the opponents of slavery will arrest the further spread of it, and place it where the public mind shall rest in the belief that it is in the course of ultimate extinction; or its advocates will push it forward, till it shall become alike lawful in all the States, old as well as new, North as well as South.
>
> Have we no tendency to the latter condition?[9]

The last sentence is invariably omitted when this passage is quoted, perhaps because from a literary standpoint it is anticlimactic. But in Lincoln's mind—and, one may guess, in the minds of those who heard him—it was not anticlimactic, but essential. Lincoln was *not* emphasizing the necessity for abolition of slavery in the near future; he was emphasizing the immediate "danger" that slavery would become a nation-wide American institution if its geographical spread were not severely restricted at once.

Once this "House Divided" speech had been made, Lincoln had to spend a great deal of time explaining it, proving that he was not an abolitionist. These efforts, together with his strategy of appealing to abolitionists and Negrophobes at once, involved him in embarrassing contradictions. In northern Illinois he spoke in one vein before abolition-minded audiences, but farther south, where settlers of Southern extraction were dominant, he spoke in another. It is instructive to compare what he said about the Negro in Chicago with what he said in Charleston.

Chicago, July 10, 1858:

> Let us discard all this quibbling about this man and the other man, this race and that race and the other race being inferior, and therefore they must be placed in an inferior position. Let us discard all these things, and unite as one people throughout this land, until we shall once more stand up declaring that all men are created equal.

Charleston, September 18, 1858:

> I will say, then, that I am not, nor ever have been, in favor of bringing about in any way the social and political equality of the white and black races [applause]: that I am not, nor ever have been, in favor of making voters or jurors of negroes, nor of qualifying them to hold office, nor to intermarry with white people. . . .
>
> And inasmuch as they cannot so live, while they do remain together there must be the position of superior and inferior, and I as much as any other man am in favor of having the superior position assigned to the white race.

It is not easy to decide whether the true Lincoln is the one who spoke in Chicago or the one who spoke in Charleston. Possibly the man devoutly believed each of the utterances at the time he delivered it; possibly his mind too was a house divided against itself. In any case it is easy to see in all this the behavior of a professional politician looking for votes.[10]

Douglas did what he could to use Lincoln's inconsistency against him. At Galesburg, with his opponent sitting on the platform behind him, he proclaimed: "I would despise myself if I thought that I was procuring your votes by concealing my opinions, and by avowing one set of principles in one part of the state, and a different set in another." Confronted by Douglas with these clashing utterances from his Chicago and Charleston speeches, Lincoln replied: "I have not supposed and do not now suppose, that there is any conflict whatever between them."

But this was politics—the premium was on strategy, not intellectual consistency—and the effectiveness of Lincoln's campaign is beyond dispute. In the ensuing elections the Republican candidates carried a majority of the voters and elected their state officers for the first time. Douglas returned to the Senate only because the Democrats, who had skillfully gerrymandered the election districts, still held their majority in the state legislature. Lincoln had contributed greatly to welding old-line Whigs and antislavery men into an effective party, and his reputation was growing by leaps and bounds. What he had done was to pick out an issue—the alleged plan to extend slavery, the alleged danger that it would spread throughout the nation—which would turn attention from the disintegrating forces in the Republican Party to the great integrating force. He was keenly aware that the party was built out of extremely heterogeneous elements, frankly speaking of it in his "House Divided" speech as composed of "strange, discordant, and even hostile elements." In addition to abolitionists and Negrophobes, it united high- and low-tariff men, hard- and soft-money men, former Whigs and former Democrats embittered by old political fights, Maine-law prohibitionists and German tipplers, Know-Nothings and immigrants. Lincoln's was the masterful diplomacy to hold such a coalition together, carry it into power, and with it win a war. . . .

Lincoln was shaken by the presidency. Back in Springfield, politics had been a sort of exhilarating game; but in the White House, politics was power, and power was responsibility. Never before had Lincoln held executive office. In public life he had always been an insignificant legislator whose votes were cast in concert with others and whose decisions in themselves had neither finality nor importance. As President he might consult others, but innumerable grave decisions were in the end his own, and with them came a burden of responsibility terrifying in its dimensions.

Lincoln's rage for personal success, his external and worldly ambition, was quieted when he entered the White House, and he was at last left alone to reckon with himself. To be confronted with the fruits of his victory only to find that it meant choosing between life and death for others was immensely sobering. That Lincoln should have shouldered the moral burden of the war was characteristic of the high seriousness into which he had grown since 1854; and it may be true, as Professor Charles W. Ramsdell suggested, that he was stricken by an awareness of his own part in whipping up the crisis. This would go far to explain the desperation with which he issued pardons and the charity that he wanted to extend to the conquered South at the war's close. In one of his rare moments of self-revelation he is reported to have said: "Now I don't know what the soul is, but whatever it is, I know that it can humble itself." The great prose of the presidential years came from a soul that had been humbled. Lincoln's utter lack of personal malice during these years, his humane detachment, his tragic sense of life, have no parallel in political history.

"Lincoln," said Herndon, "is a man of heart—aye, as gentle as a woman's and as tender. . . ." Lincoln was moved by the wounded and dying men, moved as no one in a place of power can afford to be. He had won high office by means sometimes rugged, but once there, he found he could not quite carry it off. For him it was impossible to drift into the habitual callousness of the sort of officialdom that sees men only as pawns to be shifted here and there and "expended" at the will of others. It was a symbolic thing that his office was so constantly open, that he made himself more accessible than any other chief executive in our history. "Men moving only in an official circle," he told Carpenter, "are apt to become merely official—not to say arbitrary—in their ideas, and are apter and apter with each passing day to forget that they only hold power in a representative capacity." Is it possible to recall anyone else in modern history who could exercise so much power and yet feel so slightly the private corruption that goes with it? Here, perhaps, is the best measure of Lincoln's personal eminence in the human calendar—that he was chastened and not intoxicated by power. It was almost apologetically that he remarked in response to a White House serenade after his re-election that "So long as I have been here, I have not willingly planted a thorn in any man's bosom."

There were many thorns planted in *his* bosom. The criticism was hard to bear (perhaps hardest of all that from the abolitionists, which he knew had truth in it). There was still in him a sensitivity that the years of knock-about politics had not killed, the remarkable depths of which are suddenly illumined by a casual sentence written during one of the crueler outbursts of the opposition press. Reassuring the apologetic actor James Hackett, who had unwittingly aroused a storm of hostile laughter by publishing a confidential letter, Lincoln added that he was quite used to it: "I have received a great deal of ridicule without much malice; and have received a great deal of kindness, not quite free from ridicule."

The presidency was not something that could be enjoyed. Remembering its barrenness for him, one can believe that the life of Lincoln's soul was almost entirely without consummation. Sandburg remarks that there were thirty-one rooms in the White House and that Lincoln was not at home in any of them. This was the house for which he had sacrificed so much!

As the months passed, a deathly weariness settled over him. Once when Noah Brooks suggested that he rest, he replied: "I suppose it is good for the body. But the tired part of me is *inside* and out of reach." There had always been a part of him, inside and out of reach, that had looked upon his ambition with detachment and wondered if the game was worth the candle. Now he could see the truth of what he had long dimly known and perhaps hopefully suppressed—that for a man of sensitivity and compassion to exercise great powers in a time of crisis is a grim and agonizing thing. Instead of glory, he once said, he had found only "ashes and blood." This was, for him, the end product of that success myth by which he had lived and for which he had been so persuasive a spokesman. He had had his ambitions and fulfilled them, and met heartache in his triumph.

Notes

1. For years Herndon kept on their office table the *Westminster Review*, the *Edinburgh Review*, other English periodicals, the works of Darwin, Spencer, and other English writers. He had little success in interesting Lincoln. "Occasionally he would snatch one up and peruse it for a little while, but he soon threw it down with the suggestion that it was entirely too heavy for an ordinary mind to digest."
2. William C. Howells, father of the novelist, wrote in an Ohio newspaper shortly before Lincoln's inauguration as President that he and his wife represented "the western type of Americans." "The White House," he said, "has never been occupied by better representatives of the bourgoise [*sic*] or citizen class of people, than it will be after the 4th proximo. If the idea represented by these people can only be allowed to prevail in this government, all will be well. Under such a rule, the practical individual man, who respects himself and regards the rights of others will grow to just proportions."

3. Herndon, however, attested that he heard Lincoln refer to having seen slaves on sale. *Herndon's Life of Lincoln* (Angle ed., 1930), p. 64. In a letter to Alexander H. Stephens, January 19, 1860, Lincoln wrote: "When a boy I went to New Orleans in a flat boat and there I saw slavery and slave markets as I have never seen them in Kentucky, and I heard worse of the Red River plantations."
4. Later, in the debate at Ottawa, Illinois, Lincoln repeated a larger passage containing this statement, and added: "this is the true complexion of all I have said in regard to the institution of slavery and the black race."
5. The Illinois constitutional convention of 1847 had adopted and submitted to a popular referendum a provision that instructed the legislature to pass laws prohibiting the immigration of colored persons. It was ratified by a vote of 50,261 to 21,297. If this vote can be taken as an index, the Negrophobes outnumbered their opponents by more than two to one. In 1853 the state was in effect legally closed to Negro immigration, free or slave. A Negro who entered in violation of the law was to be fined exorbitantly, and if unable to pay the fine could be sold into service. None of the states of the Northwest allowed Negro suffrage.
6. The only existing version of this speech is not a verbatim report.
7. Stephen A. Douglas's appeal to this fear was as strong as Lincoln's: "Do you desire to turn this beautiful State into a free Negro colony in order that when Missouri abolishes slavery she can send one hundred thousand emancipated slaves into Illinois to become citizens and voters, on an equality with yourselves?" But Douglas had no comparable appeal to antislavery sentiment, and Lincoln was able to exploit the fact.

   The conception that slavery was a menace to free labor throughout the nation was by no means new, nor peculiar to Lincoln. At the time of the Mexican War, Lowell had made Hosea Biglow say:

   > Wy, it's jest ez clear ez figgers,
   >   Clear ez one an' one make two.
   > Chaps that make black slaves o' niggers
   >   Want to make white slaves o' you.

   Seward, in his "Irrepressible Conflict" speech, delivered four months after Lincoln's "House Divided" speech, declared: "The United States must and will sooner or later, become either entirely a slaveholding nation or entirely a free-labor nation. Either the cotton and rice-fields of South Carolina and the sugar plantations of Louisiana will ultimately be tilled by free labor, and Charleston and New Orleans become marts for legitimate merchandise alone, or else the rye-fields and wheat-fields of Massachusetts and New York must again be surrendered by their farmers to slave culture and to the production of slaves, and Boston and New York become once more markets for trade in the bodies and souls of men." But largely because Lincoln was considered more *conservative* than Seward on the slavery question he was chosen for the party nomination in 1860.
8. Historians have dismissed these charges as untrue. Lincoln admitted that they were based on circumstantial evidence.
9. Lincoln is reported to have said to political friends of the "house divided" utterance: "I would rather be defeated with this expression in my speech, and uphold it and discuss it before the people, than be victorious without it." (Herndon refused to believe it would harm him politically, assuring: "It will make you President.") It would probably be truer to say that Lincoln was

making the great gamble of his career at this point than to say that he was sacrificing his political prospects for a principle. He had had his experience with pettifogging politics of the timid sort during his Congressional phase, and it had led only to disaster.

When Joseph Medill asked Lincoln in 1862 why he had delivered "that radical speech," Lincoln answered: "Well, after you fellows had got me into that mess and begun tempting me with offers of the Presidency, I began to think and I made up my mind that the next President of the United States would need to have a stronger anti-slavery platform than mine. So I concluded to say something." Then Lincoln asked Medill to promise not to repeat his answer to others.

10. Lincoln was fond of asserting that the Declaration of Independence, when it said that all men are created equal, included the Negro. He believed the Negro was probably inferior to the white man, he kept repeating, but in his right to eat, without anyone's leave, the bread he earned by his own labor, the Negro was the equal of any white man. Still he was opposed to citizenship for the Negro. How any man could be expected to defend his right to enjoy the fruits of his labor without having the power to defend it through his vote, Lincoln did not say. In his Peoria speech he had himself said: "No man is good enough to govern another man, without that man's consent." In one of his magnificent private memoranda on slavery Lincoln argued that anyone who defends the moral right of slavery creates an ethic by which his own enslavement may be justified. ("Fragment on Slavery," 1854.) But the same reasoning applies to anyone who would deny the Negro citizenship. It is impossible to avoid the conclusion that so far as the Negro was concerned, Lincoln could not escape the moral insensitivity that is characteristic of the average white American.

The Glorious and the Terrible

Allan Nevins

It was the American Civil War General William Tecumseh Sherman who was purported to have said "War is Hell"; yet it seems that few have truly taken his words to heart. War's pageantry and splendor, the fascination of its drama, have most often resulted in historical myopia. The slaughter and destruction which all know to be the desserts of warfare are buried as quickly as its casualties. Perhaps in no instance is this truer than with the classic confrontation between the Blue and the Gray. But the lustrous veneer, says the late Allan Nevins of the Huntington Library in San Marino, California, must be stripped away for sound historical judgment to proceed. The Civil War was not, in the words of the military historian Bruce Catton, "Glory Road." Rather, it was the testing of the character of an entire civilization. Though we are inclined to remember the glorious and forget the terrible, historical integrity requires we recognize both in order to eliminate the myth of the American Civil War.

Every great war has two sides, the glorious and the terrible. The glorious is perpetuated in multitudinous pictures, poems, novels, statues: in Meissonier's canvases of Friedland and Austerlitz, Byron's stanzas on Waterloo and Tennyson's on the Light and Heavy brigades, St. Gaudens's Sherman riding forward victory-crowned, Freeman's "Lee." The terrible is given us in a much slighter body of memorabilia: Jacques Callot's gruesome etchings of the Thirty Years War, Goya's paintings of French atrocities in Spain, Zola's "The Debacle," Walt Whitman's hospital sketches, and the thousand-page novels that drearily emerged from the Second World War.

The two aspects do exist side by side. Every student of war comes upon hundreds of veracious descriptions of its pomp and pageantry, innumerable tales of devotion and heroism. They exalt the spirit. Yet every such student falls back from this exaltation upon a sombre remembrance of the butchery, the bereavement, and the long bequest of poverty, exhaustion, and despair. In observing the centenary of the Civil War, every sensible man should keep in mind that the conflict was a terrible reproach to American civilization and a source of poison and debilities still to be felt.

If it were not true that its debits far outweighed its credits, we might conclude that the republic would profit by a civil war in every generation,

From "The Glorious and the Terrible," by Allan Nevins, in *Saturday Review* (September 2, 1961).

and that we should have commemorated Bull Run last July by again setting Yankee boys and Southern boys to killing each other. The mind recoils from the thought. But as the Civil War histories, novels, and motion pictures continue to pour forth, we shall be fortunate if we escape two very erroneous views.

The first view is that the war can somehow be detached from its context and studied as if it stood alone, without reference to causes or effects. War in fact, as Clausewitz long ago insisted, does not stand apart from and opposed to peace. It is simply a transfer of the normal inescapable conflicts of men from the realm of adjustment to that of violence. It represents not a complete transformation of national policy, but a continuance of policy by sanguinary means. That is, it cannot be understood without regarding both its causes and its results. Our Civil War, as Walt Whitman insisted, grew peculiarly out of national character. The other erroneous view is that the Civil War was, in the phrase of that graphic military historian Bruce Catton, a "Glory Road."

"Consider it not so deeply," Lady Macbeth says to her husband, stricken by the thought of red-handed murder; and "Consider it not so deeply," people instinctively say to those who remind them of war's inhuman massacre. Who wishes to while away an idle hour by looking at the harrowing pictures in the "Medical and Surgical History" of the war? It is a trick of human memories to forget, little by little, what is painful, and remember what is pleasant, and that tendency appertains to the folk memory as well. One of the finest descriptive pieces of the war was written by the true-hearted Theodore Winthrop, novelist and poet, just after his regiment crossed the Potomac on a spring night in 1861 to encamp on the Virginia side. It is rapturous in its depiction of the golden moon lighting a path over the river, the merry files of soldiers, the white tents being pitched in the dewy dawn. But ere long Winthrop was slain at Big Bethel in an engagement too blundering, shabby and piteous for any pen. We remember the happy march but forget the death.

Or take two contrasting scenes later in the war, of the same day—the day of Malvern Hill, July 1, 1862. That battle of Lee and McClellan reached its climax in the gathering dusk of a lustrous summer evening, no breath of wind stirring the air. The Union army had placed its ranks and its artillery on the slope of a great hill, a natural amphitheatre, which the Southerners assaulted. Participants never forgot the magnificence of the spectacle. From the Confederate and Union guns stately columns of black smoke towered high in the blue sky. The crash of musketry and deeper thud of artillery; the thunder of gunboat mortars from the James River, their shells curving in fiery golden lines; the cavalry on either flank, galloping to attack; the foaming horses flying from point to point with aides carrying dispatches; the steady advance of the Confederate columns and the unyielding resistance of the dense Union lines; then as darkness gathered, the varicolored signal lights flashing back and forth their messages—all this made an unforgettable panorama.

But the sequel! The troops on both sides sank exhausted on their arms. From the field the shrieking and moaning of the wounded were heart-rending, yet nothing could be done to succor them. The sky grew overcast; intense darkness shut down; and at dawn came a fierce downpour. "Such rain, and such howling set up by the wounded," wrote one Southern soldier; "such ugly wounds, sickening to the sight even of the most hardened as the rain beat upon them, washing them to a pale purple; such long-fingered corpses, and in piles, too, like cordwood—may I never see the like again!"

Both novelist and poet almost instinctively turn to the heroic aspects and picturesque incidents of war. Lowell's "Commemoration Ode," one of the half-dozen finest pieces of literature born from the conflict, necessarily eulogizes the heroes; Mary Johnston's "The Long Roll," perhaps the best Southern war novel, celebrates the ardors, not the anguishes, of Stonewall Jackson's foot-cavalry; St. Gaudens's monument on Boston Common to Robert Gould Shaw and his black infantry—the men whose dauntless hearts beat a charge right up the red rampart's slippery swell—shows the fighters, not the fallen. The historian assists in falsifying the picture. Cold, objective, he assumes that both the glorious and horrible sides exist, and need no special emphasis. He thus tends to equate the two, although the pains and penalties of war far outweigh its gleams of grandeur.

Then, too, a problem of expression impedes the realistic writer. It is not difficult to describe the pageantry of Pickett's charge. But when we come to the costs, what can we say except that the casualties were 3,000 killed, 5,000 wounded? It is impossible to describe the agony of even one soldier dying of a gangrened wound, or the heartache of one mother losing her first born; what of 10,000 such soldiers and mothers? Moreover, most historians, like the novelists and poets, have an instinctive preference for the bright side of the coin. Henry Steele Commager's otherwise fine introduction to his valuable compilation "The Blue and The Gray" has much to say about gallantry and bravery, but nothing about the squalor, the stench, and the agony.

If we protest against the prettification of the Civil War, the thoughtless glorification of what was essentially a temporary breakdown of American civilization, we must do so with an acknowledgement that it did call forth many manifestations of an admirable spirit. The pomp and circumstance, the parade and pageantry, we may dismiss as essentially empty. The valor of the host of young men who streamed to the colors we may deeply admire, but as valor we may fortunately take it for granted, for most men are brave. The patriotic ardor displayed in the first months of the war may also be taken for granted. What was highly impressive was the serious, sustained conviction, the long-enduring dedication, of countless thousands on both sides for their chosen cause. This went far beyond the transient enthusiasms of Sumter and Bull Run; far beyond ordinary battlefield courage. Lecky was correct in writing: "That which invests war with a certain grandeur is the heroic self-sacrifice which it elicits." All life is in a real sense a conflict between good and evil, in which every man or woman plays a part. A host of young Americans felt that they were enlisted in this larger struggle, and regarded their service to the North or South as part of a lifetime service to the right.

Those who seek examples of this dedication can find them scattered throughout the war records. Lincoln specially admired his young friend Elmer Ellsworth, who had endured poverty and hardship with monastic devotion to train himself for service; Lee specially admired John Pelham, the daring artillerist. Both gave their lives. Some fine illustrations of the consecrated spirit can be found in the two volumes of the "Harvard Memorial Biographies" edited by Thomas Wentworth Higginson just after the war. The ninety-eight Harvard dead were no better than the farm lads from Iowa or Alabama, the clerks from New Orleans or New York, but some of them had special gifts of self-expression. Hearken, for example, to Colonel Peter A. Porter, who wrote in his last will and testament:

> I can say, with truth, that I have entered on the course of danger with no ambitious aspirations, nor with the idea that I am fitted, by nature, or experience, to be of any important service to the government; but in obedience to the call of duty, demanding every citizen to contribute what he could, in means, labor, or life, to sustain the government of his country—a sacrifice made the more willingly by me when I consider how singularly benefitted I have been, by the institutions of the land. . . .

As we distinguish between the shining glory of the war—this readiness of countless thousands to die for an enduring moral conviction—and the false or unimportant glories, so we must distinguish between the major and the lesser debits of the conflict. Some evils and mischiefs which seemed tremendous at the time have grown less in the perspective of years; some which at first appeared small now loom large.

It was one of the bloodiest of all wars; the total deaths in the Union and Confederate armies have been computed at about 620,000; and one of the facts which appalls any careful student is the enormous amount of suffering on the field and in the hospitals. The evidence of this, while not within the view of general readers, is incontrovertible. Armies the world over in 1860 were *worse* provided with medical and surgical facilities than in Napoleon's day. The United States, after its long peace, began the war with practically no medical service whatever. Surgical application of the ideas of Pasteur and Lister lay in the future. Almost every abdominal wound meant death. Any severe laceration of a limb entailed amputation, with a good chance of mortal gangrene or erysipelas. The North systematically prevented shipments of drugs and surgical instruments to the South, a measure which did not shorten the conflict by a day, but cost the Southern troops untold agony. Had it not been for the Sanitary Commission, a body privately organized and supported, Northern armies would have duplicated the experience of British forces in the Crimea; yet Secretary of War Stanton at first deliberately impeded the Commission's work.

The story of battle after battle was the same. Night descended on a field ringing with cries of agony: Water! Water! Help!—if in winter, Blankets! Cover! All too frequently no help whatever was forthcoming. After some great conflicts the wounded lay for days, and sometimes a week, without rescue. Shiloh was fought on a Sunday and Monday. Rain set in on Sunday night, and the cold April drizzle continued through Tuesday night. On Tuesday morning nine-tenths of the wounded still lay where they fell; many had been there forty-eight hours without attention; numbers had died of shock or exhaustion; some had even drowned as the rain filled depressions from which they could not crawl. Every house in the area was converted into a hospital, where the floors were covered with wretches heavily wounded, sometimes with arms or legs torn off, who after the first bandages, got no nursing, medical care, or even nourishment. "The first day or two," wrote a newspaper reporter, "the air was filled with groans, sobs, and frenzied curses, but now the sufferers are quiet; not from cessation of pain, but mere exhaustion." Yet at this time the war was a year old.

Still more poignant versions of the same story might be given. Lee and Pope fought Second Manassas on the last Friday and Saturday in August, 1862, so near Washington that groups standing on housetops in the capital heard the rumble of artillery. The battleground, five miles long and three wide, was thickly strewn with dead and wounded. Pope retreated in confusion; many in Washington feared the city might be taken. In these circumstances, as late as the following Wednesday one member of the inadequate body of surgeons estimated that 2,000 wounded had received no attention. Many had not tasted food for four days; some were dying of hunger and thirst. A reporter for the Washington *Republican* wrote on Thursday that some dying men could yet be saved by prompt help. And on Friday, a week after the battle began, a correspondent of the New York *Tribune* told of heart-rending scenes as the doctors searched among heaps of putrefying dead men for men yet clinging to life—men who, when anyone approached, would cry, "Doctor, come to *me*; you look like a kind man; for God's sake come to *me*."

Anyone who is tempted to think of Gettysburg only in terms of its heroic episodes, its color and drama, should turn to the pages in "Battles and Leaders" in which General John D. Imboden describes the transport of the Confederate wounded, after their defeat, back into Maryland. He was ordered to ride to the head of the long wagon column as, in darkness and storm, it moved south:

> For four hours I hurried forward on my way to the front, and in all that time I was never out of hearing of the groans and cries of the wounded and dying. Scarcely one in a hundred had received adequate surgical aid, owing to the demands on the hard-working surgeons from still worse cases that had to be left behind. Many of the wounded in their wagons had been without food for thirty-six hours. Their torn and bloody clothing, matted and hardened, was rasping the tender, inflamed, and still oozing wounds. Very few of the wagons had even a layer of straw in them, and all were without springs. The road was rough and rocky from the heavy washings of the preceding day. The jolting was enough to have killed strong men, if long exposed to it. From nearly every wagon as the teams trotted on, urged by whip and shout, came such cries and shrieks as these:
>
> "My God! Why can't I die?"
>
> "My God! Will no one have mercy and kill me?"
>
> "Stop! Oh, for God's sake stop just for one minute; take me out and leave me to die on the roadside."
>
> Occasionally a wagon would be passed from which only low, deep moans could be heard. No help could be rendered to any of the sufferers. No heed could be given to any of their appeals. Mercy and duty to the many forbade the loss of a moment in the vain effort then and there to comply with the prayers of the few. On! On! We must move on. The storm continued and the darkness was appalling. There was no time even to fill a canteen with water for a dying man; for, except the drivers and the guards, all were wounded and utterly helpless in that vast procession of misery. During this one night I realized more of the horrors of war than I had in all the preceding two years.

After such a description, we can understand why a radical Northern Senator, looking across the battlefield of the Wilderness as fighting ended, told Hugh McCulloch that if in 1861 he had been given one glimpse of the agonies he there beheld, he would have said to the South: "Erring sisters, go in peace." John Esten Cooke was right in his elegy for Pelham; the living were brave and noble, but the dead were the bravest of all.

Yet *this* was far from being the ugliest side of war. Nor was the suffering in the huge prison camps, South and North, part of the worst side of war; the suffering which MacKinlay Kantor describes in his novel and to which Benét briefly adverts in "John Brown's Body":

> The triple stockade of Andersonville the damned,
> Where men corrupted like flies in their own dung
> And the gangrened sick were black with smoke and their filth.

What maims the bodies of men is less significant than what maims their spirit.

One ugly aspect of the Civil War too generally ignored is the devastation, more and more systematic, that accompanied it. For three reasons too little has been said of this devastation; the facts were kept out of official reports, the tale is too painful, and the recital easily becomes monotonous. Yet by 1862 the war in the South had become one of general depredation; by 1863, of wanton destruction; and by 1864, of an organized devastation which in terms of property anticipated the worst chapters of the two world wars. Georgia and the Shenandoah suffered in 1864 almost precisely as Belgium and Serbia suffered in 1914—the executions omitted. It was barbaric, and the only excuse to be made is that war is barbarism.

The turning point in the attitude of Northern military men was reached when General John Pope on July 18, 1862, issued from Washington headquarters a set of Draconian general orders. Order No. 5 directed that the army should subsist as far as practicable upon the country, giving vouchers for supplies seized. Order No. 7 decreed the summary execution of persons caught firing upon Union troops from houses. Order No. 11 (five days later) required officers to arrest immediately all disloyal males within reach, to make them take the oath of allegiance or go South, and to shoot all who violated their oath or who returned from the Confederacy. The order for living on the country, widely publicized East and West, changed the attitude of troops, and inspired private looting as well as public seizures of property. Pope was soon ousted, but the moral effect of his orders persisted.

Though most of the facts were excluded from official reports, their sum total, insofar as one shrewd observer could arrive at it, may be found in John T. Trowbridge's graphic volume written in 1866, "A Picture of the Desolated States." In his preface Trowbridge speaks of the Union forces not as our heroic armies but our destroying armies. Even this practiced reporter is less graphic, however, than the people who suffered under the onslaught and wrote while their emotions, like their property, still burned. Hear a lady of Louisiana tell what occurred when N. P. Banks's army passed:

> I was watching from my window the apparently orderly march of the first Yankees that appeared in view and passed up the road, when, suddenly, as if by magic, the whole plantation was covered with men, like bees from an overthrown hive; and, as far as my vision extended, an inextricable medley of men and animals met my eye. In one place, excited troopers were firing into the flock of sheep; in another, officers and men were in pursuit of the boys' ponies, and in another, a crowd were in excited chase of the work animals. The kitchen was soon filled with some, carrying off the cooking utensils and the provisions of the day; the yard with others, pursuing the poultry. . . . They penetrated under the house, into the outbuildings, and into the garden, stripping it in a moment of all its vegetables. . . . This continued during the day . . . and amid a bewildering sound of oaths and imprecations. . . . When the army had passed, we were left destitute.

Sherman believed in total war; that is, in waging war not only against the Southern armies, but the Southern people. His theory was that every man, woman, and child was "armed and at war." He wrote his wife in the summer of 1862 that the North might fall into bankruptcy, "but if they can hold on the war will soon assume a turn to extermination, not of soldiers alone, but the people." He denied, in effect, that Southerners had a right to resist invasion. When Union steamers were fired on near Randolph, Mississippi, in the fall of 1862, he destroyed Randolph, and a little later had all houses, farms, and cornfields devastated for fifteen miles along the banks.

When he drove his red plowshare across Georgia and the Carolinas, his object was to leave only scorched earth behind. He had already written of his Western operations: "Not a man is to be seen; nothing but women with houses plundered, fields open to the cattle and horses, pickets lounging on every porch, and desolation sown broadcast; servants all gone, and women and children bred in luxury . . . begging . . . for soldiers' rations." His aim was that which Phil Sheridan avowed: to leave them nothing but their eyes to weep with.

The final devastation of half the South was horrible to behold, and it was distressing to think that these savage losses had been inflicted by Americans upon fellow Americans. Yet this was far from being the worst aspect of the conflict, or the least easily reparable. Damages on which we can fix the dollar sign are important not in themselves, but as they become translated into cultural and spiritual losses; into the intellectual retardation caused by poverty, for example. The physical recovery of the South was rapid. As it was primarily an agricultural section, a few good crops at fair prices did much to restore it; and the swiftness with which housing, railroads, bridges, and public facilities were rebuilt astonished observers of the 1870s just as the swift postwar recovery of Germany and Poland has astonished observers of our day.

Infinitely worse were the biological losses—the radical hurts—inflicted by the Civil War. The killing of between 600,000 and 700,000 young men in a nation of 33,000,000 and the maiming or permanent debilitation of as many more had evil consequences projected into the far-distant future. We lost not only these men, but their children, and their children's children. Here, indeed, was a loss that proved highly cumulative. During the First World War, Lord Dunsany wrote a slender volume called "Tales of War." One of his apologues showed the Kaiser, as the embodiment of German militarism, commanded by a spirit to come on a tour. They crossed the German plain to a neat garden. Look, said the spirit:

> The Kaiser looked; and saw a window shining and a neat room in a cottage; there was nothing dreadful there, thank the good German God for that; it was all right, after all. The Kaiser had had a fright, but it was all right; there was only a woman with a baby sitting before a fire, and two small children and a man. And it was quite a jolly room. And

the man was a young soldier; and, why, he was a Prussian Guardsman —there was a helmet hanging on the wall—so everything was all right. They were jolly German children; that was well. How nice and homely the room was.... The firelight flickered, and the lamp shone on, and the children played on the floor, and the man was smoking out of a china pipe; he was strong and able and young, one of the wealth-winners of Germany.

"Have you seen?" asked the phantom.

"Yes," said the Kaiser....

At once the fire went out and the lamp faded away, the room fell sombrely into neglect and squalor, and the soldier and the children faded away with the room; all disappeared phantasmally, and nothing remained but the helmet in a kind of glow on the wall, and the woman sitting all by herself in the darkness.

"It has all gone," said the Kaiser.

"It has never been," said the phantom.

The Kaiser looked again. Yes, there was nothing there, it was just a vision....

"It might have been," said the phantom.

Just so, we can say that the multitude of Civil War dead represent hundreds of thousands of homes, and hundreds of thousands of families, that might have been, and never were. They represent millions of people who might have been part of our population today and are not. We have lost the books they might have written, the scientific discoveries they might have made, the inventions they might have perfected. Such a loss defies measurement.

The only noteworthy attempt to measure the biological losses was made by David Starr Jordan and his son Harvey in a volume called "War's Aftermath" (1914). The authors circulated carefully drawn questionnaires in Spottsylvania and Rockbridge Counties in Virginia, and in Cobb County in Georgia, inquiring particularly into the eugenic effects of the conflict. One of their queries brought out evidence that by no means all casualties were among the men; numerous girls and women succumbed to the hardships and anxieties of the conflict in the South. Another question elicited unanimous agreement that "the flower of the people" went into the war at the beginning, and of these a large part died before the end. President Jordan, weighing all the responses, reached two conclusions: first, that the evidence "leaves a decided evidence in favor of grave racial hurt," and second, that "the war has seriously impoverished this country of its best human values."

Even the terrible loss of young, productive lives, the grave biological injury to the nation, however, did not constitute the worst side of the war. One aspect of the conflict was still more serious. It was the aspect to which Lowell referred in lines written a few years after Appomattox:

> I looked to see an ampler atmosphere
> By that electric passion-gust blown clear
> I looked for this; consider what I hear....

Murmur of many voices in the air
Denounces us degenerate,
Unfaithful guardians of a noble fate. . . .

The war, as Walt Whitman truly said, had grown out of defects in the American character; of American faults it cured few, accentuated a number, and gave some a violently dangerous trend. Far behind the lines, it added to the already discreditable total of violence in American life. Applying to industry a great forcing-draft, the bellows of huge wartime appropriations, it strengthened the materialistic forces in our civilization. Its state and federal contracts, its bounty system, its innumerable opportunities for battening on the nation's woes, made speculation fashionable, and corruption almost too common for comment. Its inflation bred extravagance and dissipation.

Every month heightened the intolerance of war; it began with mobs in New York threatening newspaper offices, a mob in Philadelphia trying to lynch Senator James A. Bayard, and mobs in the South flogging and exiling Union men; as it went on, freedom of speech almost disappeared over broad areas. The atmosphere of war fostered immorality; Richmond and Washington alike became filled with saloons, brothels, and gambling dens, and such occupied cities as Memphis and Nashville were sinks of iniquity. For every knightly martyr like James Wadsworth or Albert Sidney Johnston there arose two such coarse, aggressive, selfish careerists as Ben Butler and Dan Sickles. Wadsworth and Johnston died in battle, but Butler and Sickles remained to follow postwar political careers. Seen in perspective, the war was a gigantic engine for coarsening and lowering the American character even while it quickened certain of our energies.

Parson Brownlow, a Tennessee Unionist, went from city to city in the North in 1862 demanding "grape for the Rebel masses, and hemp for their leaders"; saying that he himself would tie the rope about the necks of some rebel generals; calling for the confiscation of all Southern property; proclaiming that he would be glad to arm every wolf, bear, catamount, and crocodile, every devil in hell, to defeat the South; and declaring he would put down the rebellion "if it exterminates from God's green earth every man, woman, and child south of Mason and Dixon's Line."

In the South two famous leaders, Robert Toombs and Howell Cobb, united that year in an address to their people just as vitriolic. "The foot of the oppressor is on the soil of Georgia," it began. "He comes with lust in his eye, poverty in his purse, and hell in his heart. How shall you meet him? . . . With death for him or for yourself!" Better the charnel house for every Southerner, they continued, than "loathsome vassalage to a nation already sunk below the contempt of the civilized world." Thaddeus Stevens nursed his hatred until he spoke of "exterminating" or driving into exile *all* Southerners, just as Sherman declared he would "slay millions" to assure the safety of the Mississippi. Women of the South meanwhile expressed the most vindictive detestation of all Yankees. "I hate them," wrote one Mississippi woman after a raid on her community, "more now than I did the evening I saw them sneaking off with all we cared for, and so it will be every day I live."

Hatred was seen in its most naked form in those communities divided against themselves and racked by guerrilla war; in Missouri, Arkansas, parts of Kentucky, and east Tennessee. Writes Charles D. Drake, a distinguished Missouri leader, of his state: "Falsehood, treachery, and perjury pervaded the whole social fabric." He went on: "Could there be written a full account of all the crimes of the rebels of Missouri, and the outrages and wrongs inflicted by them upon her loyal inhabitants, during the four years of the rebellion, the world would shrink aghast from a picture which has no parallel in the previous history of any portion of the Anglo-Saxon race." Confederate sympathizers in Missouri would have said the same of Union irregulars. One atrocity provoked another. These hatreds long survived the conflict, and indeed in some spots the embers still smoulder. Typifying the whole range of spiritual injuries wrought by the war, they justify the poet Blake's cry:

> The soldier, armed with sword and gun,
> Palsied strikes the summer sun.

The historian Mendelssohn Bartholdy, in his volume entitled "War and German Society," written as part of the Carnegie Endowment's huge economic history of World War I, concluded that the moral effects of war are much worse than the material effects. He also concluded that they are radically bad, for they strike at the very heart of a country's character; "modern war, with its robot-like disregard of individual values, is bound to make the peculiar virtue of a nation an object of attack." As respects the Civil War, we can agree. If it was necessary for preserving the Union and extinguishing slavery, it was of course worth more than it cost; but should it have been necessary? Could not better leadership from 1830 to 1860 have averted it? This is a bootless question. But it is certain that the conflict, so much the greatest convulsion in our history, so tremendous in its impact on our national life, so fascinating in its drama, was in spite of all compensating elements, all the heroism, all the high example we find in Lee's character and Lincoln's wisdom, materially a disaster and morally a tragedy.

It is unfortunate that of the flood of books on the war ninety-nine in a hundred are on military topics and leaders, and that a great majority fasten attention on the floating banners, the high-ringing cheers, the humors of the camp, the ardors of the charge; the whole undeniable fascination and romance of the first true *volkskrieg* in history. It is right, within measure, to let them lift our hearts. But the long commemoration will pass essentially unimproved if it does not give us a deeper, sterner, more scientific study of the collision of two creeds and two ways of life as related to an examination of war in general.

We should probe more deeply into its roots, a process that will expose some of the weaknesses of our social fabric and governmental system. We should pay fuller attention to its darker aspects, and examine more honestly such misrepresentations as the statement it was distinguished by its generosity of spirit, the magnanimity with which the combatants treated each other; a statement absurd on its face, for no war which lasts four years and costs 600,000 lives leaves much magnanimity in its later phases. We should above all examine more closely the effects of the great and terrible war not on the nation's politics—we know that; not on its economy—we also know that; but on its character, the vital element of national life.

This examination will lead into unpleasant paths, and bring us to unhappy conclusions; but it will profit us far more than stirring battle canvases. All nations must be schooled in such studies if the world is ever to find an answer to a question uttered just after World War I by William E. Borah, a question that still rings in men's ears: "When shall we escape from war? When shall we loosen the grip of the monster?"

The Civil War and the Modern World

David M. Potter

Few historians possess the late David M. Potter's ability to convey the "feel" and texture of historical reality. In one of his most important essays, Potter, whose tenure within the profession included distinguished terms at both Yale and Stanford, questions the parochialism of Americans as regards their Civil War. In the interest of supplying a new dimension of understanding, he suggests the rather basic importance of the conflict to the fusion of nationalism and liberalism on an international scale. A view of the American Civil War that takes into account the various nineteenth-century movements toward national unification—as for example in Italy and Germany—makes the Civil War experience more intelligible to us as it asserts its broader meaning to the political life of the Western world.

It has been the curious fate of the United States to exert immense influence in the modern world, without itself quite understanding the nature of this influence. Major trends of the modern world—both constructive trends and socially injurious ones—have repeatedly become apparent in the United States before they became evident elsewhere. But though the United States has often been a step ahead in the process of social change, it has frequently been a step behind in its awareness of the meaning of new developments. The shape of things to come often became visible in America earlier than it did elsewhere, but American preconceptions about the frontier, the classless society, and the agrarian basis of democracy prevented Americans from perceiving this shape as realistically as it was perceived by social thinkers in other countries. If Americans have failed effectively to interpret their experience to people in other societies, it is in part because they have not always been able to explain it to themselves. Further, the distinctive qualities of life in America have caused a good many forces which were generically universal to take forms which seemed more restrictively peculiar to the New World than they really were.

Thus in the late eighteenth century, America executed the first democratic political revolution of a democratic age, but American society was already so equalitarian that the revolutionary implication was muted. Without any great social overturn, the American War of Independence seemed conservative when compared with the socially cataclysmic forces released in

From "Civil War," by David M. Potter, Chapter 10 in *The Comparative Approach to American History*, edited by C. Vann Woodward. Basic Books, Inc., Publishers, New York.

France a decade later. In the twentieth century the United States developed what was perhaps the first mass society, but the American cult of equality and individualism prevented Americans from analyzing their mass society in realistic terms. Often they treated it as if it were simply an infinite aggregation of Main Streets in Zenith, Ohio. America has witnessed episodes of extreme industrial conflict, but these have not been interpreted in the class terms which a Marxist society would invoke. America has experienced a sweeping revolution in sex behavior, but has not incorporated this change into the system of values by which it explains itself. Ironically, the United States has cherished a belief in its mission to spread a democracy for which it has had difficulty in finding converts, while it has led the world in technological changes which produced social transformations that it had no especial desire to bring about.

The reader need not be astonished, therefore, if the Civil War has been interpreted in terms which disguised its broader meaning. If, as some Americans asserted, its chief importance was in putting an end to chattel slavery, this could hardly be regarded as a leading development in the history of Western civilization; for slavery had disappeared from western Europe, except vestigially, while it still flourished in the Americas, and it had disappeared from most of Latin America, except Cuba and Brazil, while it still persisted in the United States. The American republic was almost destroyed therefore in a struggle over an institution which world opinion regarded as an anachronism.

If, on the other hand, the Civil War was, as some other Americans asserted, important chiefly because it preserved the American Union, this statement also was framed in restrictive terms which failed to reveal its broader implications. Beginning with the mystic phrase, *E pluribus unum*, the republic had not been able for two generations to resolve the question whether it was, in the last analysis, *pluribus* or *unum*. The Civil War gave *unum* the upper hand, and the importance of this fact became visible in world history in 1917 and again in 1941 when the strength of a consolidated American republic impinged decisively on two world wars. But at the time, in a literal sense, there was not much significance for other nations in the fact that the United States waited for fourscore years and ten to settle a question which other nations settled at their inception. There seemed little universality of significance in a war fought to find, or at least determine, a clear meaning for a cryptic federal system such as no other nation had ever had, and such as was deliberately made ambiguous in the first place in order not to lose the support which it certainly would have lost if its meaning had been clarified.

While the war was in progress, European policy makers tended to think of it simply in terms of whether it would leave the United States weaker or stronger than before. After it was over, the only people who examined it closely were military historians, looking for the lessons of strategy and tactics that might be derived from the first major conflict in which repeating arms, ironclad vessels, trench warfare, and railroads as supply lines were used on a significant scale.

Thus, while the campaigns of Lee and Grant have fascinated English and European readers, just as the campaigns of Napoleon have fascinated Americans, and while the personality of Lincoln has held an appeal for men everywhere, writers have scarcely asked the question: what was the role of the American Civil War in the history of the modern world? Did it have historical significance for anyone except Americans?

If we are seeking an answer to this question, it may be useful to begin by asking ourselves, simply, what were the prevalent tendencies of the nineteenth century, and what did the Civil War contribute in causing these tendencies to prevail? Historians have neglected the latter part of this question, but have repeatedly given an answer to the first part. They tell us, over and over, that the nineteenth century was an era of liberalism and nationalism. The basis for the generalization is obvious. Nationalism, as we know it in its modern form, scarcely existed before the French Revolution; but by the end of the nineteenth century Britain, France, Germany, Italy, and Japan had become prototypes for modern nationality, sometimes after great travail. Nationalistic forces were fermenting throughout other parts of Europe, and even in the colonial world of Asia and Africa the premonitory stirrings of a latent nationalism could already be detected. The Monroe Doctrine had done its bit to make the Western Hemisphere safe for nationalism, and the Latin Americans had responded by erecting eighteen separate nationalistic republics. Likewise with liberalism. It was scarcely more than an ideology in the minds of British and French rationalists before the French Revolution, but by the beginning of the twentieth-century representative government and other liberal institutions prevailed in Britain, France, and Italy, and to some extent even in Germany and Austria-Hungary. The Hapsburgs, the Hohenzollerns, and the Romanoffs were still on their thrones, but they stood on the defensive before the onslaughts of Social Democrats, Social Revolutionaries, and other militant reformers.

All these facts are familiar to the point of triteness and it would be parochial to exaggerate the importance of the American Civil War in connection with them. But if we are to define the place of this war in terms of world history, rather than merely of American history, there are two aspects in which it exercised a crucial effect in shaping the tendencies of world history. These aspects may or may not have served the long-range welfare of human society, and it may be argued that, ultimately, their effect was pernicious. But for good or ill, here are two things which the Civil War did: first, it turned the tide which had been running against nationalism for forty years, or ever since Waterloo; and second, it forged a bond between nationalism and liberalism at a time when it appeared that the two might draw apart and move in opposite directions.

Because of the ultimate triumph of nationalism as a worldwide force by 1900, it is easy to forget how seriously nationalism appeared to have failed at the time when the Civil War occurred. After establishing firm bridgeheads in Britain and France, it had met with disaster after disaster in its efforts to spread into southern and central Europe. Britain had moved successfully to suppress nationalism in Ireland, and Russia had taken the most repressive measures in 1830 to crush it out in Poland. After the galaxy of nationalist revolutions of 1848 the dreams of a United Italy had ended with disaster at Custozza, those of a United Germany with the anticlimax of the Frankfurt Parliament, those of Czechoslovakia with the overthrow of the Pan-Slavic Congress, and those of Hungary with the defeat of Louis Kossuth. Simultaneously, in America, the steadily rising tensions between North and South seemed increasingly likely to destroy the feeling of national unity which had appeared completely triumphant during the first two decades of the century. The forces of nationalism reasserted themselves successfully in the Italian peninsula in the two years preceding the American Civil War, but otherwise nationalism and especially liberal nationalism in Europe seemed a lost cause. Louis Napoleon had made himself emperor of France in 1852, and within another decade was busily planting a Hapsburg imperialist regime in Mexico.

Viewed from the standpoint of appearances only, the forces which opposed nationalism in Europe were entirely unlike those which opposed it in America. In Europe, one might say, the forces which thwarted nationalism were those of universalism—of the Catholic Church and of the Hapsburg and Romanoff empires, for which the nationalist impulse seemed too localizing and disruptive. In America, one might say, the forces which thwarted it were those of localism and of sectionalism, for which the nationalist impulse seemed too consolidating and centralizing. In Europe, imperial forces sought to stamp out nationalism from above; in America, particularistic forces sought to resist it from below. It is perhaps because the opposition was centripetal in Europe and centrifugal in America that historians have tended to overlook the parallel triumphs of national unification, all within a period of twelve short years, in Italy, the United States, and Germany.

But the contrast between universalism and localism, as the forces which opposed nationalism, is perhaps more apparent than real. In both Europe and America, the forces of tradition and privilege tended to be arrayed against nationalism, while the forces of liberalism and democracy tended to support it. In America, the succession of the Southern states has been accurately described as a conservative revolt—a revolution by men who were not revolutionists, and who justified their revolution less by a philosophical defense of the right of the self-determination of peoples than by refined, legalistic arguments upon the intent of the Constitution of 1787. These "Rebels," instead of advocating change, were rebelling against it and were the champions of a traditional, relatively static, hierarchical society. They feared, with some reason, as we may now conclude, the transformations that might be wrought by an industrial society. They feared the destruction of a familiar social order and defended the evil institution of slavery less because they believed in human bondage as such than because they could not conceive of their social order without slavery.

In a certain sense, then, the landed planters of the South who opposed American nationalism were not unlike the landed proprietors in central Europe who opposed German or Polish or Italian or Hungarian or Bohemian nationalism. All of them were traditionalists. All feared that nationalism was linked with a democracy which they distrusted. All feared to release from the bottle the genii of manhood suffrage, of democratic equality, of social mobility, of universal education—and in the South, of emancipation for almost four million slaves. In this sense, European and American conservatism shared much in common, and the issue in the war between North and South carried implications considerably beyond the mere question as to whether the American states should form one republic or two.

The uprising of the North in 1861, and its decision to wage a war to preserve the American Federal Union, coming in the same year in which Victor Emmanuel was crowned king of a united Italy, marked a turning of the tide which had been running against nationalism for the preceding forty-five years. For better or worse, the course was set toward a world of sovereign nation-states, subject to no ultimate control in their conduct toward one another. The process of forging additional nations would reach out, within another century, from Europe and the Americas to Asia and Africa until by 1966 there would be more than 130. As the number of "nations" increased, the beneficial effects of nationalism became increasingly uncertain, for all too many of the new sovereignties regarded the possession of nuclear destructive power as the crowning sanction of their nationhood.

Nationalism today seems something of a curse because of the paradox that while the people of the earth have been growing more and more functionally interdependent socially and economically, they have also simultaneously grown more and more irresponsibly independent of one another politically. The fragmentation of empires and other forms of supranational political authority has proceeded in ironic parallelism with increases in the cohesion of the peoples whose political relationships are being fragmented. At the same time, nationalism has shown that it can have a hideous side, undreamed of by such idealistic nationalists as Mazzini, and Lamartine, and Daniel Webster. Hitler is the supreme example, but even at the present moment a number of tyrants whose authority would command no more respect than that of a gangster if it were not sanctified by the mystique of national inviolability—a number of such tyrants have given us cause to doubt that the advancement of nationalism is necessarily a contribution to human progress. Suppose Lincoln did save the American Union, did his success in keeping one strong nation where there might have been two weaker ones really en-title him to a claim to greatness? Did it really contribute any constructive values for the modern world?

To answer these questions, it may be necessary to recognize not only that Lincoln sought to save American nationalism, but also why he sought to save it. To him, as to other idealistic nationalists, the Union—that is, the nation—was not an end in itself but a means to an end. He might affirm that "my paramount object . . . is to save the Union," and he might wage one of the most deadly wars ever fought up to that time to achieve his object. But he thought of the Union primarily as a context within which freedom might be preserved and extended. Moreover, he thought that survival of a liberal nation in America was vital as a test of the survival capacity of liberal nationalism anywhere. Thus, although personally he was distinctively and uniquely and even restrictively American—the only one of the great presidents who never went outside the United States—he thought of American democracy in the least restrictive of terms. Many years before his Presidency, he eulogized Henry Clay as one who "loved his country partly because it was his own country but mostly because it was a free country." When the Civil War came, he asserted that it involved "more than the fate of these United States" and was of concern "to the whole family of man." The Union mattered to him not because of the question of authority at Washington, but because of the "necessity that is upon us of proving that popular government is not an absurdity." In his supreme moment at Gettysburg, this American nationalist did not once use the word American, or United States. He spoke, to be sure, of the nation "which our fathers brought forth," but this one nation conceived in liberty and dedicated to equality was linked in his thought with "any other nation so conceived and so dedicated." He wanted the war to result, for his own nation, in a "new birth of freedom," but this goal was not for America alone; it was to assure "men everywhere" that "government of the people, by the people, and for the people shall not perish from the earth."

It has been well said that Lincoln fused the cause of Union with the cause of freedom, which is equivalent to saying that he fused the cause of nationalism with the cause of liberalism. A number of idealistic nationalists of the nineteenth century made this same equation, and impressed it upon the public mind so vigorously that, even a century later, when we have had fairly numerous as well as traumatic illustrations of how completely antagonistic liberalism and nationalism can sometimes be, most of us respond affirmatively to claims made in the name of national integrity. We do so because our own thought still moves in the grooves cut by the great liberal nationalists of the nineteenth century.

This equation of liberalism and nationalism is not, of course, without logical foundations. Nationalism and liberalism both share certain common assumptions. Both depend upon the awakening self-consciousness of the individual—in the one case awakening to his membership in the political community, in the other awakening to his rights to participate in the decisions of the community and to enjoy its advantages. But while logic might impel nationalism and liberalism to go hand in hand, history often violates logic, and today we have copious proof that nationalism can flourish in separation from any liberal counterpart. It did so in Fascist Italy and Nazi Germany. It does so in Red China, and in Soviet Russia (though these countries theoretically reject nationalism), and it is doing so in various dictatorships in the "emerging" nations. But if one kind of logic would prove nationalism and liberalism to be twin offspring of the idea of the free individual as patriot and as citizen, there is another logic which declares liberalism and nationalism to be opposites, since liberalism regards the state as existing for the individual and nationalism regards the individual as existing for the state.

This is only to say that the nineteenth-century conjunction of nationalism and liberalism was by no means inevitable. To regard it as inevitable is to lose the larger meaning of the Civil War, for the war was one of the important historic developments contributing to a conjunction which, in other circumstances, might never have occurred. Lincoln's dedication of nationalistic means to liberal ends went far to produce this conjunction in the cosmos of American values. But at the same time when Lincoln was fusing nationalism with liberalism in America, another of the great figures who made the nineteenth century a century of nationalism, Count Otto von Bismarck, was carefully disassociating liberalism from nationalism in Germany. Having watched how the debacle of liberalism wrecked all hopes of German unification at Frankfurt in 1848, Bismarck wedded his nationalism to a concept of power and not to ideas of freedom or popular government. He signalized this position by publicly embracing a policy of "blood and iron" when he came to the head of the Prussian ministry in the year of Lincoln's Emancipation Proclamation. Nine years and three wars later, while President Grant, as the head of an imperfectly reunited nation, was struggling to reconcile the liberal principle of home rule for the South with the liberal principle of citizenship rights for the Negro, Bismarck made his monarch emperor of a Germany which was at last firmly united under authoritarian controls.

Bismarck and Lincoln were, perhaps, the two foremost exponents of nineteenth-century nationalism, after Napoleon. No two exemplars of the same force could have been more dissimilar, and no dramatist could have designed two figures better suited to point up contrasting styles of nationalism. The Gettysburg Address would have been as foreign to Bismarck as a policy of "blood and iron" would have been to Lincoln.

The contrast, perhaps, points the way to what was significant, in world perspective, about the American Civil War. The significance lay not in the fact that it was a triumph for nationalism (though the war forged the North as well as the South into a nation larger than any in western Europe), not in the fact that it was a triumph of liberalism (though Lincoln vindicated government of the people, by the people, and for the people, and proved that democracy, with all its weaknesses, can withstand the shocks of war). The significance lay rather in the fact that the Civil War, more perhaps than any event in Europe, fused the two great forces of the nineteenth century—liberalism and nationalism. It fused them so thoroughly that their potential separateness was lost from view. The fusion gave to nationalism a sanction which, frequently since then, it has failed to deserve, and gave to liberalism a strength which, since then, it has frequently not known how to use.

Meanwhile, Americans remained in confusion as to what their war had signified for the world. Some thought they had proved the strength of democracy, forgetting that the Confederacy which they defeated was also democratic and shared democracy's weaknesses. Others thought that they had vindicated the principle of nationalism, forgetting that the loyalty which Southerners gave to the Confederacy was no less nationalistic than the loyalty which Yankees gave to the Union. Few perceived that one of the most sweeping consequences of the war was to identify with one another these two forces which were not necessarily linked. This partially fictitious identification may, in the final analysis, have done great harm by giving a spurious sanction to modern nationalism, with all its potential dangers for the larger human society. But in a more immediate sense, it was perhaps the most constructive identification made during the nineteenth century, for it gave significant moral purpose to the force of nationalism, which, without such purpose, was always in danger of degenerating into mere group egocentrism or chauvinism. At the same time, it also gave significant institutional support to the principle of freedom, which without such support would have had only the ideals of reformers to sustain it.

The Folklore Lincoln

David Donald

As Richard Hofstadter has suggested, important elements of the "Lincoln myth" were consciously sustained by Abraham Lincoln himself. But one must take into account as well the proliferation of myth after Lincoln, for it was chiefly in the postwar decades that the images of the Great Emancipator and the Great Martyr became usable material in a developing American folklore. From self-made origins emerged a national savior "with malice toward none." Though committed to objective criticism of the Lincoln lore, David Donald, Director of the Institute of Southern History at Johns Hopkins University, contends that Lincoln was in important ways one of the chief custodians of the democratic spirit. Our "reconstruction" of Abraham Lincoln should not be carried to the extreme, Donald says, for the Lincoln legends offer ready access to the workings of the American mind. "The student can use these myths for an understanding of what plain Americans wished their leaders to be."

I

The Lincoln cult is almost an American religion. It has its high priests in the form of Lincoln "authorities" and its worshippers in the thousands of "fans" who think, talk, and read Lincoln every day. The very name of its founder possesses magical significance—witness its use in advertising everything from automobiles to barbershops. Lincoln's birthday is a national holiday, commemorated with solemn ceremonies. In 1909, the centennial of his birth, Illinois teachers were directed to devote at least half of the day of February 12 to "public exercises . . . patriotic music, recitations of sayings and verses . . . and speeches." The schoolchildren were to conclude the celebration by chanting in unison, with their faces turned toward Springfield, the following ritual:

A blend of mirth and sadness, smiles and tears;
A quaint knight errant of the pioneers;
A homely hero, born of star and sod;
A Peasant Prince; a masterpiece of God.

The Lincoln birthplace in Kentucky, the memorial in Washington, and the tomb in Illinois have become national shrines visited by thousands each week.

It was probably inevitable that Lincoln should have, as Emerson said, "become mythological in a very few years." America was badly in need of a hero. By 1865 George Washington seemed so dignified and remote that it

From *Lincoln Reconsidered,* by David Donald, Vintage Books, 1961 Edition. Reprinted by permission of the author and the *Journal of the Illinois State Historical Society.*

was hard to think of him as a man, much less as a boy; he was a portrait by Peale or a Houdon bust. Davy Crockett had degenerated from frontier hero into comic legend. Andrew Jackson, Henry Clay, and Daniel Webster were already slipping into the limbo of lost souls, the history books.

The times and events of the Civil War had made a great popular leader necessary. There had been the emotional strain of war, the taut peril of defeat, the thrill of battles won, the release of peace. Then had come the calamitous, disastrous assassination. The people's grief was immediate and it was immense. Properly to describe it one would need the eloquence of a Whitman or a Sandburg. Men had a lost feeling. "The news of his going," mourned William H. Herndon, "struck me dumb, the deed being so infernally wicked . . . so huge in consequences, that it was too large to enter my brain. Hence it was incomprehensible, leaving a misty distant doubt of its truth. It *yet* does not appear like a worldly reality."

Mourning intensified grief. The trappings of death—the black-draped catafalque, the silent train that moved by a circuitous route over the land, the white-robed choirs that wailed a dirge, the crepe-veiled women, the stone-faced men—made Lincoln's passing seem even more calamitous. Over a million persons took a last sad look at the face in the casket and went away treasuring an unforgettable memory. They became of that select group who had seen Lincoln plain.

II

In those dark postwar decades there was keen interest in the Great Emancipator and Great Martyr—those two phrases, always in capitals, keep cropping up in nearly all the correspondence of the period. There were those who speculated on what Lincoln would have done had he lived, and there were more who tried to recall what he had done while alive. An avid audience looked forward eagerly to the memoirs and reminiscences that began to flood the country. Jay Monaghan's *Lincoln Bibliography* lists over four hundred and fifty speeches, sermons, and histories of Lincoln which appeared in the year of his death.

To this urgent demand for details on Lincoln's life, few would answer as did George Spears, a friend from New Salem days, who explained the brevity of his recollections by declaring: "At that time I had no idea of his ever being President therefore I did not notice his course as close as I should of." Not only persons who knew Lincoln retailed "facts" to the eager world, but also those who had merely met the President, or those who thought they had met him, or those who wished to have met him. Stories, sometimes without the slightest shadow of factual foundation, were spread by word of mouth, and by mere repetition gained authenticity. Then they appeared in Lincoln biographies and have been handed down ever since as indubitably accurate.

At the time of Lincoln's death there was no single pattern into which the stories and anecdotes about him could fit. In the blurred memories of former slaves there was the shadowy outline of a preternaturally shrewd Lincoln, half Moses, half Yankee. "I think Abe Lincoln was next to the Lord," said one ex-slave. "He done all he could for the slaves; he set 'em free." Then the aged Negro went on to "reminisce":

> 'Fore the election he [Lincoln] traveled all over the South, and he come to our house and slept in Old Mistress' bed. Didn't nobody know who he was. . . . He come to our house and he watched close. . . . When he got back up North he writ Old Master a letter and told him that he was going to have to free his slaves, that everybody was going to have to. . . . He also told him that he had visited at his house and if he doubted it to go in the room he slept in and look on the bedstead at the head and he'd see where he'd writ his name. Sure enough, there was his name: A. Lincoln.

Gradually the Negro built up a more emotional image of Lincoln, a perfect man and, in a peculiarly individual way, a personal emancipator. In Negro houses all over the nation one could find "many old pictures of Lincoln pasted on the walls of the sitting room over the mantelpiece. . . . They just had to have Lincoln near them," explains their chronicler, John E. Washington; "they loved him so." "His life to these humble people was a miracle, and his memory has become a benediction," Dr. Washington adds. "To the deeply emotional and religious slave, Lincoln was an earthly incarnation of the Savior of mankind."

At the other extreme were the stories spread by Lincoln's political enemies, legends that still persist in some parts of the South. To these the sixteenth President was only "a man of coarse nature, a self-seeking politician, who craved high office . . . to satisfy his own burning desire for distinction." ". . . his real name is Abraham Hanks," one political opponent charged. "He is the illegitimate son by an [*sic*] man named Inlow—from a Negress named Hanna Hanks." His presumptive parents were immoral, shiftless poor white trash. Unscrupulous as a lawyer, he was unprincipled as a politician. He was a man of low morality, and his "inordinate love of the lascivious, of smut," it was whispered, was "something nearly akin to lunacy."

III

Naturally the strongest growth of Lincoln legends has occurred in the North. There have been, in general, two opposing schools of tradition. One, essentially literary in character and often of New England or Eastern sponsorship, presented a prettified Lincoln, a combination of George Washington and Christ. Occasionally there were difficulties of reconciling the two ideas, and the resulting portrait looks somewhat like a Gilbert Stuart painting with a halo dubbed in by later, less skillful hands. The problem was to reconcile the standards of democracy in the gilded age with the familiar pattern of the Christ story. Fortunately for authors, consistency is not an essential in folklore.

In eulogies, sermons, birthday speeches, Republican campaign addresses, orations before the G.A.R., and in poems too numerous to count and too tedious to read, one gets a glimpse of the pattern. This Lincoln has the outlines of a mythological hero; he is a demi-god. Born in obscure circumstances, he rose over hardships, became President, was lawgiver to the Negro people, won a tremendous victory, and was killed at the height of his power. By his death he expiated the sins of his country. After one makes the obvious concessions required by mid-century morality and by the exigencies of a republican form of government, this Lincoln conforms very closely to the type of ideal hero in classical mythology.

The eulogists had some doubts as to how Lincoln's ancestry should be presented. A mythological hero should spring from unknown parentage (or at least it is concealed even from himself), sent by the gods to save his tribe. There are a number of Lincoln poets and biographers who ask: "Whence came this man?" and answer: "As if on the wings of the winds of God that blew!" On the other hand, it comported more with American notions of respectability that the hero should have at least some family connections. The Lincolns have, therefore, been traced in elaborate monographs back to the early Massachusetts settlers and even to the English family of that name. The Hankses have been "proved" to derive their name from an Egyptian dynasty, or, as an alternative explanation, they were relatives of the Lees of Virginia.

Regardless of origins, the biographers were sure of one thing. Lincoln loved his angel-mother. It is characteristic of the American attitude toward family life and of the extreme veneration for the maternal principle that the utterly unknown Nancy Hanks should be described as "a whole-hearted Christian," "a woman of marked natural abilities," of "strong mental powers and deep-toned piety," whose rigid observance of the Sabbath became a byword in frontier Kentucky—in short, "a remarkable woman." "A great man," asserted J. G. Holland in his widely circulated *Life of Abraham Lincoln,* "never drew his infant life from a purer or more womanly bosom than her own; and Mr. Lincoln always looked back to her with an unspeakable affection."

Lincoln's early life became, to this school of biography, an illustration of how determination and energy could triumph over circumstances; this Lincoln was the transcendent rail-splitter. It was a carefully manipulated symbolism that had begun at the Illinois state Republican convention of 1860 when rails that Lincoln might have split were introduced to elicit applause. The theme was drummed and piped and bugled all through the campaigns of 1860 and 1864, and the tale of Lincoln's "life of labor" that "brought forth his kingly qualities of soul" has become a part of the American tradition. Lincoln was never to escape; his Civil War administration would be appraised in terms of his early struggles:

> Out yonder splitting rails his mind had fed
> On Freedom—now he put her foes to rout.

From these origins he rose to become President of the United States, and, surprisingly enough, a successful President. There must have been, a great many people believed, some supernatural force, some divine guidance behind his rise. "Out of the unknown, and by ways that even he knew not," orated one centennial speaker, becoming more mystical with each phrase, "came to this place of power, Abraham Lincoln. He came mysteriously chosen . . . by the instinctive voice of a predestined people. Called because he was chosen; chosen, because he was already choice."

There were elements in Lincoln's personality and career which did not blend well in this portrait of a demigod. He was indubitably homely—not a major difficulty, to be sure, yet if a hero is not handsome he should at least be impressive. Rhymesters went to great length to explain the truth. Was Lincoln "ungainly, plain"? Not at all. "Grave was his visage," it was admitted, "but no cloud could dull the radiance from within that made it beautiful." A more serious obstacle was Lincoln's levity. He told jokes—a thing unprecedented in the record of mythology. Writers were more familiar with the idea of "one who knew no play, nor ever tasted rest." How could a man of sadness and tears laugh at Artemus Ward? One poet suggested that Lincoln's laughter was really a sort of anodyne "to cease his ceaseless dole." Thus Lincoln became the laughing man of sorrows.

Another difficulty was Lincoln's religion. It was embarrassing that this "soldier of his Captain Christ" belonged to no Christian church. Shortly after Lincoln's death there began to appear a veritable flood of affidavits and statements to prove, as Holland put it, that "Lincoln's power" had been the "power of a true-hearted Christian man." Reminiscences on this point probably include more nonsense than can be found anywhere else in the whole tiresome mass of spurious Lincoln recollections. To him are attributed the most improbable statements. Lincoln was supposed to have had a secret conference with Newton Bateman, Illinois superintendent of public instruction, during which he pulled a Testament from his bosom and pointed to it as "*this rock* on which I stand." "I know," he is alleged to have confided, "that liberty is right, for Christ teaches it and Christ is God."

Countless similar statements were given wide newspaper circulation. Lincoln reportedly ran upon one Benjamin B. Smith, a minister of Canton, Missouri, in a railway station, brought him into his office, and begged from the willing pastor a private, hour-long discourse upon "foreordination, election and predestination." During the darkest hours of the war Lincoln was supposed to have left his post in Washington in order to pray with Henry Ward Beecher in Brooklyn. So it went. There were those who could demonstrate that Lincoln was a Catholic, a Congregationalist, a Methodist, a Presbyterian, a Universalist, or a Spiritualist. Conflicting claims became so amusing that the editor of the Springfield *Illinois State Register* rejected them as "all wrong." "We are," he remarked whimsically, "prepared to prove by indisputable documentary evidence that he was a Mormon, and the boon companion of Joe Smith."

For these minor defects Lincoln amply compensated by the manner of his passing. His assassination at once brought to mind the tender, familiar outlines of the Christ story. Lincoln as "Savior of his country" was by his death expiating the sins of the nation. The idea had universal appeal. One has only to leaf through the pages of Lloyd Lewis's *Myths after Lincoln* to discover how frequently the idea of vicarious sacrifice recurred to Northern preachers on that dread Black Easter of 1865. Some pointed to the significance of Lincoln's martyrdom on Good Friday. "It is no blasphemy against the Son of God," asserted a Connecticut parson, "that we declare the fitness of the slaying of the second Father of our Republic on the anniversary of the day on which He was slain. Jesus Christ died for the world, Abraham Lincoln died for his country." Even so early the pattern of apotheosis was complete. America had a martyr hero, a perfect man, born to do great things, pure in heart, noble in action, and constant in principle. This was Lincoln, "President, savior of the republic, emancipator of a race, true Christian, true man."

IV

Lincoln was saved from this kind of deification by a different stream of tradition, frequently Western in origin and more truly folkloristic in quality. The grotesque hero—the Gargantua or the Till Eulenspiegel—is one of the oldest and most familiar patterns in folk literature. In America the type had been already exemplified by such favorites as Davy Crockett, Mike Fink, and Paul Bunyan. Of a like cut was the myth of Lincoln as frontier hero. This Lincoln of "folk say" was the practical joker, the teller of tall and lusty tales. Stupendously strong, he was also marvelously lazy. A true romantic, he pined over the grave of Ann Rutledge, but he also lampooned one woman who refused him and jilted another who accepted. He was Old Abe, a Westerner, and his long flapping arms were not the wings of an angel.

This folk pattern of Lincoln as frontier hero had been sketched in outline before his death. After his assassination the details were filled in. Many of the stories in the strong Western tradition can be traced back to Herndon, Lincoln's law partner, who has been called the "master myth-maker" of Lincoln folklore. Herndon did not invent the legends, but his singular personality made him peculiarly receptive to this type of Western mythology. Herndon was born in Kentucky, and, as an early German traveler put it, "the Kentuckian is a peculiar man." Moody, erratic, loquacious, addicted to high-flown "philosophical" language, but with a fondness for earthy stories, Herndon had shortly after his partner's death decided to write a biography of Lincoln. From the very outset he had in mind showing Lincoln as a Western character, shaped by the "power of mud, flowers, & mind" which he had encountered in the pioneer Northwest. Deliberately he sought to emphasize those factors which would distinguish Lincoln as a Westerner from his Eastern contemporaries. He proposed to exhibit "the type" of the "original western and south-western pioneer— . . . at times . . . somewhat open, candid, sincere, energetic, spontaneous, trusting, tolerant, brave and generous."

Seeking information about Lincoln, Herndon interviewed older settlers in central Illinois and southern Indiana at just the time when the outlines of the folk portrait were becoming firmly established. From his notes emerged the essentially fictitious picture of a semilegendary frontier hero. The stories Herndon collected fall into patterns familiar to the student of American folklore. Some remembered Lincoln as a ring-tailed roarer of the Davy Crockett type, who would wave a whisky bottle over his head to drive back his foes, shouting that "he was the big buck at the lick." There were tales of the Paul Bunyan variety, describing how Lincoln would "frequently take a barrel of whiskey by the chimes and lift it up to his face as if to drink out of the bunghole," a feat that "he could accomplish with greatest ease."

This was the Lincoln who chastely wooed Ann Rutledge and, when she died, pined sadly over her grave. "My heart," he was supposed to have said, "lies buried there." More in the frontier tradition was his courtship of Mary Owens, a well-educated Kentucky lady who refused his hand. Afterward Lincoln described her as "weather-beaten," "oversize," and lacking teeth. Of a like pattern were the tales Herndon accumulated of Lincoln's domestic unhappiness with Mary Todd, for the henpecked husband is one of the oldest comic types and was a favorite in the Western joke books of the day. Herndon also collected irreligious or, as he called them, "infidel" statements attributed to Lincoln; the folk hero is frequently anticlerical.

Many of these tales probably had a grain of historical truth, and their evolution exhibits the familiar development of folk literature. "If a man has been well known for special powers," Robert Price has pointed out in his examination of the Johnny Appleseed traditions, "folk fancies soon seize upon particular instances of these powers, begin to enhance them into facts of remarkable quality, and then proceed, as the desire for greater color grows, to invent still others that will markedly emphasize the quality admired." As the historical personage becomes absorbed in the myth, "the whole cycle of his birth, youth, education, loves, mating, maturity, and death becomes significant and grows increasingly in color and particular detail." On a rather sophisticated plane, the Lincoln of Western legend represented a true folk-hero type.

The folkloristic quality of these stories is sometimes overlooked. When Herndon visited in Indiana, he was told of verses that Lincoln had written to celebrate the wedding of his sister:

When Adam was created
He dwelt in Eden's shade,
As Moses has recorded,
And soon a bride was made.

(The poem continues for seven additional stanzas.) Dr. Milo M. Quaife has traced this ballad back to early English folk verse and has shown that it was introduced into America before the Revolutionary War. In the process of being handed down, it somehow became identified in the minds of backwoods Hoosiers with Lincoln; it was related to Herndon as such; he published the verses in his Lincoln biography; and the poem is not infrequently cited as Lincoln's original composition. Of the making of myths there is no end.

The process of evolving Western legends about Lincoln neither began nor ended with Herndon. Gossip, imagination, delayed recollection, and hearsay have all continued to multiply "Lincoln" stories. Sometimes the results of this accumulation of "folk say" are amusing. One can take, for example, a less familiar episode in Lincoln's early career—his projected duel with James Shields. The actual facts of the affair are easily ascertained. In 1842 Mary Todd and Julia Jayne published anonymously in the *Sangamo Journal* some satirical verses about Shields, then Illinois state auditor. That hot-tempered Irishman demanded of the editor the names of the writers, and Lincoln, to protect the ladies, offered to take the blame. After some stilted correspondence and much dashing back and forth of seconds, a duel with broadswords was arranged. Ultimately, however, explanations and apologies were made, and actual combat was averted. The affair remained a sore memory to Lincoln, and he disliked hearing the episode referred to. The whole affair is summarized in any good Lincoln biography.

As this same tale comes down in folklore, the whole emphasis is altered. It becomes an illustration of Lincoln the humorist and the practical joker. The duel had an amusing origin, according to one old settler who had heard another old-timer tell the story:

> Lawyer Shields and Julia Jayne were seated together at the supper table. Across the table from them sat Abe and Mary Todd. By and by the lawyer squeezed Julia's hand. In those days, you know, a pin was a woman's weapon. Julia used it when Shields squeezed her hand. And that made him scream. . . . Lincoln, who was a laughing fellow, haw-hawed right out loud, much to the embarrassment of Shields. Well to make a long story short, Shield[s] issued a duel challenge to Abe.

Another version gives a play-by-play account of the duel that never happened. "Shields fired and missed," says this "eyewitness," speaking of an encounter that was to have been fought with broadswords. "Lincoln then took steady aim and fired. A blotch of read [*sic*] appeared on the breast of Shields who fell to the ground thinking he was mortally wounded, but in fact was unhurt. Lincoln's gun was loaded with pokeberries."

To treat such statements simply as exaggerated reminiscences is to miss their significance. They are really folk stories. Seldom do they have an identifiable author, for the narrator is recounting what "they said." The very pattern of the statement is significant; "to make a long story short" is a frequent formula to conclude a folk tale. The Shields episode is only one less widely known incident about which a surprisingly large amount of folklore has accumulated. The body of tradition concerning Lincoln's courtship, his marriage, or his law practice is much more voluminous. And there is an extensive cycle of ribald and Rabelaisian stories attributed to Lincoln, for the most part unprintable and now almost forgotten.

V

Few Negroes have written books about their Great Emancipator, and the viciously anti-Lincoln publications are nearly forgotten, but the other two major currents of tradition have produced a mountainous pile of Lincoln literature. Writers who fitted Lincoln into the pattern of a mythological demigod had the early start at the printing presses. A series of widely read and often quoted biographies began to appear shortly after Lincoln's death, starting with the Arnold and the Holland lives and running without interruption through the work of Nicolay and Hay and that of Ida M. Tarbell. All were characterized by a highly laudatory tone and all presented Lincoln in an aura of great respectability.

Those who thought of Lincoln as the archetype of the frontiersman were outraged. Herndon was especially bitter at the "Finical fools," the "nice sweet smelling gentlemen" who tried to "handle things with silken gloves & 'a cammel [*sic*] hair pencil,' " but for personal reasons his own book about Lincoln was delayed for many years. The publication in 1872 of Ward Hill Lamon's biography, ghost-written from Herndonian sources, marked the first widespread circulation in print of the Western version of Lincoln's career. It was greeted as "a national misfortune." When *Herndon's Lincoln* appeared seventeen years later, it, too, met with shrill disapproval, and some shocked souls appealed to Anthony Comstock to suppress this indecent book. This food was too coarse for sensitive stomachs.

It is a mistake to consider these two opposing currents of Lincoln tradition as representing respectively the "ideal" and the "real" Lincoln. Each was legendary in character. The conflict in Lincoln biography between the Holland-Hay-Tarbell faction and the Herndon-Lamon-Weik contingent was not essentially a battle over factual differences; it was more like a religious war. One school portrayed a mythological patron saint; the other, an equally mythological frontier hero. Not all the Lincoln stories related by either school were false, but the facts were at most a secondary consideration. Acceptance or rejection of any Lincoln anecdote depended upon what was fundamentally a religious conviction. Even today this attitude is sometimes found. A recent writer has attacked certain legends that he asserts "libel" Lincoln on two grounds—first, because they "do not create a truer or finer image of him" and, second, because the myths are "unsupported by trustworthy evidence." The order of the reasons deserves notice.

It is widely recognized that the biographies of the Holland school are remote from reality. They present a conventionalized hero who is discussed from a "frankly eulogistic point of view." The temptation has naturally been to treat their opponents—such as Herndon, Lamon, and Weik—as realists, intent on giving a "true" picture of Lincoln. If there is any meaning left in the word "realism," which is rapidly becoming semantically obsolete, *Herndon's Lincoln* (a biography typical of this latter school) is realistic neither in literary style nor in biographical approach. Herndon's book was dedicated to proving a thesis—that Lincoln had his origin in a "stagnant, putrid pool" and rose through adversity to "the topmost round of the ladder." All of its contents Herndon deliberately arranged to support this contention and to enlist readers' sympathies in behalf of his protagonist. Rough and coarse elements were introduced into the biography, not primarily from conviction that these were vital aspects of human existence, but principally to serve the same function as the villain in the contemporary melodrama. Unlike the true realists, Herndon was concerned with the unusual and the sensational. It is difficult to see how anyone can find in Herndon's emotionalized treatment of the Ann Rutledge legend the work of a biographical or literary realist. Actually the biographies of the Herndon school are stylized presentations of Western folklore. Herndon's own book recounts the epic of the frontier hero, transmogrified into the pattern of the sentimental novel.

Toward the end of the century the two conceptions of Lincoln—as mythological demigod and as legendary frontier hero—began to blend, sometimes with amusing results. John T. Morse's *Abraham Lincoln,* one of the better early biographies, made no effort to reconcile the two concepts, but accepted both. For Lincoln's early years Morse followed Herndon, and for the period of the Presidency, Nicolay and Hay. The result, he admitted, tended to show that Lincoln was "physically one creature, morally and mentally two beings." In the huge file of newspaper reminiscences in the Lincoln National Life Foundation one can trace the process by which demigod and hero became inextricably scrambled. By the centennial year of Lincoln's birth the frontier stories that had been considered gamy and rough by an earlier generation had been accepted as typical Lincolnisms; and on the other side, the harshness of the Herndonian outlines was smoothed by the acceptance of many traits from the idealized Lincoln. The result was a "composite American ideal," whose "appeal is stronger than that of other heroes because on him converge so many dear traditions." The current popular conception of Lincoln is "a folk-hero who to the common folk-virtues of shrewdness and kindness adds essential wit and eloquence and loftiness of soul."

VI

One may question the value of studying these legendary accounts of Lincoln. A more conventional procedure is to assault these air castles of contemporary mythology, to use the sharp tools of historical criticism to raze the imaginary structures, to purify the ground by a liberal sprinkling of holy water in the form of footnotes, and to erect a new and "authentic" edifice. Such an approach has its merits. One cannot overestimate the importance of thoroughgoing historical investigation of Lincoln's career; far too little of the huge bibliography of Lincolniana is based upon scholarly, scientific research.

But there is also room for investigation of another sort. Referring to the debunking of historical myths and legends, W. A. Dunning, in his presidential address before the American Historical Association, reminded his hearers that in many cases "influence on the sequence of human affairs has been exercised, not by what really happened, but by what men erroneously believed to have happened." In turning to history for guidance, he observed, men have acted upon "the error that passes as history at the time, not from the truth that becomes known long after." He concluded by pointing out that "for very, very much history there is more importance in the ancient error than in the new-found truth."

His warning applies in the field of Lincoln biography. As J. Frank Dobie has put it, "The history of any public character involves not only the facts about him but what the public has taken to be facts." It is important to examine the Lincoln legends as expressing a collective wish-fulfillment of the American people. This is no psychological jargon; it is simply a way of saying that "heroes embody the qualities that we most admire or desire in ourselves." Fully realizing their general inaccuracy and almost universal distortion, the student can use these myths for an understanding of what plain Americans have wished their leaders to be. "If the folk aspiration is worthy, its dreams of great men will be worthy too."

Unless one conceives of time as ending with 1865, the Lincoln of folklore is more significant than the Lincoln of actuality. The historian may prove that the Emancipation actually freed a negligible number of slaves, yet Lincoln continues to live in men's minds as the emancipator of the Negroes. It is this folklore Lincoln who has become the central symbol in American democratic thought; he embodies what ordinary, inarticulate Americans have cherished as ideals. As Ralph H. Gabriel says, he is "first among the folk heroes of the American people." From a study of the Lincoln legends the historian can gain a more balanced insight into the workings of the American mind. As it is now written, intellectual history is too often based on printed sources—sermons, speeches, commencement addresses, books, and newspapers. The result is inevitably a distortion. The men who write books or edit papers are not average citizens. It is much as though the Gallup poll were to interrogate only college presidents. To understand the thinking of ordinary men and women, the historian must delve into their beliefs, their superstitions, their gossip, and their folklore.

The Lincoln ideal offers an excellent starting-point for the investigation. As the pattern has gradually become standardized, the folklore Lincoln is as American as the Mississippi River. Essentially national, the myth is not nationalistic. It reveals the people's faith in the democratic dogma that a poor boy can make good. It demonstrates the incurable romanticism of the American spirit. There is much in the legend which is unpleasant—Lincoln's preternatural cunning, his fondness for Rabelaisian anecdote, his difficulties with his wife—yet these traits seem to be attributed to every real folk hero. The fundamental qualities of the legendary Lincoln emphasize the essential dignity and humanity of our nation's everyday thinking. It speaks well for Americans that to the central hero in their history their folklore has attributed all the decent qualities of civilized man: patience, tolerance, humor, sympathy, kindliness, and sagacity.

The Tragic Legend of Reconstruction

Kenneth M. Stampp

Perhaps legend and myth become most debilitating when they directly affect a society's overt social and political behavior. If this is so, the legend of reconstruction qualifies as particularly tragic. Kenneth M. Stampp, an historical scholar at the University of California, Berkeley, applies a revisionist lens to the era of reconstruction in the interest of explaining American racial attitudes, past and present. Through his revisionist view of the reconstruction "radicals," Stampp brings much weight to bear against the mythology of northern postwar brutality. It was a mythology that was largely the product of the historical community itself, but one that nonetheless found an especially receptive audience both North and South.

In much serious history, as well as in a durable popular legend, two American epochs—the Civil War and the reconstruction that followed—bear an odd relationship to one another. The Civil War, though admittedly a tragedy, is nevertheless often described as a glorious time of gallantry, noble self-sacrifice, and high idealism. Even historians who have considered the war "needless" and have condemned the politicians of the 1850's for blundering into it, once they passed the firing on Fort Sumter, have usually written with reverence about Civil War heroes—the martyred Lincoln, the Christlike Lee, the intrepid Stonewall Jackson, and many others in this galaxy of demigods.

Few, of course, are so innocent as not to know that the Civil War had its seamy side. One can hardly ignore the political opportunism, the graft and profiteering in the filling of war contracts, the military blundering and needless loss of lives, the horrors of army hospitals and prison camps, and the ugly depths as well as the nobility of human nature that the war exposed with a fine impartiality. These things cannot be ignored, but they can be, and frequently are, dismissed as something alien to the essence of the war years. What was real and fundamental was the idealism and the nobility of the two contending forces: the Yankees struggling to save the Union, dying to make men free; the Confederates fighting for great constitutional principles, defending their homes from invasion. Here, indeed, is one of the secrets of the spell the Civil War has cast: it involved high-minded Americans on both sides, and there was glory enough to go around. This, in fact, is the supreme sythesis of Civil War historiography and the great balm that has healed the nation's wounds: Yankees and Confederates alike fought bravely for what they believed to be just causes. There were few villains in the drama.

But when the historian reaches the year 1865, he must take leave of the war and turn to another epoch, reconstruction, when the task was, in Lincoln's words, "to bind up the nation's wounds" and "to do all which may achieve and cherish a just and lasting peace." How, until recently, reconstruction was portrayed in both history and legend, how sharply it was believed to contrast with the years of the Civil War, is evident in the terms that were used to identify it. Various historians have called this phase of American history "The Tragic Era," "The Dreadful Decade," "The Age of Hate," and "The Blackout of Honest Government." Reconstruction represented the ultimate shame of the American people—as one historian phrased it, "the nadir of national disgrace." It was the epoch that most Americans wanted to forget.

Claude Bowers, who divided his time between politics and history, has been the chief disseminator of the traditional picture of reconstruction, for his book, *The Tragic Era*, published in 1929, has attracted more readers than any other dealing with this period. For Bowers reconstruction was a time of almost unrelieved sordidness in public and private life; whole regiments of villains march through his pages; the corrupt politicians who dominated the administration of Ulysses S. Grant; the crafty, scheming northern carpetbaggers who invaded the South after the war for political and economic plunder; the degraded and depraved southern scalawags who betrayed their own people and collaborated with the enemy; and the ignorant, barbarous, sensual Negroes who threatened to Africanize the South and destroy its Caucasian civilization.

Most of Bowers's key generalizations can be found in his preface. The years of reconstruction, he wrote, "were years of revolutionary turmoil, with the elemental passions predominant. . . . The prevailing note was one of tragedy. . . . Never have American public men in responsible positions, directing the destiny of the nation, been so brutal, hypocritical, and corrupt. The constitution was treated as a doormat on which politicians and army officers wiped their feet after wading in the muck. . . . The southern people literally were put to the torture . . . [by] rugged conspirators . . . [who] assumed the pose of philanthropists and patriots." The popularity of Bowers's book stems in part from the simplicity of his characters. None are etched in shades of gray; none are confronted with complex moral decisions. Like characters in a Victorian romance, the Republican leaders of the reconstruction era were evil through and through, and the helpless, innocent white men of the South were totally noble and pure.

If Bowers's prose is more vivid and his anger more intense, his general interpretation of reconstruction is only a slight exaggeration of a point of view shared by most serious American historians from the late nineteenth century until very recently. Writing in the 1890's, James Ford Rhodes, author of a multi-volumed history of the United States since the Compromise of

1850, branded the Republican scheme of reconstruction as "repressive" and "uncivilized," one that "pandered to the ignorant negroes, the knavish white natives and the vulturous adventurers who flocked from the North." About the same time Professor John W. Burgess, of Columbia University, called reconstruction the "most soul-sickening spectacle that Americans had ever been called upon to behold."[1] Early in the twentieth century Professor William A. Dunning, also of Columbia University, and a group of talented graduate students wrote a series of monographs that presented a crushing indictment of the Republican reconstruction program in the South—a series that made a deep and lasting impression on American historians. In the 1930's, Professor James G. Randall, of the University of Illinois, still writing in the spirit of the Dunningites, described the reconstruction era "as a time of party abuse, of corruption, of vindictive bigotry." "To use a modern phrase," wrote Randall, "government under Radical Republican rule in the South had become a kind of 'racket.' " As late as 1947, Professor E. Merton Coulter, of the University of Georgia, reminded critics of the traditional interpretation that no "amount of revision can write away the grievous mistakes made in this abnormal period of American history."[2] Thus, from Rhodes and Burgess and Dunning to Randall and Coulter the central emphasis of most historical writing about reconstruction has been upon sordid motives and human depravity. Somehow, during the summer of 1865, the nobility and idealism of the war years had died.

A synopsis of the Dunning School's version of reconstruction would run something like this: Abraham Lincoln, while the Civil War was still in progress, turned his thoughts to the great problem of reconciliation; and, "with malice toward none and charity for all," this gentle and compassionate man devised a plan that would restore the South to the Union with minimum humiliation and maximum speed. But there had already emerged in Congress a faction of radical Republicans, sometimes called Jacobins or Vindictives, who sought to defeat Lincoln's generous program. Motivated by hatred of the South, by selfish political ambitions, and by crass economic interests, the radicals tried to make the process of reconstruction as humiliating, as difficult, and as prolonged as they possibly could. Until Lincoln's tragic death, they poured their scorn upon him—and then used his coffin as a political stump to arouse the passions of the northern electorate.

The second chapter of the Dunning version begins with Andrew Johnson's succession to the presidency. Johnson, the old Jacksonian Unionist from Tennessee, took advantage of the adjournment of Congress to put Lincoln's mild plan of reconstruction into operation, and it was a striking success. In the summer and fall of 1865, Southerners organized loyal state governments, showed a willingness to deal fairly with their former slaves, and in general accepted the outcome of the Civil War in good faith. In December, when Congress assembled, President Johnson reported that the process of reconstruction was nearly completed and that the old Union had been restored. But the radicals unfortunately had their own sinister purposes: they repudiated the governments Johnson had established in the South, refused to seat southern Senators and Representatives, and then directed their fury against the new President. After a year of bitter controversy and political stalemate, the radicals, resorting to shamefully demagogic tactics, won an overwhelming victory in the congressional elections of 1866.

Now, the third chapter and the final tragedy. Riding rough-shod over presidential vetoes and federal courts, the radicals put the South under military occupation, gave the ballot to Negroes, and formed new southern state governments dominated by base and corrupt men, black and white. Not satisfied with reducing the South to political slavery and financial bankruptcy, the radicals even laid their obscene hands on the pure fabric of the federal Constitution. They impeached President Johnson and came within one vote of removing him from office, though they had no legal grounds for such action. Next, they elected Ulysses S. Grant President, and during his two administrations they indulged in such an orgy of corruption and so prostituted the civil service as to make Grantism an enduring symbol of political immorality.

The last chapter is the story of ultimate redemption. Decent southern white Democrats, their patience exhausted, organized to drive the Negroes, carpetbaggers, and scalawags from power, peacefully if possible, forcefully if necessary. One by one the southern states were redeemed, honesty and virtue triumphed, and the South's natural leaders returned to power. In the spring of 1877, the Tragic Era finally came to an end when President Hayes withdrew the federal troops from the South and restored home rule. But the legacy of radical reconstruction remained in the form of a solidly Democratic South and embittered relations between the races.

This point of view was rarely challenged until the 1930's, when a small group of revisionist historians began to give new life and a new direction to the study of reconstruction. The revisionists are a curious lot who sometimes quarrel with each other as much as they quarrel with the disciples of Dunning. At various times they have counted in their ranks Marxists of various degrees of orthodoxy, Negroes seeking historical vindication, skeptical white Southerners, and latter-day northern abolitionists. But among them are numerous scholars who have the wisdom to know that the history of an age is seldom simple and clear-cut, seldom without its tragic aspects, seldom without its redeeming virtues.

Few revisionists would claim that the Dunning interpretation of reconstruction is a pure fabrication. They recognize the shabby aspects of this era: the corruption was real, the failures obvious, the tragedy undeniable. Grant is not their idea of a model President, nor were the southern carpetbag governments worthy of their unqualified praise. They understand that the radical Republicans were not all selfless patriots, and that southern white men were not all Negro-hating rebels. In short, they have not turned history on its head, but rather, they recognize that much of what Dunning's disciples have said about reconstruction is true.

Revisionists, however, have discovered that the Dunningites overlooked a great deal, and they doubt that nobility and idealism suddenly died in 1865. They are neither surprised nor disillusioned to find that the Civil War, for all its nobility, revealed some of the ugliness of human nature as well. And they approach reconstruction with the confident expectation that here, too, every facet of human nature will be exposed. They are not satisfied with the two-dimensional characters that Dunning's disciples have painted.

What is perhaps most puzzling in the legend of reconstruction is the notion that the white people of the South were treated with unprecedented brutality, that their conquerors, in Bowers's colorful phrase, literally put them to the torture. How, in fact, *were* they treated after the failure of their rebellion against the authority of the federal government? The great mass of ordinary Southerners who voluntarily took up arms, or in other ways supported the Confederacy, were required simply to take an oath of allegiance to obtain pardon and to regain their right to vote and hold public office. But what of the Confederate leaders—the men who held high civil offices, often after resigning similar federal offices; the military leaders who had graduated from West Point and had resigned commissions in the United States Army to take commissions in the Confederate Army? Were there mass arrests, indictments for treason or conspiracy, trials and convictions, executions or imprisonments? Nothing of the sort. Officers of the Confederate Army were paroled and sent home with their men. After surrendering at Appomattox, General Lee bid farewell to his troops and rode home to live his remaining years undisturbed. Only one officer, a Captain Henry Wirtz, was arrested; and he was tried, convicted, and executed, not for treason or conspiracy, but for "war crimes." Wirtz's alleged offense, for which the evidence was rather flimsy, was the mistreatment of prisoners of war in the military prison at Andersonville, Georgia.

Of the Confederate civil officers, a handful were arrested at the close of the war, and there was talk for a time of trying a few for treason. But none, actually, was ever brought to trial, and all but Jefferson Davis were released within a few months. The former Confederate President was held in prison for nearly two years, but in 1867 he too was released. With a few exceptions, even the property of Confederate leaders was untouched, save, of course, for the emancipation of their slaves. Indeed, the only penalty imposed on most Confederate leaders was a temporary political disability provided in the Fourteenth Amendment. But in 1872 Congress pardoned all but a handful of Southerners; and soon former Confederate civil and military leaders were serving as state governors, as members of Congress, and even as Cabinet advisers of Presidents.

What, then, constituted the alleged brutality that white Southerners endured? First, the freeing of their slaves; second, the brief incarceration of a few Confederate leaders; third, a political disability imposed for a few years on most Confederate leaders; fourth, a relatively weak military occupation terminated in 1877; and, last, an attempt to extend the rights and privileges of citizenship to southern Negroes. Mistakes there were in the implementation of these measures—some of them serious—but brutality almost none. In fact, it can be said that rarely in history have the participants in an unsuccessful rebellion endured penalties as mild as those Congress imposed upon the people of the South, and particularly upon their leaders. After four years of bitter struggle costing hundreds of thousands of lives, the generosity of the federal government's terms was quite remarkable.

If northern brutality is a myth, the scandals of the Grant administration and the peculations of some of the southern reconstruction governments are sordid facts. Yet even here the Dunningites are guilty of distortion by exaggeration, by a lack of perspective, by superficial analysis, and by overemphasis. They make corruption a central theme of their narratives, but they overlook constructive accomplishments. They give insufficient attention to the men who transcended the greed of an age when, to be sure, self-serving politicians and irresponsible entrepreneurs were all too plentiful. Among these men were the humanitarians who organized Freedmen's Aid Societies to help four million southern Negroes make the difficult transition from slavery to freedom, and the missionaries and teachers who went into the South on slender budgets to build churches and schools for the freedmen. Under their auspices the Negroes first began to learn the responsibilities and obligations of freedom. Thus the training of Negroes for citizenship had its successful beginnings in the years of reconstruction.

In the nineteenth century most white Americans, North and South, had reservations about the Negro's potentialities—doubted that he had the innate intellectual capacity and moral fiber of the white man and assumed that after emancipation he would be relegated to an inferior caste. But some of the radical Republicans refused to believe that the Negroes were innately inferior and hoped passionately that they would confound their critics. The radicals then had little empirical evidence and no scientific evidence to support their belief—nothing, in fact, but faith. Their faith was derived mostly from their religion: all men, they said, are the sons of Adam and equal in the sight of God. And if Negroes are equal to white men in the sight of God, it is morally wrong for white men to withhold from Negroes the liberties and rights that white men enjoy. Here, surely, was a projection into the reconstruction era of the idealism of the abolitionist crusade and of the Civil War.

Radical idealism was in part responsible for two of the most momentous enactments of the reconstruction years: the Fourteenth Amendment to the federal Constitution which gave Negroes citizenship and promised them equal protection of the laws, and the Fifteenth Amendment which gave them the right to vote. The fact that these amendments could not have been adopted under any other circumstances, or at any other time, before or since, may suggest the crucial importance of the reconstruction era in American history. Indeed, without radical reconstruction, it would be impossible to this day for the federal government to protect Negroes from legal and political discrimination.

If all of this is true, or even part of it, why was the Dunning legend born, and why has it been so durable? Southerners, of course, have contributed much to the legend of reconstruction, but most Northerners have found the legend quite acceptable. Many of the historians who helped to create it were Northerners, among them James Ford Rhodes, William A. Dunning, Claude Bowers, and James G. Randall. Thus the legend cannot be explained simply in terms of a southern literary or historiographical conspiracy, satisfying as the legend has been to most white Southerners. What we need to know is why it also satisfies Northerners—how it became part of the intellectual baggage of so many northern historians. Why, in short, was there for so many years a kind of national, or inter-sectional, consensus that the Civil War was America's glory and reconstruction her disgrace?

The Civil War won its place in the hearts of the American people because, by the end of the nineteenth century, Northerners were willing to concede that Southerners had fought bravely for a cause that they believed to be just; whereas Southerners, with few exceptions, were willing to concede that the outcome of the war was probably best for all concerned. In an era of intense nationalism, both Northerners and Southerners agreed that the preservation of the federal Union was essential to the future power of the American people. Southerners could even say now that the abolition of slavery was one of the war's great blessings—not so much, they insisted, because slavery was an injustice to the Negroes but because it was a grievous burden upon the whites. By 1886, Henry W. Grady, the great Georgia editor and spokesman for a New South, could confess to a New York audience: "I am glad that the omniscient God held the balance of battle in His Almighty hand, and that human slavery was swept forever from American soil—the American Union saved from the wreck of war." Soon Union and Confederate veterans were holding joint reunions, exchanging anecdotes, and sharing their sentimental memories of those glorious war years. The Civil War thus took its position in the center of American folk mythology.

That the reconstruction era elicits neither pride nor sentimentality is due only in part to its moral delinquencies—remember, those of the Civil War years can be overlooked. It is also due to the white American's ambivalent attitude toward race and toward the steps that radical Republicans took to protect the Negroes. Southern white men accepted the Thirteenth Amendment to the Constitution, which abolished slavery, with a minimum of complaint, but they expected federal intervention to proceed no further than that. They assumed that the regulation of the freedmen would be left to the individual states; and clearly most of them intended to replace slavery with a caste system that would keep the Negroes perpetually subordinate to the whites.

Negroes were to remain a dependent laboring class; they were to be governed by a separate code of laws; they were to play no active part in the South's political life; and they were to be segregated socially. When radical Republicans used federal power to interfere in these matters, the majority of southern white men formed a resistance movement to fight the radical-dominated state governments until they were overthrown, after which southern whites established a caste system in defiance of federal statutes and constitutional amendments. For many decades thereafter the federal government simply admitted defeat and acquiesced; but the South refused to forget or forgive those years of humiliation when Negroes came close to winning equality. In southern mythology, then, reconstruction was a horrid nightmare.

As for the majority of northern white men, it is hard to tell how deeply they were concerned about the welfare of the American Negro after the abolition of slavery. If one were to judge from the way they treated the small number of free Negroes who resided in the northern states, one might conclude that they were, at best, indifferent to the problem—and that a considerable number of them shared the racial attitudes of the South and preferred to keep Negroes in a subordinate caste. For a time after the Civil War the radical Republicans, who were always a minority group, persuaded the northern electorate that the ultimate purpose of southern white men was to rob the North of the fruits of victory and to re-establish slavery and that federal intervention was therefore essential. In this manner radicals won approval of, or acquiescence in, their program to give civil rights and the ballot to southern Negroes. Popular support for the radical program waned rapidly, however, and by the middle of the 1870's it had all but vanished. In 1875 a Republican politician confessed that northern voters were tired of the "wornout cry of 'southern outrages,'" and they wished that "the 'nigger' the 'everlasting nigger' were in—Africa." As Northerners ceased to worry about the possibility of another southern rebellion, they became increasingly receptive to criticism of radical reconstruction.

The eventual disintegration of the radical phalanx, those root-and-branch men who, for a time, seemed bent on engineering a sweeping reformation of southern society, was another important reason for the denigration of reconstruction in American historiography. To be sure, some of the radicals, especially those who had been abolitionists before the war, never lost faith in the Negro, and in the years after reconstruction they stood by him as he struggled to break the intellectual and psychological fetters he had brought with him out of slavery. Other radicals, however, lost interest in the cause—tired of reform and spent their declining years writing their memoirs. Still others retained their crusading zeal but became disenchanted with radical reconstruction and found other crusades more attractive: civil service reform, or tariff reform, or defense of the gold standard. In 1872 they repudiated Grant and joined the Liberal Republicans; in subsequent years they considered themselves to be political independents.

This latter group had been an important element in the original radical coalition. Most of them were respectable, middle-class people in comfortable economic circumstances, well educated and highly articulate, and acutely conscious of their obligation to perform disinterested public service. They had looked upon Senator Charles Sumner of Massachusetts as their political spokesman, and upon Edwin L. Godkin of the New York *Nation* as their editorial spokesman. Like most radicals they had believed that the Negro was what slavery had made him; give the Negro equal rights and he would be quickly transformed into an industrious and responsible citizen. With the radical reconstruction program fairly launched, they had looked forward to swift and dramatic results.

But reconstruction was not as orderly and the Negro's progress was not nearly as swift and dramatic as these reformers had seemed to expect. The first signs of doubt came soon after the radicals won control of reconstruction policy, when the *Nation* warned the Negroes that the government had already done all it could for them. They were now, said the *Nation*, "on the dusty and rugged highway of competition"; henceforth "the removal of white prejudice against the Negro depends almost entirely on the Negro himself." By 1870 this bellwether of the reformers viewed with alarm the disorders and irregularities in the states governed by Negroes and carpetbaggers; by 1871 it proclaimed: "The experiment has totally failed. . . . We owe it to human nature to say that worse governments have seldom been seen in a civilized country." And three years later, looking at South Carolina, the *Nation* pronounced the ultimate epithet: "This is . . . socialism." Among the former radicals associated with the *Nation* in these years of tragic disillusionment were three prewar abolitionists: Edmund Quincy of Massachusetts, James Miller McKim of Pennsylvania, and the Reverend O. B. Frothingham of New York.

Finally, in 1890, many years after the reconstruction governments had collapsed, the *Nation*, still accurately reflecting the state of mind of the disenchanted reformers, made a full confession of its past errors. "There is," said the *Nation*, "a rapidly growing sympathy at the North with Southern perplexity over the negro problem. . . . Even those who were not shocked by the carpet-bag experiment . . . are beginning to 'view with alarm' the political prospect created by the increase of the negro population, and by the continued inability of southern society to absorb or assimilate them in any sense, physical, social, or political. . . . The sudden admission to the suffrage of a million of the recently emancipated slaves belonging to the least civilized race in the world . . . was a great leap in the dark, the ultimate consequences of which no man now living can foresee. No nation has ever done this, or anything like this for the benefit of aliens of any race or creed. Who or what is . . . [the Negro] that we should put the interests of the 55,000,000 whites on this continent in peril for his sake?" Editor Godkin answered his own question in a letter to another one-time radical: "I do not see . . . how the negro is ever to be worked into a system of government for which you and I would have much respect."

Actually, neither the obvious shortcomings of reconstruction nor an objective view of the Negro's progress in the years after emancipation can wholly explain the disillusionment of so many former radicals. Rather, their changed attitude toward the Negro and the hostile historical interpretation of reconstruction that won their favor were in part the product of social trends that severely affected the old American middle classes with whom most of them were identified. These trends had their origin in the industrial revolution; they were evident in the early nineteenth century but were enormously accelerated after the Civil War. Their institutional symbols were the giant manufacturing and railroad corporations.

In the new age of industrial enterprise there seemed to be no place for the old families with their genteel culture and strong traditions of disinterested public service. On the one hand, they were overshadowed by new and powerful industrial capitalists whose economic strength brought with it vast political influence. Legislative bodies became arenas in which the political vassals of oil, steel, and railroad barons struggled for special favors, while the interests of the public—and the old middle classes liked to think of themselves as *the public*—counted for nothing. On the other hand, they were threatened by the immigrants who came to America to work in the mines and mills and on the railroads—Italians, Slavs, and Jews from Poland and Russia. The immigrants crowded into the tenements of eastern cities, responded to the friendly overtures of urban political bosses, and used their ballots to evict the old middle-class families from power. Here was a threat to the traditional America that these families had loved—and dominated—to that once vigorous American nationality that was Protestant, Anglo-Saxon, and pure. Henry James commented bitterly about the people he met on Boston Common during a stroll one Sunday afternoon: "No sound of English, in a single instance escaped their lips; the greater number spoke a rude form of Italian, the others some outland dialect unknown to me. . . . The types and faces bore them out; the people before me were gross aliens to a man, and they were in serene and triumphant possession."

Soon the new immigrant groups had become the victims of cruel racial stereotypes. Taken collectively it would appear that they were, among other things, innately inferior to the Anglo-Saxons in their intellectual and physical traits, dirty and immoral in their habits, inclined toward criminality, receptive to dangerous political beliefs, and shiftless and irresponsible.

In due time, those who repeated these stereotypes awoke to the realization that what they were saying was not really very original—that, as a matter of fact, these generalizations were *precisely* the ones that southern white men had been making about Negroes for years. And, in their extremity, the old middle classes of the North looked with new understanding upon the problems of the beleaguered white men of the South. Perhaps all along Southerners had understood the problem better than they. Here, then, was a crucial part of the intellectual climate in which the Dunning interpretation of reconstruction was written. It was written at a time when xenophobia had become almost a national disease, when the immigration restriction movement was getting into high gear, when numerous northern cities (among them Philadelphia and Chicago) were seriously considering the establishment of racially segregated schools, and when Negroes and immigrants were being lumped together in the category of unassimilable aliens.

Several other attitudes, prevalent in the late nineteenth century, encouraged an interpretation of reconstruction that condemned radical Republicans for meddling in southern race relations. The vogue of social Darwinism discouraged governmental intervention in behalf of Negroes as well as other underprivileged groups; it encouraged the belief that a solution to the race problem could only evolve slowly as the Negroes gradually improved themselves. A rising spirit of nationalism stimulated a desire for sectional reconciliation, and part of the price was a virtual abdication of federal responsibility for the protection of the Negro's civil and political rights. An outburst of imperialism, manifested in the Spanish-American War and the annexation of the Hawaiian Islands, found one of its principal justifications in the notion that Anglo-Saxons were superior to other peoples, especially when it came to politics. In the words of Senator Albert J. Beveridge of Indiana: "God has not been preparing the English-speaking and Teutonic people for a thousand years for nothing but vain and idle self-admiration. No! He has made us the master organizers of the world to establish system where chaos reigns. . . . He has made us adept in government that we may administer government among savages and senile peoples." What folly, then, to expect Italians and Slavs to behave like Anglo-Saxons—or to accept the sentimental doctrine that Negroes deserve to be given the same political rights as white men!

Finally, at this critical juncture, sociologists, anthropologists, and psychologists presented what they regarded as convincing evidence of innate racial traits—evidence indicating that Negroes were intellectually inferior to whites and had distinctive emotional characteristics. The social scientists thus supplied the racists of the late nineteenth and early twentieth centuries with something that antebellum pro-slavery writers had always lacked: a respectable scientific argument. When, in 1916, Madison Grant, an amateur cultural anthropologist, published *The Passing of the Great Race*, his racism was only a mild caricature of a point of view shared by numerous social scientists. Examining the history of the United States, Grant easily detected her tragic blunder:

> Race consciousness . . . in the United States, down to and including the Mexican War, seems to have been very strongly developed among native Americans, and it still remains in full vigor today in the South,

> where the presence of a large negro population forces this question upon the daily attention of the whites. . . . In New England, however . . . there appeared early in the last century a wave of sentimentalism, which at that time took up the cause of the negro, and in so doing apparently destroyed, to a large extent, pride and consciousness of race in the North. The agitation over slavery was inimical to the Nordic race, because it thrust aside all national opposition to the intrusion of hordes of immigrants of inferior racial value, and prevented the fixing of a definite American type. . . . The native American by the middle of the nineteenth century was rapidly becoming a distinct type. . . . The Civil War, however, put a severe, perhaps fatal, check to the development and expansion of this splendid type, by destroying great numbers of the best breeding stock on both sides, and by breaking up the home ties of many more. If the war had not occurred these same men with their descendants would have populated the Western States instead of the racial nondescripts who are now flocking there.[3]

In this social atmosphere, armed with the knowledge of race that the social scientists had given them, historians exposed the folly of radical reconstruction. At the turn of the century, James Ford Rhodes, that intimate friend of New England Brahmins, gave his verdict on Negro suffrage—one that the Dunningites would soon develop into the central assumption, the controlling generalization, of the reconstruction legend. "No large policy in our country," concluded Rhodes, "has ever been so conspicuous a failure as that of forcing universal negro suffrage upon the South. . . . From the Republican policy came no real good to the negroes. Most of them developed no political capacity, and the few who raised themselves above the mass did not reach a high order of intelligence. . . . The negro's political activity is rarely of a nature to identify him with any movement on a high plane. . . . [He] has been politically a failure and he could not have been otherwise."[4]

In the course of time the social scientists drastically revised their notions about race, and in recent years most of them have been striving to destroy the errors in whose creation their predecessors played so crucial a part. As ideas about race have changed, historians have become increasingly critical of the Dunning interpretation of reconstruction. These changes, together with a great deal of painstaking research, have produced the revisionist writing of the past generation. It is dangerous, of course, for an historian to label himself as a revisionist, for his ultimate and inevitable fate is one day to have his own revisions revised.

But that has never discouraged revisionists, and we may hope that it never will, especially those who have been rewriting the history of the reconstruction era. One need not be disturbed about the romantic nonsense that still fills the minds of many Americans about their Civil War. This folklore is essentially harmless. But the legend of reconstruction is another matter. It has had serious consequences, because it has exerted a powerful influence upon the political behavior of many white men, North and South.

Notes

1. James Ford Rhodes: *History of the United States from the Compromise of 1850 . . .*, 7 vols. (New York, 1893–1906), Vol. VII, p. 168; John W. Burgess: *Reconstruction and the Constitution* (New York, 1902), p. 263.
2. James G. Randall: *Civil War and Reconstruction* (Boston, 1937), pp. 689, 852; E. Merton Coulter: *The South during Reconstruction, 1865–1877* (Baton Rouge, 1947), p. xi.
3. Madison Grant: *The Passing of the Great Race* (New York, 1916), pp. 77–9.
4. Rhodes: *History of the United States*, Vol. VII, pp. 168–70.

Did the Civil War Retard Industrialization?

Thomas C. Cochran

Nations in the twentieth century tend to define their existence largely in economic terms. We as Americans see our status and fate invariably interpreted in terms of the continued viability of "capitalism" as both an economic and political way of life. Thus it is not surprising that, historically speaking, we have come to attach considerable importance to the development of the American economy. In the traditional view, the Civil War was always considered basic to American economic development. It served as the convenient dividing line between limited economic growth and massive industrial expansion. In the selection here reprinted, however, Thomas C. Cochran, economic historian from the University of Pennsylvania, poses the possibility that the Civil War, rather than generating economic growth, actually retarded its development.

In most textbooks and interpretative histories of the United States the Civil War has been assigned a major role in bringing about the American Industrial Revolution. Colorful business developments in the North—adoption of new machines, the quick spread of war contracting, the boost given to profits by inflation, and the creation of a group of war millionaires—make the war years seem not only a period of rapid economic change but also one that created important forces for future growth. The superficial qualitative evidence is so persuasive that apparently few writers have examined the available long-run statistical series before adding their endorsement to the conventional interpretation. The following quotations taken from the books of two generations of leading scholars illustrate the popular view.

"The so-called Civil War," wrote Charles A. and Mary R. Beard in 1927, ". . . was a social war . . . making *vast changes* in the arrangement of classes, in the accumulation and distribution of wealth, *in the course of industrial development.*" Midway between 1927 and the present, Arthur M. Schlesinger, Sr., wrote: "On these tender industrial growths the Civil War *had the effect of a hothouse.* For reasons already clear . . . nearly every branch of industry grew lustily." Harold U. Faulkner, whose textbook sales have ranked near or at the top, said in 1954: "In the economic history of the United States the Civil War was extremely important. . . . In the North *it speeded the Industrial Revolution* and the development of capitalism by the

From "Did the Civil War Retard Industrialization?" by Thomas C. Cochran. *Mississippi Valley Historical Review* (September 1961). Reprinted by permission of *The Journal of American History.*

prosperity which it brought to industry." The leading new text of 1957, by Richard Hofstadter, William Miller, and Daniel Aaron, showed no weakening of this interpretation: "The growing demand for farm machinery as well as for the 'sinews of war' led to American industrial expansion. . . . Of necessity, *iron, coal, and copper* production boomed during the war years." A sophisticated but still essentially misleading view is presented by Gilbert C. Fite and Jim E. Reese in a text of 1959: "The Civil War proved to be a boon to Northern economic development. . . . Industry, for example, was not created by the war, but wartime demands *greatly stimulated and encouraged industrial development* which already had a good start." In a reappraisal of the Civil War, in *Harper's Magazine* for April, 1960, Denis W. Brogan, a specialist in American institutions, wrote: "It may have been only a catalyst but the War *precipitated the entry* of the United States *into the modern industrial world,* made 'the take-off' (to use Professor W. W. Rostow's brilliant metaphor) come sooner."

In all of these reiterations of the effect of the Civil War on industrialism, statistical series seem to have been largely neglected. None of the authors cited reinforce their interpretations by setting the war period in the context of important long-run indexes of industrial growth. Since 1949, series of the period 1840 to 1890 that would cast doubt on the conventional generalizations have been available in *Historical Statistics of the United States, 1789–1945*. In 1960 a new edition of *Historical Statistics* and the report of the Conference on Research in Income and Wealth on *Trends in the American Economy in the Nineteenth Century* have provided additional material to support the argument that the Civil War retarded American industrial development. These volumes give data for many growth curves for the two decades before and after the war decade—in other words, the long-run trends before and after the event in question. The pattern of these trends is a mixed one which shows no uniform type of change during the Civil War decade, but on balance for the more important series the trend is toward retardation in *rates* of growth rather than toward acceleration. This fact is evident in many series which economists would regard as basic to economic growth, but in order to keep the discussion within reasonable limits only a few can be considered here.

Robert E. Gallman has compiled new and more accurate series for both "total commodity output," including agriculture, and "value added by manufacture," the two most general measures of economic growth available for this period. He writes: "Between 1839 and 1899 total commodity output increased elevenfold, or at an average decade rate of slightly less than 50 percent. . . . Actual rates varied fairly widely, high rates appearing during the decades ending with 1854 and 1884, and a very low rate during the decade ending with 1869." From the over-all standpoint this statement indicates the immediately retarding effect of the Civil War on American economic growth, but since most of the misleading statements are made in regard to industrial growth, or particular elements in industrial growth, it is necessary to look in more detail at "value added by manufacture" and some special series. Gallman's series for value added in constant dollars of the purchasing power of 1879 shows a rise of 157 percent from 1839 to 1849; 76 percent from 1849 to 1859; and only 25 percent from 1859 to 1869. By the 1870's the more favorable prewar rates were resumed, with an increase of 82 percent for 1869–1879, and 112 percent for 1879–1889. Thus two decades of very rapid advance, the 1840's and the 1880's, are separated by thirty years of slower growth which falls to the lowest level in the decade that embraces the Civil War.

Pig-iron production in tons, perhaps the most significant commodity index of nineteenth-century American industrial growth, is available year-by-year from 1854 on. Taking total production for five-year periods, output increased 9 percent between the block of years from 1856 to 1860 and the block from 1861 to 1865. That even this slight increase might not have been registered except for the fact that 1857 to 1860 were years of intermittent depression is indicated by an 81 percent increase over the war years in the block of years from 1866 to 1870. If annual production is taken at five-year intervals, starting in 1850, the increase is 24 percent from 1850 to 1855; 17 percent from 1855 to 1860; 1 percent from 1860 to 1865; and 100 percent from 1865 to 1870. While there is no figure available for 1845, the period from 1840 to 1850 shows 97 percent increase in shipments, while for the period 1870 to 1880 the increase was 130 percent. To sum up, depression and war appear to have retarded a curve of production that was tending to rise at a high rate.

Bituminous coal production may be regarded as the next most essential commodity series. After a gain of 199 percent from 1840 to 1850 this series shows a rather steady pattern of increase at rates varying from 119 to 148 percent each decade from 1850 to 1890. The war does not appear to have markedly affected the rate of growth.

In the mid-nineteenth century copper production was not a basic series for recording American growth, but since three distinguished authors have singled it out as one of the indexes of the effect of the war on industry it is best to cite the statistics. Before 1845 production of domestic copper was negligible. By 1850 the "annual recoverable content" of copper from United States mines was 728 tons, by 1860 it was 8,064 tons, by 1865 it was 9,520 tons, and by 1870 it was 14,112 tons. In this series of very small quantities, therefore, the increase from 1850 to 1860 was just over 1,000 percent, from 1860 to 1865 it was 18 percent, and from 1865 to 1870 it was 48 percent.

Railroad track, particularly in the United States, was an essential for industrialization. Here both the depression and the war retarded the rate of growth. From 1851 through 1855 a total of 11,627 miles of new track was laid, from 1856 through 1860, only 8,721 miles, and from 1861 through 1865, only 4,076 miles. After the war the rate of growth of the early 1850's was resumed, with 16,174 miles constructed from 1866 through 1870. Looked at by decades, a rate of over 200 percent increase per decade in the twenty years before the war was slowed to 70 percent for the period from 1860 to 1870, with only a 15 percent increase during the war years. In the next two decades the rate averaged about 75 percent.

Next to food, cotton textiles may be taken as the most representative consumer-goods industry in the nineteenth century. Interference with the flow of southern cotton had a depressing effect. The number of bales of cotton consumed in United States manufacturing rose 143 percent from 1840 to 1850 and 47 percent from 1850 to 1860, but *fell* by 6 percent from 1860 to 1870. From then on consumption increased at a little higher rate than in the 1850's.

While woolen textile production is not an important series in the overall picture of industrial growth, it should be noted that, helped by protection and military needs, consumption of wool for manufacturing more than doubled during the war, and then *fell* somewhat from 1865 to 1870. But Arthur H. Cole, the historian of the woolen industry, characterizes the years from 1830 to 1870 as a period of growth "not so striking as in the decades before or afterwards."

Immigration to a nation essentially short of labor was unquestionably a stimulant to economic growth. Another country had paid for the immigrant's unproductive youthful years, and he came to the United States ready to contribute his labor at a low cost. The pattern of the curve for annual immigration shows the retarding effect of both depression and war. In the first five years of the 1850's an average of 349,685 immigrants a year came to the United States. From 1856 through 1860 the annual average fell to 169,-958, and for the war years of 1861 to 1865 it fell further to 160,345. In the first five postwar years the average rose to 302,620, but not until the first half of the 1870's did the rate equal that of the early 1850's. Had there been a return to prosperity instead of war in 1861, it seems reasonable to suppose that several hundred thousand additional immigrants would have arrived before 1865.

In the case of farm mechanization the same type of error occurs as in the annual series on copper production. "Random" statistics such as the manufacture of 90,000 reapers in 1864 are frequently cited without putting them in the proper perspective of the total number in use and the continuing trends. Reaper and mower sales started upward in the early 1850's and were large from 1856 on, in spite of the depression. William T. Hutchinson estimates that most of the 125,000 reapers and mowers in use in 1861 had been sold during the previous five years. While the business, without regard to the accidental coming of the war, was obviously in a stage of very rapid growth, the war years presented many difficulties and may actually have retarded the rate of increase. Total sales of reapers for the period 1861–1865 are estimated at 250,000—a quite ordinary increase for a young industry—but the 90,000 figure for 1864, if it is correct, reinforces the evidence from the McCormick correspondence that this was the one particularly good year of the period. During these years William S. McCormick was often of the opinion that the "uncertainties of the times" made advisable a suspension of manufacturing until the close of the war.

For a broader view of agricultural mechanization the series "value of farm implements and machinery" has special interest. Here the census gives a picture which, if correct, is explicable only on the basis of wartime destruction. Based on constant dollars the dollar value of all loans was more than 15 percent lower than just before the war. If instead of examining loans one looks at total assets of all banks the decline in constant dollars from 1860 to 1870 is reduced to 10 percent, the difference arising from a larger cash position and more investment in government bonds.

Net capital formation would be a more proper index of economic growth than bank loans or assets. Unfortunately, neither the teams of the National Bureau of Economic Research nor those of the Census Bureau have been able to carry any reliable series back of 1868. From colonial times to 1960, however, the chief single form of American capital formation has undoubtedly been building construction. Farm houses, city homes, public buildings, stores, warehouses, and factories have year-by-year constituted, in monetary value, the leading type of capital growth. Gallman has drawn up series for such construction based on estimating the flow of construction materials and adding what appear to be appropriate markups. Admittedly the process is inexact, but because of the importance of construction in reflecting general trends in capital formation it is interesting to see the results. The rate of change for the ten-year period ending in 1854 is about 140 percent; for the one ending in 1859 it is 90 percent; for 1869 it is 40 percent; and for 1879 it is 46 percent. Taking a long view, from 1839 to 1859 the average decennial rate of increase was about 70 percent, and from 1869 to 1899 it was about 40 percent. The *rate* of advance in construction was declining and the war decade added a further dip to the decline.

Since the decline in rate is for the decade, the exact effect of the war years can only be estimated, but the logic of the situation, reinforced by the record of sharp cut-backs in railroad building, seems inescapable: the Civil War, like all modern wars, checked civilian construction. The first year of war was a period of depression and tight credit in the Middle West, which checked residential and farm construction in the area that grew most rapidly before and after the war. In both the East and the West the last two years of the war were a period of rapid inflation which was regarded by businessmen as a temporary wartime phenomenon. The logical result would be to postpone construction for long-term use until after the anticipated deflation. The decline in private railroad construction to a small fraction of the normal rate exemplifies the situation.

Lavish expenditure and speculation by a small group of war contractors and market operators gambling on the inflation seem to have created a legend of high prosperity during the war years. But the general series on fluctuations in the volume of business do not bear this out. Leonard P. Ayres's estimates of business activity place the average for 1861 through 1865 below normal, and Norman J. Silberling's business index is below its normal line for all years of the war. Silberling also has an intermediate trend line for business, which smooths out annual fluctuations. This line falls steadily from 1860 to 1869. Much of Silberling's discussion in his chapter "Business Activity, Prices, and Wars" is in answer to his question: "Why does it seem to be true that despite a temporary stimulating effect of war upon some industries, wars are generally associated with a long-term retarding of business growth . . .?" He puts the Civil War in this general category.

Collectively these statistical estimates support a conclusion that the Civil War retarded American industrial growth. Presentation of this view has been the chief purpose of this article. To try to judge the non-measurable or indirect effects of the war is extremely difficult. But since further discussion of the conventional qualitative factors may help to explain the prevailing evaluation in American texts, it seems appropriate to add some conjectural obiter dicta.

Experience with the apparently stimulating effects of twentieth-century wars on production makes the conclusion that victorious war may retard the growth of an industrial state seem paradoxical, and no doubt accounts in part for the use of detached bits of quantitative data to emphasize the Civil War's industrial importance. The resolution of the paradox may be found in contemporary conditions in the United States and in the nature of the wartime demand. The essential wastefulness of war from the standpoint of economic growth was obscured by the accident that both of the great European wars of the twentieth century began when the United States had a high level of unemployment. The immediate effect of each, therefore, was to put men to work, to increase the national product, and to create an aura of prosperity. Presumably, the United States of the mid-nineteenth century tended to operate close enough to full employment in average years that any wasteful labor-consuming activities were a burden rather than a stimulant.

By modern standards the Civil War was still unmechanized. It was fought with rifles, bayonets, and sabers by men on foot or horseback. Artillery was more used than in previous wars, but was still a relatively minor consumer of iron and steel. The railroad was also brought into use, but the building of military lines offset only a small percentage of the overall drop from the prewar level of civilian railroad construction. Had all of these things not been true, the Confederacy with its small industrial development could never have fought through four years of increasingly effective blockade.

In spite of the failure of direct quantitative evidence to show accelerating effects of the war on rates of economic growth, there could be long-run effects of a qualitative type that would gradually foster a more rapid rate of economic growth. The most obvious place to look for such indirect effects would be in the results of freeing the slaves. Marxists contended that elimination of slavery was a necessary precursor of the bourgeois industrialism which would lead to the socialist revolution. The creation of a free Negro labor force was, of course, of great long-run importance. In the twentieth century it has led to readjustment of Negro population between the deep South and the northern industrial areas, and to changes in the use of southern land.

But economically the effects of war and emancipation over the period 1840 to 1880 were negative. Richard A. Easterlin writes: "In every southern state, the 1880 level of per capita income originating in commodity production and distribution was below, or at best only slightly above that of 1840. . . . [This] attests strikingly to the impact of that war and the subsequent disruption on the southern economy." In general the Negroes became sharecroppers or wage laborers, often cultivating the same land and the same crops as before the war. In qualification of the argument that free Negro labor led to more rapid industrialization it should be noted that the South did not keep up with the national pace in the growth of non-agricultural wealth until after 1900.

Two indirect effects of the war aided industrial growth to degrees that cannot accurately be measured. These were, first, a more satisfactory money market, and, secondly, more security for entrepreneurial activity than in the prewar period. The sharp wartime inflation had the usual effect of transferring income from wage, salary, and interest receivers to those making profits. This meant concentration of savings in the hands of entrepreneurs who would invest in new activities; and this no doubt helps to explain the speculative booms of the last half of the 1860's and first two years of the 1870's which have been treated as the prosperity resulting from the war. Inflation also eased the burdens of those railroads which had excessive mortgage debts. But a great deal of new research would be needed to establish causal connections between the inflationary reallocation of wealth, 1863 to 1865, and the high rate of industrial progress in the late 1870's and the 1880's.

The National Banking Act, providing a more reliable currency for interstate operations, has been hailed as a great aid to business expansion although it would be hard to demonstrate, aside from a few weeks during panics, that plentiful but occasionally unsound currency had seriously interfered with earlier industrial growth. The existence of two and a half billion dollars in federal bonds also provided a basis for credit that was larger than before the war. This led to broader and more active security markets as well as to easier personal borrowing. But two qualifications must be kept in mind. First, local bank lending to favored borrowers had probably tended to be too liberal before the war and was now put on a somewhat firmer basis. In other words, since 1800 a multiplication of banks had made credit relatively easy to obtain in the United States, and in the North this continued to be the situation. Second, the southern banking system was largely destroyed by the war and had to be rebuilt in the subsequent decades. It should also be remembered that by 1875 some 40 percent of the banks were outside the national banking system.

Because of a few colorful speculators like Jay Gould, Daniel Drew, and Jim Fisk, and the immortality conferred on them, initially by the literary ability of the Adams brothers, the New York stock exchange in the postwar decade appears to have mirrored a new era of predatory wealth. But one has only to study the scandals of the London and New York stock exchanges in 1854 to see that there was little growth in the sophistication or boldness of stock operators during these fifteen years. In any case, the exploits of market operators were seldom related in a positive way to economic growth. Even a record of new issues of securities, which is lacking for this period, would chiefly reflect the flow of capital into railroads, banks, and public utilities rather than into manufacturing. Very few "industrial" shares were publicly marketed before the decade of the 1880's; such enterprises grew chiefly from the reinvestment of earnings.

There was strong government encouragement to entrepreneurial activity during the Civil War, but to ascribe to it unusual importance for economic growth requires both analysis of the results and comparison with other periods. Government in the United States has almost always encouraged entrepreneurs. The federal and state administrations preceding the Civil War could certainly be regarded as friendly to business. They subsidized railroads by land grants, subscribed to corporate bond issues, and remitted taxes on new enterprise. Tariffs were low, but railroad men and many bankers were happy with the situation. Whether or not American industrialism was significantly accelerated by the high protection that commenced with the war is a question that economists will probably never settle.

The building of a subsidized transcontinental railroad, held back by sectional controversies in the 1850's, was authorized along a northern route with the help of federal loans and land grants when the southerners excluded themselves from Congress. Putting more than a hundred million dollars into this project in the latter half of the 1860's, however, may have had an adverse effect on industrial growth. In general, the far western roads were built for speculative and strategic purposes uneconomically ahead of demand. They may for a decade, or even two, have consumed more capital than their transportation services were then worth to the economy.

To sum up this part of the obiter dictum, those who write of the war creating a national market tied together by railroads underestimate both the achievements of the two decades before the war and the ongoing trends of the economy. The nation's business in 1855 was nearly as intersectional as in 1870. Regional animosities did not interfere with trade, nor did these feelings diminish after the war. By the late 1850's the United States was a rapidly maturing industrial state with its major cities connected by rail, its major industries selling in a national market, and blessed or cursed with financiers, security flotations, stock markets, and all the other appurtenances of industrial capitalism.

But when all specific factors of change attributable to the war have been deflated, there is still the possibility that northern victory had enhanced the capitalist spirit, that as a consequence the atmosphere of government in Washington among members of both parties was more friendly to industrial enterprise and to northern-based national business operations than had formerly been the rule. It can be argued that in spite of Greenbackers and discontented farmers legislation presumably favorable to industry could be more readily enacted. The Fourteenth Amendment, for example, had as a by-product greater security for interstate business against state regulation, although it was to be almost two decades before the Supreme Court would give force to this protection. By 1876, a year of deep depression, the two major parties were trying to outdo each other in promises of stimulating economic growth. This highly generalized type of argument is difficult to evaluate, but in qualification of any theory of a sharp change in attitude we should remember that industrialism was growing rapidly from general causes and that by the 1870's it was to be expected that major-party politics would be conforming to this change in American life.

Massive changes in physical environment such as those accompanying the rise of trade at the close of the Middle Ages or the gradual growth of industrialism from the seventeenth century on do not lend themselves readily to exact or brief periodization. If factory industry and mechanized transportation be taken as the chief indexes of early industrialism, its spread in the United States was continuous and rapid during the entire nineteenth century, but in general, advance was greater during periods of prosperity than in depressions. The first long period without a major depression, after railroads, canals, and steamboats had opened a national market, was from 1843 to 1857. Many economic historians interested in quantitative calculations would regard these years as marking the appearance of an integrated industrial society. Walter W. Rostow, incidentally, starts his "take-off" period in the 1840's and calls it completed by 1860. Others might prefer to avoid any narrow span of years. Few, however, would see a major stimulation to economic growth in the events of the Civil War.

Finally, one may speculate as to why this exaggerated conception of the role of the Civil War in industrialization gained so firm a place in American historiography. The idea fits, of course, into the Marxian frame of revolutionary changes, but it seems initially to have gained acceptance quite independently of Marxian influences. More concentrated study of the war years than of any other four-year span in the nineteenth century called attention to technological and business events usually overlooked. Isolated facts were seized upon without comparing them with similar data for other decades.

The desire of teachers for neat periodization was probably a strong factor in quickly placing the interpretation in textbooks; thus, up to 1860 the nation was agricultural, after 1865 it was industrial. Recent study of American cultural themes suggests still another reason. From most standpoints the Civil War was a national disaster, but Americans like to see their history in terms of optimism and progress. Perhaps the war was put in a perspective suited to the culture by seeing it as good because in addition to achieving freedom for the Negro it brought about industrial progress.

Suggested Further Reading for Chapter 6

Thomas A. Bailey, "The Russian Fleet Myth Re-examined," *Mississippi Valley Historical Review*, 38 (1951).

Henry Blumenthal, "Confederate Diplomacy: Popular Notions and International Realities," *Journal of Southern History*, 32 (1966).

Richard Current, *The Lincoln Nobody Knows* (New York: Hill & Wang, 1963).

Edwin Fishel, "The Mythology of Civil War Intelligence," *Civil War History*, 10 (1964).

Mark M. Krug, "On Rewriting of the Story of Reconstruction in the U.S. History Textbooks," *The Journal of Negro History*, 46 (1961).

Lloyd Lewis, *Myths After Lincoln* (New York: Grosset & Dunlap, Inc., 1957).

D. O'Flaherty, "The Blockade that Failed," *American Heritage*, 6 (1955).

Thomas J. Pressley, *Americans Interpret their Civil War* (New York: The Free Press, 1966).

Robert Penn Warren, *The Legacy of the Civil War* (New York: Vintage Books, 1964).

Bernard A. Weisberger, "The Dark and Bloody Ground of Reconstruction Historiography," *Journal of Southern History*, 5 (1939).

Arnold Whitridge, "The John Brown Legend," *History Today*, 7 (1957).

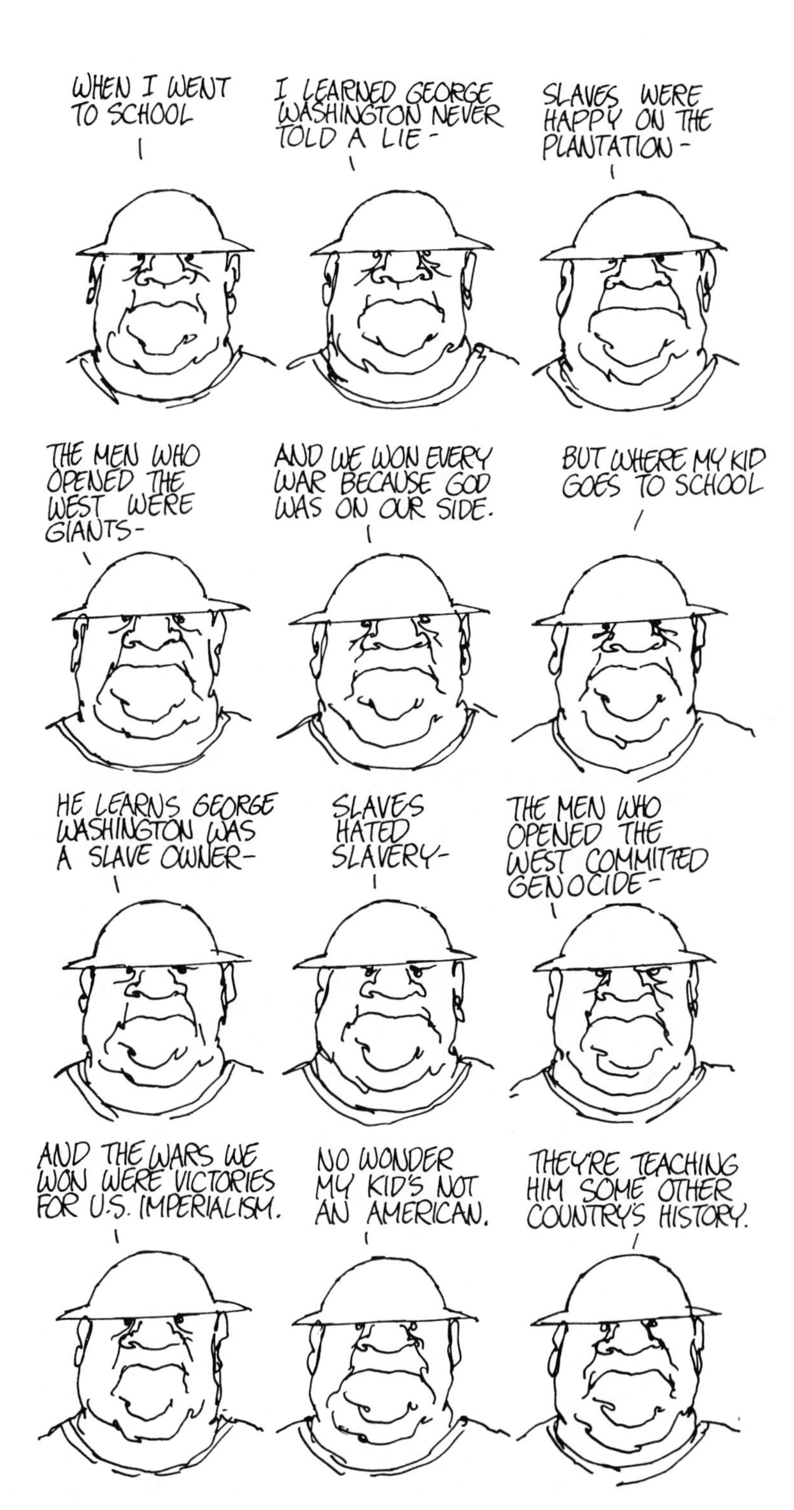
WHEN I WENT TO SCHOOL
I LEARNED GEORGE WASHINGTON NEVER TOLD A LIE-
SLAVES WERE HAPPY ON THE PLANTATION-
THE MEN WHO OPENED THE WEST WERE GIANTS-
AND WE WON EVERY WAR BECAUSE GOD WAS ON OUR SIDE.
BUT WHERE MY KID GOES TO SCHOOL
HE LEARNS GEORGE WASHINGTON WAS A SLAVE OWNER-
SLAVES HATED SLAVERY-
THE MEN WHO OPENED THE WEST COMMITTED GENOCIDE-
AND THE WARS WE WON WERE VICTORIES FOR U.S. IMPERIALISM.
NO WONDER MY KID'S NOT AN AMERICAN.
THEY'RE TEACHING HIM SOME OTHER COUNTRY'S HISTORY.